W9-AUY-999

God's Love Story

God's Love Story Ministries

Copyright © 2012 God's Love Story Ministries
All rights reserved.
ISBN: 1478241012
ISBN-13: 978-1478241010

INTRODUCTION

God's Love Story gives a broad overview of the Bible, from start to finish. It is intended to help you grasp the story and purpose of God's plan for mankind.

This book contains an assortment of verses, and is not intended to replace the complete Bible. Just like a movie trailer entices you to see the whole movie, reading God's Love Story will enable you to desire, read and understand the entire Bible as never before.

God's Love Story contains selected and compiled portions of the Bible, placed as best as possible in chronological order, as a means of giving a readable and easy to understand synopsis of the Bible. By removing verse markings, the text reads much like a novel, and actually reverts back to a form more like the original text as first written down thousands of years ago.

God's Love Story is divided into 39 compact chapters that can easily be read in one setting. Some explanations have been added, clearly marked in italicized font – these "transitional statements" are useful in bridging the gaps over sections that were not included, for the sake of brevity. They are simple, Biblical, and written without espousing any personal doctrine or beliefs - preferring to let the scriptures speak for themselves. The scriptures were taken from the World English Bible, which is not copyrighted and thus free to use.

As always, you are encouraged to "rightly divide the Word" in your own studies. We must rely solely on God's complete Word, the Bible in its entirety, not what any men teach, as we seek to base our salvation on God's plan for us.

That being said, we are excited to present God's Love Story, as we believe this can help you to grow in your understanding and application of God's Word, and thus will bring glory to Him. We hope that in your our own studies you will come to know and better understand the full Bible narrative. May God bless each of you as you seek His will, and strive to find your own place in God's Love Story.

EDITOR'S COMMENTS

I do not consider myself the author of this book. The majority of this book was not written by me, but by Yahweh God.

After all, as we read at the beginning of the New Testament book of Hebrews, "God, having in the past spoken to the fathers through the prophets at many times and in various ways, has at the end of these days spoken to us by his Son, whom he appointed heir of all things, through whom also he made the worlds."

Instead, I would prefer to be considered the editor of this book, which is just an attempt to present God's masterpiece in a different way. By no means do I consider this approach equal to or better than God's complete Word.

When I was a boy, I had some comic books called "Classics Illustrated." They presented great works of literature in an easy to read and understand format, using pictures as an aid. They did not intend to replace the works that they presented; instead, they were a tool for bringing an understanding of these works to the reader. These comic books inspired me to read many of these great masterpieces in their entirety. My intent is the same with this book.

I am by no means a great Bible scholar. I am just a common man, with an idea and a desire to help people understand the greatest story ever told.

It is my prayer that by understanding the story of God's love, knowledge will be increased, people will be drawn closer to God, and souls will be saved.

To that end, it is my intention to use the profits from the sales of this book to distribute free copies, and to have this work translated into other languages and distributed in many countries. A non-profit organization, God's Love Story Ministries, has been established to enable us reach those goals.

May God bless you and help you find your place in God's love story.

Brian Dowler
Camp Hill, Pennsylvania, USA

CHURCH CAMPAIGNS

Publicity Toolkit

God's Love Story is an excellent tool for strengthening the Biblical knowledge of your congregation, as well as an outreach tool for reaching the lost souls of your community.

There are many people who have always wanted to read the Bible, but who have never made it from cover to cover. Some people are seeking God, but are not spiritually active. But there are likely many members of your own congregation who have never read the Bible in its entirety or fully understood the primary message of God's Word.

There is a deep desire within all of us to connect with God on a higher level. We want to understand the answers to questions such as "Why was I created?", "What is the purpose of my life?" and "What will happen when I die?"

God's Love Story can help answer these questions - and enable people to understand, appreciate and connect with God as never before.

To aid congregations in using God's Love Story, a "campaign publicity kit" has been developed. This is available on our web site, www.getgodslovestory.com

The Kit Contains:

- Graphics files for printing posters. A poster has been designed for each of the 39 book chapters. These colorful, yet simple images help the readers to remember a key fact about each chapter. This in turn helps them to put each chapter into a mental timeline, thus painting a visual story through the Bible from beginning to end. These posters can be printed and displayed in your church building – we recommend "unveiling" each poster on a week-by-week basis. They can also be printed on regular-sized paper for smaller classroom or bulletin board displays.

- Graphics files for printing banners. These are great for advertising upcoming campaigns.

- Customizable flyers (Microsoft Publisher). These are terrific for handing out to neighbors and friends.

- Customizable Postcards (Microsoft Publisher). Suitable for a direct mailing campaign in your neighborhood.

- Microsoft PowerPoint slides – for projecting each chapter poster.

- Implementation Guide – suggestions to help make your church campaign successful.
- Additional files are being added as they are developed – check our web site for current details on the kit contents.

Books can be purchased from the following sources:
- An updated list of sources for printed books, E-books, and audio books is maintained at www.getgodslovestory.com
- Our Preferred Location: www.createspace.com/3936930 [We prefer that you buy individual and small lots (less than 10) of books direct from createspace.com as this maximizes income for our non-profit, at the same book prices.]
- www.amazon.com/dp/1478241012 (print and e-Book)
- BULK ORDERS: We provide discounts to groups on bulk orders at our web site, www.getgodslovestory.com – make sure you put the "get" in the address!

Get more details on God's Love Story Ministries church campaigns at www.getgodslovestory.com

Email to: godslovestory2@gmail.com

God's Love Story Ministries
PO Box 1592
Camp Hill, PA 17001
USA

CONTENTS

(cont.)

ACKNOWLEDGMENTS

First and foremost, may all glory and honor be given to Jesus, who as Paul wrote, is "… the author and perfecter of our faith."

Several reference works were consulted in the research for this publication, including:

- The Chronological Study Bible – F Lagard Smith
- Harmony of the Gospels - www.blueletterbible.org
- World English Bible – www.ebible.org

I am blessed to have so many current and former members of my congregation, the Camp Hill Church of Christ, who have great talents:

- I would like to thank Ed Dyche and Jennifer Marrs for their generous work in proofreading this book.
- The book cover was designed by Samantha Deitch.
- The posters and banners were developed by Seth Deitch, www.sethdeitch.com

My fellow elders at the Camp Hill congregation were 100% supportive of this project – so a special thank you goes out to Darren Crowden, Alan Garner, Larry Mackey, and Tim Williams. Our minister and evangelist, Doug Hamilton, was both supportive and a great inspiration in illustrating a real desire for reaching the lost. Steve Cantrell was very supportive of this effort; his desire to see this book fulfilled fueled me when fatigue set in. I also want to thank my good friend Nehemiah Gootam of Kakinada India, who expressed a keen interest in converting this book to Telugu for use in the reaching many souls in the state of Andhra Pradesh, India. I pray that will be the first of many foreign translations. Many others, too numerous to name, were supportive of the work. I thank all of you and am thankful to count you among my friends.

Also, the members of the Camp Hill Church of Christ have been so supportive in helping me with the Bible Class curriculum. To all the volunteers – from content creators, to reviewers, and artists from young to old – I thank all of you for working as a team to make this a success.

A very special "thank you" goes out to my wife Cathy, who inspires me daily by her humble heart, caring attitude, and righteous life. She is a special person, the most genuine person I have ever met, and I am ever so lucky to have her as my wife, friend, life companion, and the mother of our children.

This book is dedicated to the memory of our dear Brother Paul Cantrell, who was a tireless servant of God, a caring man who dedicated his life to preaching and teaching the Word of God. Since his passing on September 1, 2011, he is greatly missed.

Brian Dowler, August 2012

1 THE BEGINNING

From Creation to Destruction

The Bible is called "The greatest story ever told," and for good reason. Men through the ages have asked the questions, "Who put me here?", "Why am I here?" and "What will happen to me when I die?" The Bible answers these questions, laying out the purpose for our existence and giving us answers to these important questions.

Starting at the beginning, we see God's hand controlling the creation of our world and universe, as well as influencing major and minor events among the people of the world. From the majesty of the heavens to the beauty of the earth, his work is marvelous; but the crowning glory of his creation is man, who is made in God's own image. The purpose of the entire creation is for our benefit. And the purpose of our creation is for the glorification of God.

Behind every event that God puts into motion, is his grand plan. Whether God speaks to one of his believers in a dream, or causes a nation's course to be changed by war, like a grand master at the chessboard, there is a purpose behind every move. And that purpose is to provide a means of salvation for mankind.

In the Old Testament portion of the Bible, the stage is being set for the coming of the "Messiah," Jesus Christ, God's only son, to be the perfect sacrifice that makes it possible for the sins of man to be washed away. In the New Testament portion of the Bible, the life and teachings of Jesus are given. The son of God takes on a fleshly form, living a perfect life, culminating with His death, burial and resurrection from the grave. With this sacrifice, God has given us the gift of eternal life. Just as God raised Jesus from the dead, we can have confidence that He can also raise us from the dead, to live a joyful existence in heaven with him eternally.

The New Testament portion continues with the story of the church, the body of believers in Christ Jesus. The church, lovingly called the "Bride of Christ," grows rapidly, but then suffers from persecution. Despite this suffering, the church continues to prosper. The Bible ends with the book of Revelation, a book of prophesy about the church and end of time, giving hope to those who are being persecuted for the name of Jesus. In this final prophesy we receive confirmation that Jesus will reign supreme in heaven with those who obey him.

The purpose of our life is to obey God, thus bringing him glory. Despite the difficulties of life, if we are faithful to God, who loves each of us, he will reward us beyond measure.

This grand narrative, the Bible, is truly God's love story.

In the beginning God created the heavens and the earth. Now the earth was formless and empty. Darkness was on the surface of the deep. God's Spirit was hovering over the surface of the waters.

God said, "Let there be light," and there was light. God saw the light, and saw that it was good. God divided the light from the darkness. God called the light "day," and the darkness he called "night." There was evening and there was morning, one day.

God said, "Let there be an expanse in the middle of the waters, and let it divide the waters from the waters." God made the expanse, and divided the waters which were under the expanse from the waters which were above the expanse; and it was so. God called the expanse "sky." There was evening and there was morning, a second day.

God said, "Let the waters under the sky be gathered together to one place, and let the dry land appear"; and it was so. God called the dry land "earth," and the gathering together of the waters he called "seas." God saw that it was good. God said, "Let the earth yield grass, herbs yielding seed, and fruit trees bearing fruit after their kind, with its seed in it, on the earth"; and it was so. The earth yielded grass, herbs yielding seed after their kind, and trees bearing fruit, with its seed in it, after their kind; and God saw that it was good. There was evening and there was morning, a third day.

God said, "Let there be lights in the expanse of sky to divide the day from the night; and let them be for signs, and for seasons, and for days and years; and let them be for lights in the expanse of sky to give light on the earth"; and it was so. God made the two great lights: the greater light to rule the day, and the lesser light to rule the night. He also made the stars. God set them in the expanse of sky to give light to the earth, and to rule over the day and over the night, and to divide the light from the darkness. God saw that it was good. There was evening and there was morning, a fourth day.

God said, "Let the waters swarm with swarms of living creatures, and let birds fly above the earth in the open expanse of sky." God created the large sea creatures, and every living creature that moves, with which the waters swarmed, after their kind, and every winged bird after its kind. God saw that it was good. God blessed them, saying, "Be fruitful, and multiply, and fill the waters in the seas, and let birds multiply on the earth." There was evening and there was morning, a fifth day.

God said, "Let the earth produce living creatures after their kind, livestock, creeping things, and animals of the earth after their kind"; and it was so. God made the animals of the earth after their kind, and the livestock after their kind, and everything that creeps on the ground after its kind. God saw that it was good.

God said, "Let us make man in our image, after our likeness: and let them have dominion over the fish of the sea, and over the birds of the sky, and over the livestock, and over all the earth, and over every creeping thing that creeps on the earth." God created man in his own image. In God's image he created him; male and female he created them. God blessed them. God said to them, "Be fruitful, multiply, fill the earth, and subdue it. Have dominion over the fish of the sea, over the birds of the sky, and over every living thing that moves on the earth." God said, "Behold, I have given you every herb yielding seed, which is on the surface of all the earth, and every tree, which bears fruit yielding seed. It will be your food. To every animal of the earth, and to every bird of the sky, and to everything that creeps on the earth, in which there is life, I have given every green herb for food"; and it was so.

God saw everything that he had made, and, behold, it was very good. There was evening and there was morning, a sixth day.

The heavens and the earth were finished, and all their vast array. On the seventh day God finished his work which he had made; and he rested on the seventh day from all his work which he had made. God blessed the seventh day, and made it holy, because he rested in it from all his work which he had created and made.

This is the history of the generations of the heavens and of the earth when they were created, in the day that Yahweh God made the earth and the heavens. No plant of the field was yet in the earth, and no herb of the field had yet sprung up; for Yahweh God had not caused it to rain on the earth. There was not a man to till the ground, but a mist went up from the earth, and watered the whole surface of the ground. Yahweh God formed man from the dust of the ground, and breathed into his nostrils the breath of life; and man became a living soul. Yahweh God planted a garden eastward, in Eden, and there he put the man whom he had formed. Out of the ground Yahweh God made every tree to grow that is pleasant to the sight, and good for food; the tree of life also in the middle of the garden, and the tree of the knowledge of good and evil. A river went out of Eden to water the garden; and from there it was parted, and became four heads. The name of the first is Pishon: this is the one which flows through the whole land of Havilah, where there is gold; and the gold of that land is good. There is aromatic resin and the onyx stone. The name of the second river is Gihon: the same river that flows through the whole land of Cush. The name of the third river is Hiddekel: this is the one which flows in front of Assyria. The fourth river is the Euphrates. Yahweh God took the man, and put him into the garden of Eden to dress it and to keep it. Yahweh God commanded the man, saying, "Of every tree of the garden you may freely eat; but of the tree of the knowledge of good and evil, you shall not eat of it; for in the day that you eat of it you will surely die."

Yahweh God said, "It is not good that the man should be alone; I will make him a helper suitable for him." Out of the ground Yahweh God formed every animal of the field, and every bird of the sky, and brought them to the man to see what he would call them. Whatever the man called every living creature, that was its name. The man gave names to all livestock, and to the birds of the sky, and to every animal of the field; but for man there was not found a helper suitable for him. Yahweh God caused a deep sleep to fall on the man, and he slept; and he took one of his ribs, and closed up the flesh in its place. He made the rib, which Yahweh God had taken from the man, into a woman, and brought her to the man. The man said, "This is now bone of my bones, and flesh of my flesh. She will be called 'woman,' because she was taken out of Man." Therefore a man will leave his father and his mother, and will join with his wife, and they will be one flesh. They were both naked, the man and his wife, and were not ashamed.

Now the serpent was more subtle than any animal of the field which Yahweh God had made. He said to the woman, "Has God really said, 'You shall not eat of any tree of the garden?'"

The woman said to the serpent, "Of the fruit of the trees of the garden we may eat, but of the fruit of the tree which is in the middle of the garden, God has said, 'You shall not eat of it, neither shall you touch it, lest you die.'"

The serpent said to the woman, "You won't surely die, for God knows that in the day you eat it, your eyes will be opened, and you will be like God, knowing good and evil."

When the woman saw that the tree was good for food, and that it was a delight to the eyes, and that the tree was to be desired to make one wise, she took of its fruit, and ate; and she gave some to her husband with her, and he ate. The eyes of both of them were opened, and they knew that they were naked. They sewed fig leaves together, and made themselves aprons. They heard the voice of Yahweh God walking in the garden in the cool of the day, and the man and his wife hid themselves from the presence of Yahweh God among the trees of the garden.

Yahweh God called to the man, and said to him, "Where are you?"

The man said, "I heard your voice in the garden, and I was afraid, because I was naked; and I hid myself."

God said, "Who told you that you were naked? Have you eaten from the tree that I commanded you not to eat from?"

The man said, "The woman whom you gave to be with me, she gave me of the tree, and I ate."

Yahweh God said to the woman, "What is this you have done?"

The woman said, "The serpent deceived me, and I ate."

Yahweh God said to the serpent, "Because you have done this, you are cursed above all livestock, and above every animal of the field. On your belly you shall go, and you shall eat dust all the days of your life. I will put enmity between you and the woman, and between your offspring and her offspring. He will bruise your head, and you will bruise his heel."

To the woman he said, "I will greatly multiply your pain in childbirth. In pain you will bear children. Your desire will be for your husband, and he will rule over you."

To Adam he said, "Because you have listened to your wife's voice, and have eaten of the tree, of which I commanded you, saying, 'You shall not eat of it,' cursed is the ground for your sake. In toil you will eat of it all the days of your life. It will yield thorns and thistles to you; and you will eat the herb of the field. By the sweat of your face will you eat bread until you return to the ground, for out of it you were taken. For you are dust, and to dust you shall return."

The man called his wife Eve, because she was the mother of all living. Yahweh God made coats of skins for Adam and for his wife, and clothed them.

Yahweh God said, "Behold, the man has become like one of us, knowing good and evil. Now, lest he reach out his hand, and also take of the tree of life, and eat, and live forever..." Therefore Yahweh God sent him out from the garden of Eden, to till the ground from which he was taken. So he drove out the man; and he placed Cherubs at the east of the garden of Eden, and the flame of a sword which turned every way, to guard the way to the tree of life.

The man knew Eve his wife. She conceived, and gave birth to Cain, and said, "I have gotten a man with Yahweh's help." Again she gave birth, to Cain's brother Abel. Abel was a keeper of sheep, but Cain was a tiller of the ground. As time passed, it happened that Cain brought an offering to Yahweh from the fruit of the ground. Abel also brought some of the firstborn of his flock and of its fat. Yahweh respected Abel and his offering, but he didn't respect Cain and his offering. Cain was very angry, and the expression on his face fell. Yahweh said to Cain, "Why are you angry? Why has the expression of your face fallen? If you do well, will it not be lifted up? If you don't do well, sin crouches at the door. Its desire is for you, but you are to rule over it." Cain said to Abel, his brother, "Let's go into the field." It happened when they were in the field, that Cain rose up against Abel, his brother, and killed him.

Yahweh said to Cain, "Where is Abel, your brother?" He said, "I don't know. Am I my brother's keeper?"

Yahweh said, "What have you done? The voice of your brother's blood cries to me from the ground. Now you are cursed because of the ground, which has opened its mouth to receive your brother's blood from your hand. From now on, when you till the ground, it won't yield its strength to you. You shall be a fugitive and a wanderer in the earth."

Cain said to Yahweh, "My punishment is greater than I can bear. Behold, you have driven me out this day from the surface of the ground. I will be hidden from your face, and I will be a fugitive and a wanderer in the earth. It will happen that whoever finds me will kill me."

Yahweh said to him, "Therefore whoever slays Cain, vengeance will be taken on him sevenfold." Yahweh appointed a sign for Cain, lest any finding him should strike him.

After Cain was cursed, he married, and bands of his descendants became known for the keeping of livestock, for the playing of musical instruments, and for the forging of brass and iron. Carrying on the tradition of Cain, one of his descendants, Lamech, also was known for murdering a young man.

From Adam and Eve's son Seth, a line of descendants populated the earth. In those days, men lived for hundreds of years, with the pinnacle reached by Methuselah, who lived to the advanced age of 969 years. Enoch, who was taken to be with God without dying at the age 365, was actually an exception to the longevity among the lineage from Seth to Noah, which totaled eight generations. Unfortunately, by this time nearly all men were consumed by wickedness.

This is the history of the generations of Noah. Noah was a righteous man, blameless among the people of his time. Noah walked with God. Noah became the father of three sons: Shem, Ham, and Japheth. The earth was corrupt before God, and the earth was filled with violence. God saw the earth, and saw that it was corrupt, for all flesh had corrupted their way on the earth.

God said to Noah, "The end of all flesh has come before me, for the earth is filled with violence through them. Behold, I will destroy them with the earth. Make a ship of gopher wood. You shall make rooms in the ship, and shall seal it inside and outside with pitch. This is how you shall make it. The length of the ship will be three hundred cubits, its breadth fifty cubits, and its height thirty cubits. You shall make a roof in the ship, and you shall finish it to a cubit upward. You shall set the door of the ship in its side. You shall make it with lower, second, and third levels. I, even I, do bring the flood of waters on this earth, to destroy all flesh having the breath of life from under the sky. Everything that is in the earth will die. But I will establish my covenant with you. You shall come into the ship, you, your sons, your wife, and your sons' wives with you. Of every living thing of all flesh, you shall bring two of every sort into the ship, to keep them alive with you. They shall be male and female. Of the birds after their kind, of the livestock after their kind, of every creeping thing of the ground after its kind, two of every sort shall come to you, to keep them alive. Take with you of all food that is eaten, and gather it to yourself; and it will be for food for you, and for them." Thus Noah did. According to all that God commanded him, so he did.

Yahweh said to Noah, "Come with all of your household into the ship, for I have seen your righteousness before me in this generation. You shall take seven pairs of every clean animal with you, the male and his female. Of the animals that are not clean, take two, the male and his female. Also of the birds of the sky, seven and seven, male and female, to keep seed alive on the surface of all the earth. In seven days, I will cause it to rain on the earth for forty days and forty nights. Every living thing that I have made, I will destroy from the surface of the ground."

Noah did everything that Yahweh commanded him.

Noah was six hundred years old when the flood of waters came on the earth. Noah went into the ship with his sons, his wife, and his sons' wives, because of the waters of the flood. Clean animals, animals that are not clean, birds, and everything that creeps on the ground went by pairs to Noah into the ship, male and female, as God commanded Noah. It happened after the seven days, that the waters of the flood came on the earth. In the six hundredth year of Noah's life, in the second month, on the seventeenth day of the month, on the same day all the fountains of the great deep were burst open, and the sky's windows were opened. The rain was on the earth forty days and forty nights.

The waters prevailed fifteen cubits upward, and the mountains were covered. All flesh died that moved on the earth, including birds, livestock, animals, every creeping thing that creeps on the earth, and every man. All in whose nostrils was the breath of the spirit of life, of all that was on the dry land, died. Every living thing was destroyed that was on the surface of the ground, including man, livestock, creeping things, and birds of the sky. They were destroyed from the earth. Only Noah was left, and those who were with him in the ship. The waters prevailed on the earth one hundred fifty days.

God remembered Noah, all the animals, and all the livestock that were with him in the ship; and God made a wind to pass over the earth. The waters subsided. The deep's fountains and the sky's windows were also stopped, and the rain from the sky was restrained. The waters receded from the earth continually. After the end of one hundred fifty days the waters decreased. The ship rested in the seventh month, on the seventeenth day of the month, on Ararat's mountains. The waters receded continually until the tenth month. In the tenth month, on the first day of the month, the tops of the mountains were seen.

It happened in the six hundred first year, in the first month, the first day of the month, the waters were dried up from the earth. Noah removed the covering of the ship, and looked. He saw that the surface of the ground was dried. In the second month, on the twenty-seventh day of the month, the earth was dry.

God spoke to Noah, saying, "Go out of the ship, you, and your wife, and your sons, and your sons' wives with you. Bring out with you every living thing that is with you of all flesh, including birds, livestock, and every creeping thing that creeps on the earth, that they may breed abundantly in the earth, and be fruitful, and multiply on the earth."

Noah went out, with his sons, his wife, and his sons' wives with him. Every animal, every creeping thing, and every bird, whatever moves on the earth, after their families, went out of the ship.

Noah built an altar to Yahweh, and took of every clean animal, and of every clean bird, and offered burnt offerings on the altar. Yahweh smelled the pleasant aroma. Yahweh said in his heart, "I will not again curse the ground any more for man's sake, because the imagination of man's heart is evil from his youth; neither will I ever again strike everything living, as I have done. While the earth remains, seed time and harvest, and cold and heat, and summer and winter, and day and night shall not cease."

God blessed Noah and his sons, and said to them, "Be fruitful, and multiply, and replenish the earth. The fear of you and the dread of you will be on every animal of the earth, and on every bird of the sky. Everything that the ground teems with, and all the fish of the sea are delivered into your hand. Every moving thing that lives will be food for you. As the green herb, I have given everything to you. But flesh with its life, its blood, you shall not eat. I will surely require your blood of your lives. At the hand of every animal I will require it. At the hand of man, even at the hand of every man's brother, I will require the life of man. Whoever sheds man's blood, his blood will be shed by man, for God made man in his own image. Be fruitful and multiply. Increase abundantly in the earth, and multiply in it."

I will establish my covenant with you: all flesh will not be cut off any more by the waters of the flood, neither will there ever again be a flood to destroy the earth." God said, "This is the token of the covenant which I make between me and you and every living creature that is with you, for perpetual generations: I set my rainbow in the cloud, and it will be for a sign of a covenant between me and the earth. It will happen, when I bring a cloud over the earth, that the rainbow will be seen in the cloud, and I will remember my covenant, which is between me and you and every living creature of all flesh, and the waters will no more become a flood to destroy all flesh. The rainbow will be in the cloud. I will look at it, that I may remember the everlasting covenant between God and every living creature of all flesh that is on the earth." God said to Noah, "This is the token of the covenant which I have established between me and all flesh that is on the earth."

The sons of Noah who went out from the ship were Shem, Ham, and Japheth. Ham is the father of Canaan. These three were the sons of Noah, and from these, the whole earth was populated.

Noah lived three hundred fifty years after the flood. All the days of Noah were nine hundred fifty years, then he died.

After the flood, Shem, Ham and Japheth began families, and they eventually divided into nations. But when their pride led them to intend to "make a name for themselves" God intervened.

The whole earth was of one language and of one speech. It happened, as they traveled east, that they found a plain in the land of Shinar, and they lived there. They said one to another, "Come, let's make bricks, and burn them thoroughly." They had brick for stone, and they used tar for mortar. They said, "Come, let's build ourselves a city, and a tower whose top reaches to the sky, and let's make ourselves a name, lest we be scattered abroad on the surface of the whole earth."

Yahweh came down to see the city and the tower, which the children of men built. Yahweh said, "Behold, they are one people, and they have all one language, and this is what they begin to do. Now nothing will be withheld from them, which they intend to do. Come, let's go down, and there confuse their language, that they may not understand one another's speech." So Yahweh scattered them abroad from there on the surface of all the earth. They stopped building the city. Therefore its name was called Babel, because there Yahweh confused the language of all the earth. From there, Yahweh scattered them

land at that time. Abram said to Lot, "Please, let there be no strife between me and you, and between my herdsmen and your herdsmen; for we are relatives. Isn't the whole land before you? Please separate yourself from me. If you go to the left hand, then I will go to the right. Or if you go to the right hand, then I will go to the left."

Lot lifted up his eyes, and saw all the plain of the Jordan, that it was well-watered everywhere, before Yahweh destroyed Sodom and Gomorrah, like the garden of Yahweh, like the land of Egypt, as you go to Zoar. So Lot chose the Plain of the Jordan for himself. Lot traveled east, and they separated themselves the one from the other. Abram lived in the land of Canaan, and Lot lived in the cities of the plain, and moved his tent as far as Sodom. Now the men of Sodom were exceedingly wicked and sinners against Yahweh.

Yahweh said to Abram, after Lot was separated from him, "Now, lift up your eyes, and look from the place where you are, northward and southward and eastward and westward, for all the land which you see, I will give to you, and to your offspring forever. I will make your offspring as the dust of the earth, so that if a man can number the dust of the earth, then your seed may also be numbered. Arise, walk through the land in its length and in its breadth; for I will give it to you."

Abram moved his tent, and came and lived by the oaks of Mamre, which are in Hebron, and built an altar there to Yahweh.

After some time, there was a war among the various kings of the region. In the battle, Sodom and Gomorrah was overcome, and Lot and his family were led away as captives. When told of this, Abram took 318 fighting men from his household and pursued the bands which had captured Lot. Overcoming them in a night raid, they rescued Lot, his family, and all his goods. On his triumphant return, Abram was blessed by Melchizedek king of Salem, who was priest of God Most High.

After these things the word of Yahweh came to Abram in a vision, saying, "Don't be afraid, Abram. I am your shield, your exceedingly great reward."

Abram said, "Lord Yahweh, what will you give me, since I go childless, and he who will inherit my estate is Eliezer of Damascus?" Abram said, "Behold, to me you have given no seed: and, behold, one born in my house is my heir."

Behold, the word of Yahweh came to him, saying, "This man will not be your heir, but he who will come out of your own body will be your heir." Yahweh brought him outside, and said, "Look now toward the sky, and count the stars, if you are able to count them." He said to Abram, "So shall your seed be." He believed in Yahweh; and he reckoned it to him for righteousness.

14

Now Sarai, Abram's wife, bore him no children. She had a handmaid, an Egyptian, whose name was Hagar. Sarai said to Abram, "See now, Yahweh has restrained me from bearing. Please go in to my handmaid. It may be that I will obtain children by her." Abram listened to the voice of Sarai. Sarai, Abram's wife, took Hagar the Egyptian, her handmaid, after Abram had lived ten years in the land of Canaan, and gave her to Abram her husband to be his wife. He went in to Hagar, and she conceived. When she saw that she had conceived, her mistress was despised in her eyes. Sarai said to Abram, "This wrong is your fault. I gave my handmaid into your bosom, and when she saw that she had conceived, I was despised in her eyes. Yahweh judge between me and you."

But Abram said to Sarai, "Behold, your maid is in your hand. Do to her whatever is good in your eyes." Sarai dealt harshly with her, and she fled from her face.

The angel of Yahweh found her by a fountain of water in the wilderness, by the fountain in the way to Shur. He said, "Hagar, Sarai's handmaid, where did you come from? Where are you going?"

She said, "I am fleeing from the face of my mistress Sarai."

The angel of Yahweh said to her, "Return to your mistress, and submit yourself under her hands." The angel of Yahweh said to her, "I will greatly multiply your seed, that they will not be numbered for multitude." The angel of Yahweh said to her, "Behold, you are with child, and will bear a son. You shall call his name Ishmael, because Yahweh has heard your affliction. He will be like a wild donkey among men. His hand will be against every man, and every man's hand against him. He will live opposite all of his brothers."

Hagar bore a son for Abram. Abram called the name of his son, whom Hagar bore, Ishmael. Abram was eighty-six years old when Hagar bore Ishmael to Abram.

When Abram was ninety-nine years old, Yahweh appeared to Abram, and said to him, "I am God Almighty. Walk before me, and be blameless. I will make my covenant between me and you, and will multiply you exceedingly."

Abram fell on his face. God talked with him, saying, "As for me, behold, my covenant is with you. You will be the father of a multitude of nations. Neither will your name any more be called Abram, but your name will be Abraham; for I have made you the father of a multitude of nations. I will make you exceedingly fruitful, and I will make nations of you. Kings will come out of you. I will establish my covenant between me and you and your seed after you throughout their generations for an everlasting covenant, to be a God to you and to your seed after you. I will give to you, and to your seed after you, the land where you are traveling, all the land of Canaan, for an everlasting possession. I will be their God."

God said to Abraham, "As for you, you will keep my covenant, you and your seed after you throughout their generations. This is my covenant, which you shall keep, between me and you and your seed after you. Every male among you shall be circumcised. You shall be circumcised in the flesh of your foreskin. It will be a token of the covenant between me and you. He who is eight days old will be circumcised among you, every male throughout your generations, he who is born in the house, or bought with money from any foreigner who is not of your seed. He who is born in your house, and he who is bought with your money, must be circumcised. My covenant will be in your flesh for an everlasting covenant. The uncircumcised male who is not circumcised in the flesh of his foreskin, that soul shall be cut off from his people. He has broken my covenant."

God said to Abraham, "As for Sarai your wife, you shall not call her name Sarai, but her name will be Sarah. I will bless her, and moreover I will give you a son by her. Yes, I will bless her, and she will be a mother of nations. Kings of peoples will come from her."

Then Abraham fell on his face, and laughed, and said in his heart, "Will a child be born to him who is one hundred years old? Will Sarah, who is ninety years old, give birth?" Abraham said to God, "Oh that Ishmael might live before you!"

God said, "No, but Sarah, your wife, will bear you a son. You shall call his name Isaac. I will establish my covenant with him for an everlasting covenant for his seed after him. As for Ishmael, I have heard you. Behold, I have blessed him, and will make him fruitful, and will multiply him exceedingly. He will become the father of twelve princes, and I will make him a great nation. But my covenant I establish with Isaac, whom Sarah will bear to you at this set time next year."

Yahweh visited Sarah as he had said, and Yahweh did to Sarah as he had spoken. Sarah conceived, and bore Abraham a son in his old age, at the set time of which God had spoken to him. Abraham called his son who was born to him, whom Sarah bore to him, Isaac. Abraham circumcised his son, Isaac, when he was eight days old, as God had commanded him. Abraham was one hundred years old when his son, Isaac, was born to him. Sarah said, "God has made me laugh. Everyone who hears will laugh with me." She said, "Who would have said to Abraham, that Sarah would nurse children? For I have borne him a son in his old age."

The child grew, and was weaned. Abraham made a great feast on the day that Isaac was weaned. Sarah saw the son of Hagar the Egyptian, whom she had borne to Abraham, mocking. Therefore she said to Abraham, "Cast out this handmaid and her son! For the son of this handmaid will not be heir with my son, Isaac."

The thing was very grievous in Abraham's sight on account of his son. God said to Abraham, "Don't let it be grievous in your sight because of the boy, and because of your handmaid. In all that Sarah says to you, listen to her voice. For from Isaac will your seed be called. I will also make a nation of the son of the handmaid, because he is your seed." Abraham rose up early in the morning, and took bread and a bottle of water, and gave it to Hagar, putting it on her shoulder; and gave her the child, and sent her away. She departed, and wandered in the wilderness of Beersheba. The water in the bottle was spent, and she cast the child under one of the shrubs. She went and sat down opposite him, a good way off, about a bow shot away. For she said, "Don't let me see the death of the child." She sat over against him, and lifted up her voice, and wept. God heard the voice of the boy. The angel of God called to Hagar out of the sky, and said to her, "What ails you, Hagar? Don't be afraid. For God has heard the voice of the boy where he is. Get up, lift up the boy, and hold him in your hand. For I will make him a great nation."

God opened her eyes, and she saw a well of water. She went, filled the bottle with water, and gave the boy drink. God was with the boy, and he grew. He lived in the wilderness, and became, as he grew up, an archer.

It happened after these things, that God tested Abraham, and said to him, "Abraham!"

He said, "Here I am."

He said, "Now take your son, your only son, whom you love, even Isaac, and go into the land of Moriah. Offer him there for a burnt offering on one of the mountains which I will tell you of."

Abraham rose early in the morning, and saddled his donkey, and took two of his young men with him, and Isaac his son. He split the wood for the burnt offering, and rose up, and went to the place of which God had told him. On the third day Abraham lifted up his eyes, and saw the place far off. Abraham said to his young men, "Stay here with the donkey. The boy and I will go yonder. We will worship, and come back to you." Abraham took the wood of the burnt offering and laid it on Isaac his son. He took in his hand the fire and the knife. They both went together. Isaac spoke to Abraham his father, and said, "My father?"

He said, "Here I am, my son."

He said, "Here is the fire and the wood, but where is the lamb for a burnt offering?"

Abraham said, "God will provide himself the lamb for a burnt offering, my son." So they both went together. They came to the place which God had told him of. Abraham built the altar there, and laid the wood in order, bound Isaac his son, and laid him on the altar, on the wood. Abraham stretched out his hand, and took the knife to kill his son.

The angel of Yahweh called to him out of the sky, and said, "Abraham,

Abraham!"

He said, "Here I am."

He said, "Don't lay your hand on the boy, neither do anything to him. For now I know that you fear God, since you have not withheld your son, your only son, from me."

Abraham lifted up his eyes, and looked, and saw that behind him was a ram caught in the thicket by his horns. Abraham went and took the ram, and offered him up for a burnt offering instead of his son. Abraham called the name of that place Yahweh Will Provide. As it is said to this day, "On Yahweh's mountain, it will be provided."

The angel of Yahweh called to Abraham a second time out of the sky, and said, "I have sworn by myself, says Yahweh, because you have done this thing, and have not withheld your son, your only son, that I will bless you greatly, and I will multiply your seed greatly like the stars of the heavens, and like the sand which is on the seashore. Your seed will possess the gate of his enemies. In your seed will all the nations of the earth be blessed, because you have obeyed my voice."

Abraham was old, and well stricken in age. Yahweh had blessed Abraham in all things. Abraham said to his servant, the elder of his house, who ruled over all that he had, "Please put your hand under my thigh. I will make you swear by Yahweh, the God of heaven and the God of the earth, that you shall not take a wife for my son of the daughters of the Canaanites, among whom I live. But you shall go to my country, and to my relatives, and take a wife for my son Isaac."

The servant put his hand under the thigh of Abraham his master, and swore to him concerning this matter. The servant took ten camels, of his master's camels, and departed, having a variety of good things of his master's with him. He arose, and went to Mesopotamia, to the city of Nahor. He made the camels kneel down outside the city by the well of water at the time of evening, the time that women go out to draw water. He said, "Yahweh, the God of my master Abraham, please give me success this day, and show kindness to my master Abraham. Behold, I am standing by the spring of water. The daughters of the men of the city are coming out to draw water. Let it happen, that the young lady to whom I will say, 'Please let down your pitcher, that I may drink,' and she will say, 'Drink, and I will also give your camels a drink,'—let her be the one you have appointed for your servant Isaac. By this I will know that you have shown kindness to my master."

It happened, before he had finished speaking, that behold, Rebekah came out, who was born to Bethuel the son of Milcah, the wife of Nahor, Abraham's brother, with her pitcher on her shoulder. The young lady was very beautiful to look at, a virgin, neither had any man known her. She went down to the spring, filled her pitcher, and came up. The servant ran to meet her, and said, "Please give me a drink, a little water from your pitcher."

She said, "Drink, my lord." She hurried, and let down her pitcher on her hand, and gave him drink. When she had done giving him drink, she said, "I will also draw for your camels, until they have done drinking." She hurried, and emptied her pitcher into the trough, and ran again to the well to draw, and drew for all his camels.

The man looked steadfastly at her, remaining silent, to know whether Yahweh had made his journey prosperous or not. It happened, as the camels had done drinking, that the man took a golden ring of half a shekel weight, and two bracelets for her hands of ten shekels weight of gold, and said, "Whose daughter are you? Please tell me. Is there room in your father's house for us to lodge in?"

She said to him, "I am the daughter of Bethuel the son of Milcah, whom she bore to Nahor." She said moreover to him, "We have both straw and provender enough, and room to lodge in."

The man bowed his head, and worshiped Yahweh. He said, "Blessed be Yahweh, the God of my master Abraham, who has not forsaken his loving kindness and his truth toward my master. As for me, Yahweh has led me in the way to the house of my master's relatives."

Rebekah's family, relatives of Abraham, agreed to allow her to return with Abraham's servant to become Isaac's wife. Isaac loved her, and he was comforted after his mother's death. Rebekah became pregnant with twins; these two sons would have a tumultuous history.

Isaac was forty years old when he took Rebekah, the daughter of Bethuel the Syrian of Paddan Aram, the sister of Laban the Syrian, to be his wife. Isaac entreated Yahweh for his wife, because she was barren. Yahweh was entreated by him, and Rebekah his wife conceived. The children struggled together within her. She said, "If it be so, why do I live?" She went to inquire of Yahweh. Yahweh said to her,

"Two nations are in your womb.

Two peoples will be separated from your body.

The one people will be stronger than the other people.

The elder will serve the younger."

When her days to be delivered were fulfilled, behold, there were twins in her womb. The first came out red all over, like a hairy garment. They named him Esau. After that, his brother came out, and his hand had hold on Esau's heel. He was named Jacob. Isaac was sixty years old when she bore them.

The boys grew. Esau was a skillful hunter, a man of the field. Jacob was a quiet man, living in tents. Now Isaac loved Esau, because he ate his venison. Rebekah

saddle, and sat on them. Laban felt about all the tent, but didn't find them. She said to her father, "Don't let my lord be angry that I can't rise up before you; for I'm having my period." He searched, but didn't find the teraphim.

Jacob was angry, and argued with Laban. Jacob answered Laban, "What is my trespass? What is my sin, that you have hotly pursued after me? Now that you have felt around in all my stuff, what have you found of all your household stuff? Set it here before my relatives and your relatives, that they may judge between us two.

"These twenty years I have been with you. Your ewes and your female goats have not cast their young, and I haven't eaten the rams of your flocks. That which was torn of animals, I didn't bring to you. I bore its loss. Of my hand you required it, whether stolen by day or stolen by night. This was my situation: in the day the drought consumed me, and the frost by night; and my sleep fled from my eyes. These twenty years I have been in your house. I served you fourteen years for your two daughters, and six years for your flock, and you have changed my wages ten times. Unless the God of my father, the God of Abraham, and the fear of Isaac, had been with me, surely now you would have sent me away empty. God has seen my affliction and the labor of my hands, and rebuked you last night."

Laban answered Jacob, "The daughters are my daughters, the children are my children, the flocks are my flocks, and all that you see is mine: and what can I do this day to these my daughters, or to their children whom they have borne? Now come, let us make a covenant, you and I; and let it be for a witness between me and you."

Jacob took a stone, and set it up for a pillar. Jacob said to his relatives, "Gather stones." They took stones, and made a heap. They ate there by the heap. Laban called it Jegar Sahadutha, but Jacob called it Galeed. Laban said, "This heap is witness between me and you this day." Therefore it was named Galeed and Mizpah, for he said, "Yahweh watch between me and you, when we are absent one from another.

Having overcome the strife with Laban, Jacob next faced the prospect of reuniting with his brother Esau, who had his birthright taken by Jacob in an act of deceit. After 20 years, Jacob was not sure what kind of reception he would receive from his brother. During the night, Jacob wrestled with God, who changed Jacob's name to Israel.

Jacob sent messengers in front of him to Esau, his brother, to the land of Seir, the field of Edom. He commanded them, saying, "This is what you shall tell my lord, Esau: 'This is what your servant, Jacob, says. I have lived as a foreigner with Laban, and stayed until now. I have cattle, donkeys, flocks, male servants, and female servants. I have sent to tell my lord, that I may find favor in your sight.'" The messengers returned to Jacob, saying, "We came to your brother Esau. Not only that, but he comes to meet you, and four hundred men with him." Then Jacob was greatly afraid and was distressed. He divided the people who were with him, and the flocks, and the herds, and the camels, into two companies; and he said, "If Esau comes to the one company, and strikes it, then the company which is left will escape." Jacob said, "God of my father Abraham, and God of my father Isaac, Yahweh, who said to me, 'Return to your country, and to your relatives, and I will do you good,' I am not worthy of the least of all the loving kindnesses, and of all the truth, which you have shown to your servant; for with just my staff I passed over this Jordan; and now I have become two companies. Please deliver me from the hand of my brother, from the hand of Esau: for I fear him, lest he come and strike me, and the mothers with the children. You said, 'I will surely do you good, and make your seed as the sand of the sea, which can't be numbered because there are so many.'"

He lodged there that night, and took from that which he had with him, a present for Esau, his brother: two hundred female goats and twenty male goats, two hundred ewes and twenty rams, thirty milk camels and their colts, forty cows, ten bulls, twenty female donkeys and ten foals. He delivered them into the hands of his servants, every herd by itself, and said to his servants, "Pass over before me, and put a space between herd and herd." He commanded the foremost, saying, "When Esau, my brother, meets you, and asks you, saying, 'Whose are you? Where are you going? Whose are these before you?' Then you shall say, 'They are your servant, Jacob's. It is a present sent to my lord, Esau. Behold, he also is behind us.'" He commanded also the second, and the third, and all that followed the herds, saying, "This is how you shall speak to Esau, when you find him. You shall say, 'Not only that, but behold, your servant, Jacob, is behind us.'" For, he said, "I will appease him with the present that goes before me, and afterward I will see his face. Perhaps he will accept me."

So the present passed over before him, and he himself lodged that night in the camp.

He rose up that night, and took his two wives, and his two handmaids, and his eleven sons, and passed over the ford of the Jabbok. He took them, and sent them over the stream, and sent over that which he had. Jacob was left alone, and wrestled with a man there until the breaking of the day. When he saw that he didn't prevail against him, he touched the hollow of his thigh, and the hollow of Jacob's thigh was strained, as he wrestled. The man said, "Let me go, for the day breaks."

Jacob said, "I won't let you go, unless you bless me."

He said to him, "What is your name?"

He said, "Jacob." He said, "Your name will no longer be called Jacob, but Israel; for you have fought with God and with men, and have prevailed."

Jacob asked him, "Please tell me your name."

He said, "Why is it that you ask what my name is?" He blessed him there.

Jacob called the name of the place Peniel: for, he said, "I have seen God face to face, and my life is preserved." The sun rose on him as he passed over Peniel, and he limped because of his thigh. Therefore the children of Israel don't eat the sinew of the hip, which is on the hollow of the thigh, to this day, because he touched the hollow of Jacob's thigh in the sinew of the hip.

Jacob lifted up his eyes, and looked, and, behold, Esau was coming, and with him four hundred men. He divided the children between Leah, Rachel, and the two handmaids. He put the handmaids and their children in front, Leah and her children after, and Rachel and Joseph at the rear. He himself passed over in front of them, and bowed himself to the ground seven times, until he came near to his brother.

Esau ran to meet him, embraced him, fell on his neck, kissed him, and they wept. He lifted up his eyes, and saw the women and the children; and said, "Who are these with you?"

He said, "The children whom God has graciously given your servant." Then the handmaids came near with their children, and they bowed themselves. Leah also and her children came near, and bowed themselves. After them, Joseph came near with Rachel, and they bowed themselves.

Esau said, "What do you mean by all this company which I met?"

Jacob said, "To find favor in the sight of my lord."

Esau said, "I have enough, my brother; let that which you have be yours."

Jacob said, "Please, no, if I have now found favor in your sight, then receive my present at my hand, because I have seen your face, as one sees the face of God, and you were pleased with me. Please take the gift that I brought to you, because God has dealt graciously with me, and because I have enough." He urged him, and he took it.

God said to Jacob, "Arise, go up to Bethel, and live there. Make there an altar to God, who appeared to you when you fled from the face of Esau your brother."

Then Jacob said to his household, and to all who were with him, "Put away the foreign gods that are among you, purify yourselves, change your garments. Let us arise, and go up to Bethel. I will make there an altar to God, who answered me in the day of my distress, and was with me in the way which I went."

They gave to Jacob all the foreign gods which were in their hands, and the rings which were in their ears; and Jacob hid them under the oak which was by

Shechem. They traveled, and a terror of God was on the cities that were around them, and they didn't pursue the sons of Jacob. So Jacob came to Luz (that is, Bethel), which is in the land of Canaan, he and all the people who were with him. He built an altar there, and called the place El Beth El; because there God was revealed to him, when he fled from the face of his brother. Deborah, Rebekah's nurse, died, and she was buried below Bethel under the oak; and its name was called Allon Bacuth.

God appeared to Jacob again, when he came from Paddan Aram, and blessed him. God said to him, "Your name is Jacob. Your name shall not be Jacob any more, but your name will be Israel." He named him Israel. God said to him, "I am God Almighty. Be fruitful and multiply. A nation and a company of nations will be from you, and kings will come out of your body. The land which I gave to Abraham and Isaac, I will give it to you, and to your seed after you will I give the land."

They traveled from Bethel. There was still some distance to come to Ephrath, and Rachel travailed. She had hard labor. When she was in hard labor, the midwife said to her, "Don't be afraid, for now you will have another son."

It happened, as her soul was departing (for she died), that she named him Benoni, but his father named him Benjamin. Rachel died, and was buried in the way to Ephrath (the same is Bethlehem).

The days of Isaac were one hundred eighty years. Isaac gave up the spirit, and died, and was gathered to his people, old and full of days. Esau and Jacob, his sons, buried him.

3 DREAMS AND DELIVERANCE

From Hebrew Slave to Egyptian Ruler

Now Israel loved Joseph more than all his children, because he was the son of his old age, and he made him a coat of many colors. His brothers saw that their father loved him more than all his brothers, and they hated him, and couldn't speak peaceably to him.

Joseph dreamed a dream, and he told it to his brothers, and they hated him all the more. He said to them, "Please hear this dream which I have dreamed: for behold, we were binding sheaves in the field, and behold, my sheaf arose and also stood upright; and behold, your sheaves came around, and bowed down to my sheaf."

His brothers said to him, "Will you indeed reign over us? Or will you indeed have dominion over us?" They hated him all the more for his dreams and for his words. He dreamed yet another dream, and told it to his brothers, and said, "Behold, I have dreamed yet another dream: and behold, the sun and the moon and eleven stars bowed down to me." He told it to his father and to his brothers. His father rebuked him, and said to him, "What is this dream that you have dreamed? Will I and your mother and your brothers indeed come to bow ourselves down to you to the earth?" His brothers envied him, but his father kept this saying in mind.

His brothers went to feed their father's flock in Shechem. Israel said to Joseph, "Aren't your brothers feeding the flock in Shechem? Come, and I will send you to them." He said to him, "Here I am."

Joseph went after his brothers, and found them in Dothan. They saw him afar off, and before he came near to them, they conspired against him to kill him. They said one to another, "Behold, this dreamer comes. Come now therefore, and let's kill him, and cast him into one of the pits, and we will say, 'An evil animal has devoured him.' We will see what will become of his dreams."

Reuben heard it, and delivered him out of their hand, and said, "Let's not take his life." Reuben said to them, "Shed no blood. Throw him into this pit that is in the wilderness, but lay no hand on him"—that he might deliver him out of their hand, to restore him to his father. It happened, when Joseph came to his brothers, that they stripped Joseph of his coat, the coat of many colors that was on him; and they took him, and threw him into the pit. The pit was empty. There was no water in it.

They sat down to eat bread, and they lifted up their eyes and looked, and saw a caravan of Ishmaelites was coming from Gilead, with their camels bearing spices and balm and myrrh, going to carry it down to Egypt. Judah said to his brothers, "What profit is it if we kill our brother and conceal his blood? Come, and let's sell him to the Ishmaelites, and not let our hand be on him; for he is our brother, our flesh." His brothers listened to him. Midianites who were merchants passed by, and they drew and lifted up Joseph out of the pit, and sold Joseph to the Ishmaelites for twenty pieces of silver. They brought Joseph into Egypt.

Reuben returned to the pit; and saw that Joseph wasn't in the pit; and he tore his clothes. He returned to his brothers, and said, "The child is no more; and I, where will I go?" They took Joseph's coat, and killed a male goat, and dipped the coat in the blood. They took the coat of many colors, and they brought it to their father, and said, "We have found this. Examine it, now, whether it is your son's coat or not."

He recognized it, and said, "It is my son's coat. An evil animal has devoured him. Joseph is without doubt torn in pieces." Jacob tore his clothes, and put sackcloth on his waist, and mourned for his son many days. All his sons and all his daughters rose up to comfort him, but he refused to be comforted. He said, "For I will go down to Sheol to my son mourning." His father wept for him. The Midianites sold him into Egypt to Potiphar, an officer of Pharaoh's, the captain of the guard.

Joseph was brought down to Egypt. Potiphar, an officer of Pharaoh's, the captain of the guard, an Egyptian, bought him from the hand of the Ishmaelites that had brought him down there. Yahweh was with Joseph, and he was a prosperous man. He was in the house of his master the Egyptian. His master saw that Yahweh was with him, and that Yahweh made all that he did prosper in his hand. Joseph found favor in his sight. He ministered to him, and he made him overseer over his house, and all that he had he put into his hand. It happened from the time that he made him overseer in his house, and over all that he had, that Yahweh blessed the Egyptian's house for Joseph's sake; and the blessing of Yahweh was on all that he had, in the house and in the field. He left all that he had in Joseph's hand. He didn't concern himself with anything, except for the food which he ate.

Joseph was well-built and handsome. It happened after these things, that his master's wife cast her eyes on Joseph; and she said, "Lie with me."

But he refused, and said to his master's wife, "Behold, my master doesn't know what is with me in the house, and he has put all that he has into my hand. He isn't greater in this house than I, neither has he kept back anything from me but you, because you are his wife. How then can I do this great wickedness, and sin against God?"

As she spoke to Joseph day by day, he didn't listen to her, to lie by her, or to be with her. About this time, he went into the house to do his work, and there were none of the men of the house inside. She caught him by his garment, saying, "Lie with me!"

He left his garment in her hand, and ran outside. When she saw that he had left his garment in her hand, and had run outside, she called to the men of her house, and spoke to them, saying, "Behold, he has brought in a Hebrew to us to mock us. He came in to me to lie with me, and I cried with a loud voice. It happened, when he heard that I lifted up my voice and cried, that he left his garment by me, and ran outside." She laid up his garment by her, until his master came home. She spoke to him according to these words, saying, "The Hebrew servant, whom you have brought to us, came in to me to mock me, and it happened, as I lifted up my voice and cried, that he left his garment by me, and ran outside."

It happened, when his master heard the words of his wife, which she spoke to him, saying, "This is what your servant did to me," that his wrath was kindled. Joseph's master took him, and put him into the prison, the place where the king's prisoners were bound, and he was there in custody. But Yahweh was with Joseph, and showed kindness to him, and gave him favor in the sight of the keeper of the prison. The keeper of the prison committed to Joseph's hand all the prisoners who were in the prison. Whatever they did there, he was responsible for it. The keeper of the prison didn't look after anything that was under his hand, because Yahweh was with him; and that which he did, Yahweh made it prosper

While in prison, God blessed Joseph and worked through him to interpret dreams. Joseph interpreted dreams for the butler and baker of Pharaoh, who had also been thrown into prison. As Joseph predicted, the baker was put to death, but the butler was restored to his position in Pharaoh's palace. One day, when Pharaoh was troubled by a dream, the butler remembered Joseph and his ability. Joseph was called from prison to stand before Pharaoh, the ruler of mighty Egypt.

Then Pharaoh sent and called Joseph, and they brought him hastily out of the dungeon. He shaved himself, changed his clothing, and came in to Pharaoh. Pharaoh said to Joseph, "I have dreamed a dream, and there is no one who can interpret it. I have heard it said of you, that when you hear a dream you can interpret it."

Joseph answered Pharaoh, saying, "It isn't in me. God will give Pharaoh an answer of peace."

Pharaoh spoke to Joseph, "In my dream, behold, I stood on the brink of the river: and behold, there came up out of the river seven cattle, fat and sleek. They fed in the marsh grass, and behold, seven other cattle came up after them, poor and very ugly and thin, such as I never saw in all the land of Egypt for ugliness. The thin and ugly cattle ate up the first seven fat cattle, and when they had eaten them up, it couldn't be known that they had eaten them, but they were still ugly, as at the beginning. So I awoke. I saw in my dream, and behold, seven heads of grain came up on one stalk, full and good: and behold, seven heads of grain, withered, thin, and blasted with the east wind, sprung up after them. The thin heads of grain swallowed up the seven good heads of grain. I told it to the magicians, but there was no one who could explain it to me."

Joseph said to Pharaoh, "The dream of Pharaoh is one. What God is about to do he has declared to Pharaoh. The seven good cattle are seven years; and the seven good heads of grain are seven years. The dream is one. The seven thin and ugly cattle that came up after them are seven years, and also the seven empty heads of grain blasted with the east wind; they will be seven years of famine. That is the thing which I spoke to Pharaoh. What God is about to do he has shown to Pharaoh. Behold, there come seven years of great plenty throughout all the land of Egypt. There will arise after them seven years of famine, and all the plenty will be forgotten in the land of Egypt. The famine will consume the land, and the plenty will not be known in the land by reason of that famine which follows; for it will be very grievous. The dream was doubled to Pharaoh, because the thing is established by God, and God will shortly bring it to pass.

"Now therefore let Pharaoh look for a discreet and wise man, and set him over the land of Egypt. Let Pharaoh do this, and let him appoint overseers over the land, and take up the fifth part of the land of Egypt's produce in the seven plenteous years. Let them gather all the food of these good years that come, and lay up grain under the hand of Pharaoh for food in the cities, and let them keep it. The food will be for a store to the land against the seven years of famine, which will be in the land of Egypt; that the land not perish through the famine."

The thing was good in the eyes of Pharaoh, and in the eyes of all his servants. Pharaoh said to his servants, "Can we find such a one as this, a man in whom is the Spirit of God?" Pharaoh said to Joseph, "Because God has shown you all of this, there is none so discreet and wise as you. You shall be over my house, and according to your word will all my people be ruled. Only in the throne I will be greater than you." Pharaoh said to Joseph, "Behold, I have set you over all the land of Egypt." Pharaoh took off his signet ring from his hand, and put it on Joseph's hand, and arrayed him in robes of fine linen, and put a gold chain about his neck, and he made him to ride in the second chariot which he had. They cried before him, "Bow the knee!" He set him over all the land of Egypt. Pharaoh said to Joseph, "I am Pharaoh, and without you shall no man lift up his hand or his foot in all the land of Egypt." Pharaoh called Joseph's name Zaphenath-Paneah; and he gave him Asenath, the daughter of Potiphera priest of On as a wife. Joseph went out over the land of Egypt.

Joseph was thirty years old when he stood before Pharaoh king of Egypt. Joseph went out from the presence of Pharaoh, and went throughout all the land of Egypt. In the seven plenteous years the earth produced abundantly. He gathered up all the food of the seven years which were in the land of Egypt, and laid up the food in the cities: the food of the field, which was around every city, he laid up in the same. Joseph laid up grain as the sand of the sea, very much, until he stopped counting, for it was without number. To Joseph were born two sons before the year of famine came, whom Asenath, the daughter of Potiphera priest of On, bore to him. Joseph called the name of the firstborn Manasseh, "For," he said, "God has made me forget all my toil, and all my father's house." The name of the second, he called Ephraim: "For God has made me fruitful in the land of my affliction."

The seven years of plenty, that were in the land of Egypt, came to an end. The seven years of famine began to come, just as Joseph had said. There was famine in all lands, but in all the land of Egypt there was bread. When all the land of Egypt was famished, the people cried to Pharaoh for bread, and Pharaoh said to all the Egyptians, "Go to Joseph. What he says to you, do." The famine was over all the surface of the earth. Joseph opened all the store houses, and sold to the Egyptians. The famine was severe in the land of Egypt. All countries came into Egypt, to Joseph, to buy grain, because the famine was severe in all the earth.

Now Jacob saw that there was grain in Egypt, and Jacob said to his sons, "Why do you look at one another?" He said, "Behold, I have heard that there is grain in Egypt. Go down there, and buy for us from there, so that we may live, and not die." Joseph's ten brothers went down to buy grain from Egypt. But Jacob didn't send Benjamin, Joseph's brother, with his brothers; for he said, "Lest perhaps harm happen to him." The sons of Israel came to buy among those who came, for the famine was in the land of Canaan. Joseph was the governor over the land. It was he who sold to all the people of the land. Joseph's brothers came, and bowed themselves down to him with their faces to the earth. Joseph saw his brothers, and he recognized them, but acted like a stranger to them, and spoke roughly with them. He said to them, "Where did you come from?"

They said, "From the land of Canaan to buy food."

Joseph recognized his brothers, but they didn't recognize him. Joseph remembered the dreams which he dreamed about them, and said to them, "You are spies! You have come to see the nakedness of the land."

They said to him, "No, my lord, but your servants have come to buy food. We are all one man's sons; we are honest men. Your servants are not spies."

He said to them, "No, but you have come to see the nakedness of the land!"

They said, "We, your servants, are twelve brothers, the sons of one man in the land of Canaan; and behold, the youngest is this day with our father, and one is no more."

Joseph said to them, "It is like I told you, saying, 'You are spies!' By this you shall be tested. By the life of Pharaoh, you shall not go out from here, unless your youngest brother comes here.

So Joseph knew his brothers, but they did not recognize him. This gave Joseph a chance to put them to a test; he kept Simeon as a prisoner in Egypt, and sent the rest of his brothers back to their father Jacob. But he advised them not to return without their youngest brother, Benjamin. He also had their money secretly put back into their sacks, to make it appear that they had stolen the money from Egypt. This "trick" ensured that they would have to muster bravery to return to Egypt.

The famine was severe in the land. It happened, when they had eaten up the grain which they had brought out of Egypt, their father said to them, "Go again, buy us a little more food."

Judah spoke to him, saying, "The man solemnly warned us, saying, 'You shall not see my face, unless your brother is with you.' If you'll send our brother with us, we'll go down and buy you food, but if you'll not send him, we'll not go down, for the man said to us, 'You shall not see my face, unless your brother is with you.'"

Their father, Israel, said to them, "If it must be so, then do this. Take from the choice fruits of the land in your bags, and carry down a present for the man, a little balm, a little honey, spices and myrrh, nuts, and almonds; and take double money in your hand, and take back the money that was returned in the mouth of your sacks. Perhaps it was an oversight. Take your brother also, get up, and return to the man. May God Almighty give you mercy before the man, that he may release to you your other brother and Benjamin. If I am bereaved of my children, I am bereaved."

The men took that present, and they took double money in their hand, and

Benjamin; and got up, went down to Egypt, and stood before Joseph.

When Joseph came home, they brought him the present which was in their hand into the house, and bowed themselves down to him to the earth. He asked them of their welfare, and said, "Is your father well, the old man of whom you spoke? Is he yet alive?"

They said, "Your servant, our father, is well. He is still alive." They bowed down humbly. He lifted up his eyes, and saw Benjamin, his brother, his mother's son, and said, "Is this your youngest brother, of whom you spoke to me?" He said, "God be gracious to you, my son." Joseph hurried, for his heart yearned over his brother; and he sought a place to weep. He entered into his room, and wept there. He washed his face, and came out. He controlled himself, and said, "Serve the meal."

They served him by himself, and them by themselves, and the Egyptians, that ate with him, by themselves, because the Egyptians don't eat bread with the Hebrews, for that is an abomination to the Egyptians. They sat before him, the firstborn according to his birthright, and the youngest according to his youth, and the men marveled one with another. He sent portions to them from before him, but Benjamin's portion was five times as much as any of theirs. They drank, and were merry with him.

He commanded the steward of his house, saying, "Fill the men's sacks with food, as much as they can carry, and put each man's money in his sack's mouth. Put my cup, the silver cup, in the sack's mouth of the youngest, with his grain money." He did according to the word that Joseph had spoken. As soon as the morning was light, the men were sent away, they and their donkeys. When they had gone out of the city, and were not yet far off, Joseph said to his steward, "Up, follow after the men. When you overtake them, ask them, 'Why have you rewarded evil for good? Isn't this that from which my lord drinks, and by which he indeed divines? You have done evil in so doing.'" He overtook them, and he spoke these words to them.

They said to him, "Why does my lord speak such words as these? Far be it from your servants that they should do such a thing! Behold, the money, which we found in our sacks' mouths, we brought again to you out of the land of Canaan. How then should we steal silver or gold out of your lord's house? With whomever of your servants it is found, let him die, and we also will be my lord's bondservants."

He said, "Now also let it be according to your words: he with whom it is found will be my bondservant; and you will be blameless."

Then they hurried, and each man took his sack down to the ground, and each man opened his sack. He searched, beginning with the eldest, and ending at the youngest. The cup was found in Benjamin's sack. Then they tore their clothes, and each man loaded his donkey, and returned to the city.

Judah and his brothers came to Joseph's house, and he was still there. They fell on the ground before him. Joseph said to them, "What deed is this that you have done? Don't you know that such a man as I can indeed divine?"

Judah said, "What will we tell my lord? What will we speak? Or how will we clear ourselves? God has found out the iniquity of your servants. Behold, we are my lord's bondservants, both we, and he also in whose hand the cup is found."

He said, "Far be it from me that I should do so. The man in whose hand the cup is found, he will be my bondservant; but as for you, go up in peace to your father."

Then Judah came near to him, and said, "Oh, my lord, please let your servant speak a word in my lord's ears, and don't let your anger burn against your servant; for you are even as Pharaoh. My lord asked his servants, saying, 'Have you a father, or a brother?' We said to my lord, 'We have a father, an old man, and a child of his old age, a little one; and his brother is dead, and he alone is left of his mother; and his father loves him.' You said to your servants, 'Bring him down to me, that I may set my eyes on him.' We said to my lord, 'The boy can't leave his father: for if he should leave his father, his father would die.' You said to your servants, 'Unless your youngest brother comes down with you, you will see my face no more.' It happened when we came up to your servant my father, we told him the words of my lord. Our father said, 'Go again, buy us a little food.' We said, 'We can't go down. If our youngest brother is with us, then we will go down: for we may not see the man's face, unless our youngest brother is with us.' Your servant, my father, said to us, 'You know that my wife bore me two sons: and the one went out from me, and I said, "Surely he is torn in pieces"; and I haven't seen him since. If you take this one also from me, and harm happens to him, you will bring down my gray hairs with sorrow to Sheol.' Now therefore when I come to your servant my father, and the boy is not with us; since his life is bound up in the boy's life; it will happen, when he sees that the boy is no more, that he will die. Your servants will bring down the gray hairs of your servant, our father, with sorrow to Sheol. For your servant became collateral for the boy to my father, saying, 'If I don't bring him to you, then I will bear the blame to my father forever.' Now therefore, please let your servant stay instead of the boy, a bondservant to my lord; and let the boy go up with his brothers. For how will I go up to my father, if the boy isn't with me?—lest I see the evil that will come on my father."

Then Joseph couldn't control himself before all those who stood before him, and he cried, "Cause everyone to go out from me!" No one else stood with him, while Joseph made himself known to his brothers. He wept aloud. The Egyptians heard, and the house of Pharaoh heard. Joseph said to his brothers, "I am Joseph! Does my father still live?"

His brothers couldn't answer him; for they were terrified at his presence. Joseph said to his brothers, "Come near to me, please."

They came near. "He said, I am Joseph, your brother, whom you sold into Egypt. Now don't be grieved, nor angry with yourselves, that you sold me here, for God sent me before you to preserve life. For these two years the famine has been in the land, and there are yet five years, in which there will be neither plowing nor harvest. God sent me before you to preserve for you a remnant in the earth, and to save you alive by a great deliverance. So now it wasn't you who sent me here, but God, and he has made me a father to Pharaoh, lord of all his house, and ruler over all the land of Egypt. Hurry, and go up to my father, and tell him, 'This is what your son Joseph says, "God has made me lord of all Egypt. Come down to me. Don't wait. You shall dwell in the land of Goshen, and you will be near to me, you, your children, your children's children, your flocks, your herds, and all that you have. There I will nourish you; for there are yet five years of famine; lest you come to poverty, you, and your household, and all that you have."' Behold, your eyes see, and the eyes of my brother Benjamin, that it is my mouth that speaks to you. You shall tell my father of all my glory in Egypt, and of all that you have seen. You shall hurry and bring my father down here." He fell on his brother Benjamin's neck, and wept, and Benjamin wept on his neck. He kissed all his brothers, and wept on them. After that his brothers talked with him.

The report of it was heard in Pharaoh's house, saying, "Joseph's brothers have come." It pleased Pharaoh well, and his servants. Pharaoh said to Joseph, "Tell your brothers, 'Do this. Load your animals, and go, travel to the land of Canaan. Take your father and your households, and come to me, and I will give you the good of the land of Egypt, and you will eat the fat of the land.'

They went up out of Egypt, and came into the land of Canaan, to Jacob their father. They told him, saying, "Joseph is still alive, and he is ruler over all the land of Egypt." His heart fainted, for he didn't believe them. They told him all the words of Joseph, which he had said to them. When he saw the wagons which Joseph had sent to carry him, the spirit of Jacob, their father, revived. Israel said, "It is enough. Joseph my son is still alive. I will go and see him before I die."

Israel traveled with all that he had, and came to Beersheba, and offered sacrifices to the God of his father, Isaac. God spoke to Israel in the visions of the night, and said, "Jacob, Jacob!"

He said, "Here I am."

He said, "I am God, the God of your father. Don't be afraid to go down into

Egypt, for there I will make of you a great nation. I will go down with you into Egypt. I will also surely bring you up again. Joseph will close your eyes."

Jacob rose up from Beersheba, and the sons of Israel carried Jacob, their father, their little ones, and their wives, in the wagons which Pharaoh had sent to carry him.

He sent Judah before him to Joseph, to show the way before him to Goshen, and they came into the land of Goshen. Joseph prepared his chariot, and went up to meet Israel, his father, in Goshen. He presented himself to him, and fell on his neck, and wept on his neck a good while. Israel said to Joseph, "Now let me die, since I have seen your face, that you are still alive."

Joseph placed his father and his brothers, and gave them a possession in the land of Egypt, in the best of the land, in the land of Rameses, as Pharaoh had commanded. Joseph nourished his father, his brothers, and all of his father's household, with bread, according to their families.

As Joseph had predicted, the famine was very severe. Joseph wisely sold the food and grain that was stored, thus greatly increasing the wealth and power of Pharaoh. The people used all of their money, then they sold their livestock, then their land, and then finally they indentured themselves to Pharaoh in return for food. After the famine, Joseph gave the people seed to plant, but made them promise to give one fifth of their crop to Pharaoh from that point onward.

Israel lived in the land of Egypt, in the land of Goshen; and they got themselves possessions therein, and were fruitful, and multiplied exceedingly. Jacob lived in the land of Egypt seventeen years. So the days of Jacob, the years of his life, were one hundred forty-seven years. The time drew near that Israel must die, and he called his son Joseph, and said to him, "If now I have found favor in your sight, please put your hand under my thigh, and deal kindly and truly with me. Please don't bury me in Egypt, but when I sleep with my fathers, you shall carry me out of Egypt, and bury me in their burying place."

He said, "I will do as you have said."

He said, "Swear to me," and he swore to him. Israel bowed himself on the bed's head.

Israel also gave blessings to his other 11 sons, as well as to the two sons of Joseph. On his deathbed, he made his sons promise to return his body to his homeland in Canaan, to be buried with his ancestors. Joseph commanded his physicians to embalm Israel, and after 70 days of mourning, Joseph and his brothers carried his body to Canaan, and Israel was buried as he had requested.

God dealt well with the midwives, and the people multiplied, and grew very mighty. It happened, because the midwives feared God, that he gave them families. Pharaoh commanded all his people, saying, "You shall cast every son who is born into the river, and every daughter you shall save alive."

A man of the house of Levi went and took a daughter of Levi as his wife. The woman conceived, and bore a son. When she saw that he was a fine child, she hid him three months. When she could no longer hide him, she took a papyrus basket for him, and coated it with tar and with pitch. She put the child in it, and laid it in the reeds by the river's bank. His sister stood far off, to see what would be done to him. Pharaoh's daughter came down to bathe at the river. Her maidens walked along by the riverside. She saw the basket among the reeds, and sent her handmaid to get it. She opened it, and saw the child, and behold, the baby cried. She had compassion on him, and said, "This is one of the Hebrews' children."

Then his sister said to Pharaoh's daughter, "Should I go and call a nurse for you from the Hebrew women, that she may nurse the child for you?"

Pharaoh's daughter said to her, "Go." The maiden went and called the child's mother. Pharaoh's daughter said to her, "Take this child away, and nurse him for me, and I will give you your wages."

The woman took the child, and nursed it. The child grew, and she brought him to Pharaoh's daughter, and he became her son. She named him Moses, and said, "Because I drew him out of the water."

It happened in those days, when Moses had grown up, that he went out to his brothers, and looked at their burdens. He saw an Egyptian striking a Hebrew, one of his brothers. He looked this way and that way, and when he saw that there was no one, he killed the Egyptian, and hid him in the sand. He went out the second day, and behold, two men of the Hebrews were fighting with each other. He said to him who did the wrong, "Why do you strike your fellow?"

He said, "Who made you a prince and a judge over us? Do you plan to kill me, as you killed the Egyptian?"

Moses was afraid, and said, "Surely this thing is known." Now when Pharaoh heard this thing, he sought to kill Moses. But Moses fled from the face of Pharaoh, and lived in the land of Midian, and he sat down by a well.

Now the priest of Midian had seven daughters. They came and drew water, and filled the troughs to water their father's flock. The shepherds came and drove them away; but Moses stood up and helped them, and watered their flock.

When they came to Reuel, their father, he said, "How is it that you have returned so early today?"

They said, "An Egyptian delivered us out of the hand of the shepherds, and moreover he drew water for us, and watered the flock."

He said to his daughters, "Where is he? Why is it that you have left the man? Call him, that he may eat bread."

Moses was content to dwell with the man. He gave Moses Zipporah, his daughter. She bore a son, and he named him Gershom, for he said, "I have lived as a foreigner in a foreign land."

It happened in the course of those many days, that the king of Egypt died, and the children of Israel sighed because of the bondage, and they cried, and their cry came up to God because of the bondage. God heard their groaning, and God remembered his covenant with Abraham, with Isaac, and with Jacob. God saw the children of Israel, and God was concerned about them.

Now Moses was keeping the flock of Jethro, his father-in-law, the priest of Midian, and he led the flock to the back of the wilderness, and came to God's mountain, to Horeb. The angel of Yahweh appeared to him in a flame of fire out of the midst of a bush. He looked, and behold, the bush burned with fire, and the bush was not consumed. Moses said, "I will turn aside now, and see this great sight, why the bush is not burnt."

When Yahweh saw that he turned aside to see, God called to him out of the midst of the bush, and said, "Moses! Moses!"

He said, "Here I am."

He said, "Don't come close. Take your sandals off of your feet, for the place you are standing on is holy ground." Moreover he said, "I am the God of your father, the God of Abraham, the God of Isaac, and the God of Jacob."

Moses hid his face; for he was afraid to look at God.

Yahweh said, "I have surely seen the affliction of my people who are in Egypt, and have heard their cry because of their taskmasters, for I know their sorrows. I have come down to deliver them out of the hand of the Egyptians, and to bring them up out of that land to a good and large land, to a land flowing with milk and honey; to the place of the Canaanite, the Hittite, the Amorite, the Perizzite, the Hivite, and the Jebusite. Now, behold, the cry of the children of Israel has come to me. Moreover I have seen the oppression with which the Egyptians oppress them. Come now therefore, and I will send you to Pharaoh, that you may bring my people, the children of Israel, out of Egypt."

Moses said to God, "Who am I, that I should go to Pharaoh, and that I should bring the children of Israel out of Egypt?"

He said, "Certainly I will be with you. This will be the token to you, that I have sent you: when you have brought the people out of Egypt, you shall serve God on this mountain."

Moses said to God, "Behold, when I come to the children of Israel, and tell them, 'The God of your fathers has sent me to you;' and they ask me, 'What is his name?' What should I tell them?"

God said to Moses, "I AM WHO I AM," and he said, "You shall tell the children of Israel this: 'I AM has sent me to you.'" God said moreover to Moses, "You shall tell the children of Israel this, 'Yahweh, the God of your fathers, the God of Abraham, the God of Isaac, and the God of Jacob, has sent me to you.' This is my name forever, and this is my memorial to all generations.

They will listen to your voice, and you shall come, you and the elders of Israel, to the king of Egypt, and you shall tell him, 'Yahweh, the God of the Hebrews, has met with us. Now please let us go three days' journey into the wilderness, that we may sacrifice to Yahweh, our God.' I know that the king of Egypt won't give you permission to go, no, not by a mighty hand. I will reach out my hand and strike Egypt with all my wonders which I will do in its midst, and after that he will let you go. I will give this people favor in the sight of the Egyptians, and it will happen that when you go, you shall not go empty-handed. But every woman shall ask of her neighbor, and of her who visits her house, jewels of silver, jewels of gold, and clothing; and you shall put them on your sons, and on your daughters. You shall plunder the Egyptians."

Moses answered, "But, behold, they will not believe me, nor listen to my voice; for they will say, 'Yahweh has not appeared to you.'"

Yahweh said to him, "What is that in your hand?" He said, "A rod." He said, "Throw it on the ground." He threw it on the ground, and it became a snake; and Moses ran away from it.

Yahweh said to Moses, "Stretch out your hand, and take it by the tail."

He stretched out his hand, and took hold of it, and it became a rod in his hand.

"That they may believe that Yahweh, the God of their fathers, the God of Abraham, the God of Isaac, and the God of Jacob, has appeared to you." Yahweh said furthermore to him, "Now put your hand inside your cloak."

He put his hand inside his cloak, and when he took it out, behold, his hand was leprous, as white as snow.

He said, "Put your hand inside your cloak again."

He put his hand inside his cloak again, and when he took it out of his cloak, behold, it had turned again as his other flesh.

"It will happen, if they will neither believe you nor listen to the voice of the first sign, that they will believe the voice of the latter sign. It will happen, if they will not believe even these two signs, neither listen to your voice, that you shall take of the water of the river, and pour it on the dry land. The water which you take out of the river will become blood on the dry land."

Moses said to Yahweh, "O Lord, I am not eloquent, neither before now, nor since you have spoken to your servant; for I am slow of speech, and of a slow tongue."

Yahweh said to him, "Who made man's mouth? Or who makes one mute, or deaf, or seeing, or blind? Isn't it I, Yahweh? Now therefore go, and I will be with your mouth, and teach you what you shall speak."

He said, "Oh, Lord, please send someone else."

The anger of Yahweh was kindled against Moses, and he said, "What about Aaron, your brother, the Levite? I know that he can speak well. Also, behold, he comes out to meet you. When he sees you, he will be glad in his heart. You shall speak to him, and put the words in his mouth. I will be with your mouth, and with his mouth, and will teach you what you shall do. He will be your spokesman to the people; and it will happen, that he will be to you a mouth, and you will be to him as God. You shall take this rod in your hand, with which you shall do the signs."

Moses went and returned to Jethro his father-in-law, and said to him, "Please let me go and return to my brothers who are in Egypt, and see whether they are still alive." Jethro said to Moses, "Go in peace."

Yahweh said to Aaron, "Go into the wilderness to meet Moses."

He went, and met him on God's mountain, and kissed him. Moses told Aaron all the words of Yahweh with which he had sent him, and all the signs with which he had instructed him. Moses and Aaron went and gathered together all the elders of the children of Israel. Aaron spoke all the words which Yahweh had spoken to Moses, and did the signs in the sight of the people. The people believed, and when they heard that Yahweh had visited the children of Israel, and that he had seen their affliction, then they bowed their heads and worshiped.

Afterward Moses and Aaron came, and said to Pharaoh, "This is what Yahweh, the God of Israel, says, 'Let my people go, that they may hold a feast to me in the wilderness.'"

Pharaoh said, "Who is Yahweh, that I should listen to his voice to let Israel go? I don't know Yahweh, and moreover I will not let Israel go."

They said, "The God of the Hebrews has met with us. Please let us go three days' journey into the wilderness, and sacrifice to Yahweh, our God, lest he fall on us with pestilence, or with the sword."

The king of Egypt said to them, "Why do you, Moses and Aaron, take the people from their work? Get back to your burdens!" Pharaoh said, "Behold, the people of the land are now many, and you make them rest from their burdens." The same day Pharaoh commanded the taskmasters of the people, and their officers, saying, "You shall no longer give the people straw to make brick, as before. Let them go and gather straw for themselves. The number of the bricks, which they made before, you require from them. You shall not diminish anything of it, for they are idle; therefore they cry, saying, 'Let us go and sacrifice to our

God.' Let heavier work be laid on the men, that they may labor therein; and don't let them pay any attention to lying words."

The brutal taskmasters pushed the Israelites as Pharaoh had commanded, forcing them to gather straw and to make the same allotment of bricks. When they could not meet the daily quotas, the Egyptians beat the officers of the children of Israel, and they mocked their request to worship God in the wilderness. Soon, the Israelite officers grumbled against Moses and Aaron, saying "...you have made us a stench to be abhorred in the eyes of Pharaoh, and in the eyes of his servants, to put a sword in their hand to kill us." Moses then plead to God, who reassured him that he would bring the children of Israel out from their burdens and deliver them to the Promised Land. But the Israelites did not listen to him, due to their bondage and anguish of spirit. God then sent Moses to deal directly with Pharaoh, promising him that He would bring great signs and wonders in Egypt.

Yahweh said to Moses, "Behold, I have made you as God to Pharaoh; and Aaron your brother shall be your prophet. You shall speak all that I command you; and Aaron your brother shall speak to Pharaoh, that he let the children of Israel go out of his land. I will harden Pharaoh's heart, and multiply my signs and my wonders in the land of Egypt. But Pharaoh will not listen to you, and I will lay my hand on Egypt, and bring out my armies, my people the children of Israel, out of the land of Egypt by great judgments. The Egyptians shall know that I am Yahweh, when I stretch out my hand on Egypt, and bring out the children of Israel from among them."

Moses and Aaron did so. As Yahweh commanded them, so they did. Moses was eighty years old, and Aaron eighty-three years old, when they spoke to Pharaoh.

Yahweh spoke to Moses and to Aaron, saying, "When Pharaoh speaks to you, saying, 'Perform a miracle!' then you shall tell Aaron, 'Take your rod, and cast it down before Pharaoh, that it become a serpent.'"

Moses and Aaron went in to Pharaoh, and they did so, as Yahweh had commanded: and Aaron cast down his rod before Pharaoh and before his servants, and it became a serpent. Then Pharaoh also called for the wise men and the sorcerers. They also, the magicians of Egypt, did the same thing with their enchantments. For they each cast down their rods, and they became serpents: but Aaron's rod swallowed up their rods. Pharaoh's heart was hardened, and he didn't listen to them; as Yahweh had spoken.

Having refused to believe this miracle from God, Pharaoh's heart hardened. Yahweh then began a series of 10 plagues against the Egyptians, starting with turning the water of Egypt into blood. Despite the overwhelming power of these plagues, Pharaoh did not allow the Israelites to leave.

Yahweh said to Moses, "Pharaoh's heart is stubborn. He refuses to let the people go. Go to Pharaoh in the morning. Behold, he goes out to the water; and you shall stand by the river's bank to meet him; and the rod which was turned to a serpent you shall take in your hand. You shall tell him, 'Yahweh, the God of the Hebrews, has sent me to you, saying, "Let my people go, that they may serve me in the wilderness:" and behold, until now you haven't listened. Thus says Yahweh, "In this you shall know that I am Yahweh. Behold, I will strike with the rod that is in my hand on the waters which are in the river, and they shall be turned to blood. The fish that are in the river shall die, and the river shall become foul; and the Egyptians shall loathe to drink water from the river." Yahweh said to Moses, "Tell Aaron, 'Take your rod, and stretch out your hand over the waters of Egypt, over their rivers, over their streams, and over their pools, and over all their ponds of water, that they may become blood; and there shall be blood throughout all the land of Egypt, both in vessels of wood and in vessels of stone.'"

Moses and Aaron did so, as Yahweh commanded; and he lifted up the rod, and struck the waters that were in the river, in the sight of Pharaoh, and in the sight of his servants; and all the waters that were in the river were turned to blood. The fish that were in the river died; and the river became foul, and the Egyptians couldn't drink water from the river; and the blood was throughout all the land of Egypt. The magicians of Egypt did the same thing with their enchantments; and Pharaoh's heart was hardened, and he didn't listen to them; as Yahweh had spoken. Pharaoh turned and went into his house, and he didn't even take this to heart. All the Egyptians dug around the river for water to drink; for they couldn't drink of the water of the river. Seven days were fulfilled, after Yahweh had struck the river.

A pattern then developed. God sent a plague on Egypt, until Pharaoh agreed to allow the nation of Israel to leave in return for relief. Then, when God removed the plague, Pharaoh again hardened his heart, and recanted his approval. In return, God sent another plague. Wave after wave of disaster and destruction ravaged the land of Egypt; but Goshen, where the Israelites live, was spared from any effect. The plagues were as follows:

1   *The water of Egypt was turned to blood.*
2   *Frogs swarmed over the land, even into the houses and ovens of the Egyptians.*
3   *Aaron struck his rod to the ground, and all the dust of the earth became lice throughout all the land of Egypt. There were lice on the people and on the animals.*
4   *Swarms of flies invaded the land and houses of Egypt.*

5   *A plague brought death to the livestock of Egypt, but none of the livestock of the children of Israel was affected.*

6   *Moses sprinkled ashes of a furnace, and severe boils broke out on the people and animals of Egypt.*

7   *Yahweh sent a very severe hail, mixed with lightning, which struck both man and animals; the hail struck every herb of the field, and broke every tree of the field.*

8   *Yahweh sent an east wind, which brought swarms of locusts. They covered the surface of the whole earth, so that the land was darkened. There remained nothing green, either tree or herb of the field, through all the land of Egypt.*

9   *God caused a thick darkness in all the land of Egypt for three days.*

10   *After these nine plagues, God purposed to send one more plague, so horrible, that it would finally drive Pharaoh to his knees and force the Egyptians to relent.*

But Yahweh hardened Pharaoh's heart, and he wouldn't let them go. Pharaoh said to him, "Get away from me! Be careful to see my face no more; for in the day you see my face you shall die!"

Moses said, "You have spoken well. I will see your face again no more."

Yahweh said to Moses, "Yet one plague more will I bring on Pharaoh, and on Egypt; afterward he will let you go. When he lets you go, he will surely thrust you out altogether. Speak now in the ears of the people, and let them ask every man of his neighbor, and every woman of her neighbor, jewels of silver, and jewels of gold." Yahweh gave the people favor in the sight of the Egyptians. Moreover the man Moses was very great in the land of Egypt, in the sight of Pharaoh's servants, and in the sight of the people.

Moses said, "This is what Yahweh says: 'About midnight I will go out into the midst of Egypt, and all the firstborn in the land of Egypt shall die, from the firstborn of Pharaoh who sits on his throne, even to the firstborn of the female servant who is behind the mill; and all the firstborn of livestock. There shall be a great cry throughout all the land of Egypt, such as there has not been, nor shall be any more. But against any of the children of Israel a dog won't even bark or move its tongue, against man or animal; that you may know that Yahweh makes a distinction between the Egyptians and Israel. All these your servants shall come down to me, and bow down themselves to me, saying, "Get out, with all the people who follow you"; and after that I will go out.'" He went out from Pharaoh in hot anger.

God informed Moses that Pharaoh once again would not listen to him. But this time, the Egyptians would pay a very steep price for Pharaoh's arrogance. God then outlined the Passover feast, which served two purposes: the initial one would be for the purpose of saving the Israelites from the last plague and the second one was that the feast, from that point on, would commemorate their deliverance from Egypt.

Speak to all the congregation of Israel, saying, 'On the tenth day of this month, they shall take to them every man a lamb, according to their fathers' houses, a lamb for a household; and if the household is too little for a lamb, then he and his neighbor next to his house shall take one according to the number of the souls; according to what everyone can eat you shall make your count for the lamb. Your lamb shall be without blemish, a male a year old. You shall take it from the sheep, or from the goats: and you shall keep it until the fourteenth day of the same month; and the whole assembly of the congregation of Israel shall kill it at evening. They shall take some of the blood, and put it on the two doorposts and on the lintel, on the houses in which they shall eat it. They shall eat the flesh in that night, roasted with fire, and unleavened bread. They shall eat it with bitter herbs. Don't eat it raw, nor boiled at all with water, but roasted with fire; with its head, its legs and its inner parts. You shall let nothing of it remain until the morning; but that which remains of it until the morning you shall burn with fire. This is how you shall eat it: with your belt on your waist, your shoes on your feet, and your staff in your hand; and you shall eat it in haste: it is Yahweh's Passover. For I will go through the land of Egypt in that night, and will strike all the firstborn in the land of Egypt, both man and animal. Against all the gods of Egypt I will execute judgments: I am Yahweh. The blood shall be to you for a token on the houses where you are: and when I see the blood, I will pass over you, and there shall no plague be on you to destroy you, when I strike the land of Egypt. This day shall be to you for a memorial, and you shall keep it a feast to Yahweh: throughout your generations you shall keep it a feast by an ordinance forever.

It shall happen when you have come to the land which Yahweh will give you, according as he has promised, that you shall keep this service. It will happen, when your children ask you, 'What do you mean by this service?' that you shall say, 'It is the sacrifice of Yahweh's Passover, who passed over the houses of the children of Israel in Egypt, when he struck the Egyptians, and spared our houses.'"

The people bowed their heads and worshiped. The children of Israel went and did so; as Yahweh had commanded Moses and Aaron, so they did.

It happened at midnight, that Yahweh struck all the firstborn in the land of Egypt, from the firstborn of Pharaoh who sat on his throne to the firstborn of the captive who was in the dungeon; and all the firstborn of livestock. Pharaoh rose up in the night, he, and all his servants, and all the Egyptians; and there was a great cry in Egypt, for there was not a house where there was not one dead. He called for Moses and Aaron by night, and said, "Rise up, get out from among my people, both you and the children of Israel; and go, serve Yahweh, as you have said! Take both your flocks and your herds, as you have said, and be gone; and bless me also!"

The Egyptians were urgent with the people, to send them out of the land in haste, for they said, "We are all dead men." The people took their dough before it was leavened, their kneading troughs being bound up in their clothes on their shoulders. The children of Israel did according to the word of Moses; and they asked of the Egyptians jewels of silver, and jewels of gold, and clothing. Yahweh gave the people favor in the sight of the Egyptians, so that they let them have what they asked. They despoiled the Egyptians.

The children of Israel traveled from Rameses to Succoth, about six hundred thousand on foot who were men, besides children. A mixed multitude went up also with them, with flocks, herds, and even very much livestock. They baked unleavened cakes of the dough which they brought out of Egypt; for it wasn't leavened, because they were thrust out of Egypt, and couldn't wait, neither had they prepared for themselves any food. Now the time that the children of Israel lived in Egypt was four hundred thirty years. It happened at the end of four hundred thirty years, even the same day it happened, that all the armies of Yahweh went out from the land of Egypt.

5 OUT OF EGYPT

An Independent Nation of God's Own People

It happened, when Pharaoh had let the people go, that God didn't lead them by the way of the land of the Philistines, although that was near; for God said, "Lest perhaps the people change their minds when they see war, and they return to Egypt"; but God led the people around by the way of the wilderness by the Red Sea; and the children of Israel went up armed out of the land of Egypt. Moses took the bones of Joseph with him, for he had made the children of Israel swear, saying, "God will surely visit you, and you shall carry up my bones away from here with you." They took their journey from Succoth, and encamped in Etham, in the edge of the wilderness. Yahweh went before them by day in a pillar of cloud, to lead them on their way, and by night in a pillar of fire, to give them light, that they might go by day and by night: the pillar of cloud by day, and the pillar of fire by night, didn't depart from before the people.

Following the mighty plagues, the Israelite nation made a clean break from Egypt. But Pharaoh was not yet finished; with one more change of heart, he decided to send his army after Israel, to return them to slavery.

It was told the king of Egypt that the people had fled; and the heart of Pharaoh and of his servants was changed towards the people, and they said, "What is this we have done, that we have let Israel go from serving us?" He prepared his chariot, and took his army with him; and he took six hundred chosen chariots, and all the chariots of Egypt, and captains over all of them. Yahweh hardened the heart of Pharaoh king of Egypt, and he pursued after the children of Israel; for the children of Israel went out with a high hand. The Egyptians pursued after them: all the horses and chariots of Pharaoh, his horsemen, and his army; and overtook them encamping by the sea, beside Pihahiroth, before Baal Zephon.

When Pharaoh drew near, the children of Israel lifted up their eyes, and behold, the Egyptians were marching after them; and they were very afraid. The children of Israel cried out to Yahweh. They said to Moses, "Because there were no graves in Egypt, have you taken us away to die in the wilderness? Why have you treated us this way, to bring us out of Egypt? Isn't this the word that we spoke to you in Egypt, saying, 'Leave us alone, that we may serve the Egyptians?' For it were better for us to serve the Egyptians, than that we should die in the wilderness."

Moses said to the people, "Don't be afraid. Stand still, and see the salvation of Yahweh, which he will work for you today: for the Egyptians whom you have seen today, you shall never see them again. Yahweh will fight for you, and you shall be still."

Yahweh said to Moses, "Why do you cry to me? Speak to the children of Israel, that they go forward. Lift up your rod, and stretch out your hand over the sea, and divide it: and the children of Israel shall go into the midst of the sea on dry ground. I, behold, I will harden the hearts of the Egyptians, and they shall go in after them: and I will get myself honor over Pharaoh, and over all his armies, over his chariots, and over his horsemen. The Egyptians shall know that I am Yahweh, when I have gotten myself honor over Pharaoh, over his chariots, and over his horsemen." The angel of God, who went before the camp of Israel, moved and went behind them; and the pillar of cloud moved from before them, and stood behind them. It came between the camp of Egypt and the camp of Israel; and there was the cloud and the darkness, yet gave it light by night: and the one didn't come near the other all the night.

Moses stretched out his hand over the sea, and Yahweh caused the sea to go back by a strong east wind all the night, and made the sea dry land, and the waters were divided. The children of Israel went into the midst of the sea on the dry ground, and the waters were a wall to them on their right hand, and on their left. The Egyptians pursued, and went in after them into the midst of the sea: all of Pharaoh's horses, his chariots, and his horsemen. It happened in the morning watch, that Yahweh looked out on the Egyptian army through the pillar of fire and of cloud, and confused the Egyptian army. He took off their chariot wheels, and they drove them heavily; so that the Egyptians said, "Let's flee from the face of Israel, for Yahweh fights for them against the Egyptians!"

Yahweh said to Moses, "Stretch out your hand over the sea, that the waters may come again on the Egyptians, on their chariots, and on their horsemen." Moses stretched out his hand over the sea, and the sea returned to its strength when the morning appeared; and the Egyptians fled against it. Yahweh overthrew the Egyptians in the midst of the sea. The waters returned, and covered the chariots and the horsemen, even all Pharaoh's army that went in after them into the sea. There remained not so much as one of them. But the children of Israel walked on dry land in the midst of the sea, and the waters were a wall to them on their right hand, and on their left. Thus Yahweh saved Israel that day out of the hand of the Egyptians; and Israel saw the Egyptians dead on the seashore. Israel saw the great work which Yahweh did to the Egyptians, and the people feared Yahweh; and they believed in Yahweh, and in his servant Moses.

The deliverance from the army of Egypt made a strong impression on the nation of Israel. They sang praises to God, and reveled in their deliverance from Egypt. Yet, it would not take long before the nation had begun to lose its trust in God and the people grumbled against him. Thus began a long and repetitive pattern; the Israelites grumbled against God, God provided for them, they were initially thankful, but then they fell back into their same bad habits.

Moses led Israel onward from the Red Sea, and they went out into the wilderness of Shur; and they went three days in the wilderness, and found no water. When they came to Marah, they couldn't drink from the waters of Marah, for they were bitter. Therefore its name was called Marah. The people murmured against Moses, saying, "What shall we drink?" Then he cried to Yahweh. Yahweh showed him a tree, and he threw it into the waters, and the waters were made sweet. There he made a statute and an ordinance for them, and there he tested them; and he said, "If you will diligently listen to the voice of Yahweh your God, and will do that which is right in his eyes, and will pay attention to his commandments, and keep all his statutes, I will put none of the diseases on you, which I have put on the Egyptians; for I am Yahweh who heals you."

They came to Elim, where there were twelve springs of water, and seventy palm trees: and they encamped there by the waters.

They took their journey from Elim, and all the congregation of the children of Israel came to the wilderness of Sin, which is between Elim and Sinai, on the fifteenth day of the second month after their departing out of the land of Egypt. The whole congregation of the children of Israel murmured against Moses and against Aaron in the wilderness; and the children of Israel said to them, "We wish that we had died by the hand of Yahweh in the land of Egypt, when we sat by the meat pots, when we ate our fill of bread, for you have brought us out into this wilderness, to kill this whole assembly with hunger."

Moses and Aaron said to all the children of Israel, "At evening, then you shall know that Yahweh has brought you out from the land of Egypt; and in the morning, then you shall see the glory of Yahweh; because he hears your murmurings against Yahweh. Who are we, that you murmur against us?" Moses said, "Now Yahweh shall give you meat to eat in the evening, and in the morning bread to satisfy you; because Yahweh hears your murmurings which you murmur

mountain quaked greatly. When the sound of the trumpet grew louder and louder, Moses spoke, and God answered him by a voice. Yahweh came down on Mount Sinai, to the top of the mountain. Yahweh called Moses to the top of the mountain, and Moses went up.

Yahweh said to Moses, "Go down, warn the people, lest they break through to Yahweh to gaze, and many of them perish. Let the priests also, who come near to Yahweh, sanctify themselves, lest Yahweh break forth on them."

Moses said to Yahweh, "The people can't come up to Mount Sinai, for you warned us, saying, 'Set bounds around the mountain, and sanctify it.'"

Yahweh said to him, "Go down and you shall bring Aaron up with you, but don't let the priests and the people break through to come up to Yahweh, lest he break forth on them."

So Moses went down to the people, and told them.

God spoke to Moses the famous "Ten Commandments," which became the cornerstone of laws for the nation of Israel. Many of the laws of civilized countries are based upon the principles that are outlined by God in these key commandments. These laws discuss how man is to relate to God, as well as to his fellow man.

God spoke all these words, saying, "I am Yahweh your God, who brought you out of the land of Egypt, out of the house of bondage.

"You shall have no other gods before me.

"You shall not make for yourselves an idol, nor any image of anything that is in the heavens above, or that is in the earth beneath, or that is in the water under the earth: you shall not bow yourself down to them, nor serve them, for I, Yahweh your God, am a jealous God, visiting the iniquity of the fathers on the children, on the third and on the fourth generation of those who hate me, and showing loving kindness to thousands of those who love me and keep my commandments.

"You shall not take the name of Yahweh your God in vain, for Yahweh will not hold him guiltless who takes his name in vain.

"Remember the Sabbath day, to keep it holy. You shall labor six days, and do all your work, but the seventh day is a Sabbath to Yahweh your God. You shall not do any work in it, you, nor your son, nor your daughter, your male servant, nor your female servant, nor your livestock, nor your stranger who is within your gates; for in six days Yahweh made heaven and earth, the sea, and all that is in them, and rested the seventh day; therefore Yahweh blessed the Sabbath day, and made it holy.

"Honor your father and your mother, that your days may be long in the land which Yahweh your God gives you.

"You shall not murder.

"You shall not commit adultery.

"You shall not steal.

"You shall not give false testimony against your neighbor.

"You shall not covet your neighbor's house. You shall not covet your neighbor's wife, nor his male servant, nor his female servant, nor his ox, nor his donkey, nor anything that is your neighbor's."

All the people perceived the thunderings, the lightnings, the sound of the trumpet, and the mountain smoking. When the people saw it, they trembled, and stayed at a distance. They said to Moses, "Speak with us yourself, and we will listen; but don't let God speak with us, lest we die."

Moses came and told the people all the words of Yahweh, and all the ordinances; and all the people answered with one voice, and said, "All the words which Yahweh has spoken will we do."

Moses wrote all the words of Yahweh, and rose up early in the morning, and built an altar under the mountain, and twelve pillars for the twelve tribes of Israel. He sent young men of the children of Israel, who offered burnt offerings and sacrificed peace offerings of cattle to Yahweh. Moses took half of the blood and put it in basins, and half of the blood he sprinkled on the altar. He took the book of the covenant and read it in the hearing of the people, and they said, "All that Yahweh has spoken will we do, and be obedient."

Moses took the blood, and sprinkled it on the people, and said, "Look, this is the blood of the covenant, which Yahweh has made with you concerning all these words."

Moses went up on the mountain, and the cloud covered the mountain. The glory of Yahweh settled on Mount Sinai, and the cloud covered it six days. The seventh day he called to Moses out of the midst of the cloud. The appearance of the glory of Yahweh was like devouring fire on the top of the mountain in the eyes of the children of Israel. Moses entered into the midst of the cloud, and went up on the mountain; and Moses was on the mountain forty days and forty nights.

Yahweh spoke to Moses, saying, "Speak to the children of Israel, that they take an offering for me. From everyone whose heart makes him willing you shall take my offering.

Let them make me a sanctuary, that I may dwell among them. According to all that I show you, the pattern of the tabernacle, and the pattern of all of its furniture, even so you shall make it.

God gave detailed instructions to Moses for the building of a tabernacle, a structure that would become the center of worship for the nation of Israel until a permanent temple would be built by future generations. Included in these instructions were plans for the ark of the covenant, an ornate box which would contain the stone tablets with the ten commandments, the rod of Aaron, and a jar of manna.

"Bring Aaron your brother, and his sons with him, near to you from among the children of Israel, that he may minister to me in the priest's office, even Aaron, Nadab and Abihu, Eleazar and Ithamar, Aaron's sons. You shall make holy garments for Aaron your brother, for glory and for beauty. You shall speak to all who are wise-hearted, whom I have filled with the spirit of wisdom, that they make Aaron's garments to sanctify him, that he may minister to me in the priest's office. These are the garments which they shall make: a breastplate, and an ephod, and a robe, and a coat of checker work, a turban, and a sash: and they shall make holy garments for Aaron your brother, and his sons, that he may minister to me in the priest's office.

God also gave instructions to Moses on how the priests were to minister to the nation of Israel. This included instructions for ritual sacrifices to atone for their sins, as well as the sins of the Israelite people. The priests, who were from the tribe of Levi, also had to go through purification rituals and had to be consecrated as they began their duties in the tabernacle.

When the people saw that Moses delayed to come down from the mountain, the people gathered themselves together to Aaron, and said to him, "Come, make us gods, which shall go before us; for as for this Moses, the man who brought us up out of the land of Egypt, we don't know what has become of him."

Aaron said to them, "Take off the golden rings, which are in the ears of your wives, of your sons, and of your daughters, and bring them to me."

All the people took off the golden rings which were in their ears, and brought them to Aaron. He received what they handed him, and fashioned it with an engraving tool, and made it a molten calf; and they said, "These are your gods, Israel, which brought you up out of the land of Egypt."

When Aaron saw this, he built an altar before it; and Aaron made a proclamation, and said, "Tomorrow shall be a feast to Yahweh."

They rose up early on the next day, and offered burnt offerings, and brought peace offerings; and the people sat down to eat and to drink, and rose up to play.

Yahweh spoke to Moses, "Go, get down; for your people, who you brought up out of the land of Egypt, have corrupted themselves! They have turned aside quickly out of the way which I commanded them. They have made themselves a molten calf, and have worshiped it, and have sacrificed to it, and said, 'These are your gods, Israel, which brought you up out of the land of Egypt.'"

Yahweh said to Moses, "I have seen these people, and behold, they are a stiff-necked people. Now therefore leave me alone, that my wrath may burn hot against them, and that I may consume them; and I will make of you a great nation."

Moses begged Yahweh his God, and said, "Yahweh, why does your wrath burn hot against your people, that you have brought out of the land of Egypt with great power and with a mighty hand? Why should the Egyptians speak, saying, 'He brought them forth for evil, to kill them in the mountains, and to consume them from the surface of the earth?' Turn from your fierce wrath, and repent of this evil against your people. Remember Abraham, Isaac, and Israel, your servants, to whom you swore by your own self, and said to them, 'I will multiply your seed as the stars of the sky, and all this land that I have spoken of I will give to your seed, and they shall inherit it forever.'"

Yahweh repented of the evil which he said he would do to his people.

Moses turned, and went down from the mountain, with the two tablets of the testimony in his hand; tablets that were written on both their sides; on the one side and on the other they were written. The tablets were the work of God, and the writing was the writing of God, engraved on the tables.

When Joshua heard the noise of the people as they shouted, he said to Moses, "There is the noise of war in the camp."

He said, "It isn't the voice of those who shout for victory, neither is it the voice of those who cry for being overcome; but the noise of those who sing that I hear." It happened, as soon as he came near to the camp, that he saw the calf and the dancing: and Moses' anger grew hot, and he threw the tablets out of his hands, and broke them beneath the mountain. He took the calf which they had made, and burnt it with fire, ground it to powder, and scattered it on the water, and made the children of Israel drink of it.

Moses said to Aaron, "What did these people do to you, that you have brought a great sin on them?"

Aaron said, "Don't let the anger of my lord grow hot. You know the people, that they are set on evil. For they said to me, 'Make us gods, which shall go before us; for as for this Moses, the man who brought us up out of the land of Egypt, we don't know what has become of him.' I said to them, 'Whoever has any gold, let them take it off:' so they gave it to me; and I threw it into the fire, and out came this calf."

When Moses saw that the people had broken loose, (for Aaron had let them loose for a derision among their enemies), then Moses stood in the gate of the camp, and said, "Whoever is on Yahweh's side, come to me!"

All the sons of Levi gathered themselves together to him. He said to them, "Thus says Yahweh, the God of Israel, 'Every man put his sword on his thigh, and go back and forth from gate to gate throughout the camp, and every man kill his brother, and every man his companion, and every man his neighbor.'" The sons of Levi did according to the word of Moses: and there fell of the people that day about three thousand men. Moses said, "Consecrate yourselves today to Yahweh, yes, every man against his son, and against his brother; that he may bestow on you a blessing this day."

It happened on the next day, that Moses said to the people, "You have sinned a great sin. Now I will go up to Yahweh. Perhaps I shall make atonement for your sin."

Moses returned to Yahweh, and said, "Oh, this people have sinned a great sin, and have made themselves gods of gold. Yet now, if you will, forgive their sin— and if not, please blot me out of your book which you have written."

Yahweh said to Moses, "Whoever has sinned against me, him will I blot out of my book. Now go, lead the people to the place of which I have spoken to you. Behold, my angel shall go before you. Nevertheless in the day when I punish, I will punish them for their sin."

Now Moses used to take the tent and to pitch it outside the camp, far away from the camp, and he called it "The Tent of Meeting." It happened that everyone who sought Yahweh went out to the Tent of Meeting, which was outside the camp. It happened that when Moses went out to the Tent, that all the people rose up, and stood, everyone at their tent door, and watched Moses, until he had gone into the Tent. It happened, when Moses entered into the Tent, that the pillar of cloud descended, stood at the door of the Tent, and spoke with Moses. All the people saw the pillar of cloud stand at the door of the Tent, and all the people rose up and worshiped, everyone at their tent door. Yahweh spoke to Moses face to face, as a man speaks to his friend. He turned again into the camp, but his servant Joshua, the son of Nun, a young man, didn't depart out of the Tent.

Moses said to Yahweh, "Behold, you tell me, 'Bring up this people:' and you haven't let me know whom you will send with me. Yet you have said, 'I know you by name, and you have also found favor in my sight.' Now therefore, if I have found favor in your sight, please show me now your ways, that I may know you, so that I may find favor in your sight: and consider that this nation is your people."

He said, "My presence will go with you, and I will give you rest."

He said to him, "If your presence doesn't go with me, don't carry us up from here. For how would people know that I have found favor in your sight, I and your people? Isn't it in that you go with us, so that we are separated, I and your people, from all the people who are on the surface of the earth?"

Yahweh said to Moses, "I will do this thing also that you have spoken; for you have found favor in my sight, and I know you by name."

He said, "Please show me your glory."

He said, "I will make all my goodness pass before you, and will proclaim the name of Yahweh before you. I will be gracious to whom I will be gracious, and will show mercy on whom I will show mercy." He said, "You cannot see my face, for man may not see me and live." Yahweh also said, "Behold, there is a place by me, and you shall stand on the rock. It will happen, while my glory passes by, that I will put you in a cleft of the rock, and will cover you with my hand until I have passed by; then I will take away my hand, and you will see my back; but my face shall not be seen."

Yahweh said to Moses, "Chisel two stone tablets like the first: and I will write on the tablets the words that were on the first tablets, which you broke. Be ready by the morning, and come up in the morning to Mount Sinai, and present yourself there to me on the top of the mountain. No one shall come up with you; neither let anyone be seen throughout all the mountain; neither let the flocks nor herds feed before that mountain."

He chiseled two tablets of stone like the first; and Moses rose up early in the morning, and went up to Mount Sinai, as Yahweh had commanded him, and took in his hand two stone tablets. Yahweh descended in the cloud, and stood with him there, and proclaimed the name of Yahweh. Yahweh passed by before him, and proclaimed, "Yahweh! Yahweh, a merciful and gracious God, slow to anger, and abundant in loving kindness and truth, keeping loving kindness for thousands, forgiving iniquity and disobedience and sin; and that will by no means clear the guilty, visiting the iniquity of the fathers on the children, and on the children's children, on the third and on the fourth generation."

Moses hurried and bowed his head toward the earth, and worshiped. He said, "If now I have found favor in your sight, Lord, please let the Lord go in the midst of us; although this is a stiff-necked people; pardon our iniquity and our sin, and take us for your inheritance."

He said, "Behold, I make a covenant: before all your people I will do marvels, such as have not been worked in all the earth, nor in any nation; and all the people among which you are shall see the work of Yahweh; for it is an awesome thing that I do with you.

Yahweh said to Moses, "Write you these words: for in accordance with these words I have made a covenant with you and with Israel."

He was there with Yahweh forty days and forty nights; he neither ate bread, nor drank water. He wrote on the tablets the words of the covenant, the ten commandments.

It happened, when Moses came down from Mount Sinai with the two tablets of the testimony in Moses' hand, when he came down from the mountain, that Moses didn't know that the skin of his face shone by reason of his speaking with him. When Aaron and all the children of Israel saw Moses, behold, the skin of his face shone; and they were afraid to come near him. Moses called to them, and Aaron and all the rulers of the congregation returned to him; and Moses spoke to them. Afterward all the children of Israel came near, and he gave them all of the commandments that Yahweh had spoken with him on Mount Sinai. When Moses was done speaking with them, he put a veil on his face. But when Moses went in before Yahweh to speak with him, he took the veil off, until he came out; and he came out, and spoke to the children of Israel that which he was commanded. The children of Israel saw Moses' face, that the skin of Moses' face shone: and Moses put the veil on his face again, until he went in to speak with him.

All the congregation of the children of Israel departed from the presence of Moses. They came, everyone whose heart stirred him up, and everyone whom his spirit made willing, and brought Yahweh's offering, for the work of the Tent of Meeting, and for all of its service, and for the holy garments.

Using detailed instructions from God, the Israelites built the tabernacle as a central point in their worship to God. A beautiful, elaborate tent-like structure, the tabernacle contained ornate items such as the Ark of the Covenant, tables, lampstands, basins and an altar for sacrifices. Using the spoils of gold, skins, stones and other riches they brought out of Egypt, the people donated so much toward the building of the tabernacle that they had to be told to stop giving.

Thus all the work of the tabernacle of the Tent of Meeting was finished. The children of Israel did according to all that Yahweh commanded Moses; so they did. They brought the tabernacle to Moses, the tent, with all its furniture, its clasps, its boards, its bars, its pillars, its sockets, the covering of rams' skins dyed red, the covering of sea cow hides, the veil of the screen, the ark of the testimony with its poles, the mercy seat, the table, all its vessels, the show bread, the pure lampstand, its lamps, even the lamps to be set in order, all its vessels, the oil for the light, the golden altar, the anointing oil, the sweet incense, the screen for the door of the Tent, the bronze altar, its grating of brass, its poles, all of its vessels, the basin and its base, the hangings of the court, its pillars, its sockets, the screen for the gate of the court, its cords, its pins, all the instruments of the service of the tabernacle, for the Tent of Meeting, the finely worked garments for ministering in the holy place, the holy garments for Aaron the priest, and the garments of his sons, to minister in the priest's office.

According to all that Yahweh commanded Moses, so the children of Israel did all the work. Moses saw all the work, and behold, they had done it as Yahweh had commanded, even so had they done it: and Moses blessed them.

It happened in the first month in the second year, on the first day of the month, that the tabernacle was raised up.

Then the cloud covered the Tent of Meeting, and the glory of Yahweh filled the tabernacle. Moses wasn't able to enter into the Tent of Meeting, because the cloud stayed on it, and Yahweh's glory filled the tabernacle. When the cloud was taken up from over the tabernacle, the children of Israel went onward, throughout all their journeys; but if the cloud wasn't taken up, then they didn't travel until the day that it was taken up. For the cloud of Yahweh was on the tabernacle by day, and there was fire in the cloud by night, in the sight of all the house of Israel, throughout all their journeys.

6 THE COVENANT

God's Detailed Instructions to Israel

While many people are familiar with the Ten Commandments, these were just a small part of the detailed instructions that God gave to Moses on Mount Sinai. Among these instructions were items such as:

- *Instructions for giving animal and grain sacrifices, both for individuals and the entire Israelite assembly.*
- *Laws instructing how to handle intentional and unintentional actions that caused harm to another person or to the property of others.*
- *The introduction of the concept of things that caused a person to become "unclean," such as touching an unclean animal, a specific illness, or coming into contact with a dead body. Thousands of years before people understood the role of viruses and bacteria in spreading disease, these laws served to protect the Israelites by ensuring proper separation or cleansing in the event of an unsafe situation.*
- *How to deal with people who broke an oath, trespassed against anther's property, or committed various sins.*

God showed his love for his chosen people, by providing regulations that protected them from sickness and disease. The laws of behavior given here, written to provide fairness, justice, and protection, became the cornerstone of laws throughout the civilized world in centuries to come.

Among the ordinances handed down by God were laws dictating the proper actions and sacrifices of people and the priests, to deal properly with sin. As an example, here are some of the ordinances covering what became known as a trespass offering:

Yahweh spoke to Moses, saying, "If anyone sins, and commits a trespass against Yahweh, and deals falsely with his neighbor in a matter of deposit, or of bargain, or of robbery, or has oppressed his neighbor, or has found that which was lost, and dealt falsely therein, and swearing to a lie; in any of all these things that a man does, sinning therein; then it shall be, if he has sinned, and is guilty, he shall restore that which he took by robbery, or the thing which he has gotten by oppression, or the deposit which was committed to him, or the lost thing which he found, or anything about which he has sworn falsely; he shall restore it even in full, and shall add a fifth part more to it. To him to whom it belongs he shall give it, in the day of his being found guilty. He shall bring his trespass offering to Yahweh, a ram without blemish from the flock, according to your estimation, for a trespass offering, to the priest. The priest shall make atonement for him before Yahweh, and he will be forgiven concerning whatever he does to become guilty."

Yahweh spoke to Moses, saying, "Speak to Aaron and to his sons, saying, 'This is the law of the sin offering: in the place where the burnt offering is killed, the sin offering shall be killed before Yahweh. It is most holy. The priest who offers it for sin shall eat it. It shall be eaten in a holy place, in the court of the Tent of Meeting. Whatever shall touch its flesh shall be holy. When there is any of its blood sprinkled on a garment, you shall wash that on which it was sprinkled in a holy place. But the earthen vessel in which it is boiled shall be broken; and if it is boiled in a bronze vessel, it shall be scoured, and rinsed in water. Every male among the priests shall eat of it: it is most holy. No sin offering, of which any of the blood is brought into the Tent of Meeting to make atonement in the Holy Place, shall be eaten: it shall be burned with fire.

"'This is the law of the trespass offering. It is most holy. In the place where they kill the burnt offering, he shall kill the trespass offering; and its blood he shall sprinkle around on the altar. He shall offer all of its fat: the fat tail, and the fat that covers the innards, and the two kidneys, and the fat that is on them, which is by the loins, and the cover on the liver, with the kidneys, shall he take away; and the priest shall burn them on the altar for an offering made by fire to Yahweh: it is a trespass offering. Every male among the priests may eat of it. It shall be eaten in a holy place. It is most holy.

In addition to a trespass offering, there were other sin offerings and peace offerings. God also dictated a consecration ceremony for Aaron and the priests. This involved purification rituals, special clothing, and elaborate sacrifices. After Moses and Aaron supervised the fulfillment of this consecration of the priests, God showed his pleasure in a mighty way.

Moses and Aaron went into the Tent of Meeting, and came out, and blessed the people: and the glory of Yahweh appeared to all the people. There came forth fire from before Yahweh, and consumed the burnt offering and the fat upon the altar: and when all the people saw it, they shouted, and fell on their faces.

God was serious about the laws and procedures he handed down to Moses, Aaron and the priests, and to the Israelite nation. An example of this occurred when two of the sons of Aaron offered "strange fire" before God, paying the ultimate price for their carelessness.

Nadab and Abihu, the sons of Aaron, each took his censer, and put fire in it, and laid incense on it, and offered strange fire before Yahweh, which he had not commanded them. And fire came forth from before Yahweh, and devoured them, and they died before Yahweh.

Then Moses said to Aaron, "This is what Yahweh spoke of, saying,

'I will show myself holy to those who come near me, and before all the people I will be glorified.'"

Aaron held his peace. Moses called Mishael and Elzaphan, the sons of Uzziel the uncle of Aaron, and said to them, "Draw near, carry your brothers from before the sanctuary out of the camp." So they drew near, and carried them in their coats out of the camp, as Moses had said.

Moses said to Aaron, and to Eleazar and to Ithamar, his sons, "Don't let the hair of your heads go loose, neither tear your clothes; that you don't die, and that he not be angry with all the congregation: but let your brothers, the whole house of Israel, bewail the burning which Yahweh has kindled. You shall not go out from the door of the Tent of Meeting, lest you die; for the anointing oil of Yahweh is on you." They did according to the word of Moses.

God also passed down many laws on what was considered "clean" (OK to eat) and "unclean" (forbidden to eat). These laws also gave instructions on how to become "clean" again after touching an unclean animal, including the washing of bodies and clothing, waiting times, and even on the destruction or washing of various types of containers.

Yahweh spoke to Moses and to Aaron, saying to them, "Speak to the children of Israel, saying, 'These are the living things which you may eat among all the animals that are on the earth. Whatever parts the hoof, and is cloven-footed, and chews the cud among the animals, that you may eat.

"'Nevertheless these you shall not eat of those that chew the cud, or of those who part the hoof: the camel, because he chews the cud but doesn't have a parted hoof, he is unclean to you. The coney, because he chews the cud but doesn't have a parted hoof, he is unclean to you. The hare, because she chews the cud but doesn't part the hoof, she is unclean to you. The pig, because he has a split hoof, and is cloven-footed, but doesn't chew the cud, he is unclean to you. Of their flesh you shall not eat, and their carcasses you shall not touch; they are unclean to you.

"'These you may eat of all that are in the waters: whatever has fins and scales in the waters, in the seas, and in the rivers, that you may eat. All that don't have fins and scales in the seas, and in the rivers, of all that move in the waters, and of all the living creatures that are in the waters, they are an abomination to you, and you detest them. You shall not eat of their flesh, and you shall detest their carcasses.

"'Every animal which parts the hoof, and is not cloven-footed, nor chews the cud, is unclean to you. Everyone who touches them shall be unclean. Whatever goes on its paws, among all animals that go on all fours, they are unclean to you. Whoever touches their carcass shall be unclean until the evening. He who carries their carcass shall wash his clothes, and be unclean until the evening. They are unclean to you.

Additional regulations covered proper procedures after childbirth, the medical examination of boils, scabs, open sores, leprosy, and burns by the priests, and whether various conditions were to be considered unclean. If unclean, further regulations governed how one could again be pronounced clean by the priests - after proper tasks such as separation from the assembly for a specified time, washings, re-examination, and offerings if the medical condition was resolved.

Most everyone has heard the term "scapegoat." This comes from the procedure outlined by God to purify the high priest every year before he entered the "Holy of Holies," the innermost part of the tabernacle. In this location, the Ark of the Covenant resided. Only the high priest was allowed to enter this room, and only once per year. Part of this procedure involved sending a live "scapegoat" into the wilderness, which symbolically carried the sins of Israel away.

Yahweh spoke to Moses, after the death of the two sons of Aaron, when they drew near before Yahweh, and died; and Yahweh said to Moses, "Tell Aaron your brother, not to come at all times into the Most Holy Place within the veil, before the mercy seat which is on the ark; lest he die: for I will appear in the cloud on the mercy seat.

"Herewith shall Aaron come into the sanctuary: with a young bull for a sin offering, and a ram for a burnt offering. He shall put on the holy linen coat, and he shall have the linen breeches on his body, and shall put on the linen sash, and he shall be clothed with the linen turban. They are the holy garments. He shall bathe his body in water, and put them on. He shall take from the congregation of the children of Israel two male goats for a sin offering, and one ram for a burnt offering.

"Aaron shall offer the bull of the sin offering, which is for himself, and make atonement for himself and for his house. He shall take the two goats, and set them before Yahweh at the door of the Tent of Meeting. Aaron shall cast lots for the two goats; one lot for Yahweh, and the other lot for the scapegoat. Aaron shall present the goat on which the lot fell for Yahweh, and offer him for a sin offering. But the goat, on which the lot fell for the scapegoat, shall be presented alive before Yahweh, to make atonement for him, to send him away for the scapegoat into the wilderness.

"When he has made an end of atoning for the Holy Place, the Tent of Meeting, and the altar, he shall present the live goat. Aaron shall lay both his hands on the head of the live goat, and confess over him all the iniquities of the children of Israel, and all their transgressions, even all their sins; and he shall put them on the head of the goat, and shall send him away into the wilderness by the hand of a man who is in readiness. The goat shall carry all their iniquities on himself to a solitary land, and he shall let the goat go in the wilderness.

Yahweh said to Moses, "Speak to the children of Israel, and say to them, 'I am Yahweh your God. You shall not do as they do in the land of Egypt, where you lived: and you shall not do as they do in the land of Canaan, where I am bringing you; neither shall you walk in their statutes. You shall do my ordinances, and you shall keep my statutes, and walk in them: I am Yahweh your God. You shall therefore keep my statutes and my ordinances; which if a man does, he shall live in them: I am Yahweh.

"'For whoever shall do any of these abominations, even the souls that do them shall be cut off from among their people. Therefore you shall keep my requirements, that you do not practice any of these abominable customs, which were practiced before you, and that you do not defile yourselves with them: I am Yahweh your God.'"

God was preparing his people to become a holy nation. It was necessary to prepare them to seek spiritual purity, due to the corruption and abominable practices of the nations that they were to drive out of the Canaan land. God wanted them to be strong in resisting the temptations of sin and idolatry that was prevalent in the land of Canaan. Regulations that may seem strict by today's standards were necessary to strengthen his chosen people for the task ahead. Only through this spiritual purification would they have the strength to achieve the greatness God desired for their nation.

"'You shall not steal. "'You shall not lie. "'You shall not deceive one another.

"'You shall not swear by my name falsely, and profane the name of your God. I am Yahweh.

"'You shall not oppress your neighbor, nor rob him.

"'The wages of a hired servant shall not remain with you all night until the morning.

"'You shall not curse the deaf, nor put a stumbling block before the blind; but you shall fear your God. I am Yahweh.

"'You shall do no injustice in judgment: you shall not be partial to the poor, nor show favoritism to the great; but you shall judge your neighbor in righteousness.

"'You shall not go up and down as a slanderer among your people.

"'You shall not endanger the life of your neighbor. I am Yahweh.

"'You shall not hate your brother in your heart. You shall surely rebuke your neighbor, and not bear sin because of him.

"'You shall not take vengeance, nor bear any grudge against the children of your people; but you shall love your neighbor as yourself. I am Yahweh.

"'If a stranger lives as a foreigner with you in your land, you shall not do him wrong. The stranger who lives as a foreigner with you shall be to you as the native-born among you, and you shall love him as yourself; for you lived as foreigners in the land of Egypt. I am Yahweh your God.

"'You shall do no unrighteousness in judgment, in measures of length, of weight, or of quantity. You shall have just balances, just weights, a just ephah, and a just liquid measure. I am Yahweh your God, who brought you out of the land of Egypt.

"'When you reap the harvest of your land, you shall not wholly reap into the corners of your field, neither shall you gather the gleanings of your harvest: you shall leave them for the poor, and for the foreigner. I am Yahweh your God.'"

"'He who strikes any man mortally shall surely be put to death. He who strikes an animal mortally shall make it good, life for life. If anyone injures his neighbor; as he has done, so shall it be done to him: fracture for fracture, eye for eye, tooth for tooth; as he has injured someone, so shall it be done to him. He who kills an animal shall make it good; and he who kills a man shall be put to death. You shall have one kind of law, for the foreigner as well as the native-born: for I am Yahweh your God.'"

Yahweh said to Moses in Mount Sinai, "Speak to the children of Israel, and tell them, 'When you come into the land which I give you, then the land shall keep a Sabbath to Yahweh. Six years you shall sow your field, and six years you shall prune your vineyard, and gather in its fruits; but in the seventh year there shall be a Sabbath of solemn rest for the land, a Sabbath to Yahweh. You shall not sow your field or prune your vineyard. What grows of itself in your harvest you shall not reap, and the grapes of your undressed vine you shall not gather. It shall be a year of solemn rest for the land. The Sabbath of the land shall be for food for you; for yourself, for your servant, for your maid, for your hired servant, and for your stranger, who lives as a foreigner with you. For your livestock also, and for the animals that are in your land, shall all its increase be for food.

"'You shall count off seven Sabbaths of years, seven times seven years; and there shall be to you the days of seven Sabbaths of years, even forty-nine years. Then you shall sound the loud trumpet on the tenth day of the seventh month. On the Day of Atonement you shall sound the trumpet throughout all your land. You shall make the fiftieth year holy, and proclaim liberty throughout the land to

break my covenant with them; for I am Yahweh their God; but I will for their sake remember the covenant of their ancestors, whom I brought out of the land of Egypt in the sight of the nations, that I might be their God. I am Yahweh.'"

These are the statutes, ordinances and laws, which Yahweh made between him and the children of Israel in Mount Sinai by Moses.

7 DESERT WANDERINGS

From Quick Escape to Exhausting Detour

Free from bondage in Egypt, protected by mighty acts of God, and benefiting from a new set of laws and rituals prescribed to Moses on Mount Sinai, the Israelites seem poised for greatness. Only a journey of about two weeks separates them from the Promised Land of Canaan, and the covenant God first made with Abraham seems only weeks away from fulfillment. A military census taken not long after their departure from Egypt listed the number of fighting men 20 years of age and older as 603,550 - not counting the priests of the tribe of Levi. Thus, the total Israelite population of the beginning of their desert wanderings has been estimated at two to three million. They were indeed a large and powerful force.

But the grumblings and complaining of Israel turned what should have been a quick journey into an exhausting detour. The people of God, rather than acting as God-enable conquerors instead fell into grumblings and open rebellion. Time and time again the people disappoint both Moses and God. Only God's promise to fulfill their destiny keeps him from destroying the nation and starting over. They are forced to wander in the desert for 40 years, surrounded by hostile nations, and suffering from heat and exhaustion. Of the entire nation, only two men, Joshua and Caleb, would survive to enter the Promised Land.

Yahweh spoke to Moses in the wilderness of Sinai, in the Tent of Meeting, on the first day of the second month, in the second year after they had come out of the land of Egypt, saying, "Take a census of all the congregation of the children of Israel, by their families, by their fathers' houses, according to the number of the names, every male, one by one; from twenty years old and upward, all who are able to go out to war in Israel. You and Aaron shall number them by their divisions.

They assembled all the congregation together on the first day of the second month; and they declared their ancestry by their families, by their fathers' houses, according to the number of the names, from twenty years old and upward, one by one. As Yahweh commanded Moses, so he numbered them in the wilderness of Sinai.

The numbers of fighting men in each Israelite tribe were totaled by Moses and Aaron as follows: Reuben - 46,500; Simeon - 59,300; Gad - 45,650; Judah - 64,600; Issachar - 54,400; Zebulun - 57,400; Ephraim - 40,500; Manasseh - 32,200; Benjamin - 35,400; Dan - 62,700; Asher - 41,500; Naphtali - 53,400.

So all those who were numbered of the children of Israel by their fathers' houses, from twenty years old and upward, all who were able to go out to war in Israel; even all those who were numbered were six hundred three thousand five hundred fifty.

But the Levites after the tribe of their fathers were not numbered among them. For Yahweh spoke to Moses, saying, "Only the tribe of Levi you shall not number, neither shall you take a census of them among the children of Israel; but appoint the Levites over the Tabernacle of the Testimony, and over all its furnishings, and over all that belongs to it. They shall carry the tabernacle, and all its furnishings; and they shall take care of it, and shall encamp around it. When the tabernacle is to move, the Levites shall take it down; and when the tabernacle is to be set up, the Levites shall set it up. The stranger who comes near shall be put to death. The children of Israel shall pitch their tents, every man by his own camp, and every man by his own standard, according to their divisions. But the Levites shall encamp around the Tabernacle of the Testimony, that there may be no wrath on the congregation of the children of Israel: and the Levites shall be responsible for the Tabernacle of the Testimony."

Thus the children of Israel did. According to all that Yahweh commanded Moses, so they did.

Yahweh spoke to Moses in the wilderness of Sinai, saying, "Count the children of Levi by their fathers' houses, by their families. You shall count every male from a month old and upward."

Moses numbered them according to the word of Yahweh, as he was commanded.

These were the sons of Levi by their names: Gershon, and Kohath, and Merari.

All who were numbered of the Levites, whom Moses and Aaron numbered at the commandment of Yahweh, by their families, all the males from a month old and upward, were twenty-two thousand.

After the counting of the Levite men, God gave detailed instructions to Moses and Aaron for the duties of the priests; their tasks in making sacrifices, in the keeping of the tabernacle, in the tear-down, moving and re-assembly of the tabernacle, and in serving the people.

Among the statutes given to Moses were provisions for an Israelite to take a "Nazirite vow," dedicating their lives to the service of God. The famous Bible characters Samson and Samuel would live as a Nazirite, and it is likely that John the Baptist also lived as a Nazirite.

Yahweh spoke to Moses, saying, "Speak to the children of Israel, and tell them: 'When either man or woman shall make a special vow, the vow of a Nazirite, to separate himself to Yahweh, he shall separate himself from wine and strong drink. He shall drink no vinegar of wine, or vinegar of fermented drink, neither shall he drink any juice of grapes, nor eat fresh grapes or dried. All the days of his separation he shall eat nothing that is made of the grapevine, from the seeds even to the skins.

"'All the days of his vow of separation no razor shall come on his head, until the days are fulfilled, in which he separates himself to Yahweh. He shall be holy. He shall let the locks of the hair of his head grow long.

It happened on the day that Moses had finished setting up the tabernacle, and had anointed it and sanctified it, with all its furniture, and the altar with all its vessels, and had anointed and sanctified them; that the princes of Israel, the heads of their fathers' houses, offered. These were the princes of the tribes. These are they who were over those who were numbered: and they brought their offering before Yahweh, six covered wagons, and twelve oxen; a wagon for every two of the princes, and for each one an ox: and they presented them before the tabernacle. Yahweh spoke to Moses, saying, "Accept these from them, that they may be used in doing the service of the Tent of Meeting; and you shall give them to the Levites, to every man according to his service."

The wagons were loaded down with gifts given by the Israelites for the sanctification of the tabernacle. The nation was blessed with items of gold, silver and other rich goods given to them by the Egyptians, as God opened their hearts and caused them to give many such items to the Israelites when they left Egypt.

This was the dedication of the altar, on the day when it was anointed, by the princes of Israel: twelve silver platters, twelve silver bowls, twelve golden ladles; each silver platter weighing one hundred thirty shekels, and each bowl seventy; all the silver of the vessels two thousand four hundred shekels, after the shekel of the sanctuary; the twelve golden ladles, full of incense, weighing ten shekels apiece, after the shekel of the sanctuary; all the gold of the ladles weighed one hundred twenty shekels; all the cattle for the burnt offering twelve bulls, the rams twelve, the male lambs a year old twelve, and their meal offering; and the male goats for a sin offering twelve; and all the cattle for the sacrifice of peace offerings twenty-four bulls, the rams sixty, the male goats sixty, the male lambs a year old sixty. This was the dedication of the altar, after it was anointed.

They set forward from the Mount of Yahweh three days' journey. The ark of the covenant of Yahweh went before them three days' journey, to seek out a resting place for them. The cloud of Yahweh was over them by day, when they set forward from the camp. It happened, when the ark went forward, that Moses said, "Rise up, Yahweh, and let your enemies be scattered! Let those who hate you flee before you!" When it rested, he said, "Return, Yahweh, to the ten thousands of the thousands of Israel."

The people were complaining in the ears of Yahweh. When Yahweh heard it, his anger was kindled; and Yahweh's fire burnt among them, and consumed some of the outskirts of the camp. The people cried to Moses; and Moses prayed to Yahweh, and the fire abated. The name of that place was called Taberah, because Yahweh's fire burnt among them.

The mixed multitude that was among them lusted exceedingly: and the children of Israel also wept again, and said, "Who will give us flesh to eat? We remember the fish, which we ate in Egypt for nothing; the cucumbers, and the melons, and the leeks, and the onions, and the garlic; but now we have lost our appetite. There is nothing at all except this manna to look at." The manna was like coriander seed, and its appearance like the appearance of bdellium. The people went around, gathered it, and ground it in mills, or beat it in mortars, and boiled it in pots, and made cakes of it. Its taste was like the taste of fresh oil. When the dew fell on the camp in the night, the manna fell on it.

Moses said, "The people, among whom I am, are six hundred thousand men on foot; and you have said, 'I will give them flesh, that they may eat a whole month.' Shall flocks and herds be slaughtered for them, to be sufficient for them? Shall all the fish of the sea be gathered together for them, to be sufficient for them?"

Yahweh said to Moses, "Has Yahweh's hand grown short? Now you will see whether my word will happen to you or not."

Moses went into the camp, he and the elders of Israel. A wind from Yahweh went out and brought quails from the sea, and let them fall by the camp, about a day's journey on this side, and a day's journey on the other side, around the camp, and about two cubits above the surface of the earth. The people rose up all that day, and all the night, and all the next day, and gathered the quails. He who gathered least gathered ten homers; and they spread them all abroad for themselves around the camp. While the flesh was yet between their teeth, before it was chewed, the anger of Yahweh was kindled against the people, and Yahweh struck the people with a very great plague. The name of that place was called Kibroth Hattaavah, because there they buried the people who lusted.

On the day that the tabernacle was raised up, the cloud covered the tabernacle, even the Tent of the Testimony: and at evening it was over the tabernacle as it were the appearance of fire, until morning. So it was continually. The cloud covered it, and the appearance of fire by night. Whenever the cloud was taken up from over the Tent, then after that the children of Israel traveled; and in the place where the cloud remained, there the children of Israel encamped.

Yahweh spoke to Moses, saying, "Send men, that they may spy out the land of Canaan, which I give to the children of Israel. Of every tribe of their fathers, you shall send a man, every one a prince among them."

Moses sent them from the wilderness of Paran according to the commandment of Yahweh: all of them men who were heads of the children of Israel.

They returned from spying out the land at the end of forty days. They went and came to Moses, and to Aaron, and to all the congregation of the children of Israel, to the wilderness of Paran, to Kadesh; and brought back word to them, and to all the congregation, and showed them the fruit of the land. They told him, and said, "We came to the land where you sent us; and surely it flows with milk and honey; and this is its fruit. However the people who dwell in the land are strong, and the cities are fortified and very large. Moreover, we saw the children of Anak there. Amalek dwells in the land of the South: and the Hittite, and the Jebusite, and the Amorite, dwell in the hill country; and the Canaanite dwells by the sea, and along by the side of the Jordan." Caleb stilled the people before Moses, and said, "Let us go up at once, and possess it; for we are well able to overcome it." But the men who went up with him said, "We aren't able to go up against the people; for they are stronger than we." They brought up an evil report of the land which they had spied out to the children of Israel, saying, "The land, through which we have gone to spy it out, is a land that eats up its inhabitants; and all the people who we saw in it are men of great stature. There we saw the Nephilim, the sons of Anak, who come of the Nephilim: and we were in our own sight as grasshoppers, and so we were in their sight."

All the congregation lifted up their voice, and cried; and the people wept that night. All the children of Israel murmured against Moses and against Aaron: and the whole congregation said to them, "Would that we had died in the land of Egypt! or would that we had died in this wilderness! Why does Yahweh bring us to this land, to fall by the sword? Our wives and our little ones will be a prey: wouldn't it be better for us to return into Egypt?" They said one to another, "Let us make a captain, and let us return into Egypt." Then Moses and Aaron fell on their faces before all the assembly of the congregation of the children of Israel. Joshua the son of Nun and Caleb the son of Jephunneh, who were of those who spied out the land, tore their clothes: and they spoke to all the congregation of the children of Israel, saying, "The land, which we passed through to spy it out, is an exceeding good land. If Yahweh delights in us, then he will bring us into this land, and give it to us; a land which flows with milk and honey. Only don't rebel against Yahweh, neither fear the people of the land; for they are bread for us: their defense is removed from over them, and Yahweh is with us. Don't fear them." But all the congregation threatened to stone them with stones. The glory of Yahweh appeared in the Tent of Meeting to all the children of Israel.

Yahweh said to Moses, "How long will this people despise me? and how long will they not believe in me, for all the signs which I have worked among them? I will strike them with the pestilence, and disinherit them, and will make of you a nation greater and mightier than they." Moses said to Yahweh, "Then the Egyptians will hear it; for you brought up this people in your might from among them; and they will tell it to the inhabitants of this land. They have heard that you Yahweh are in the midst of this people; for you Yahweh are seen face to face, and your cloud stands over them, and you go before them, in a pillar of cloud by day, and in a pillar of fire by night. Now if you killed this people as one man, then the nations which have heard the fame of you will speak, saying, 'Because Yahweh was not able to bring this people into the land which he swore to them, therefore he has slain them in the wilderness.' Now please let the power of the Lord be great, according as you have spoken, saying, 'Yahweh is slow to anger, and abundant in loving kindness, forgiving iniquity and disobedience; and that will by no means clear the guilty, visiting the iniquity of the fathers on the children, on the third and on the fourth generation.' Please pardon the iniquity of this people according to the greatness of your loving kindness, and according as you have forgiven this people, from Egypt even until now."

Yahweh spoke to Moses and to Aaron, saying, "How long shall I bear with this evil congregation, that murmur against me? I have heard the murmurings of the children of Israel, which they murmur against me. Tell them, 'As I live, says Yahweh, surely as you have spoken in my ears, so will I do to you: your dead bodies shall fall in this wilderness; and all who were numbered of you, according to your whole number, from twenty years old and upward, who have murmured against me, surely you shall not come into the land, concerning which I swore that I would make you dwell therein, except Caleb the son of Jephunneh, and Joshua the son of Nun. But your little ones, that you said should be a prey, them will I bring in, and they shall know the land which you have rejected. But as for you, your dead bodies shall fall in this wilderness. Your children shall be wanderers in the wilderness forty years, and shall bear your prostitution, until your dead bodies be consumed in the wilderness. After the number of the days in which you spied out the land, even forty days, for every day a year, you will bear your iniquities, even forty years, and you will know my alienation.'

Once again, the people of Israel grumbled, this time over a lack of water. Rather than asking God for help, they fell into their normal pattern of complaining. But this time Moses gets pulled into trouble; instead of speaking to the rock to bring forth water, as God commanded, he struck the rock with his rod twice and seemed to take for himself credit for this great miracle. Because of this, God denied him the right to enter the Promised Land. Once again, we see that while God has great love for man, this love in turn demands strict obedience to his will.

The children of Israel, even the whole congregation, came into the wilderness of Zin in the first month: and the people stayed in Kadesh; and Miriam died there, and was buried there. There was no water for the congregation: and they assembled themselves together against Moses and against Aaron. The people strove with Moses, and spoke, saying, "We wish that we had died when our brothers died before Yahweh! Why have you brought the assembly of Yahweh into this wilderness, that we should die there, we and our animals? Why have you made us to come up out of Egypt, to bring us in to this evil place? It is no place of seed, or of figs, or of vines, or of pomegranates; neither is there any water to drink."

Moses and Aaron went from the presence of the assembly to the door of the Tent of Meeting, and fell on their faces: and the glory of Yahweh appeared to them. Yahweh spoke to Moses, saying, "Take the rod, and assemble the congregation, you, and Aaron your brother, and speak to the rock before their eyes, that it give forth its water; and you shall bring forth to them water out of the rock; so you shall give the congregation and their livestock drink."

Moses took the rod from before Yahweh, as he commanded him. Moses and Aaron gathered the assembly together before the rock, and he said to them, "Hear now, you rebels; shall we bring you water out of this rock for you?" Moses lifted up his hand, and struck the rock with his rod twice: and water came forth abundantly, and the congregation drank, and their livestock.

Yahweh said to Moses and Aaron, "Because you didn't believe in me, to sanctify me in the eyes of the children of Israel, therefore you shall not bring this assembly into the land which I have given them."

The nation quickly forgot that God delivered the Canaanites into their hands, and they complained about the journey around the land of Edom. In response, God sent poisonous snakes among the people. When Moses prayed for the people, God instructed him to lift a brass serpent on a stake; when the people looked at this serpent, they would not die. To this day, the image of a snake on a pole is a universally recognized symbol of the medical profession.

They traveled from Mount Hor by the way to the Red Sea, to compass the land of Edom: and the soul of the people was much discouraged because of the way. The people spoke against God, and against Moses, "Why have you brought us up out of Egypt to die in the wilderness? For there is no bread, and there is no water; and our soul loathes this light bread."

Yahweh sent fiery serpents among the people, and they bit the people; and many people of Israel died. The people came to Moses, and said, "We have sinned, because we have spoken against Yahweh, and against you. Pray to Yahweh, that he take away the serpents from us." Moses prayed for the people.

Yahweh said to Moses, "Make a fiery serpent, and set it on a standard: and it shall happen, that everyone who is bitten, when he sees it, shall live." Moses made a serpent of brass, and set it on the standard: and it happened, that if a serpent had bitten any man, when he looked to the serpent of brass, he lived.

The Israelites enjoyed battle victories against the Amorites, and then set their sights on Moab. Then Balak, the king of Moab, sent for a pagan prophet, Balaam, hoping he will curse the Israelites. But God appeared to Balaam in a dream and warned him not to speak out against his blessed people. When Balaam did not follow God's instructions fully, there was a very interesting chain of events involving a talking donkey and an angel.

Balaam answered the servants of Balak, "If Balak would give me his house full of silver and gold, I can't go beyond the word of Yahweh my God, to do less or more. Now therefore, please wait also here this night, that I may know what Yahweh will speak to me more."

God came to Balaam at night, and said to him, "If the men have come to call you, rise up, go with them; but only the word which I speak to you, that you shall do."

Balaam rose up in the morning, and saddled his donkey, and went with the princes of Moab. God's anger was kindled because he went; and the angel of Yahweh placed himself in the way for an adversary against him. Now he was riding on his donkey, and his two servants were with him. The donkey saw the angel of Yahweh standing in the way, with his sword drawn in his hand; and the donkey turned aside out of the way, and went into the field: and Balaam struck the donkey, to turn her into the way. Then the angel of Yahweh stood in a narrow path between the vineyards, a wall being on this side, and a wall on that side. The donkey saw the angel of Yahweh, and she thrust herself to the wall, and crushed Balaam's foot against the wall: and he struck her again.

The angel of Yahweh went further, and stood in a narrow place, where there was no way to turn either to the right hand or to the left. The donkey saw the angel of Yahweh, and she lay down under Balaam: and Balaam's anger was kindled, and he struck the donkey with his staff.

Yahweh opened the mouth of the donkey, and she said to Balaam, "What have I done to you, that you have struck me these three times?"

Balaam said to the donkey, "Because you have mocked me, I wish there were a sword in my hand, for now I would have killed you."

The donkey said to Balaam, "Am I not your donkey, on which you have ridden all your life long to this day? Was I ever in the habit of doing so to you?"

He said, "No."

Then Yahweh opened the eyes of Balaam, and he saw the angel of Yahweh standing in the way, with his sword drawn in his hand; and he bowed his head, and fell on his face. The angel of Yahweh said to him, "Why have you struck your donkey these three times? Behold, I have come forth as an adversary, because your way is perverse before me: and the donkey saw me, and turned aside before me these three times. Unless she had turned aside from me, surely now I would have killed you, and saved her alive."

Balaam said to the angel of Yahweh, "I have sinned; for I didn't know that you stood in the way against me. Now therefore, if it displeases you, I will go back again."

The angel of Yahweh said to Balaam, "Go with the men; but only the word that I shall speak to you, that you shall speak."

Yahweh put a word in Balaam's mouth, and said, "Return to Balak, and thus you shall speak."

He returned to him, and behold, he was standing by his burnt offering, he, and all the princes of Moab. He took up his parable, and said,

"From Aram has Balak brought me,
the king of Moab from the mountains of the East.
Come, curse Jacob for me.
Come, defy Israel.
How shall I curse whom God has not cursed?
How shall I defy whom Yahweh has not defied?
For from the top of the rocks I see him.
From the hills I see him.
Behold, it is a people that dwells alone,
and shall not be reckoned among the nations.
Who can count the dust of Jacob,
or number the fourth part of Israel?
Let me die the death of the righteous!
Let my last end be like his!"

Although not yet in the Promised Land, the nation of Israel began to be unduly influenced by the pagan nations around them. Moabite and Midianite women were corrupting the men through sexual trysts and by encouraging them to practice idolatry. On one occasion, one of the grandsons of Aaron took matters into his own hands in dramatic fashion, in order to restore proper spiritual purity to Israel.

Israel stayed in Shittim; and the people began to play the prostitute with the daughters of Moab: for they called the people to the sacrifices of their gods; and the people ate, and bowed down to their gods. Israel joined himself to Baal Peor: and the anger of Yahweh was kindled against Israel. Yahweh said to Moses, "Take all the chiefs of the people, and hang them up to Yahweh before the sun, that the fierce anger of Yahweh may turn away from Israel."

Moses said to the judges of Israel, "Everyone kill his men who have joined themselves to Baal Peor."

Behold, one of the children of Israel came and brought to his brothers a Midianite woman in the sight of Moses, and in the sight of all the congregation of the children of Israel, while they were weeping at the door of the Tent of Meeting. When Phinehas, the son of Eleazar, the son of Aaron the priest, saw it, he rose up from the midst of the congregation, and took a spear in his hand; and he went after the man of Israel into the pavilion, and thrust both of them through, the man of Israel, and the woman through her body. So the plague was stayed from the children of Israel. Those who died by the plague were twenty-four thousand. Yahweh spoke to Moses, saying, "Phinehas, the son of Eleazar, the son of Aaron the priest, has turned my wrath away from the children of Israel, in that he was jealous with my jealousy among them, so that I didn't consume the children of Israel in my jealousy. Therefore say, 'Behold, I give to him my covenant of peace: and it shall be to him, and to his seed after him, the covenant of an everlasting priesthood; because he was jealous for his God, and made atonement for the children of Israel.'"

Moses spoke to Yahweh, saying, "Let Yahweh, the God of the spirits of all flesh, appoint a man over the congregation, who may go out before them, and who may come in before them, and who may lead them out, and who may bring them in; that the congregation of Yahweh not be as sheep which have no shepherd."

Yahweh said to Moses, "Take Joshua the son of Nun, a man in whom is the Spirit, and lay your hand on him; and set him before Eleazar the priest, and before all the congregation; and commission him in their sight. You shall put of your honor on him, that all the congregation of the children of Israel may obey. He shall stand before Eleazar the priest, who shall inquire for him by the judgment of the Urim before Yahweh: at his word shall they go out, and at his word they shall come in, both he, and all the children of Israel with him, even all the congregation."

Moses did as Yahweh commanded him; and he took Joshua, and set him before Eleazar the priest, and before all the congregation: and he laid his hands on him, and commissioned him, as Yahweh spoke by Moses.

As the Israelite nation prepared to enter the Promised Land, God gave instructions to Moses on how to divide the land among the tribes. By agreement, the tribes of Reuben, Gad and part of the tribe of Manasseh were allowed to take possession of fertile land suitable for grazing that was east of the Jordan River, as they had many livestock. In return, they agreed to enter the Promised Land with the other tribes to help conquer the land in battle. God also established "cities of refuge," where one who accidentally killed another person could flee, escaping the wrath of the murdered person's family until a fair trial could be given.

Because the idolatry and sins of the Canaanite people was so ingrained, it was necessary for God to give instructions that they should be totally driven out and destroyed. Otherwise Israel would never be able to withstand the corrupting influence of their wicked practices, such as child sacrifices, idol worship, and temple prostitution.

Yahweh spoke to Moses in the plains of Moab by the Jordan at Jericho, saying, Speak to the children of Israel, and tell them, "When you pass over the Jordan into the land of Canaan, then you shall drive out all the inhabitants of the land from before you, destroy all their stone idols, destroy all their molten images, and demolish all their high places. You shall take possession of the land, and dwell therein; for I have given the land to you to possess it. You shall inherit the land by lot according to your families; to the more you shall give the more inheritance, and to the fewer you shall give the less inheritance: wherever the lot falls to any man, that shall be his. You shall inherit according to the tribes of your fathers.

"But if you do not drive out the inhabitants of the land from before you, then those you let remain of them will be as pricks in your eyes and as thorns in your sides, and they will harass you in the land in which you dwell. It shall happen that as I thought to do to them, so will I do to you."

8 PREPARING FOR CONQUEST

On The Verge of the Promised Land

After 40 years of wandering in the Sinai desert, the nation of Israel was finally ready to enter the Promised Land. Over these 40 years, God worked a subtle miracle; their clothes and shoes did not wear out, and they remained as good as the day when they left Egypt. Moses, now 120 years old, knew it was near his time to die, as God had told him that he could not enter the Promised Land.

To prepare the nation for their task, Moses assembled the people together, and delivered one last statement to them. In this statement, Moses implored the people to remember what God did for them in delivering them from the Egyptians and from their enemies over the last 40 years. He pleaded with them to remain faithful to God, and warned them what would happen if they did not walk in the ways commanded. Moses predicted a glorious victory to the nation of Israel, but he also warned them of their prevalence to ignore God when times are good. Moses went over many of the commands given to him by God for the nation, in painstaking detail. He commanded them to set up a monument once they crossed the Jordan River, so as to help them to remember their dependence upon God.

Having established Joshua as his successor, Moses was now ready to claim his heavenly reward.

These are the words which Moses spoke to all Israel beyond the Jordan in the wilderness, in the Arabah over against Suph, between Paran, and Tophel, and Laban, and Hazeroth, and Dizahab.

For Yahweh your God has blessed you in all the work of your hand; he has known your walking through this great wilderness: these forty years Yahweh your God has been with you; you have lacked nothing.

Now, Israel, listen to the statutes and to the ordinances, which I teach you, to do them; that you may live, and go in and possess the land which Yahweh, the God of your fathers, gives you. You shall not add to the word which I command you, neither shall you diminish from it, that you may keep the commandments of Yahweh your God which I command you. Your eyes have seen what Yahweh did because of Baal Peor; for all the men who followed Baal Peor, Yahweh your God has destroyed them from the midst of you. But you who were faithful to Yahweh your God are all alive this day.

But Yahweh has taken you, and brought you forth out of the iron furnace, out of Egypt, to be to him a people of inheritance, as at this day. Furthermore, Yahweh was angry with me for your sakes, and swore that I should not go over the Jordan, and that I should not go in to that good land, which Yahweh your God gives you for an inheritance: but I must die in this land, I must not go over the Jordan; but you shall go over, and possess that good land. Take heed to yourselves, lest you forget the covenant of Yahweh your God, which he made with you, and make you an engraved image in the form of anything which Yahweh your God has forbidden you. For Yahweh your God is a devouring fire, a jealous God.

For ask now of the days that are past, which were before you, since the day that God created man on the earth, and from the one end of the sky to the other, whether there has been anything as this great thing is, or has been heard like it? Did a people ever hear the voice of God speaking out of the midst of the fire, as you have heard, and live? Or has God tried to go and take a nation for himself from the midst of another nation, by trials, by signs, and by wonders, and by war, and by a mighty hand, and by an outstretched arm, and by great terrors, according to all that Yahweh your God did for you in Egypt before your eyes? It was shown to you so that you might know that Yahweh is God. There is no one else besides him. Out of heaven he made you to hear his voice, that he might instruct you: and on earth he made you to see his great fire; and you heard his words out of the midst of the fire. Because he loved your fathers, therefore he chose their seed after them, and brought you out with his presence, with his great power, out of Egypt; to drive out nations from before you greater and mightier than you, to bring you in, to give you their land for an inheritance, as at this day. Know therefore this day, and lay it to your heart, that Yahweh is God in heaven above and on the earth beneath; there is none else. You shall keep his statutes, and his commandments, which I command you this day, that it may go well with you, and with your children after you, and that you may prolong your days in the land, which Yahweh your God gives you, forever.

Hear therefore, Israel, and observe to do it; that it may be well with you, and that you may increase mightily, as Yahweh, the God of your fathers, has promised to you, in a land flowing with milk and honey. Hear, Israel: Yahweh is our God; Yahweh is one: and you shall love Yahweh your God with all your heart, and with all your soul, and with all your might. These words, which I command you this day, shall be on your heart; and you shall teach them diligently to your children, and shall talk of them when you sit in your house, and when you walk by the way, and when you lie down, and when you rise up. You shall bind them for a sign on your hand, and they shall be for symbols between your eyes. You shall write them on the door posts of your house, and on your gates. It shall be, when Yahweh your God shall bring you into the land which he swore to your fathers, to Abraham, to Isaac, and to Jacob, to give you, great and goodly cities, which you didn't build, and houses full of all good things, which you didn't fill, and cisterns dug out, which you didn't dig, vineyards and olive trees, which you didn't plant, and you shall eat and be full; then beware lest you forget Yahweh, who brought you forth out of the land of Egypt, out of the house of bondage.

When your son asks you in time to come, saying, "What do the testimonies, the statutes, and the ordinances, which Yahweh our God has commanded you mean?" then you shall tell your son, "We were Pharaoh's bondservants in Egypt: and Yahweh brought us out of Egypt with a mighty hand; and Yahweh showed great and awesome signs and wonders on Egypt, on Pharaoh, and on all his house, before our eyes; and he brought us out from there, that he might bring us in, to give us the land which he swore to our fathers.

You shall consume all the peoples whom Yahweh your God shall deliver to you; your eye shall not pity them: neither shall you serve their gods; for that will be a snare to you. If you shall say in your heart, "These nations are more than I; how can I dispossess them?" you shall not be afraid of them: you shall well remember what Yahweh your God did to Pharaoh, and to all Egypt; the great trials which your eyes saw, and the signs, and the wonders, and the mighty hand, and the outstretched arm, by which Yahweh your God brought you out: so shall Yahweh your God do to all the peoples of whom you are afraid. Moreover Yahweh your God will send the hornet among them, until those who are left, and hide themselves, perish from before you. You shall not be scared of them; for Yahweh your God is in the midst of you, a great and awesome God.

You shall observe to do all the commandment which I command you this day, that you may live, and multiply, and go in and possess the land which Yahweh swore to your fathers. You shall remember all the way which Yahweh your God has led you these forty years in the wilderness, that he might humble you, to prove you, to know what was in your heart, whether you would keep his commandments, or not. He humbled you, and allowed you to be hungry, and fed you with manna, which you didn't know, neither did your fathers know; that he might make you know that man does not live by bread only, but man lives by everything that proceeds out of the mouth of Yahweh. Your clothing didn't grow old on you, neither did your foot swell, these forty years. You shall consider in your heart that as a man chastens his son, so Yahweh your God chastens you.

Hear, Israel: you are to pass over the Jordan this day, to go in to dispossess nations greater and mightier than yourself, cities great and fortified up to the sky, a people great and tall, the sons of the Anakim, whom you know, and of whom you have heard say, "Who can stand before the sons of Anak?" Know therefore this day, that Yahweh your God is he who goes over before you as a devouring fire; he will destroy them, and he will bring them down before you: so you shall drive them out, and make them to perish quickly, as Yahweh has spoken to you.

Don't say in your heart, after Yahweh your God has thrust them out from before you, saying, "For my righteousness Yahweh has brought me in to possess this land"; because Yahweh drives them out before you because of the wickedness of these nations. Not for your righteousness, or for the uprightness of your heart, do you go in to possess their land; but for the wickedness of these nations Yahweh your God does drive them out from before you, and that he may establish the word which Yahweh swore to your fathers, to Abraham, to Isaac, and to Jacob. Know therefore, that Yahweh your God doesn't give you this good land to possess it for your righteousness; for you are a stiff-necked people.

These are the statutes and the ordinances which you shall observe to do in the land which Yahweh, the God of your fathers, has given you to possess it, all the days that you live on the earth. You shall surely destroy all the places in which the nations that you shall dispossess served their gods, on the high mountains, and on the hills, and under every green tree: and you shall break down their altars, and dash in pieces their pillars, and burn their Asherim with fire; and you shall cut down the engraved images of their gods; and you shall destroy their name out of that place.

Moses and the elders of Israel commanded the people, saying, "Keep all the commandment which I command you this day. It shall be on the day when you shall pass over the Jordan to the land which Yahweh your God gives you, that you shall set yourself up great stones, and plaster them with plaster: and you shall write on them all the words of this law, when you have passed over; that you may go in to the land which Yahweh your God gives you, a land flowing with milk and honey, as Yahweh, the God of your fathers, has promised you. It shall be, when you have passed over the Jordan, that you shall set up these stones, which I command you this day, in Mount Ebal, and you shall plaster them with plaster. There you shall build an altar to Yahweh your God, an altar of stones: you shall lift up no iron on them. You shall build the altar of Yahweh your God of uncut stones; and you shall offer burnt offerings thereon to Yahweh your God: and you shall sacrifice peace offerings, and shall eat there; and you shall rejoice before Yahweh your God. You shall write on the stones all the words of this law very plainly."

Moses and the priests, the Levites, spoke to all Israel, saying, "Keep silence, and listen, Israel: this day you have become the people of Yahweh your God. You shall therefore obey the voice of Yahweh your God, and do his commandments and his statutes, which I command you this day."

It shall happen, if you shall listen diligently to the voice of Yahweh your God, to observe to do all his commandments which I command you this day, that Yahweh your God will set you on high above all the nations of the earth: and all these blessings shall come on you, and overtake you, if you shall listen to the voice of Yahweh your God. You shall be blessed in the city, and you shall be blessed in the field. You shall be blessed in the fruit of your body, the fruit of your ground, the fruit of your animals, the increase of your livestock, and the young of your flock. Your basket and your kneading trough shall be blessed. You shall be blessed when you come in, and you shall be blessed when you go out.

Moses called to all Israel, and said to them, You have seen all that Yahweh did before your eyes in the land of Egypt to Pharaoh, and to all his servants, and to all his land; the great trials which your eyes saw, the signs, and those great wonders: but Yahweh has not given you a heart to know, and eyes to see, and ears to hear, to this day. I have led you forty years in the wilderness: your clothes have not grown old on you, and your shoes have not grown old on your feet. You have not eaten bread, neither have you drunk wine or strong drink; that you may know that I am Yahweh your God.

For this commandment which I command you this day, it is not too hard for you, neither is it far off. It is not in heaven, that you should say, "Who shall go up for us to heaven, and bring it to us, and make us to hear it, that we may do it?" Neither is it beyond the sea, that you should say, "Who shall go over the sea for us, and bring it to us, and make us to hear it, that we may do it?" But the word is very near to you, in your mouth, and in your heart, that you may do it. Behold, I have set before you this day life and good, and death and evil; in that I command you this day to love Yahweh your God, to walk in his ways, and to keep his commandments and his statutes and his ordinances, that you may live and multiply, and that Yahweh your God may bless you in the land where you go in to possess it. But if your heart turns away, and you will not hear, but shall be drawn away, and worship other gods, and serve them; I denounce to you this day, that you shall surely perish; you shall not prolong your days in the land, where you pass over the Jordan to go in to possess it. I call heaven and earth to witness against you this day, that I have set before you life and death, the blessing and the curse: therefore choose life, that you may live, you and your seed; to love Yahweh your God, to obey his voice, and to cling to him; for he is your life, and the length of your days; that you may dwell in the land which Yahweh swore to your fathers, to Abraham, to Isaac, and to Jacob, to give them.

Moses, one of the great leaders of the Bible, was near death. But before he could consider his work complete, he made sure to once again remind the nation of Israel, in great detail, of their responsibility to keep all the commands of God. Another important task remained as well - to pass on his leadership to another person who would lead the nation after he was gone. For this, he selected Joshua, who had demonstrated his trust in God 40 years earlier, as one of the spies who returned from Canaan. His choice of Joshua expressed his faith that, with God's help, they could conquer the Promised Land.

Moses went and spoke these words to all Israel. He said to them, "I am one hundred twenty years old this day; I can no more go out and come in: and Yahweh has said to me, 'You shall not go over this Jordan.' Yahweh your God, he will go over before you; he will destroy these nations from before you, and you shall dispossess them. Joshua shall go over before you, as Yahweh has spoken. Yahweh will do to them as he did to Sihon and to Og, the kings of the Amorites, and to their land; whom he destroyed. Yahweh will deliver them up before you, and you shall do to them according to all the commandment which I have commanded you. Be strong and courageous, don't be afraid, nor be scared of them: for Yahweh your God, he it is who does go with you; he will not fail you, nor forsake you."

Moses called to Joshua, and said to him in the sight of all Israel, "Be strong and courageous: for you shall go with this people into the land which Yahweh has sworn to their fathers to give them; and you shall cause them to inherit it. Yahweh, he it is who does go before you; he will be with you, he will not fail you, neither forsake you: don't be afraid, neither be dismayed."

It happened, when Moses had made an end of writing the words of this law in a book, until they were finished, that Moses commanded the Levites, who bore the ark of the covenant of Yahweh, saying, "Take this book of the law, and put it by the side of the ark of the covenant of Yahweh your God, that it may be there for a witness against you.

Yahweh spoke to Moses that same day, saying, "Go up into this mountain of Abarim, to Mount Nebo, which is in the land of Moab, that is over against Jericho; and see the land of Canaan, which I give to the children of Israel for a possession; and die on the mountain where you go up, and be gathered to your people, as Aaron your brother died on Mount Hor, and was gathered to his people: because you trespassed against me in the midst of the children of Israel at the waters of Meribah of Kadesh, in the wilderness of Zin; because you didn't sanctify me in the midst of the children of Israel. For you shall see the land before you; but you shall not go there into the land which I give the children of Israel."

Moses went up from the plains of Moab to Mount Nebo, to the top of Pisgah, that is over against Jericho. Yahweh showed him all the land of Gilead, to Dan, and all Naphtali, and the land of Ephraim and Manasseh, and all the land of Judah, to the hinder sea, and the South, and the Plain of the valley of Jericho the city of palm trees, to Zoar. Yahweh said to him, "This is the land which I swore to Abraham, to Isaac, and to Jacob, saying, 'I will give it to your seed.' I have caused you to see it with your eyes, but you shall not go over there."

So Moses the servant of Yahweh died there in the land of Moab, according to the word of Yahweh. He buried him in the valley in the land of Moab over against Beth Peor: but no man knows of his tomb to this day. Moses was one hundred twenty years old when he died: his eye was not dim, nor his natural force abated. The children of Israel wept for Moses in the plains of Moab thirty days: so the days of weeping in the mourning for Moses were ended. Joshua the son of Nun was full of the spirit of wisdom; for Moses had laid his hands on him: and the children of Israel listened to him, and did as Yahweh commanded Moses. There has not arisen a prophet since in Israel like Moses, whom Yahweh knew face to face, in all the signs and the wonders, which Yahweh sent him to do in the land of Egypt, to Pharaoh, and to all his servants, and to all his land, and in all the mighty hand, and in all the great terror, which Moses worked in the sight of all Israel.

9 FINALLY HOME

Entering the Promised Land

After 40 years of wandering in the wilderness, it was now time for the Israelite nation to finally claim the land that was promised to Abraham hundreds of years before. Still, even as the nation was poised on the Jordan River, obstacles remained. The death of Moses had the potential of creating a leadership vacuum; fortunately, Joshua demonstrated through his actions and faith in God that he was up for the task.

Joshua, through his obedience to God, helped Israel overcome overwhelming odds to finally accomplish what they were destined for. He made sure that the Israelites put God first. At times, they acted very much unlike a conquering army; pausing for circumcision rituals and stopping to worship God, erecting stone monuments, and even walking around cities without attacking until God was ready. But, by doing as God desired, despite being outnumbered and fighting against superior, well-trained and well-equipped armies, they were victorious.

Entering Canaan, a land "flowing with milk and honey," they fully conquered and inhabited the Promised Land in a period of around seven years. And, they seemed to have learned a valuable lesson in the wilderness; the nation put God first, and did not grumble or complain as they went about the business of fighting and conquering the land. God rewarded their faith in Him by showering them with victory, then peace and prosperity.

Now it happened after the death of Moses the servant of Yahweh, that Yahweh spoke to Joshua the son of Nun, Moses' servant, saying, "Moses my servant is dead; now therefore arise, go over this Jordan, you, and all this people, to the land which I give to them, even to the children of Israel. I have given you every place that the sole of your foot will tread on, as I told Moses.

Only be strong and very courageous, to observe to do according to all the law, which Moses my servant commanded you. Don't turn from it to the right hand or to the left, that you may have good success wherever you go. This book of the law shall not depart out of your mouth, but you shall meditate on it day and night, that you may observe to do according to all that is written therein: for then you shall make your way prosperous, and then you shall have good success.

Then Joshua commanded the officers of the people, saying, "Pass through the midst of the camp, and command the people, saying, 'Prepare food; for within three days you are to pass over this Jordan, to go in to possess the land, which Yahweh your God gives you to possess it.'"

Joshua the son of Nun secretly sent two men out of Shittim as spies, saying, "Go, view the land, including Jericho." They went and came into the house of a prostitute whose name was Rahab, and slept there.

The king of Jericho was told, "Behold, men of the children of Israel came in here tonight to spy out the land."

The king of Jericho sent to Rahab, saying, "Bring out the men who have come to you, who have entered into your house; for they have come to spy out all the land."

The woman took the two men and hid them. Then she said, "Yes, the men came to me, but I didn't know where they came from. It happened about the time of the shutting of the gate, when it was dark, that the men went out. Where the men went, I don't know. Pursue them quickly; for you will overtake them." But she had brought them up to the roof, and hid them with the stalks of flax, which she had laid in order on the roof. The men pursued them the way to the Jordan to the fords: and as soon as those who pursued them had gone out, they shut the gate. Before they had laid down, she came up to them on the roof; and she said to the men, "I know that Yahweh has given you the land, and that the fear of you has fallen on us, and that all the inhabitants of the land melt away before you. For we have heard how Yahweh dried up the water of the Red Sea before you, when you came out of Egypt; and what you did to the two kings of the Amorites, who were beyond the Jordan, to Sihon and to Og, whom you utterly destroyed. As soon as we had heard it, our hearts melted, neither did there remain any more spirit in any man, because of you: for Yahweh your God, he is God in heaven above, and on earth beneath. Now therefore, please swear to me by Yahweh, since I have dealt kindly with you, that you also will deal kindly with my father's house, and give me a true token; and that you will save alive my father, my mother, my brothers, and my sisters, and all that they have, and will deliver our lives from death."

The men said to her, "Our life for yours, if you don't talk about this business of ours; and it shall be, when Yahweh gives us the land, that we will deal kindly and truly with you."

Then she let them down by a cord through the window; for her house was on the side of the wall, and she lived on the wall. She said to them, "Go to the mountain, lest the pursuers find you; and hide yourselves there three days, until the pursuers have returned. Afterward, you may go your way."

The men said to her, "We will be guiltless of this your oath which you have made us to swear. Behold, when we come into the land, you shall bind this line of scarlet thread in the window which you used to let us down. You shall gather to yourself into the house your father, your mother, your brothers, and all your father's household.

Forty years ago, Moses had sent spies into Canaan. Only Joshua and Caleb had faith that they would conquer the land; the rest of Israel withered without proper faith in God. Now, 40 years later, the spies sent out by Joshua returned full of confidence and faith in the delivering power of God. Encouraged by this report, the nation made plans to begin the invasion immediately.

They went, and came to the mountain, and stayed there three days, until the pursuers had returned. The pursuers sought them throughout all the way, but didn't find them. Then the two men returned, descended from the mountain, passed over, and came to Joshua the son of Nun; and they told him all that had happened to them. They said to Joshua, "Truly Yahweh has delivered into our hands all the land. Moreover, all the inhabitants of the land melt away before us."

Joshua said to the people, "Sanctify yourselves; for tomorrow Yahweh will do wonders among you."

Joshua spoke to the priests, saying, "Take up the ark of the covenant, and pass over before the people." They took up the ark of the covenant, and went before the people.

Yahweh said to Joshua, "Today I will begin to magnify you in the sight of all Israel, that they may know that as I was with Moses, so I will be with you. You shall command the priests who bear the ark of the covenant, saying, 'When you come to the brink of the waters of the Jordan, you shall stand still in the Jordan.'"

Joshua said to the children of Israel, "Come here, and hear the words of Yahweh your God." Joshua said, "Hereby you shall know that the living God is among you, and that he will without fail drive the Canaanite, and the Hittite, and the Hivite, and the Perizzite, and the Girgashite, and the Amorite, and the Jebusite out from before you. Behold, the ark of the covenant of the Lord of all the earth passes over before you into the Jordan. Now therefore take twelve men out of the tribes of Israel, for every tribe a man. It shall come to pass, when the soles of the feet of the priests who bear the ark of Yahweh, the Lord of all the earth, rest in the waters of the Jordan, that the waters of the Jordan will be cut off, even the waters that come down from above; and they shall stand in one heap."

It happened, when the people moved from their tents to pass over the Jordan, the priests who bore the ark of the covenant being before the people, and when those who bore the ark had come to the Jordan, and the feet of the priests who bore the ark had dipped in the edge of the water (for the Jordan overflows all its banks all the time of harvest), that the waters which came down from above stood, and rose up in one heap, a great way off, at Adam, the city that is beside Zarethan; and those that went down toward the sea of the Arabah, even the Salt Sea, were wholly cut off. Then the people passed over right against Jericho. The priests who bore the ark of the covenant of Yahweh stood firm on dry ground in the middle of the Jordan; and all Israel passed over on dry ground, until all the nation had passed completely over the Jordan.

It happened, when all the nation had completely passed over the Jordan, that Yahweh spoke to Joshua, saying, "Take twelve men out of the people, out of every tribe a man, and command them, saying, 'Take from out of the middle of the Jordan, out of the place where the priests' feet stood firm, twelve stones, and carry them over with you, and lay them down in the lodging place, where you will lodge tonight.'"

On that day, Yahweh magnified Joshua in the sight of all Israel; and they feared him, as they feared Moses, all the days of his life.

Yahweh spoke to Joshua, saying, "Command the priests who bear the ark of the testimony, that they come up out of the Jordan."

Joshua therefore commanded the priests, saying, "Come up out of the Jordan!" It happened, when the priests who bore the ark of the covenant of Yahweh had come up out of the middle of the Jordan, and the soles of the priests' feet were lifted up to the dry ground, that the waters of the Jordan returned to their place, and went over all its banks, as before. The people came up out of the Jordan on the tenth day of the first month, and encamped in Gilgal, on the east border of Jericho.

Before battle could begin, Joshua made sure that Israel paid proper respect to God. This involved setting up a monument of stones to commemorate the work of God in allowing them to cross the Jordan River, as well as keeping the Passover feast. When word reached the nations around them that Israel had crossed the Jordan River, aided by the miraculous power of God, the hearts of the nations melted with fear. God was on the move.

Joshua set up those twelve stones, which they took out of the Jordan, in Gilgal. He spoke to the children of Israel, saying, "When your children ask their fathers in time to come, saying, 'What do these stones mean?' Then you shall let your children know, saying, 'Israel came over this Jordan on dry land. For Yahweh your God dried up the waters of the Jordan from before you, until you had passed over, as Yahweh your God did to the Red Sea, which he dried up from before us, until we had passed over; that all the peoples of the earth may know the hand of

Yahweh, that it is mighty; that you may fear Yahweh your God forever.'"

It happened, when all the kings of the Amorites, who were beyond the Jordan westward, and all the kings of the Canaanites, who were by the sea, heard how that Yahweh had dried up the waters of the Jordan from before the children of Israel, until we had passed over, that their heart melted, neither was there spirit in them any more, because of the children of Israel.

The children of Israel encamped in Gilgal. They kept the Passover on the fourteenth day of the month at evening in the plains of Jericho. They ate unleavened cakes and parched grain of the produce of the land on the next day after the Passover, in the same day. The manna ceased on the next day, after they had eaten of the produce of the land. The children of Israel didn't have manna any more; but they ate of the fruit of the land of Canaan that year.

The first city to be conquered was Jericho. God immediately put the faith of Israel in his power and the leadership of Joshua to the test. The unconventional approach to the battle created one of the most interesting stories of conquest in human history.

Now Jericho was tightly shut up because of the children of Israel. No one went out, and no one came in. Yahweh said to Joshua, "Behold, I have given Jericho into your hand, with its king and the mighty men of valor. All your men of war shall march around the city, going around the city once. You shall do this six days. Seven priests shall bear seven trumpets of rams' horns before the ark. On the seventh day, you shall march around the city seven times, and the priests shall blow the trumpets. It shall be that when they make a long blast with the ram's horn, and when you hear the sound of the trumpet, all the people shall shout with a great shout; and the wall of the city shall fall down flat, and the people shall go up every man straight before him."

Joshua the son of Nun called the priests, and said to them, "Take up the ark of the covenant, and let seven priests bear seven trumpets of rams' horns before the ark of Yahweh."

They said to the people, "Advance! March around the city, and let the armed men pass on before Yahweh's ark."

It was so, that when Joshua had spoken to the people, the seven priests bearing the seven trumpets of rams' horns before Yahweh advanced, and blew the trumpets; and the ark of the covenant of Yahweh followed them. The armed men went before the priests who blew the trumpets, and the ark went after them. The trumpets sounded as they went.

Joshua commanded the people, saying, "You shall not shout, nor let your voice be heard, neither shall any word proceed out of your mouth, until the day I tell

peace offerings.

Afterward he read all the words of the law, the blessing and the curse, according to all that is written in the book of the law. There was not a word of all that Moses commanded, which Joshua didn't read before all the assembly of Israel, with the women, the little ones, and the foreigners who were among them.

The nation of Israel continued its battles. Success piled upon success, and in a steady forward march, the nation of Israel laid claim to more and more of the Promised Land. Time and time again, God aided their military power, by casting confusion on the enemies, raining stones from the sky, sending hornets to drive the opposing armies away, and on one occasion, even stopping the sun in the sky so the battle could continue. Joshua left nothing undone that was commanded to him by Moses.

Now it happened when Adoni-Zedek king of Jerusalem heard how Joshua had taken Ai, and had utterly destroyed it; as he had done to Jericho and her king, so he had done to Ai and her king; and how the inhabitants of Gibeon had made peace with Israel, and were among them; that they were very afraid, because Gibeon was a great city, as one of the royal cities, and because it was greater than Ai, and all its men were mighty. Therefore Adoni-Zedek king of Jerusalem sent to Hoham king of Hebron, to Piram king of Jarmuth, to Japhia king of Lachish, and to Debir king of Eglon, saying, "Come up to me, and help me, and let us strike Gibeon; for it has made peace with Joshua and with the children of Israel." Therefore the five kings of the Amorites, the king of Jerusalem, the king of Hebron, the king of Jarmuth, the king of Lachish, the king of Eglon, gathered themselves together, and went up, they and all their armies, and encamped against Gibeon, and made war against it. The men of Gibeon sent to Joshua to the camp to Gilgal, saying, "Don't abandon your servants! Come up to us quickly, and save us, and help us; for all the kings of the Amorites that dwell in the hill country have gathered together against us."

So Joshua went up from Gilgal, he, and all the people of war with him, and all the mighty men of valor. Yahweh said to Joshua, "Don't fear them, for I have delivered them into your hands. Not a man of them will stand before you."

Joshua therefore came on them suddenly. He went up from Gilgal all night. Yahweh confused them before Israel, and he killed them with a great slaughter at Gibeon, and chased them by the way of the ascent of Beth Horon, and struck them to Azekah and to Makkedah. It happened, as they fled from before Israel, while they were at the descent of Beth Horon, that Yahweh cast down great stones from the sky on them to Azekah, and they died. There were more who died from the hailstones than who the children of Israel killed with the sword.

Then Joshua spoke to Yahweh in the day when Yahweh delivered up the Amorites before the children of Israel; and he said in the sight of Israel, "Sun, stand still on Gibeon! You, moon, stop in the valley of Aijalon!"

The sun stood still, and the moon stayed, until the nation had avenged themselves of their enemies. Isn't this written in the book of Jashar? The sun stayed in the midst of the sky, and didn't hurry to go down about a whole day. There was no day like that before it or after it, that Yahweh listened to the voice of a man; for Yahweh fought for Israel.

Joshua returned, and all Israel with him, to the camp to Gilgal. These five kings fled, and hid themselves in the cave at Makkedah. Joshua was told, saying, "The five kings are found, hidden in the cave at Makkedah."

Joshua said, "Roll large stones to the mouth of the cave, and set men by it to guard them; but don't stay. Pursue your enemies, and them from the rear. Don't allow them to enter into their cities; for Yahweh your God has delivered them into your hand."

It happened, when Joshua and the children of Israel had finished killing them with a very great slaughter until they were consumed, and the remnant which remained of them had entered into the fortified cities, that all the people returned to the camp to Joshua at Makkedah in peace. None moved his tongue against any of the children of Israel. Then Joshua said, "Open the mouth of the cave, and bring those five kings out of the cave to me."

They did so, and brought those five kings out of the cave to him: the king of Jerusalem, the king of Hebron, the king of Jarmuth, the king of Lachish, and the king of Eglon. It happened, when they brought those kings out to Joshua, that Joshua called for all the men of Israel, and said to the chiefs of the men of war who went with him, "Come near, put your feet on the necks of these kings."

They came near, and put their feet on their necks.

Joshua said to them, "Don't be afraid, nor be dismayed. Be strong and courageous, for Yahweh will do this to all your enemies against whom you fight."

Afterward Joshua struck them, put them to death, and hanged them on five trees. They were hanging on the trees until the evening. It happened at the time of the going down of the sun, that Joshua commanded, and they took them down off the trees, and cast them into the cave in which they had hidden themselves, and laid great stones on the mouth of the cave, which remain to this very day.

Joshua took Makkedah on that day, and struck it with the edge of the sword, with its king. He utterly destroyed them and all the souls who were in it. He left none remaining. He did to the king of Makkedah as he had done to the king of Jericho.

So Joshua struck all the land, the hill country, and the South, and the lowland,

and the slopes, and all their kings. He left none remaining, but he utterly destroyed all that breathed, as Yahweh, the God of Israel, commanded. Joshua struck them from Kadesh Barnea even to Gaza, and all the country of Goshen, even to Gibeon. Joshua took all these kings and their land at one time, because Yahweh, the God of Israel, fought for Israel. Joshua returned, and all Israel with him, to the camp to Gilgal.

It happened, when Jabin king of Hazor heard of it, that he sent to Jobab king of Madon, to the king of Shimron, to the king of Achshaph, and to the kings who were on the north, in the hill country, in the Arabah south of Chinneroth, in the lowland, and in the heights of Dor on the west, to the Canaanite on the east and on the west, and the Amorite, and the Hittite, and the Perizzite, and the Jebusite in the hill country, and the Hivite under Hermon in the land of Mizpah. They went out, they and all their armies with them, many people, even as the sand that is on the seashore in multitude, with very many horses and chariots. All these kings met together; and they came and encamped together at the waters of Merom, to fight with Israel.

Yahweh said to Joshua, "Don't be afraid because of them; for tomorrow at this time, I will deliver them up all slain before Israel. You shall hamstring their horses and burn their chariots with fire."

So Joshua came, and all the people of war with him, against them by the waters of Merom suddenly, and fell on them. Yahweh delivered them into the hand of Israel, and they struck them, and chased them to great Sidon, and to Misrephoth Maim, and to the valley of Mizpeh eastward. They struck them until they left them none remaining. Joshua did to them as Yahweh told him. He hamstrung their horses and burnt their chariots with fire. Joshua turned back at that time, and took Hazor, and struck its king with the sword: for Hazor used to be the head of all those kingdoms. They struck all the souls who were in it with the edge of the sword, utterly destroying them. There was no one left who breathed. He burnt Hazor with fire. Joshua captured all the cities of those kings, with their kings, and he struck them with the edge of the sword, and utterly destroyed them; as Moses the servant of Yahweh commanded. But as for the cities that stood on their mounds, Israel burned none of them, except Hazor only. Joshua burned that. The children of Israel took all the spoil of these cities, with the livestock, as spoils for themselves; but every man they struck with the edge of the sword, until they had destroyed them. They didn't leave any who breathed.

As Yahweh commanded Moses his servant, so Moses commanded Joshua. Joshua did so. He left nothing undone of all that Yahweh commanded Moses.

So Joshua took the whole land, according to all that Yahweh spoke to Moses; and Joshua gave it for an inheritance to Israel according to their divisions by their tribes. The land had rest from war.

The nation of Israel now moved from a time of war to a time of prosperity. Joshua divided the land among the people by tribes and families. Although the focus shifted to settling in the Promised Land, there were still pockets of resistance - places where Canaanite people still were not driven from the land. Joshua gave God's instructions to the tribes on where to settle, and what additional work remained to drive out the unwanted Canaanite people.

With the nation of Israel now fully established in the Promised Land, Joshua prepared the nation to move past his leadership. Advanced in years, and ready to die, Joshua made one last farewell address to the nation, in which he reminded them of the importance of following God and keeping his laws and commands. Like all great leaders, Joshua ensured that the people under his command had a good understanding of their purpose, and that they would continue to function properly after his departure. At the age of 110, Joshua died, leaving behind a legacy as one of the great leaders in the Bible.

It happened after many days, when Yahweh had given rest to Israel from their enemies all around, and Joshua was old and well advanced in years, that Joshua called for all Israel, for their elders and for their heads, and for their judges and for their officers, and said to them, "I am old and well advanced in years. You have seen all that Yahweh your God has done to all these nations because of you; for it is Yahweh your God who has fought for you. Behold, I have allotted to you these nations that remain, to be an inheritance for your tribes, from the Jordan, with all the nations that I have cut off, even to the great sea toward the going down of the sun. Yahweh your God will thrust them out from before you, and drive them from out of your sight. You shall possess their land, as Yahweh your God spoke to you.

"Therefore be very courageous to keep and to do all that is written in the book of the law of Moses, that you not turn aside from it to the right hand or to the left; that you not come among these nations, these that remain among you; neither make mention of the name of their gods, nor cause to swear by them, neither serve them, nor bow down yourselves to them; but hold fast to Yahweh your God, as you have done to this day.

"For Yahweh has driven great and strong nations out from before you. But as for you, no man has stood before you to this day. One man of you shall chase a thousand; for it is Yahweh your God who fights for you, as he spoke to you. Take good heed therefore to yourselves, that you love Yahweh your God.

"But if you do at all go back, and hold fast to the remnant of these nations, even these who remain among you, and make marriages with them, and go in to them, and they to you; know for a certainty that Yahweh your God will no longer drive these nations from out of your sight; but they shall be a snare and a trap to you, a scourge in your sides, and thorns in your eyes, until you perish from off this good land which Yahweh your God has given you.

"Behold, today I am going the way of all the earth. You know in all your hearts and in all your souls that not one thing has failed of all the good things which Yahweh your God spoke concerning you. All have happened to you. Not one thing has failed of it. It shall happen that as all the good things have come on you of which Yahweh your God spoke to you, so Yahweh will bring on you all the evil things, until he has destroyed you from off this good land which Yahweh your God has given you, when you disobey the covenant of Yahweh your God, which he commanded you, and go and serve other gods, and bow down yourselves to them. Then the anger of Yahweh will be kindled against you, and you will perish quickly from off the good land which he has given to you."

Joshua gathered all the tribes of Israel to Shechem, and called for the elders of Israel, for their heads, for their judges, and for their officers; and they presented themselves before God. Joshua said to all the people, "Thus says Yahweh, the God of Israel, 'Your fathers lived of old time beyond the River, even Terah, the father of Abraham, and the father of Nahor: and they served other gods. I took your father Abraham from beyond the River, and led him throughout all the land of Canaan, and multiplied his seed, and gave him Isaac. I gave to Isaac Jacob and Esau: and I gave to Esau Mount Seir, to possess it. Jacob and his children went down into Egypt.

"'I sent Moses and Aaron, and I plagued Egypt, according to that which I did in its midst: and afterward I brought you out. I brought your fathers out of Egypt: and you came to the sea. The Egyptians pursued after your fathers with chariots and with horsemen to the Red Sea. When they cried out to Yahweh, he put darkness between you and the Egyptians, and brought the sea on them, and covered them; and your eyes saw what I did in Egypt: and you lived in the wilderness many days.

"'I brought you into the land of the Amorites, that lived beyond the Jordan: and they fought with you; and I gave them into your hand. You possessed their land; and I destroyed them from before you. Then Balak the son of Zippor, king of Moab, arose and fought against Israel. He sent and called Balaam the son of Beor to curse you; but I would not listen to Balaam; therefore he blessed you still. So I delivered you out of his hand.

"'You went over the Jordan, and came to Jericho. The men of Jericho fought against you, the Amorite, the Perizzite, the Canaanite, the Hittite, the Girgashite, the Hivite, and the Jebusite; and I delivered them into your hand. I sent the hornet before you, which drove them out from before you, even the two kings of the Amorites; not with your sword, nor with your bow. I gave you a land whereon you had not labored, and cities which you didn't build, and you live in them. You eat of vineyards and olive groves which you didn't plant.'

"Now therefore fear Yahweh, and serve him in sincerity and in truth. Put away the gods which your fathers served beyond the River, in Egypt; and serve Yahweh. If it seems evil to you to serve Yahweh, choose this day whom you will serve; whether the gods which your fathers served that were beyond the River, or the gods of the Amorites, in whose land you dwell: but as for me and my house, we will serve Yahweh."

The people said to Joshua, "We will serve Yahweh our God, and we will listen to his voice."

So Joshua made a covenant with the people that day, and made for them a statute and an ordinance in Shechem. Joshua wrote these words in the book of the law of God; and he took a great stone, and set it up there under the oak that was by the sanctuary of Yahweh. Joshua said to all the people, "Behold, this stone shall be a witness against us; for it has heard all the words of Yahweh which he spoke to us. It shall be therefore a witness against you, lest you deny your God." So Joshua sent the people away, every man to his inheritance.

It happened after these things, that Joshua the son of Nun, the servant of Yahweh, died, being one hundred and ten years old. They buried him in the border of his inheritance in Timnathserah, which is in the hill country of Ephraim, on the north of the mountain of Gaash. Israel served Yahweh all the days of Joshua, and all the days of the elders who outlived Joshua, and had known all the work of Yahweh, that he had worked for Israel.

10 BEFORE THE KINGS

The Dark Days of the Judges

After the death of Joshua and the next generation of leaders that grew up in his shadow, the nation of Israel slowly but surely fell into their old patterns, and began to lose their focus and love for God. After a brief period of glory, capped by military victory and peace, the nation lost its moral clarity.

For many generations, a pattern developed. The people turned from God, and began to be influenced by the pagan practices of the nations around them, turning to idol worship and forgetting the one true God. God then allowed nations to rise in power, so that the Israelites suffered under their oppression. Often Israel controlled the mountain regions, while their enemies controlled the fertile plains with horses, chariots and advanced military weaponry. After some time, the Israelites repented, and cried out to God. God, remembering his promises, then raised "judges" to deliver them from their oppressions.

These "judges" were not lawyers or courtroom advocates, but military leaders chosen by God to bring deliverance. They rescued Israel through military victories, often accompanied by miraculous assistance from God and using very unconventional tactics. They were normal men and women, thrust into positions of leadership, who often struggled with their faults, made mistakes and displayed poor judgment.

In this dark chapter of Israel's history, once again God showed his love for his people, by allowing them to suffer when they turned from Him, but by rescuing them when they displayed repentance.

Now when Joshua had sent the people away, the children of Israel went every man to his inheritance to possess the land. The people served Yahweh all the days of Joshua, and all the days of the elders who outlived Joshua, who had seen all the great work of Yahweh that he had worked for Israel. Joshua the son of Nun, the servant of Yahweh, died, being one hundred ten years old. They buried him in the border of his inheritance in Timnath Heres, in the hill country of Ephraim, on the north of the mountain of Gaash. Also all that generation were gathered to their fathers: and there arose another generation after them, who didn't know Yahweh, nor yet the work which he had worked for Israel. The children of Israel did that which was evil in the sight of Yahweh, and served the Baals; and they forsook Yahweh, the God of their fathers, who brought them out of the land of Egypt, and followed other gods, of the gods of the peoples who were around them, and bowed themselves down to them: and they provoked Yahweh to anger. They forsook Yahweh, and served Baal and the Ashtaroth. The anger of Yahweh was kindled against Israel, and he delivered them into the hands of spoilers who despoiled them; and he sold them into the hands of their enemies all around, so that they could not any longer stand before their enemies. Wherever they went out, the hand of Yahweh was against them for evil, as Yahweh had spoken, and as Yahweh had sworn to them: and they were very distressed. Yahweh raised up judges, who saved them out of the hand of those who despoiled them.

Yet they didn't listen to their judges; for they played the prostitute after other gods, and bowed themselves down to them: they turned aside quickly out of the way in which their fathers walked, obeying the commandments of Yahweh. They didn't do so. When Yahweh raised them up judges, then Yahweh was with the judge, and saved them out of the hand of their enemies all the days of the judge: for it grieved Yahweh because of their groaning by reason of those who oppressed them and troubled them. But it happened, when the judge was dead, that they turned back, and dealt more corruptly than their fathers, in following other gods to serve them, and to bow down to them; they didn't cease from their doings, nor from their stubborn way. The anger of Yahweh was kindled against Israel; and he said, "Because this nation have transgressed my covenant which I commanded their fathers, and have not listened to my voice; I also will not henceforth drive out any from before them of the nations that Joshua left when he died; that by them I may prove Israel, whether they will keep the way of Yahweh to walk therein, as their fathers kept it, or not." So Yahweh left those nations, without driving them out hastily; neither delivered he them into the hand of Joshua.

The children of Israel did that which was evil in the sight of Yahweh, and forgot Yahweh their God, and served the Baals and the Asheroth. Therefore the anger of Yahweh was kindled against Israel, and he sold them into the hand of Cushan Rishathaim king of Mesopotamia: and the children of Israel served Cushan Rishathaim eight years. When the children of Israel cried to Yahweh, Yahweh raised up a savior to the children of Israel, who saved them, even Othniel the son of Kenaz, Caleb's younger brother. The Spirit of Yahweh came on him, and he judged Israel; and he went out to war, and Yahweh delivered Cushan Rishathaim king of Mesopotamia into his hand: and his hand prevailed against Cushan Rishathaim. The land had rest forty years. Othniel the son of Kenaz died. The children of Israel again did that which was evil in the sight of Yahweh: and Yahweh strengthened Eglon the king of Moab against Israel, because they had done that which was evil in the sight of Yahweh.

After Othniel, God sent additional judges, including Ehud the left-handed Benjamite, who killed Eglon, the fat king of Moab. After him God sent Shamgar, who killed 600 Philistines with an ox goad. God then raised up a woman judge, Deborah, and a reluctant judge, Barak, to save Israel.

The children of Israel again did that which was evil in the sight of Yahweh, when Ehud was dead. Yahweh sold them into the hand of Jabin king of Canaan, who reigned in Hazor; the captain of whose army was Sisera, who lived in Harosheth of the Gentiles. The children of Israel cried to Yahweh: for he had nine hundred chariots of iron; and twenty years he mightily oppressed the children of Israel. Now Deborah, a prophetess, the wife of Lappidoth, she judged Israel at that time. She lived under the palm tree of Deborah between Ramah and Bethel in the hill country of Ephraim: and the children of Israel came up to her for judgment. She sent and called Barak the son of Abinoam out of Kedesh Naphtali, and said to him, "Hasn't Yahweh, the God of Israel, commanded, 'Go and draw to Mount Tabor, and take with you ten thousand men of the children of Naphtali and of the children of Zebulun? I will draw to you, to the river Kishon, Sisera, the captain of Jabin's army, with his chariots and his multitude; and I will deliver him into your hand.'"

Barak said to her, "If you will go with me, then I will go; but if you will not go with me, I will not go."

She said, "I will surely go with you: nevertheless, the journey that you take shall not be for your honor; for Yahweh will sell Sisera into the hand of a woman." Deborah arose, and went with Barak to Kedesh.

Barak called Zebulun and Naphtali together to Kedesh; and there went up ten thousand men at his feet: and Deborah went up with him. Now Heber the Kenite had separated himself from the Kenites, even from the children of Hobab the brother-in-law of Moses, and had pitched his tent as far as the oak in Zaanannim, which is by Kedesh. They told Sisera that Barak the son of Abinoam was gone up to Mount Tabor. Sisera gathered together all his chariots, even nine hundred chariots of iron, and all the people who were with him, from Harosheth of the Gentiles, to the river Kishon.

Deborah said to Barak, "Go; for this is the day in which Yahweh has delivered Sisera into your hand. Hasn't Yahweh gone out before you?" So Barak went down from Mount Tabor, and ten thousand men after him. Yahweh confused Sisera, and all his chariots, and all his army, with the edge of the sword before Barak; and Sisera alighted from his chariot, and fled away on his feet. But Barak pursued after the chariots, and after the army, to Harosheth of the Gentiles: and all the army of Sisera fell by the edge of the sword; there was not a man left.

However Sisera fled away on his feet to the tent of Jael the wife of Heber the Kenite; for there was peace between Jabin the king of Hazor and the house of Heber the Kenite. Jael went out to meet Sisera, and said to him, "Turn in, my lord, turn in to me; don't be afraid." He came in to her into the tent, and she covered him with a rug.

He said to her, "Please give me a little water to drink; for I am thirsty."

She opened a bottle of milk, and gave him drink, and covered him.

He said to her, "Stand in the door of the tent, and it shall be, when any man comes and inquires of you, and says, 'Is there any man here?' that you shall say, 'No.'"

Then Jael Heber's wife took a tent peg, and took a hammer in her hand, and went softly to him, and struck the pin into his temples, and it pierced through into the ground; for he was in a deep sleep; so he swooned and died. Behold, as Barak pursued Sisera, Jael came out to meet him, and said to him, "Come, and I will show you the man whom you seek." He came to her; and behold, Sisera lay dead, and the tent peg was in his temples. So God subdued on that day Jabin the king of Canaan before the children of Israel. The hand of the children of Israel prevailed more and more against Jabin the king of Canaan, until they had destroyed Jabin king of Canaan.

After deliverance from Canaan, Israel had rest for 40 years. But after again falling away from God, the Midianites began to oppress the nation. God then raised up Gideon, a doubtful man, to rescue Israel once again. The story of his unconventional victory is another fascinating military record from the Bible.

The children of Israel did that which was evil in the sight of Yahweh: and Yahweh delivered them into the hand of Midian seven years. The hand of Midian prevailed against Israel; and because of Midian the children of Israel made them the dens which are in the mountains, and the caves, and the strongholds. So it was, when Israel had sown, that the Midianites came up, and the Amalekites, and the children of the east; they came up against them; and they encamped against them, and destroyed the increase of the earth, until you come to Gaza, and left no sustenance in Israel, neither sheep, nor ox, nor donkey. For they came up with their livestock and their tents; they came in as locusts for multitude; both they and their camels were without number: and they came into the land to destroy it. Israel was brought very low because of Midian; and the children of Israel cried to Yahweh.

It happened, when the children of Israel cried to Yahweh because of Midian, that Yahweh sent a prophet to the children of Israel: and he said to them, "Thus says Yahweh, the God of Israel, 'I brought you up from Egypt, and brought you forth out of the house of bondage; and I delivered you out of the hand of the Egyptians, and out of the hand of all who oppressed you, and drove them out from before you, and gave you their land; and I said to you, "I am Yahweh your God; you shall not fear the gods of the Amorites, in whose land you dwell." But you have not listened to my voice.'"

The angel of Yahweh came, and sat under the oak which was in Ophrah, that pertained to Joash the Abiezrite: and his son Gideon was beating out wheat in the wine press, to hide it from the Midianites. The angel of Yahweh appeared to him, and said to him, "Yahweh is with you, you mighty man of valor!"

Gideon said to him, "Oh, my lord, if Yahweh is with us, why then has all this happened to us? Where are all his wondrous works which our fathers told us of, saying, 'Didn't Yahweh bring us up from Egypt?' But now Yahweh has cast us off, and delivered us into the hand of Midian."

Yahweh looked at him, and said, "Go in this with your might, and save Israel from the hand of Midian. Haven't I sent you?"

He said to him, "O Lord, how shall I save Israel? Behold, my family is the poorest in Manasseh, and I am the least in my father's house."

Yahweh said to him, "Surely I will be with you, and you shall strike the Midianites as one man."

He said to him, "If now I have found favor in your sight, then show me a sign that it is you who talk with me. Please don't go away, until I come to you, and bring out my present, and lay it before you."

He said, "I will wait until you come back."

Gideon went in, and prepared a young goat, and unleavened cakes of an ephah of meal. He put the meat in a basket and he put the broth in a pot, and brought it out to him under the oak, and presented it.

The angel of God said to him, "Take the meat and the unleavened cakes, and lay them on this rock, and pour out the broth."

He did so. Then the angel of Yahweh stretched out the end of the staff that was in his hand, and touched the meat and the unleavened cakes; and fire went up out of the rock, and consumed the meat and the unleavened cakes; and the angel of Yahweh departed out of his sight.

Gideon saw that he was the angel of Yahweh; and Gideon said, "Alas, Lord Yahweh! Because I have seen the angel of Yahweh face to face!"

Yahweh said to him, "Peace be to you! Don't be afraid. You shall not die."

Then Gideon built an altar there to Yahweh, and called it "Yahweh is Peace." To this day it is still in Ophrah of the Abiezrites.

Then all the Midianites and the Amalekites and the children of the east assembled themselves together; and they passed over, and encamped in the valley of Jezreel. But the Spirit of Yahweh came on Gideon; and he blew a trumpet; and Abiezer was gathered together after him. He sent messengers throughout all Manasseh; and they also were gathered together after him: and he sent messengers to Asher, and to Zebulun, and to Naphtali; and they came up to meet them.

Gideon said to God, "If you will save Israel by my hand, as you have spoken, behold, I will put a fleece of wool on the threshing floor; if there is dew on the fleece only, and it is dry on all the ground, then shall I know that you will save Israel by my hand, as you have spoken."

It was so; for he rose up early on the next day, and pressed the fleece together, and wrung the dew out of the fleece, a bowl full of water.

Gideon said to God, "Don't let your anger be kindled against me, and I will speak but this once. Please let me make a trial just this once with the fleece. Let it now be dry only on the fleece, and on all the ground let there be dew."

God did so that night: for it was dry on the fleece only, and there was dew on all the ground.

Then Jerubbaal, who is Gideon, and all the people who were with him, rose up early, and encamped beside the spring of Harod: and the camp of Midian was on the north side of them, by the hill of Moreh, in the valley. Yahweh said to Gideon, "The people who are with you are too many for me to give the Midianites into their hand, lest Israel vaunt themselves against me, saying, 'My own hand has saved me.' Now therefore proclaim in the ears of the people, saying, 'Whoever is fearful and trembling, let him return and depart from Mount Gilead.'" Twenty-two thousand of the people returned, and ten thousand remained.

Yahweh said to Gideon, "The people are still too many. Bring them down to the water, and I will test them for you there. It shall be, that of whom I tell you, 'This shall go with you,' the same shall go with you; and of whoever I tell you, 'This shall not go with you,' the same shall not go." So he brought down the people to the water; and Yahweh said to Gideon, "Everyone who laps of the water with his tongue, like a dog laps, you shall set him by himself; likewise everyone who bows down on his knees to drink." The number of those who lapped, putting their hand to their mouth, was three hundred men; but all the rest of the people bowed down on their knees to drink water. Yahweh said to Gideon, "By the three hundred men who lapped will I save you, and deliver the Midianites into your hand. Let all the other people go, each to his own place."

So the people took food in their hand, and their trumpets; and he sent all the men of Israel every man to his tent, but retained the three hundred men: and the camp of Midian was beneath him in the valley. It happened the same night, that Yahweh said to him, "Arise, go down into the camp; for I have delivered it into your hand. But if you are afraid to go down, go with Purah your servant down to the camp: and you shall hear what they say; and afterward your hands will be strengthened to go down into the camp." Then went he down with Purah his servant to the outermost part of the armed men who were in the camp.

The Midianites and the Amalekites and all the children of the east lay along in the valley like locusts for multitude; and their camels were without number, as the sand which is on the seashore for multitude.

When Gideon had come, behold, there was a man telling a dream to his fellow; and he said, "Behold, I dreamed a dream; and behold, a cake of barley bread tumbled into the camp of Midian, and came to the tent, and struck it so that it fell, and turned it upside down, so that the tent lay flat."

His fellow answered, "This is nothing other than the sword of Gideon the son of Joash, a man of Israel. God has delivered Midian into his hand, with all the army."

It was so, when Gideon heard the telling of the dream, and its interpretation, that he worshiped; and he returned into the camp of Israel, and said, "Arise; for Yahweh has delivered the army of Midian into your hand!"

He divided the three hundred men into three companies, and he put into the hands of all of them trumpets, and empty pitchers, with torches within the pitchers.

He said to them, "Watch me, and do likewise. Behold, when I come to the outermost part of the camp, it shall be that, as I do, so you shall do. When I blow the trumpet, I and all who are with me, then blow the trumpets also on every side of all the camp, and shout, 'For Yahweh and for Gideon!'"

So Gideon, and the hundred men who were with him, came to the outermost part of the camp in the beginning of the middle watch, when they had but newly set the watch: and they blew the trumpets, and broke in pieces the pitchers that were in their hands. The three companies blew the trumpets, and broke the pitchers, and held the torches in their left hands, and the trumpets in their right hands with which to blow; and they shouted, "The sword of Yahweh and of Gideon!"

They each stood in his place around the camp; and all the army ran; and they shouted, and put them to flight. They blew the three hundred trumpets, and Yahweh set every man's sword against his fellow, and against all the army; and the army fled as far as Beth Shittah toward Zererah, as far as the border of Abel Meholah, by Tabbath. The men of Israel were gathered together out of Naphtali, and out of Asher, and out of all Manasseh, and pursued after Midian. Gideon sent messengers throughout all the hill country of Ephraim, saying, "Come down against Midian, and take before them the waters, as far as Beth Barah, even the Jordan!" So all the men of Ephraim were gathered together, and took the waters as far as Beth Barah, even the Jordan. They took the two princes of Midian, Oreb and Zeeb; and they killed Oreb at the rock of Oreb, and Zeeb they killed at the wine press of Zeeb, and pursued Midian: and they brought the heads of Oreb and Zeeb to Gideon beyond the Jordan.

So Midian was subdued before the children of Israel, and they lifted up their heads no more. The land had rest forty years in the days of Gideon.

It happened, as soon as Gideon was dead, that the children of Israel turned again, and played the prostitute after the Baals, and made Baal Berith their god. The children of Israel didn't remember Yahweh their God, who had delivered them out of the hand of all their enemies on every side; neither did they show kindness to the house of Jerubbaal, Gideon, according to all the goodness which he had shown to Israel.

For many more generations the nation of Israel fell into their same old patterns. When the Philistines grew in might, God raised up a strong man from the tribe of Dan, Samson, to deliver Israel.

The children of Israel again did that which was evil in the sight of Yahweh; and Yahweh delivered them into the hand of the Philistines forty years. There was a certain man of Zorah, of the family of the Danites, whose name was Manoah; and his wife was barren, and didn't bear. The angel of Yahweh appeared to the woman, and said to her, "See now, you are barren, and don't bear; but you shall conceive, and bear a son. Now therefore please beware and drink no wine nor strong drink, and don't eat any unclean thing: for, behold, you shall conceive, and bear a son; and no razor shall come on his head; for the child shall be a Nazirite to God from the womb: and he shall begin to save Israel out of the hand of the Philistines."

The woman bore a son, and named him Samson: and the child grew, and Yahweh blessed him. The Spirit of Yahweh began to move him in Mahaneh Dan, between Zorah and Eshtaol.

Samson went down to Timnah, and saw a woman in Timnah of the daughters of the Philistines. He came up, and told his father and his mother, and said, "I have seen a woman in Timnah of the daughters of the Philistines: now therefore get her for me as wife."

Then his father and his mother said to him, "Is there never a woman among the daughters of your brothers, or among all my people, that you go to take a wife of the uncircumcised Philistines?"

Samson said to his father, "Get her for me; for she pleases me well."

But his father and his mother didn't know that it was of Yahweh; for he sought an occasion against the Philistines. Now at that time the Philistines had rule over Israel. Then went Samson down, and his father and his mother, to Timnah, and came to the vineyards of Timnah: and behold, a young lion roared against him. The Spirit of Yahweh came mightily on him, and he tore him as he would have torn a young goat; and he had nothing in his hand: but he didn't tell his father or his mother what he had done. He went down, and talked with the woman, and she pleased Samson well. After a while he returned to take her; and he turned aside to see the carcass of the lion: and behold, there was a swarm of bees in the body of the lion, and honey. He took it into his hands, and went on, eating as he went; and he came to his father and mother, and gave to them, and they ate: but he didn't tell them that he had taken the honey out of the body of the lion. His father went down to the woman: and Samson made there a feast; for so used the young men to do. It happened, when they saw him, that they brought thirty companions to be with him.

Samson said to them, "Let me tell you a riddle now. If you can declare it to me within the seven days of the feast, and find it out, then I will give you thirty linen garments and thirty changes of clothing; but if you can't declare it to me, then you shall give me thirty linen garments and thirty changes of clothing."

They said to him, "Put forth your riddle, that we may hear it." He said to them,

"Out of the eater came forth food. Out of the strong came forth sweetness." They couldn't in three days declare the riddle.

It happened on the seventh day, that they said to Samson's wife, "Entice your husband, that he may declare to us the riddle, lest we burn you and your father's house with fire. Have you called us to impoverish us? Is it not so?"

Samson's wife wept before him, and said, "You just hate me, and don't love me. You have put forth a riddle to the children of my people, and haven't told it me." He said to her, "Behold, I haven't told it my father nor my mother, and shall I tell you?"

She wept before him the seven days, while their feast lasted: and it happened on the seventh day, that he told her, because she pressed him severely; and she told the riddle to the children of her people. The men of the city said to him on the seventh day before the sun went down, "What is sweeter than honey? What is stronger than a lion?"

He said to them, "If you hadn't plowed with my heifer, you wouldn't have found out my riddle."

The Spirit of Yahweh came mightily on him, and he went down to Ashkelon, and struck thirty men of them, and took their spoil, and gave the changes of clothing to those who declared the riddle. His anger was kindled, and he went up to his father's house. But Samson's wife was given to his companion, whom he had used as his friend.

But it happened after a while, in the time of wheat harvest, that Samson visited his wife with a young goat; and he said, "I will go in to my wife into the room."

But her father wouldn't allow him to go in. Her father said, "I most certainly thought that you had utterly hated her; therefore I gave her to your companion. Isn't her younger sister more beautiful than she? Please take her, instead."

Samson said to them, "This time I will be blameless in regard of the Philistines, when I harm them." Samson went and caught three hundred foxes, and took torches, and turned tail to tail, and put a torch in the midst between every two tails. When he had set the brands on fire, he let them go into the standing grain of the Philistines, and burnt up both the shocks and the standing grain, and also the olive groves.

Then the Philistines said, "Who has done this?"

They said, "Samson, the son-in-law of the Timnite, because he has taken his wife, and given her to his companion." The Philistines came up, and burnt her and her father with fire.

Samson said to them, "If you behave like this, surely I will be avenged of you, and after that I will cease." He struck them hip and thigh with a great slaughter: and he went down and lived in the cleft of the rock of Etam. Then the Philistines went up, and encamped in Judah, and spread themselves in Lehi.

The men of Judah said, "Why have you come up against us?"

They said, "We have come up to bind Samson, to do to him as he has done to us."

Then three thousand men of Judah went down to the cleft of the rock of Etam, and said to Samson, "Don't you know that the Philistines are rulers over us? What then is this that you have done to us?"

He said to them, "As they did to me, so have I done to them."

They said to him, "We have come down to bind you, that we may deliver you into the hand of the Philistines."

Samson said to them, "Swear to me that you will not fall on me yourselves."

They spoke to him, saying, "No; but we will bind you fast, and deliver you into their hand; but surely we will not kill you." They bound him with two new ropes, and brought him up from the rock.

When he came to Lehi, the Philistines shouted as they met him: and the Spirit of Yahweh came mightily on him, and the ropes that were on his arms became as flax that was burnt with fire, and his bands dropped from off his hands. He found a fresh jawbone of a donkey, and put forth his hand, and took it, and struck a thousand men therewith. Samson said, "With the jawbone of a donkey, heaps on heaps; with the jawbone of a donkey I have struck a thousand men." It happened, when he had made an end of speaking, that he cast away the jawbone out of his hand; and that place was called Ramath Lehi. He was very thirsty, and called on Yahweh, and said, "You have given this great deliverance by the hand of your servant; and now shall I die for thirst, and fall into the hand of the uncircumcised?"

But God split the hollow place that is in Lehi, and water came out of it. When he had drunk, his spirit came again, and he revived: therefore its name was called En Hakkore, which is in Lehi, to this day. He judged Israel in the days of the Philistines twenty years.

Samson went to Gaza, and saw there a prostitute, and went in to her. The Gazites were told, "Samson is here!" They surrounded him, and laid wait for him all night in the gate of the city, and were quiet all the night, saying, "Wait until morning light, then we will kill him." Samson lay until midnight, and arose at midnight, and laid hold of the doors of the gate of the city, and the two posts, and plucked them up, bar and all, and put them on his shoulders, and carried them up to the top of the mountain that is before Hebron.

It came to pass afterward, that he loved a woman in the valley of Sorek, whose name was Delilah. The lords of the Philistines came up to her, and said to her, "Entice him, and see in which his great strength lies, and by what means we may prevail against him, that we may bind him to afflict him; and we will each give you eleven hundred pieces of silver."

Delilah said to Samson, "Please tell me where your great strength lies, and what you might be bound to afflict you."

Samson said to her, "If they bind me with seven green cords that were never dried, then shall I become weak, and be as another man."

Then the lords of the Philistines brought up to her seven green cords which had not been dried, and she bound him with them. Now she had an ambush waiting in the inner room. She said to him, "The Philistines are on you,

Samson!" He broke the cords, as a string of tow is broken when it touches the fire. So his strength was not known.

Delilah said to Samson, "Behold, you have mocked me, and told me lies: now please tell me with which you might be bound."

He said to her, "If they only bind me with new ropes with which no work has been done, then shall I become weak, and be as another man."

So Delilah took new ropes, and bound him therewith, and said to him, "The Philistines are on you, Samson!" The ambush was waiting in the inner room. He broke them off his arms like a thread.

Delilah said to Samson, "Until now, you have mocked me and told me lies. Tell me with what you might be bound." He said to her, "If you weave the seven locks of my head with the web."

She fastened it with the pin, and said to him, "The Philistines are on you, Samson!" He awakened out of his sleep, and plucked away the pin of the beam, and the web.

She said to him, "How can you say, 'I love you,' when your heart is not with me? You have mocked me these three times, and have not told me where your great strength lies."

It happened, when she pressed him daily with her words, and urged him, that his soul was troubled to death. He told her all his heart, and said to her, "No razor has ever come on my head; for I have been a Nazirite to God from my mother's womb. If I am shaved, then my strength will go from me, and I will become weak, and be like any other man."

When Delilah saw that he had told her all his heart, she sent and called for the lords of the Philistines, saying, "Come up this once, for he has told me all his heart." Then the lords of the Philistines came up to her, and brought the money in their hand. She made him sleep on her knees; and she called for a man, and shaved off the seven locks of his head; and she began to afflict him, and his strength went from him. She said, "The Philistines are upon you, Samson!"

He awoke out of his sleep, and said, "I will go out as at other times, and shake myself free." But he didn't know that Yahweh had departed from him. The Philistines laid hold on him, and put out his eyes; and they brought him down to Gaza, and bound him with fetters of brass; and he ground at the mill in the prison.

However the hair of his head began to grow again after he was shaved.

The lords of the Philistines gathered them together to offer a great sacrifice to Dagon their god, and to rejoice; for they said, "Our god has delivered Samson our enemy into our hand." When the people saw him, they praised their god; for they said, "Our god has delivered our enemy and the destroyer of our country, who has slain many of us, into our hand."

It happened, when their hearts were merry, that they said, "Call for Samson, that he may entertain us." They called for Samson out of the prison; and he performed before them. They set him between the pillars; and Samson said to the boy who held him by the hand, "Allow me to feel the pillars whereupon the house rests, that I may lean on them."

Now the house was full of men and women; and all the lords of the Philistines were there; and there were on the roof about three thousand men and women, who saw while Samson performed. Samson called to Yahweh, and said, "Lord Yahweh, remember me, please, and strengthen me, please, only this once, God, that I may be at once avenged of the Philistines for my two eyes." Samson took hold of the two middle pillars on which the house rested, and leaned on them, the one with his right hand, and the other with his left. Samson said, "Let me die with the Philistines!" He bowed himself with all his might; and the house fell on the lords, and on all the people who were therein. So the dead that he killed at his death were more than those who he killed in his life. Then his brothers and all the house of his father came down, and took him, and brought him up, and buried him between Zorah and Eshtaol in the burial site of Manoah his father. He judged Israel twenty years.

In those days there was no king in Israel: every man did that which was right in his own eyes.

11 YOUR GOD, MY GOD

A Moabite Daughter-In-Law Earns God's Favor

During the time of the judges, we have one of the most incredible love stories of the Bible. Here we find Ruth, a woman from the nation of Moab, who married a man from Israel. When her husband died, an incredible bond grew between Ruth and Naomi, her mother-in-law. These two women grew to rely on each other, in a time when they have no man to rely upon.

With God's help, they found a "kinsman redeemer," Boaz, a relative of Naomi who showed kind favor to Ruth due to her good reputation.

It happened in the days when the judges judged, that there was a famine in the land. A certain man of Bethlehem Judah went to live in the country of Moab, he, and his wife, and his two sons. The name of the man was Elimelech, and the name of his wife Naomi, and the name of his two sons Mahlon and Chilion, Ephrathites of Bethlehem Judah. They came into the country of Moab, and continued there. Elimelech, Naomi's husband, died; and she was left, and her two sons. They took them wives of the women of Moab; the name of the one was Orpah, and the name of the other Ruth: and they lived there about ten years. Mahlon and Chilion both died, and the woman was bereaved of her two children and of her husband. Then she arose with her daughters-in-law, that she might return from the country of Moab: for she had heard in the country of Moab how that Yahweh had visited his people in giving them bread. She went forth out of the place where she was, and her two daughters-in-law with her; and they went on the way to return to the land of Judah. Naomi said to her two daughters-in-law, "Go, return each of you to her mother's house: Yahweh deal kindly with you, as you have dealt with the dead, and with me. Yahweh grant you that you may find rest, each of you in the house of her husband."

Then she kissed them, and they lifted up their voice, and wept. They said to her, "No, but we will return with you to your people."

Naomi said, "Go back, my daughters. Why do you want to go with me? Do I still have sons in my womb, that they may be your husbands? Go back, my daughters, go your way; for I am too old to have a husband. If I should say, 'I have hope,' if I should even have a husband tonight, and should also bear sons; would you then wait until they were grown? Would you then refrain from having husbands? No, my daughters, for it grieves me much for your sakes, for the hand of Yahweh has gone out against me."

They lifted up their voice, and wept again: and Orpah kissed her mother-in-law, but Ruth joined with her. She said, "Behold, your sister-in-law has gone back to her people, and to her god. Follow your sister-in-law."

The next statement from Ruth, in which she professed her love and devotion to her mother-in-law Naomi, is one of the most beloved passages of the Bible. Her love for Naomi was a stirring example, and her devotion to Naomi and God set in motion an incredible turn of events that would affect the entire nation of Israel in years to come.

Ruth said, "Don't entreat me to leave you, and to return from following after you, for where you go, I will go; and where you lodge, I will lodge; your people shall be my people, and your God my God; where you die, will I die, and there will I be buried. Yahweh do so to me, and more also, if anything but death part you and me."

When she saw that she was steadfastly minded to go with her, she left off speaking to her.

So they two went until they came to Bethlehem. It happened, when they had come to Bethlehem, that all the city was moved about them, and they asked, "Is this Naomi?"

She said to them, "Don't call me Naomi. Call me Mara; for the Almighty has dealt very bitterly with me. I went out full, and Yahweh has brought me home again empty; why do you call me Naomi, since Yahweh has testified against me, and the Almighty has afflicted me?"

So Naomi returned, and Ruth the Moabitess, her daughter-in-law, with her, who returned out of the country of Moab: and they came to Bethlehem in the beginning of barley harvest.

By laws passed down from Moses, God had provided means for the poor to share in the harvest of the land. Farmers were to leave behind "gleanings," the corners and edges of the fields, or spots they missed when harvesting.

These crops were set aside to be harvested by the poor, widows, fatherless children, and others who did not have the means to grow their own food. By doing this, God showed his love for mankind. Also by law, Ruth was allowed to take advantage of this provision, even though she was a foreigner living in Israel.

Naomi had a kinsman of her husband's, a mighty man of wealth, of the family of Elimelech, and his name was Boaz. Ruth the Moabitess said to Naomi, "Let me now go to the field, and glean among the ears of grain after him in whose sight I shall find favor."

She said to her, "Go, my daughter." She went, and came and gleaned in the field after the reapers: and she happened to come to the portion of the field belonging to Boaz, who was of the family of Elimelech.

Behold, Boaz came from Bethlehem, and said to the reapers, "Yahweh be with you."

They answered him, "Yahweh bless you."

Then Boaz said to his servant who was set over the reapers, "Whose young lady is this?"

The servant who was set over the reapers answered, "It is the Moabite lady who came back with Naomi out of the country of Moab. She said, 'Please let me glean and gather after the reapers among the sheaves.' So she came, and has continued even from the morning until now, except that she stayed a little in the house."

Then Boaz said to Ruth, "Listen, my daughter. Don't go to glean in another field, and don't go from here, but stay here close to my maidens. Let your eyes be on the field that they reap, and go after them. Haven't I commanded the young men not to touch you? When you are thirsty, go to the vessels, and drink from that which the young men have drawn."

Then she fell on her face, and bowed herself to the ground, and said to him, "Why have I found favor in your sight, that you should take knowledge of me, since I am a foreigner?"

Boaz answered her, "It has fully been shown me, all that you have done to your mother-in-law since the death of your husband; and how you have left your father and your mother, and the land of your birth, and have come to a people that you didn't know before. May Yahweh repay your work, and a full reward be given you from Yahweh, the God of Israel, under whose wings you have come to take refuge."

Then she said, "Let me find favor in your sight, my lord, because you have comforted me, and because you have spoken kindly to your handmaid, though I am not as one of your handmaidens."

At meal time Boaz said to her, "Come here, and eat of the bread, and dip your morsel in the vinegar."

She sat beside the reapers, and they reached her parched grain, and she ate, and was satisfied, and left some of it. When she had risen up to glean, Boaz commanded his young men, saying, "Let her glean even among the sheaves, and don't reproach her. Also pull out some for her from the bundles, and leave it, and let her glean, and don't rebuke her."

So she gleaned in the field until evening; and she beat out that which she had gleaned, and it was about an ephah of barley. She took it up, and went into the city; and her mother-in-law saw what she had gleaned: and she brought out and gave to her that which she had left after she was sufficed.

Her mother-in-law said to her, "Where have you gleaned today? Where have you worked? Blessed be he who noticed you."

She showed her mother-in-law with whom she had worked, and said, "The man's name with whom I worked today is Boaz." Naomi said to her daughter-in-law, "Blessed be he of Yahweh, who has not left off his kindness to the living and to the dead." Naomi said to her, "The man is a close relative to us, one of our near kinsmen."

Ruth the Moabitess said, "Yes, he said to me, 'You shall stay close to my young men, until they have ended all my harvest.'"

Naomi said to Ruth her daughter-in-law, "It is good, my daughter, that you go out with his maidens, and that they not meet you in any other field." So she stayed close to the maidens of Boaz, to glean to the end of barley harvest and of wheat harvest; and she lived with her mother-in-law.

Encouraged by the kindness of Boaz, Naomi set in motion a plan for Ruth to show her willingness to marry this kind man. As a relative of Naomi, Boaz was a "kinsman redeemer," who had the rights to marry Ruth in order to protect the lineage of Naomi and her family. But, there was one small problem - Boaz was actually second in line for the right to marry Ruth; if he was to fulfill this role, he had to first secure the first right of marriage from the primary kinsman-redeemer.

Naomi her mother-in-law said to her, "My daughter, shall I not seek rest for you, that it may be well with you? Now isn't Boaz our kinsman, with whose maidens you were? Behold, he winnows barley tonight in the threshing floor. Therefore wash yourself, anoint yourself, get dressed, and go down to the threshing floor, but don't make yourself known to the man until he has finished eating and drinking. It shall be, when he lies down, that you shall mark the place where he shall lie, and you shall go in, and uncover his feet, and lay down; then he will tell you what you shall do."

She said to her, "All that you say I will do." She went down to the threshing floor, and did according to all that her mother-in-law told her. When Boaz had eaten and drunk, and his heart was merry, he went to lie down at the end of the heap of grain. She came softly, uncovered his feet, and laid her down. It happened at midnight, that the man was startled and turned himself; and behold, a woman lay at his feet. He said, "Who are you?"

She answered, "I am Ruth your handmaid. Therefore spread your skirt over your handmaid; for you are a near kinsman."

He said, "Blessed are you by Yahweh, my daughter. You have shown more kindness in the latter end than at the beginning, inasmuch as you didn't follow young men, whether poor or rich. Now, my daughter, don't be afraid; I will do to you all that you say; for all the city of my people does know that you are a worthy woman. Now it is true that I am a near kinsman; however there is a kinsman nearer than I. Stay this night, and it shall be in the morning, that if he will perform for you the part of a kinsman, well; let him do the kinsman's part. But if he will not do the part of a kinsman for you, then will I do the part of a kinsman for you, as Yahweh lives. Lie down until the morning."

She lay at his feet until the morning. She rose up before one could discern another. For he said, "Let it not be known that the woman came to the threshing floor." He said, "Bring the mantle that is on you, and hold it." She held it; and he measured six measures of barley, and laid it on her; and he went into the city.

When she came to her mother-in-law, she said, "How did it go, my daughter?"

She told her all that the man had done to her. She said, "He gave me these six measures of barley; for he said, 'Don't go empty to your mother-in-law.'"

Then she said, "Sit still, my daughter, until you know how the matter will fall; for the man will not rest, until he has finished the thing this day."

Now Boaz went up to the gate, and sat down there. Behold, the near kinsman of whom Boaz spoke came by; to whom he said, "Come over here, friend, and sit down!" He turned aside, and sat down. He took ten men of the elders of the city, and said, "Sit down here." They sat down. He said to the near kinsman, "Naomi, who has come back out of the country of Moab, is selling the parcel of land, which was our brother Elimelech's. I thought to disclose it to you, saying, 'Buy it before those who sit here, and before the elders of my people.' If you will redeem it, redeem it; but if you will not redeem it, then tell me, that I may know. For there is no one to redeem it besides you; and I am after you."

He said, "I will redeem it."

Then Boaz said, "On the day you buy the field from the hand of Naomi, you must buy it also from Ruth the Moabitess, the wife of the dead, to raise up the name of the dead on his inheritance."

The near kinsman said, "I can't redeem it for myself, lest I mar my own inheritance. Take my right of redemption for yourself; for I can't redeem it."

Now this was the custom in former time in Israel concerning redeeming and concerning exchanging, to confirm all things: a man took off his shoe, and gave it to his neighbor; and this was the way of attestation in Israel. So the near kinsman said to Boaz, "Buy it for yourself." He took off his shoe.

Boaz said to the elders, and to all the people, "You are witnesses this day, that I have bought all that was Elimelech's, and all that was Chilion's and Mahlon's, from the hand of Naomi. Moreover Ruth the Moabitess, the wife of Mahlon, I have purchased to be my wife, to raise up the name of the dead on his inheritance, that the name of the dead not be cut off from among his brothers, and from the gate of his place. You are witnesses this day."

All the people who were in the gate, and the elders, said, "We are witnesses. May Yahweh make the woman who has come into your house like Rachel and like Leah, which two built the house of Israel; and treat you worthily in Ephrathah, and be famous in Bethlehem. Let your house be like the house of Perez, whom Tamar bore to Judah, of the seed which Yahweh shall give you of this young woman."

So Boaz took Ruth, and she became his wife; and he went in to her, and Yahweh gave her conception, and she bore a son. The women said to Naomi, "Blessed be Yahweh, who has not left you this day without a near kinsman; and let his name be famous in Israel. He shall be to you a restorer of life, and sustain you in your old age, for your daughter-in-law, who loves you, who is better to you than seven sons, has borne him." Naomi took the child, and laid it in her bosom, and became nurse to it. The women, her neighbors, gave him a name, saying, "There is a son born to Naomi"; and they named him Obed. He is the father of Jesse, the father of David.

In an incredible turn of events, Boaz and Ruth were married, and through this union the Moabite woman Ruth became a descendant of David, the greatest king of Israel. Once again, God showed his love for his people, by inserting a Godly foreign woman into the lineage of David, and ultimately, the savior of all mankind, Jesus Christ.

12 GREAT PROPHET, DISOBEDIENT KING

Samuel and Saul

One of the greatest of the judges of Israel was Samuel. His birth was brought about when God heard the cries of a barren woman, who pledged that if God would grant her the ability to have a son, that she would dedicate her child to a life of service in the temple. God answered her prayers, and young Samuel was brought to the care of the temple. The birth of Samuel is great evidence of the love of God, who listens to and answers the prayers of his believers.

Like Samson, Samuel lived as a Nazirite, with no razor touching his head. Although not granted the physical strength that God gave to Samson, Samuel excelled in spiritual leadership, and brought great deliverance to Israel from the powerful Philistine nation, which was concentrated near the Mediterranean coast, but was constantly pushing deeper into the territory of Israel.

Israel had no real central leadership - they were organized by 12 tribes, and seemed to fully cooperate only in times of extreme duress. In this background, it was God who chose Samuel to lead the nation. In the time before Israel had kings, the strong spiritual leadership of Samuel was just what was needed.

Now there was a certain man of Ramathaim Zophim, of the hill country of Ephraim, and his name was Elkanah, the son of Jeroham, the son of Elihu, the son of Tohu, the son of Zuph, an Ephraimite: and he had two wives; the name of the one was Hannah, and the name of other Peninnah: and Peninnah had children, but Hannah had no children. This man went up out of his city from year to year to worship and to sacrifice to Yahweh of Armies in Shiloh. The two sons of Eli, Hophni and Phinehas, priests to Yahweh, were there. When the day came that Elkanah sacrificed, he gave to Peninnah his wife, and to all her sons and her daughters, portions: but to Hannah he gave a double portion; for he loved Hannah, but Yahweh had shut up her womb. Her rival provoked her severely, to make her fret, because Yahweh had shut up her womb. As he did so year by year, when she went up to the house of Yahweh, so she provoked her; therefore she wept, and didn't eat. Elkanah her husband said to her, "Hannah, why do you weep? Why don't you eat? Why is your heart grieved? Am I not better to you than ten sons?"

So Hannah rose up after they had eaten in Shiloh, and after they had drunk. Now Eli the priest was sitting on his seat by the doorpost of Yahweh's temple. She was in bitterness of soul, and prayed to Yahweh, and wept bitterly. She vowed a vow, and said, "Yahweh of Armies, if you will indeed look on the affliction of your handmaid, and remember me, and not forget your handmaid, but will give to your handmaid a boy, then I will give him to Yahweh all the days of his life, and no razor shall come on his head."

It happened, as she continued praying before Yahweh, that Eli saw her mouth. Now Hannah spoke in her heart. Only her lips moved, but her voice was not heard. Therefore Eli thought she had been drunken. Eli said to her, "How long will you be drunken? Put away your wine from you."

Hannah answered, "No, my lord, I am a woman of a sorrowful spirit. I have drunk neither wine nor strong drink, but I poured out my soul before Yahweh. Don't count your handmaid for a wicked woman; for I have been speaking out of the abundance of my complaint and my provocation."

Then Eli answered, "Go in peace; and may the God of Israel grant your petition that you have asked of him."

She said, "Let your handmaid find favor in your sight." So the woman went her way, and ate; and her facial expression wasn't sad any more. They rose up in the morning early, and worshiped before Yahweh, and returned, and came to their house to Ramah: and Elkanah knew Hannah his wife; and Yahweh remembered her. It happened, when the time had come, that Hannah conceived, and bore a son; and she named him Samuel, saying, "Because I have asked him of Yahweh."

The man Elkanah, and all his house, went up to offer to Yahweh the yearly sacrifice, and his vow. But Hannah didn't go up; for she said to her husband, "Not until the child is weaned; then I will bring him, that he may appear before Yahweh, and stay there forever."

Elkanah her husband said to her, "Do what seems good to you. Wait until you have weaned him; only may Yahweh establish his word."

So the woman waited and nursed her son, until she weaned him. When she had weaned him, she took him up with her, with three bulls, and one ephah of meal, and a bottle of wine, and brought him to Yahweh's house in Shiloh. The child was young. They killed the bull, and brought the child to Eli. She said, "Oh, my lord, as your soul lives, my lord, I am the woman who stood by you here, praying to Yahweh. For this child I prayed; and Yahweh has given me my petition which I asked of him. Therefore also I have granted him to Yahweh. As long as he lives he is granted to Yahweh." He worshiped Yahweh there.

Elkanah went to Ramah to his house.

But Samuel ministered before Yahweh, being a child, clothed with a linen ephod. Moreover his mother made him a little robe, and brought it to him from year to year, when she came up with her husband to offer the yearly sacrifice. Eli blessed Elkanah and his wife, and said, "Yahweh give you seed of this woman for the petition which was asked of Yahweh." They went to their own home. Yahweh visited Hannah, and she conceived, and bore three sons and two daughters. The child Samuel grew before Yahweh.

The child Samuel was given to Eli, to be raised in the temple of Yahweh. But there was deep trouble there; the two sons of Eli, in their duties as priests, sinned against God by not treating properly the sacrifices being brought by the people. These two sons also committed other sins that defiled the priesthood. Because of this, God told Eli that his descendants would be cut off from Israel. Instead, God began to prepare Samuel for future leadership.

The child Samuel ministered to Yahweh before Eli. The word of Yahweh was precious in those days; there was no frequent vision. It happened at that time, when Eli was laid down in his place (now his eyes had begun to grow dim, so that he could not see), and the lamp of God hadn't yet gone out, and Samuel had laid down in Yahweh's temple, where the ark of God was; that Yahweh called Samuel; and he said, "Here I am." He ran to Eli, and said, "Here I am; for you called me."

He said, "I didn't call; lie down again."

He went and lay down. Yahweh called yet again, "Samuel!"

Samuel arose and went to Eli, and said, "Here I am; for you called me."

He answered, "I didn't call, my son; lie down again." Now Samuel didn't yet know Yahweh, neither was the word of Yahweh yet revealed to him. Yahweh called Samuel again the third time. He arose and went to Eli, and said, "Here I am; for you called me."

Eli perceived that Yahweh had called the child. Therefore Eli said to Samuel, "Go, lie down: and it shall be, if he calls you, that you shall say, 'Speak, Yahweh; for your servant hears.'" So Samuel went and lay down in his place. Yahweh came, and stood, and called as at other times, "Samuel! Samuel!"

Then Samuel said, "Speak; for your servant hears."

Yahweh said to Samuel, "Behold, I will do a thing in Israel, at which both the ears of everyone who hears it shall tingle. In that day I will perform against Eli all that I have spoken concerning his house, from the beginning even to the end.

For I have told him that I will judge his house forever, for the iniquity which he knew, because his sons brought a curse on themselves, and he didn't restrain them. Therefore I have sworn to the house of Eli, that the iniquity of Eli's house shall not be removed with sacrifice nor offering forever."

Samuel lay until the morning, and opened the doors of the house of Yahweh. Samuel feared to show Eli the vision. Then Eli called Samuel, and said, "Samuel, my son!"

He said, "Here I am."

He said, "What is the thing that he has spoken to you? Please don't hide it from me. God do so to you, and more also, if you hide anything from me of all the things that he spoke to you."

Samuel told him every bit, and hid nothing from him.

He said, "It is Yahweh. Let him do what seems good to him."

Samuel grew, and Yahweh was with him, and let none of his words fall to the ground. All Israel from Dan even to Beersheba knew that Samuel was established to be a prophet of Yahweh. Yahweh appeared again in Shiloh; for Yahweh revealed himself to Samuel in Shiloh by the word of Yahweh.

The word of Samuel came to all Israel. Now Israel went out against the Philistines to battle, and encamped beside Ebenezer: and the Philistines encamped in Aphek. The Philistines put themselves in array against Israel: and when they joined battle, Israel was struck before the Philistines; and they killed of the army in the field about four thousand men. When the people had come into the camp, the elders of Israel said, "Why has Yahweh struck us today before the Philistines? Let us get the ark of the covenant of Yahweh out of Shiloh to us, that it may come among us, and save us out of the hand of our enemies."

So the people sent to Shiloh; and they brought from there the ark of the covenant of Yahweh of Armies, who sits above the cherubim: and the two sons of Eli, Hophni and Phinehas, were there with the ark of the covenant of God. When the ark of the covenant of Yahweh came into the camp, all Israel shouted with a great shout, so that the earth rang again. When the Philistines heard the noise of the shout, they said, "What does the noise of this great shout in the camp of the Hebrews mean?" They understood that the ark of Yahweh had come into the camp.

The Philistines were afraid, for they said, "God has come into the camp." They said, "Woe to us! For there has not been such a thing before. Woe to us! Who shall deliver us out of the hand of these mighty gods? These are the gods that struck the Egyptians with all kinds of plagues in the wilderness. Be strong, and behave like men, O you Philistines, that you not be servants to the Hebrews, as they have been to you. Strengthen yourselves like men, and fight!" The Philistines fought, and Israel was struck, and they fled every man to his tent: and there was a very great slaughter; for there fell of Israel thirty thousand footmen. The ark of God was taken; and the two sons of Eli, Hophni and Phinehas, were slain. There ran a man of Benjamin out of the army, and came to Shiloh the same day, with his clothes torn, and with earth on his head. When he came, behold, Eli was sitting on his seat by the road watching; for his heart trembled for the ark of God. When the man came into the city, and told it, all the city cried out.

When Eli heard the noise of the crying, he said, "What does the noise of this tumult mean?"

The man hurried, and came and told Eli. Now Eli was ninety-eight years old; and his eyes were set, so that he could not see. The man said to Eli, "I am he who came out of the army, and I fled today out of the army."

He said, "How did the matter go, my son?"

He who brought the news answered, "Israel has fled before the Philistines, and there has been also a great slaughter among the people. Your two sons also, Hophni and Phinehas, are dead, and the ark of God has been captured."

It happened, when he made mention of the ark of God, that Eli fell from off his seat backward by the side of the gate; and his neck broke, and he died; for he was an old man, and heavy. He had judged Israel forty years.

Although the Philistines captured the ark, God caused hardship among the towns where the ark was stored - tumors, confusion, deaths, and their idols crashing to the ground overnight. Finally, the Philistines resolved to return the ark to Israel to avoid these plagues. The Philistines created trespass offerings of gold, in the shapes of tumors and mice, and placed these on a cart, along with the ark. The cart, being pulled by two cows, arrived at Beth Shemesh in Israel. The men there rejoiced, sacrificing to God when the ark was recovered. But they made a grave error, by looking into the ark, and God showed his wrath at this trespass in a powerful way.

They of Beth Shemesh were reaping their wheat harvest in the valley; and they lifted up their eyes, and saw the ark, and rejoiced to see it. The cart came into the field of Joshua of Beth Shemesh, and stood there, where there was a great stone: and they split the wood of the cart, and offered up the cows for a burnt offering to Yahweh. The Levites took down the ark of Yahweh, and the coffer that was with it, in which the jewels of gold were, and put them on the great stone: and the men of Beth Shemesh offered burnt offerings and sacrificed sacrifices the same day to Yahweh.

He struck of the men of Beth Shemesh, because they had looked into the ark of Yahweh, he struck of the people fifty thousand seventy men; and the people mourned, because Yahweh had struck the people with a great slaughter. The men of Beth Shemesh said, "Who is able to stand before Yahweh, this holy God? To whom shall he go up from us?"

With Eli dead, Samuel took on the role of Israel's spiritual leader. After 20 years under his guidance, the nation of Israel was finally repentant and ready to turn back to God. Samuel encouraged the nation to finally break the oppression of the Philistines. With great thunder from God confusing the Philistines, the Israelite army routed them, and restored all of their cities to the control of Israel.

As in the case of his mentor Eli, the sons of Samuel also turned away from the righteous ways of God. Seeing no viable leadership in place to come after Samuel, the people of Israel began to desire a king. Although this was displeasing to Samuel, God agreed to establish a king over the nation once they were warned of the price the nation would pay for this arrangement.

It happened, when Samuel was old, that he made his sons judges over Israel. Now the name of his firstborn was Joel; and the name of his second, Abijah: they were judges in Beersheba. His sons didn't walk in his ways, but turned aside after lucre, and took bribes, and perverted justice. Then all the elders of Israel gathered themselves together, and came to Samuel to Ramah; and they said to him, "Behold, you are old, and your sons don't walk in your ways: now make us a king to judge us like all the nations." But the thing displeased Samuel, when they said, "Give us a king to judge us."

Samuel prayed to Yahweh. Yahweh said to Samuel, "Listen to the voice of the people in all that they tell you; for they have not rejected you, but they have rejected me, that I should not be king over them. According to all the works which they have done since the day that I brought them up out of Egypt even to this day, in that they have forsaken me, and served other gods, so do they also to you. Now therefore listen to their voice: however you shall protest solemnly to them, and shall show them the way of the king who shall reign over them."

Samuel told all the words of Yahweh to the people who asked of him a king. He said, "This will be the way of the king who shall reign over you: he will take your sons, and appoint them to him, for his chariots, and to be his horsemen; and they shall run before his chariots; and he will appoint them to him for captains of thousands, and captains of fifties; and he will assign some to plow his ground, and to reap his harvest, and to make his instruments of war, and the instruments of his chariots. He will take your daughters to be perfumers, and to be cooks, and to be bakers. He will take your fields, and your vineyards, and your olive groves, even their best, and give them to his servants. He will take the tenth of your seed, and of your vineyards, and give to his officers, and to his servants. He will take your male servants, and your female servants, and your best young men, and your donkeys, and put them to his work. He will take the tenth of your flocks: and you shall be his servants. You shall cry out in that day because of your king whom you shall have chosen you; and Yahweh will not answer you in that day."

But the people refused to listen to the voice of Samuel; and they said, "No; but we will have a king over us, that we also may be like all the nations, and that our king may judge us, and go out before us, and fight our battles."

Samuel heard all the words of the people, and he rehearsed them in the ears of Yahweh. Yahweh said to Samuel, "Listen to their voice, and make them a king."

Samuel said to the men of Israel, "Every man go to his city."

In the anointing of Israel's first King, Saul, there is a valuable lesson in human behavior. No matter how good we are, we can always fall away from righteousness. With great wealth and adoration it is difficult to remain humble and obedient to God. In the beginning of Saul's reign, the Bible tells us that "there was not among the children of Israel a better person than he..." However, over time, the nation paid a price for the gradual, but steady decline in Saul's leadership and morality.

Now there was a man of Benjamin, whose name was Kish, the son of Abiel, the son of Zeror, the son of Becorath, the son of Aphiah, the son of a Benjamite, a mighty man of valor. He had a son, whose name was Saul, an impressive young man; and there was not among the children of Israel a better person than he. From his shoulders and upward he was higher than any of the people.

The donkeys of Kish, Saul's father, were lost. Kish said to Saul his son, "Take now one of the servants with you, and arise, go seek the donkeys." He passed through the hill country of Ephraim, and passed through the land of Shalishah, but they didn't find them: then they passed through the land of Shaalim, and there they weren't there: and he passed through the land of the Benjamites, but they didn't find them.

When they had come to the land of Zuph, Saul said to his servant who was with him, "Come, and let us return, lest my father stop caring about the donkeys, and be anxious for us."

He said to him, "See now, there is in this city a man of God, and he is a man who is held in honor. All that he says comes surely to pass. Now let us go there. Perhaps he can tell us concerning our journey whereon we go."

They went up to the city. As they came within the city, behold, Samuel came out toward them, to go up to the high place.

Now Yahweh had revealed to Samuel a day before Saul came, saying, "Tomorrow about this time I will send you a man out of the land of Benjamin, and you shall anoint him to be prince over my people Israel; and he shall save my people out of the hand of the Philistines: for I have looked on my people, because their cry has come to me."

When Samuel saw Saul, Yahweh said to him, "Behold, the man of whom I spoke to you! this same shall have authority over my people."

Then Saul drew near to Samuel in the gate, and said, "Please tell me where the seer's house is."

Samuel answered Saul, and said, "I am the seer. Go up before me to the high place, for you shall eat with me today. In the morning I will let you go, and will tell you all that is in your heart. As for your donkeys who were lost three days ago, don't set your mind on them; for they are found. For whom is all that is desirable in Israel? Is it not for you, and for all your father's house?"

Saul answered, "Am I not a Benjamite, of the smallest of the tribes of Israel? And my family the least of all the families of the tribe of Benjamin? Why then do you speak to me like this?"

Then Samuel took the vial of oil, and poured it on his head, and kissed him, and said, "Isn't it that Yahweh has anointed you to be prince over his inheritance?

Samuel called the people together to Yahweh to Mizpah; and he said to the children of Israel, "Thus says Yahweh, the God of Israel, 'I brought up Israel out of Egypt, and I delivered you out of the hand of the Egyptians, and out of the hand of all the kingdoms that oppressed you:' but you have this day rejected your God, who himself saves you out of all your calamities and your distresses; and you have said to him, 'No! Set a king over us.' Now therefore present yourselves before Yahweh by your tribes, and by your thousands."

So Samuel brought all the tribes of Israel near, and the tribe of Benjamin was taken. He brought the tribe of Benjamin near by their families; and the family of the Matrites was taken; and Saul the son of Kish was taken: but when they sought him, he could not be found. Therefore they asked of Yahweh further, "Is there yet a man to come here?"

Yahweh answered, "Behold, he has hidden himself among the baggage."

They ran and fetched him there; and when he stood among the people, he was higher than any of the people from his shoulders and upward. Samuel said to all the people, "You see him whom Yahweh has chosen, that there is none like him among all the people?"

All the people shouted, and said, "Let the king live!" Then Samuel told the people the regulations of the kingdom, and wrote it in a book, and laid it up before Yahweh. Samuel sent all the people away, every man to his house.

Saul did not immediately take on the role of a king; in fact, when we next read about him, he was plowing a field with his oxen. But the Spirit of God moved upon him, and he organized a great deliverance of Jabesh Gilead against the Ammonites. After this event, Saul began to assume his role as king in a more traditional manner.

Then Nahash the Ammonite came up, and encamped against Jabesh Gilead: and all the men of Jabesh said to Nahash, "Make a covenant with us, and we will serve you." Nahash said to them, "On this condition I will make it with you, that all your right eyes be put out; and I will lay it for a reproach on all Israel."

The elders of Jabesh said to him, "Give us seven days, that we may send messengers to all the borders of Israel; and then, if there is no one to save us, we will come out to you." Then the messengers came to Saul, and spoke these words in the ears of the people: and all the people lifted up their voice, and wept.

Behold, Saul came following the oxen out of the field; and Saul said, "What ails the people that they weep?" They told him the words of the men of Jabesh. The Spirit of God came mightily on Saul when he heard those words, and his anger was kindled greatly. He took a yoke of oxen, and cut them in pieces, and sent them throughout all the borders of Israel by the hand of messengers, saying, "Whoever doesn't come forth after Saul and after Samuel, so shall it be done to his oxen." The dread of Yahweh fell on the people, and they came out as one man.

He numbered them in Bezek; and the children of Israel were three hundred thousand, and the men of Judah thirty thousand. They said to the messengers who came, "Thus you shall tell the men of Jabesh Gilead, 'Tomorrow, by the time the sun is hot, you shall have deliverance.'" The messengers came and told the men of Jabesh; and they were glad. Therefore the men of Jabesh said, "Tomorrow we will come out to you, and you shall do with us all that seems good to you." It was so on the next day, that Saul put the people in three companies; and they came into the midst of the camp in the morning watch, and struck the Ammonites until the heat of the day: and it happened, that those who remained were scattered, so that no two of them were left together.

Samuel said to all Israel, "Behold, I have listened to your voice in all that you said to me, and have made a king over you. Now, behold, the king walks before you; and I am old and gray-headed; and behold, my sons are with you: and I have walked before you from my youth to this day. Here I am. Witness against me before Yahweh, and before his anointed. Whose ox have I taken? Whose donkey have I taken? Whom have I defrauded? Whom have I oppressed? Of whose hand have I taken a ransom to blind my eyes therewith? I will restore it to you."

They said, "You have not defrauded us, nor oppressed us, neither have you taken anything of any man's hand."

He said to them, "Yahweh is witness against you, and his anointed is witness this day, that you have not found anything in my hand."

They said, "He is witness."

Saul reigned a year; and when he had reigned two years over Israel, Saul chose for himself three thousand men of Israel, of which two thousand were with Saul in Michmash and in the Mount of Bethel, and one thousand were with Jonathan in Gibeah of Benjamin: and the rest of the people he sent every man to his tent. Jonathan struck the garrison of the Philistines that was in Geba: and the Philistines heard of it. Saul blew the trumpet throughout all the land, saying, "Let the Hebrews hear!" All Israel heard that Saul had struck the garrison of the Philistines, and also that Israel was had in abomination with the Philistines. The people were gathered together after Saul to Gilgal. The Philistines assembled themselves together to fight with Israel, thirty thousand chariots, and six thousand horsemen, and people as the sand which is on the seashore in multitude: and they came up, and encamped in Michmash, eastward of Beth Aven. When the men of Israel saw that they were in a strait (for the people were distressed), then the people hid themselves in caves, and in thickets, and in rocks, and in coverts, and in pits. Now some of the Hebrews had gone over the Jordan to the land of Gad and Gilead; but as for Saul, he was yet in Gilgal, and all the people followed him trembling. He stayed seven days, according to the time set by Samuel: but Samuel didn't come to Gilgal; and the people were scattered from him. Saul said, "Bring here the burnt offering to me, and the peace offerings." He offered the burnt offering.

It came to pass that as soon as he had made an end of offering the burnt offering, behold, Samuel came; and Saul went out to meet him, that he might greet him. Samuel said, "What have you done?"

Saul said, "Because I saw that the people were scattered from me, and that you didn't come within the days appointed, and that the Philistines assembled themselves together at Michmash; therefore I said, 'Now the Philistines will come down on me to Gilgal, and I haven't entreated the favor of Yahweh.' I forced myself therefore, and offered the burnt offering."

Samuel said to Saul, "You have done foolishly. You have not kept the commandment of Yahweh your God, which he commanded you; for now

Yahweh would have established your kingdom on Israel forever. But now your kingdom shall not continue. Yahweh has sought for himself a man after his own heart, and Yahweh has appointed him to be prince over his people, because you have not kept that which Yahweh commanded you."

Saul's impatience was just one of many mistakes he would make during his reign. Despite his flaws, Saul and his son, Jonathan, led Israel to many great victories. They directed the nation as they triumphed against enemies on all sides, including the Moabites, Ammonites, Edomites, Philistines, Ammonites and Amalekites.

Samuel said to Saul, "Yahweh sent me to anoint you to be king over his people, over Israel. Now therefore listen to the voice of the words of Yahweh. Thus says Yahweh of Armies, 'I have marked that which Amalek did to Israel, how he set himself against him in the way, when he came up out of Egypt. Now go and strike Amalek, and utterly destroy all that they have, and don't spare them; but kill both man and woman, infant and nursing baby, ox and sheep, camel and donkey.'"

Saul summoned the people, and numbered them in Telaim, two hundred thousand footmen, and ten thousand men of Judah.

Saul struck the Amalekites, from Havilah as you go to Shur, that is before Egypt. He took Agag the king of the Amalekites alive, and utterly destroyed all the people with the edge of the sword. But Saul and the people spared Agag, and the best of the sheep, and of the cattle, and of the fatlings, and the lambs, and all that was good, and wouldn't utterly destroy them: but everything that was vile and refuse, that they destroyed utterly. Then the word of Yahweh came to Samuel, saying, "It grieves me that I have set up Saul to be king; for he is turned back from following me, and has not performed my commandments." Samuel was angry; and he cried to Yahweh all night.

Saul again grieved God, this time by not utterly destroying the Amalekites, as commanded. God sent Samuel to inform Saul that he had been rejected as the king of Israel due to his disobedience. It was time for a new king, one that would treasure God and lead the people to follow righteously.

Then Samuel went to Ramah; and Saul went up to his house to Gibeah of Saul. Samuel came no more to see Saul until the day of his death; for Samuel mourned for Saul: and Yahweh grieved that he had made Saul king over Israel.

13 THE ANOINTED SHEPHERD

From Humble Shepherd to God's Anointed

Yahweh said to Samuel, "How long will you mourn for Saul, since I have rejected him from being king over Israel? Fill your horn with oil, and go. I will send you to Jesse the Bethlehemite; for I have provided a king for myself among his sons."

Samuel said, "How can I go? If Saul hears it, he will kill me."

Yahweh said, "Take a heifer with you, and say, I have come to sacrifice to Yahweh.

Call Jesse to the sacrifice, and I will show you what you shall do. You shall anoint to me him whom I name to you."

Samuel did that which Yahweh spoke, and came to Bethlehem. The elders of the city came to meet him trembling, and said, "Do you come peaceably?"

He said, "Peaceably; I have come to sacrifice to Yahweh. Sanctify yourselves, and come with me to the sacrifice." He sanctified Jesse and his sons, and called them to the sacrifice. It happened, when they had come, that he looked at Eliab, and said, "Surely Yahweh's anointed is before him."

But Yahweh said to Samuel, "Don't look on his face, or on the height of his stature; because I have rejected him: for I see not as man sees; for man looks at the outward appearance, but Yahweh looks at the heart." Then Jesse called Abinadab, and made him pass before Samuel. He said, "Neither has Yahweh chosen this one." Then Jesse made Shammah to pass by. He said, "Neither has Yahweh chosen this one." Jesse made seven of his sons to pass before Samuel. Samuel said to Jesse, "Yahweh has not chosen these." Samuel said to Jesse, "Are all your children here?"

He said, "There remains yet the youngest, and behold, he is keeping the sheep."

Samuel said to Jesse, "Send and get him; for we will not sit down until he comes here."

He sent, and brought him in. Now he was ruddy, and withal of a beautiful face, and goodly to look on. Yahweh said, "Arise, anoint him; for this is he."

Then Samuel took the horn of oil, and anointed him in the midst of his brothers: and the Spirit of Yahweh came mightily on David from that day forward. So Samuel rose up, and went to Ramah.

In a strange turn of events, David ended up in the court of Saul by his reputation as a harp player. The time David spent observing King Saul and the workings of the royal court helped prepare him for his future kingship. But when David had a great victory against the champion of the Philistine army, he rose from an obscure harp player to a champion of Israel.

Now the Philistines gathered together their armies to battle; and they were gathered together at Socoh, which belongs to Judah, and encamped between Socoh and Azekah, in Ephesdammim. Saul and the men of Israel were gathered together, and encamped in the valley of Elah, and set the battle in array against the Philistines. The Philistines stood on the mountain on the one side, and Israel stood on the mountain on the other side: and there was a valley between them. There went out a champion out of the camp of the Philistines, named Goliath, of Gath, whose height was six cubits and a span. He had a helmet of brass on his head, and he was clad with a coat of mail; and the weight of the coat was five thousand shekels of brass. He had brass shin armor on his legs, and a javelin of brass between his shoulders. The staff of his spear was like a weaver's beam; and his spear's head weighed six hundred shekels of iron: and his shield bearer went before him. He stood and cried to the armies of Israel, and said to them, "Why have you come out to set your battle in array? Am I not a Philistine, and you servants to Saul? Choose a man for yourselves, and let him come down to me. If he be able to fight with me, and kill me, then will we be your servants; but if I prevail against him, and kill him, then you will be our servants, and serve us." The Philistine said, "I defy the armies of Israel this day! Give me a man, that we may fight together!"

When Saul and all Israel heard those words of the Philistine, they were dismayed, and greatly afraid.

The Philistine drew near morning and evening, and presented himself forty days. Jesse said to David his son, "Now take for your brothers an ephah of this parched grain, and these ten loaves, and carry them quickly to the camp to your brothers; and bring these ten cheeses to the captain of their thousand, and see how your brothers are doing, and bring back news." Now Saul, and they, and all the men of Israel, were in the valley of Elah, fighting with the Philistines. David rose up early in the morning, and left the sheep with a keeper, and took, and went, as Jesse had commanded him; and he came to the place of the wagons, as the army which was going forth to the fight shouted for the battle. Israel and the Philistines put the battle in array, army against army.

David left his baggage in the hand of the keeper of the baggage, and ran to the army, and came and greeted his brothers. As he talked with them, behold, there came up the champion, the Philistine of Gath, Goliath by name, out of the ranks of the Philistines, and spoke according to the same words: and David heard them. All the men of Israel, when they saw the man, fled from him, and were terrified. The men of Israel said, "Have you seen this man who has come up? He has surely come up to defy Israel. It shall be, that the man who kills him, the king will enrich him with great riches, and will give him his daughter, and make his father's house free in Israel."

David spoke to the men who stood by him, saying, "What shall be done to the man who kills this Philistine, and takes away the reproach from Israel? For who is this uncircumcised Philistine, that he should defy the armies of the living God?"

The people answered him in this way, saying, "So shall it be done to the man who kills him."

Eliab his eldest brother heard when he spoke to the men; and Eliab's anger was kindled against David, and he said, "Why have you come down? With whom have you left those few sheep in the wilderness? I know your pride, and the naughtiness of your heart; for you have come down that you might see the battle."

David said, "What have I now done? Is there not a cause?" He turned away from him toward another, and spoke like that again; and the people answered him again the same way. When the words were heard which David spoke, they rehearsed them before Saul; and he sent for him. David said to Saul, "Let no man's heart fail because of him. Your servant will go and fight with this Philistine."

Saul said to David, "You are not able to go against this Philistine to fight with him; for you are but a youth, and he a man of war from his youth."

David said to Saul, "Your servant was keeping his father's sheep; and when a lion or a bear came, and took a lamb out of the flock, I went out after him, and struck him, and rescued it out of his mouth. When he arose against me, I caught him by his beard, and struck him, and killed him. Your servant struck both the lion and the bear. This uncircumcised Philistine shall be as one of them, since he has defied the armies of the living God." David said, "Yahweh who delivered me out of the paw of the lion, and out of the paw of the bear, he will deliver me out of the hand of this Philistine."

Saul said to David, "Go; and Yahweh shall be with you." Saul dressed David with his clothing. He put a helmet of brass on his head, and he clad him with a coat of mail. David strapped his sword on his clothing, and he tried to move; for he had not tested it. David said to Saul, "I can't go with these; for I have not tested them." David took them off.

He took his staff in his hand, and chose for himself five smooth stones out of the brook, and put them in the shepherd's bag which he had, even in his wallet. His sling was in his hand; and he drew near to the Philistine. The Philistine came on and drew near to David; and the man who bore the shield went before him. When the Philistine looked about, and saw David, he disdained him; for he was but a youth, and ruddy, and withal of a fair face. The Philistine said to David, "Am I a dog, that you come to me with sticks?" The Philistine cursed David by his gods. The Philistine said to David, "Come to me, and I will give your flesh to the birds of the sky, and to the animals of the field."

Then David said to the Philistine, "You come to me with a sword, and with a spear, and with a javelin: but I come to you in the name of Yahweh of Armies, the God of the armies of Israel, whom you have defied. Today, Yahweh will deliver you into my hand. I will strike you, and take your head from off you. I will give the dead bodies of the army of the Philistines this day to the birds of the sky, and to the wild animals of the earth; that all the earth may know that there is a God in Israel, and that all this assembly may know that Yahweh doesn't save with sword and spear: for the battle is Yahweh's, and he will give you into our hand."

It happened, when the Philistine arose, and came and drew near to meet David, that David hurried, and ran toward the army to meet the Philistine. David put his hand in his bag, took a stone, and slung it, and struck the Philistine in his forehead; and the stone sank into his forehead, and he fell on his face to the earth.

So David prevailed over the Philistine with a sling and with a stone, and struck the Philistine, and killed him; but there was no sword in the hand of David. Then David ran, and stood over the Philistine, and took his sword, and drew it out of its sheath, and killed him, and cut off his head therewith. When the Philistines saw that their champion was dead, they fled. The men of Israel and of Judah arose, and shouted, and pursued the Philistines, until you come to Gai, and to the gates of Ekron. The wounded of the Philistines fell down by the way to Shaaraim, even to Gath, and to Ekron. The children of Israel returned from chasing after the Philistines, and they plundered their camp. David took the head of the Philistine, and brought it to Jerusalem; but he put his armor in his tent. When Saul saw David go forth against the Philistine, he said to Abner, the captain of the army, "Abner, whose son is this youth?"

Abner said, "As your soul lives, O king, I can't tell."

The king said, "Inquire whose son the young man is!"

As David returned from the slaughter of the Philistine, Abner took him, and brought him before Saul with the head of the Philistine in his hand. Saul said to him, "Whose son are you, you young man?"

David answered, "I am the son of your servant Jesse the Bethlehemite."

It happened, when he had made an end of speaking to Saul, that the soul of Jonathan was knit with the soul of David, and Jonathan loved him as his own soul. Saul took him that day, and would let him go no more home to his father's house. Then Jonathan and David made a covenant, because he loved him as his own soul. Jonathan stripped himself of the robe that was on him, and gave it to David, and his clothing, even to his sword, and to his bow, and to his sash. David went out wherever Saul sent him, and behaved himself wisely: and Saul set him over the men of war, and it was good in the sight of all the people, and also in the sight of Saul's servants. It happened as they came, when David returned from the slaughter of the Philistine, that the women came out of all the cities of Israel, singing and dancing, to meet king Saul, with tambourines, with joy, and with instruments of music. The women sang one to another as they played, and said,

"Saul has slain his thousands, David his ten thousands."

Saul spoke to Jonathan his son, and to all his servants, that they should kill David. But Jonathan, Saul's son, delighted much in David. Jonathan told David, saying, "Saul my father seeks to kill you. Now therefore, please take care of yourself in the morning, and live in a secret place, and hide yourself. I will go out and stand beside my father in the field where you are, and I will talk with my father about you; and if I see anything, I will tell you."

Jonathan spoke good of David to Saul his father, and said to him, "Don't let the king sin against his servant, against David; because he has not sinned against you, and because his works have been very good toward you; for he put his life in his hand, and struck the Philistine, and Yahweh worked a great victory for all Israel. You saw it, and rejoiced. Why then will you sin against innocent blood, to kill David without a cause?"

Saul listened to the voice of Jonathan: and Saul swore, "As Yahweh lives, he shall not be put to death."

Saul soon went back on his word, trying on several occasions to kill young David. But Saul's son Jonathan, who loved David, agreed to help David determine whether it was safe for him to stay in the court of Saul.

David said to Jonathan, "Behold, tomorrow is the new moon, and I should not fail to dine with the king; but let me go, that I may hide myself in the field to the third day at evening.

Jonathan said to David, "Come, and let us go out into the field." They both went out into the field. Jonathan said to David, "By Yahweh, the God of Israel, when I have sounded my father about this time tomorrow, or the third day, behold, if there is good toward David, shall I not then send to you, and disclose it to you?

Jonathan caused David to swear again, for the love that he had to him; for he loved him as he loved his own soul. Then Jonathan said to him, "Tomorrow is the new moon: and you will be missed, because your seat will be empty. When you have stayed three days, you shall go down quickly, and come to the place where you hid yourself when this started, and shall remain by the stone Ezel. I will shoot three arrows on its side, as though I shot at a mark. Behold, I will send the boy, saying, 'Go, find the arrows!' If I tell the boy, 'Behold, the arrows are on this side of you. Take them;' then come; for there is peace to you and no hurt, as Yahweh lives. But if I say this to the boy, 'Behold, the arrows are beyond you;' then go your way; for Yahweh has sent you away. Concerning the matter which you and I have spoken of, behold, Yahweh is between you and me forever."

King Saul was seemingly becoming more mentally unstable by the day. He even went so far as to throw his spear at his son Jonathan, when Jonathan stood up for David. It became obvious to Jonathan that it was no longer safe for David to remain in the court of King Saul. Despite the great love David and Jonathan had for each other, it was time for them to separate, for their own safety.

It happened in the morning, that Jonathan went out into the field at the time appointed with David, and a little boy with him. He said to his boy, "Run, find now the arrows which I shoot." As the boy ran, he shot an arrow beyond him. When the boy had come to the place of the arrow which Jonathan had shot, Jonathan cried after the boy, and said, "Isn't the arrow beyond you?" Jonathan cried after the boy, "Go fast! Hurry! Don't delay!" Jonathan's boy gathered up the arrows, and came to his master. But the boy didn't know anything. Only Jonathan and David knew the matter. Jonathan gave his weapons to his boy, and said to him, "Go, carry them to the city."

As soon as the boy was gone, David arose out of the south, and fell on his face to the ground, and bowed himself three times. They kissed one another, and wept one with another, and David wept the most. Jonathan said to David, "Go in peace, because we have both sworn in the name of Yahweh, saying, 'Yahweh shall be between me and you, and between my seed and your seed, forever.'" He arose and departed; and Jonathan went into the city.

David fled from Saul, and found himself in Nob, where Abimelech is serving as a priest. Abimelech helped David, giving him food and the sword of Goliath the Philistine giant, which was kept in the temple there for safe keeping. But an Edomite man, Doeg, saw this transaction. Saul became consumed with preserving his kingship by seeking to kill David. It is in this pursuit that Saul turned completely away from God, even ordering a massacre of priests.

David therefore departed there, and escaped to the cave of Adullam. When his brothers and all his father's house heard it, they went down there to him.

Everyone who was in distress, and everyone who was in debt, and everyone who was discontented, gathered themselves to him; and he became captain over them: and there were with him about four hundred men. David went there to Mizpeh of Moab, and he said to the king of Moab, "Please let my father and my mother come out with you, until I know what God will do for me." He brought them before the king of Moab; and they lived with him all the while that David was in the stronghold. The prophet Gad said to David, "Don't stay in the stronghold. Depart, and go into the land of Judah."

Then David departed, and came into the forest of Hereth.

Saul heard that David was discovered, and the men who were with him. Now Saul was sitting in Gibeah, under the tamarisk tree in Ramah, with his spear in his hand, and all his servants were standing about him. Saul said to his servants who stood about him, "Hear now, you Benjamites! Will the son of Jesse give everyone of you fields and vineyards, will he make you all captains of thousands and captains of hundreds, that all of you have conspired against me, and there is none who discloses to me when my son makes a treaty with the son of Jesse, and there is none of you who is sorry for me, or discloses to me that my son has stirred up my servant against me, to lie in wait, as at this day?"

Then Doeg the Edomite, who stood by the servants of Saul, answered and said, "I saw the son of Jesse coming to Nob, to Ahimelech the son of Ahitub. He inquired of Yahweh for him, gave him food, and gave him the sword of Goliath the Philistine."

Then the king sent to call Ahimelech the priest, the son of Ahitub, and all his father's house, the priests who were in Nob: and they came all of them to the king. Saul said, "Hear now, you son of Ahitub."

He answered, "Here I am, my lord."

Saul said to him, "Why have you conspired against me, you and the son of Jesse, in that you have given him bread, and a sword, and have inquired of God for him, that he should rise against me, to lie in wait, as at this day?"

Then Ahimelech answered the king, and said, "Who among all your servants is so faithful as David, who is the king's son-in-law, and is taken into your council, and is honorable in your house? Have I today begun to inquire of God for him? Be it far from me! Don't let the king impute anything to his servant, nor to all the house of my father; for your servant knows nothing of all this, less or more."

The king said, "You shall surely die, Ahimelech, you, and all your father's house." The king said to the guard who stood about him, "Turn, and kill the priests of Yahweh; because their hand also is with David, and because they knew that he fled, and didn't disclose it to me." But the servants of the king wouldn't put forth their hand to fall on the priests of Yahweh. The king said to Doeg, "Turn and attack the priests!"

Doeg the Edomite turned, and he attacked the priests, and he killed on that day eighty-five people who wore a linen ephod. He struck Nob, the city of the priests, with the edge of the sword, both men and women, children and nursing babies, and cattle and donkeys and sheep, with the edge of the sword.

It happened, when Saul was returned from following the Philistines, that it was told him, saying, "Behold, David is in the wilderness of En Gedi." Then Saul took three thousand chosen men out of all Israel, and went to seek David and his men on the rocks of the wild goats. He came to the sheep pens by the way, where there was a cave; and Saul went in to relieve himself. Now David and his men were abiding in the innermost parts of the cave. The men of David said to him, "Behold, the day of which Yahweh said to you, 'Behold, I will deliver your enemy into your hand, and you shall do to him as it shall seem good to you.'" Then David arose, and cut off the skirt of Saul's robe secretly. It happened afterward, that David's heart struck him, because he had cut off Saul's skirt. He said to his men, "Yahweh forbid that I should do this thing to my lord, Yahweh's anointed, to put forth my hand against him, since he is Yahweh's anointed." So David checked his men with these words, and didn't allow them to rise against Saul. Saul rose up out of the cave, and went on his way. David also arose afterward, and went out of the cave, and cried after Saul, saying, "My lord the king!"

When Saul looked behind him, David bowed with his face to the earth, and showed respect. David said to Saul, "Why do you listen to men's words, saying, 'Behold, David seeks your hurt?' Behold, this day your eyes have seen how that Yahweh had delivered you today into my hand in the cave. Some urged me to

139

kill you; but I spared you; and I said, I will not put forth my hand against my lord; for he is Yahweh's anointed. Moreover, my father, behold, yes, see the skirt of your robe in my hand; for in that I cut off the skirt of your robe, and didn't kill you, know and see that there is neither evil nor disobedience in my hand, and I have not sinned against you, though you hunt for my life to take it. May Yahweh judge between me and you, and may Yahweh avenge me of you; but my hand shall not be on you. As the proverb of the ancients says, 'Out of the wicked comes forth wickedness;' but my hand shall not be on you. Against whom has the king of Israel come out? Whom do you pursue? A dead dog? A flea? May Yahweh therefore be judge, and give sentence between me and you, and see, and plead my cause, and deliver me out of your hand."

It came to pass, when David had made an end of speaking these words to Saul, that Saul said, "Is this your voice, my son David?" Saul lifted up his voice, and wept. He said to David, "You are more righteous than I; for you have done good to me, whereas I have done evil to you. You have declared this day how you have dealt well with me, because when Yahweh had delivered me up into your hand, you didn't kill me. For if a man finds his enemy, will he let him go away unharmed? Therefore may Yahweh reward you good for that which you have done to me this day. Now, behold, I know that you shall surely be king, and that the kingdom of Israel shall be established in your hand. Swear now therefore to me by Yahweh, that you will not cut off my seed after me, and that you will not destroy my name out of my father's house."

David swore to Saul. Saul went home; but David and his men went up to the stronghold.

David spoke to Yahweh the words of this song in the day that Yahweh delivered him out of the hand of all his enemies, and out of the hand of Saul: and he said, "Yahweh is my rock, my fortress, and my deliverer, even mine;

God, my rock, in him I will take refuge; my shield, and the horn of my salvation, my high tower, and my refuge. My savior, you save me from violence.

I will call on Yahweh, who is worthy to be praised: So shall I be saved from my enemies.

For the waves of death surrounded me. The floods of ungodliness made me afraid.

The cords of Sheol were around me. The snares of death caught me. In my distress I called on Yahweh. Yes, I called to my God. He heard my voice out of his temple. My cry came into his ears.

Yahweh lives! Blessed be my rock! Exalted be God, the rock of my salvation,

even the God who executes vengeance for me, who brings down peoples under me, who brings me away from my enemies. Yes, you lift me up above those who rise up against me. You deliver me from the violent man.

Therefore I will give thanks to you, Yahweh, among the nations. Will sing praises to your name.

He gives great deliverance to his king, and shows loving kindness to his anointed, to David and to his seed, forevermore."

Samuel died; and all Israel gathered themselves together, and lamented him, and buried him in his house at Ramah. David arose, and went down to the wilderness of Paran.

Once again Saul returned to his evil ways, and pursued David in an attempt to murder him. David was again given a chance to kill Saul, but refused to lay a hand on the Lord's anointed king. David joined forces with the Philistines; he and his 600 fighting men lived among them for protection, and in return, he fought against their non-Israelite enemies with great success. When the Philistines went to war against Israel, the Philistine captains sent David and his men away, fearing that they would turn against them and fight for Israel. In this battle, Saul and his three sons were killed, and the reign of the first king of Israel came to an end.

Now the Philistines fought against Israel: and the men of Israel fled from before the Philistines, and fell down slain on Mount Gilboa. The Philistines followed hard on Saul and on his sons; and the Philistines killed Jonathan, and Abinadab, and Malchishua, the sons of Saul. The battle went hard against Saul, and the archers overtook him; and he was greatly distressed by reason of the archers. Then Saul said to his armor bearer, "Draw your sword, and thrust me through with it, lest these uncircumcised come and thrust me through, and abuse me!" But his armor bearer would not; for he was terrified. Therefore Saul took his sword, and fell on it. When his armor bearer saw that Saul was dead, he likewise fell on his sword, and died with him. So Saul died, and his three sons, and his armor bearer, and all his men, that same day together. When the men of Israel who were on the other side of the valley, and those who were beyond the Jordan, saw that the men of Israel fled, and that Saul and his sons were dead, they forsook the cities, and fled; and the Philistines came and lived in them.

It happened on the next day, when the Philistines came to strip the slain, that they found Saul and his three sons fallen on Mount Gilboa. They cut off his head, and stripped off his armor, and sent into the land of the Philistines all around, to carry the news to the house of their idols, and to the people. They put his armor in the house of the Ashtaroth; and they fastened his body to the wall of Beth Shan. When the inhabitants of Jabesh Gilead heard concerning him that which the Philistines had done to Saul, all the valiant men arose, and went all night, and took the body of Saul and the bodies of his sons from the wall of Beth Shan; and they came to Jabesh, and burnt them there. They took their bones, and buried them under the tamarisk tree in Jabesh, and fasted seven days.

14 BROKEN GLORY

Victories and Struggles of a King

After the death of Saul and his sons, David did not rejoice, as in the death of an enemy, but he grieved their deaths as that of a friend. In his heartfelt lament over their deaths, David wrote a song to commemorate Saul and Jonathan.

"Your glory, Israel, is slain on your high places! How the mighty have fallen!

Don't tell it in Gath. Don't publish it in the streets of Ashkelon, lest the daughters of the Philistines rejoice, lest the daughters of the uncircumcised triumph.

From the blood of the slain, from the fat of the mighty, Jonathan's bow didn't turn back. Saul's sword didn't return empty.

Saul and Jonathan were lovely and pleasant in their lives. In their death, they were not divided. They were swifter than eagles. They were stronger than lions.

How are the mighty fallen in the midst of the battle! Jonathan is slain on your high places.

I am distressed for you, my brother Jonathan. You have been very pleasant to me. Your love to me was wonderful, passing the love of women.

How are the mighty fallen, and the weapons of war perished!"

It happened after this, that David inquired of Yahweh, saying, "Shall I go up into any of the cities of Judah?"

Yahweh said to him, "Go up." David said, "Where shall I go up?"

He said, "To Hebron."

The men of Judah came, and there they anointed David king over the house of Judah.

Now there was long war between the house of Saul and the house of David: and David grew stronger and stronger, but the house of Saul grew weaker and weaker.

After a disagreement with Ishbosheth, the surviving son of King Saul, Abner, the commander of Saul's army, joined David, and sought to restore the entire nation of Israel to him. But Joab, the commander of David's army, distrusted Abner and murdered him. When David found out about this, he was severely grieved. When the nation saw David's sincere sorrow at the death of Abner, they drew to him.

Then came all the tribes of Israel to David to Hebron, and spoke, saying, "Behold, we are your bone and your flesh. In times past, when Saul was king over us, it was you who led out and brought in Israel. Yahweh said to you, 'You shall be shepherd of my people Israel, and you shall be prince over Israel.'" So all the elders of Israel came to the king to Hebron; and king David made a covenant with them in Hebron before Yahweh; and they anointed David king over Israel. David was thirty years old when he began to reign, and he reigned forty years. In Hebron he reigned over Judah seven years and six months; and in Jerusalem he reigned thirty-three years over all Israel and Judah.

David grew greater and greater; for Yahweh, the God of Armies, was with him. Hiram king of Tyre sent messengers to David, and cedar trees, and carpenters, and masons; and they built David a house. David perceived that Yahweh had established him king over Israel, and that he had exalted his kingdom for his people Israel's sake.

God was with David, giving him many children, consolidating the kingdom under his rule, and aiding his armies so that they subdued the mighty Philistines. The love that David had for God became evident when the nation of Israel gloriously returned the Ark of the covenant to Jerusalem.

David again gathered together all the chosen men of Israel, thirty thousand. David arose, and went with all the people who were with him, from Baale Judah, to bring up from there the ark of God, which is called by the Name, even the name of Yahweh of Armies who sits above the cherubim. They set the ark of God on a new cart, and brought it out of the house of Abinadab that was in the hill: and Uzzah and Ahio, the sons of Abinadab, drove the new cart. They brought it out of the house of Abinadab, which was in the hill, with the ark of God: and Ahio went before the ark. David and all the house of Israel played before Yahweh with all kinds of instruments made of fir wood, and with harps, and with stringed instruments, and with tambourines, and with castanets, and with cymbals.

When they came to the threshing floor of Nacon, Uzzah reached for the ark of God, and took hold of it; for the cattle stumbled. The anger of Yahweh was kindled against Uzzah; and God struck him there for his error; and there he died by the ark of God. David was displeased, because Yahweh had broken forth on Uzzah; and he called that place Perez Uzzah, to this day. David was afraid of Yahweh that day; and he said, "How shall the ark of Yahweh come to me?" So David would not move the ark of Yahweh to be with him in the city of David; but David carried it aside into the house of Obed-Edom the Gittite. The ark of Yahweh remained in the house of Obed-Edom the Gittite three months: and Yahweh blessed Obed-Edom, and all his house. It was told king David, saying, "Yahweh has blessed the house of Obed-Edom, and all that pertains to him, because of the ark of God."

David went and brought up the ark of God from the house of Obed-Edom into the city of David with joy. It was so, that, when those who bore the ark of Yahweh had gone six paces, he sacrificed an ox and a fattened calf. David danced before Yahweh with all his might; and David was clothed in a linen ephod. So David and all the house of Israel brought up the ark of Yahweh with shouting, and with the sound of the trumpet. It was so, as the ark of Yahweh came into the city of David, that Michal the daughter of Saul looked out at the window, and saw king David leaping and dancing before Yahweh; and she despised him in her heart. They brought in the ark of Yahweh, and set it in its place, in the midst of the tent that David had pitched for it; and David offered burnt offerings and peace offerings before Yahweh. When David had made an end of offering the burnt offering and the peace offerings, he blessed the people in the name of Yahweh of Armies. He gave to all the people, even among the whole multitude of Israel, both to men and women, to everyone a portion of bread, dates, and raisins. So all the people departed everyone to his house. Then David returned to bless his household. Michal the daughter of Saul came out to meet David, and said, "How glorious the king of Israel was today, who uncovered himself today in the eyes of the handmaids of his servants, as one of the vain fellows shamelessly uncovers himself!"

David said to Michal, "It was before Yahweh, who chose me above your father, and above all his house, to appoint me prince over the people of Yahweh, over Israel. Therefore will I celebrate before Yahweh. I will be yet more vile than this, and will be base in my own sight. But of the handmaids of whom you have spoken, they shall honor me." Michal the daughter of Saul had no child to the day of her death.

David desired to build a temple for God. Although his intention was honorable, God decreed that David, being a king of war, was not the right ruler to build this house. So while David was allowed to make plans for a temple, it would be up to his successor to build this edifice.

It happened, when the king lived in his house, and Yahweh had given him rest from all his enemies all around, that the king said to Nathan the prophet, "See now, I dwell in a house of cedar, but the ark of God dwells within curtains."

Nathan said to the king, "Go, do all that is in your heart; for Yahweh is with you."

It happened the same night, that the word of Yahweh came to Nathan, saying, "Go and tell my servant David, 'Thus says Yahweh, "Shall you build me a house for me to dwell in?

I have been with you wherever you went, and have cut off all your enemies from before you. I will make you a great name, like the name of the great ones who are in the earth.

When your days are fulfilled, and you shall sleep with your fathers, I will set up your seed after you, who shall proceed out of your bowels, and I will establish his kingdom. He shall build a house for my name, and I will establish the throne of his kingdom forever.

Then David the king went in, and sat before Yahweh; and he said, "Who am I, Lord Yahweh, and what is my house, that you have brought me thus far?

Now, Yahweh God, the word that you have spoken concerning your servant, and concerning his house, confirm it forever, and do as you have spoken.

God gave victory to David wherever he went. David had great victories over the Philistines, the Moabites, Syrians, Amelikites, and Ammonites. War in those days was brutal; in one battle, the armies of Israel killed 22,000 Syrian soldiers, and they followed this up with another battle in which they killed 18,000 Syrians. In another conflict, David killed of the Syrians seven hundred charioteers and forty thousand horsemen. But against the backdrop of these great military victories, David succumbed to temptation and the Bible records his greatest downfall.

The Bible is unique among ancient books, in that it records the weaknesses as well as the strengths of its characters. This gives great credibility to the Bible as a historical record. But, more importantly, it shows us that God's love for us can also overcome our own weaknesses and faults.

It happened, at the return of the year, at the time when kings go out, that David sent Joab, and his servants with him, and all Israel; and they destroyed the children of Ammon, and besieged Rabbah. But David stayed at Jerusalem. It happened at evening, that David arose from off his bed, and walked on the roof of the king's house: and from the roof he saw a woman bathing; and the woman was very beautiful to look on. David sent and inquired after the woman. One said, "Isn't this Bathsheba, the daughter of Eliam, the wife of Uriah the Hittite?"

David sent messengers, and took her; and she came in to him, and he lay with her (for she was purified from her uncleanness); and she returned to her house. The woman conceived; and she sent and told David, and said, "I am with child."

David sent to Joab, "Send me Uriah the Hittite." Joab sent Uriah to David. When Uriah had come to him, David asked of him how Joab did, and how the people fared, and how the war prospered. David said to Uriah, "Go down to your house, and wash your feet." Uriah departed out of the king's house, and a gift from the king was sent after him. But Uriah slept at the door of the king's house with all the servants of his lord, and didn't go down to his house. When they had told David, saying, "Uriah didn't go down to his house," David said to Uriah, "Haven't you come from a journey? Why didn't you go down to your house?"

Uriah said to David, "The ark, Israel, and Judah, are staying in tents; and my lord Joab, and the servants of my lord, are encamped in the open field. Shall I then go into my house to eat and to drink, and to lie with my wife? As you live, and as your soul lives, I will not do this thing!"

David said to Uriah, "Stay here today also, and tomorrow I will let you depart." So Uriah stayed in Jerusalem that day, and the next day. When David had called him, he ate and drink before him; and he made him drunk. At evening, he went out to lie on his bed with the servants of his lord, but didn't go down to his house. It happened in the morning, that David wrote a letter to Joab, and sent it by the hand of Uriah. He wrote in the letter, saying, "Send Uriah to the forefront of the hottest battle, and retreat from him, that he may be struck, and die."

It happened, when Joab kept watch on the city, that he assigned Uriah to the place where he knew that valiant men were. The men of the city went out, and fought with Joab. Some of the people fell, even of the servants of David; and Uriah the Hittite died also.

When the wife of Uriah heard that Uriah her husband was dead, she made lamentation for her husband. When the mourning was past, David sent and took her home to his house, and she became his wife, and bore him a son. But the thing that David had done displeased Yahweh.

Yahweh sent Nathan to David. He came to him, and said to him, "There were two men in one city; the one rich, and the other poor. The rich man had very many flocks and herds, but the poor man had nothing, except one little ewe lamb, which he had bought and raised. It grew up together with him, and with his children. It ate of his own food, drank of his own cup, and lay in his bosom, and was to him like a daughter. A traveler came to the rich man, and he spared to take of his own flock and of his own herd, to dress for the wayfaring man who had come to him, but took the poor man's lamb, and dressed it for the man who had come to him."

David's anger was greatly kindled against the man, and he said to Nathan, "As Yahweh lives, the man who has done this is worthy to die! He shall restore the lamb fourfold, because he did this thing, and because he had no pity!"

Nathan said to David, "You are the man. This is what Yahweh, the God of Israel, says: 'I anointed you king over Israel, and I delivered you out of the hand of Saul. I gave you your master's house, and your master's wives into your bosom, and gave you the house of Israel and of Judah; and if that would have been too little, I would have added to you many more such things. Why have you despised the word of Yahweh, to do that which is evil in his sight? You have struck Uriah the Hittite with the sword, and have taken his wife to be your wife, and have slain him with the sword of the children of Ammon. Now therefore the sword will never depart from your house, because you have despised me, and have taken the wife of Uriah the Hittite to be your wife.'

"This is what Yahweh says: 'Behold, I will raise up evil against you out of your own house; and I will take your wives before your eyes, and give them to your neighbor, and he will lie with your wives in the sight of this sun. For you did it secretly, but I will do this thing before all Israel, and before the sun.'"

David said to Nathan, "I have sinned against Yahweh."

Nathan said to David, "Yahweh also has put away your sin. You will not die. However, because by this deed you have given great occasion to Yahweh's enemies to blaspheme, the child also who is born to you shall surely die." Nathan departed to his house.

Yahweh struck the child that Uriah's wife bore to David, and it was very sick. David therefore begged God for the child; and David fasted, and went in, and lay all night on the earth. The elders of his house arose beside him, to raise him up from the earth: but he would not, neither did he eat bread with them. It happened on the seventh day, that the child died. The servants of David feared to tell him that the child was dead; for they said, "Behold, while the child was yet alive, we spoke to him, and he didn't listen to our voice. How will he then harm himself, if we tell him that the child is dead?"

But when David saw that his servants were whispering together, David perceived that the child was dead; and David said to his servants, "Is the child dead?"

They said, "He is dead."

Then David arose from the earth, and washed, and anointed himself, and changed his clothing; and he came into the house of Yahweh, and worshiped: then he came to his own house; and when he required, they set bread before him, and he ate. Then his servants said to him, "What is this that you have done? You fasted and wept for the child while he was alive; but when the child was dead, you rose up and ate bread."

He said, "While the child was yet alive, I fasted and wept; for I said, 'Who knows whether Yahweh will not be gracious to me, that the child may live?' But now he is dead, why should I fast? Can I bring him back again? I shall go to him, but he will not return to me."

David comforted Bathsheba his wife, and went in to her, and lay with her. She bore a son, and he called his name Solomon. Yahweh loved him; and he sent by the hand of Nathan the prophet; and he named him Jedidiah, for Yahweh's sake.

Now in all Israel there was none to be so much praised as Absalom for his beauty: from the sole of his foot even to the crown of his head there was no blemish in him. When he cut the hair of his head (now it was at every year's end that he cut it; because it was heavy on him, therefore he cut it); he weighed the hair of his head at two hundred shekels, after the king's weight.

To Absalom there were born three sons, and one daughter, whose name was Tamar: she was a woman of a beautiful face. Absalom lived two full years in Jerusalem; and he didn't see the king's face. Then Absalom sent for Joab, to send him to the king; but he would not come to him: and he sent again a second time, but he would not come. Therefore he said to his servants, "Behold, Joab's field is near mine, and he has barley there. Go and set it on fire." Absalom's servants set the field on fire.

Then Joab arose, and came to Absalom to his house, and said to him, "Why have your servants set my field on fire?"

Absalom answered Joab, "Behold, I sent to you, saying, 'Come here, that I may send you to the king, to say, "Why have I come from Geshur? It would be better for me to be there still. Now therefore let me see the king's face; and if there is iniquity in me, let him kill me."

So Joab came to the king, and told him; and when he had called for Absalom, he came to the king, and bowed himself on his face to the ground before the king: and the king kissed Absalom.

It happened after this, that Absalom prepared him a chariot and horses, and fifty men to run before him. Absalom rose up early, and stood beside the way of the gate. It was so, that when any man had a suit which should come to the king for judgment, then Absalom called to him, and said, "What city are you from?"

149

He said, "Your servant is of one of the tribes of Israel."

Absalom said to him, "Behold, your matters are good and right; but there is no man deputized by the king to hear you." Absalom said moreover, "Oh that I were made judge in the land, that every man who has any suit or cause might come to me, and I would do him justice!" It was so, that when any man came near to do him obeisance, he put forth his hand, and took hold of him, and kissed him. Absalom did this sort of thing to all Israel who came to the king for judgment. So Absalom stole the hearts of the men of Israel.

It happened at the end of forty years, that Absalom said to the king, "Please let me go and pay my vow, which I have vowed to Yahweh, in Hebron. For your servant vowed a vow while I stayed at Geshur in Syria, saying, 'If Yahweh shall indeed bring me again to Jerusalem, then I will serve Yahweh.'"

The king said to him, "Go in peace."

So he arose, and went to Hebron. But Absalom sent spies throughout all the tribes of Israel, saying, "As soon as you hear the sound of the trumpet, then you shall say, 'Absalom is king in Hebron!'" Two hundred men went with Absalom out of Jerusalem, who were invited, and went in their simplicity; and they didn't know anything. Absalom sent for Ahithophel the Gilonite, David's counselor, from his city, even from Giloh, while he was offering the sacrifices. The conspiracy was strong; for the people increased continually with Absalom. A messenger came to David, saying, "The hearts of the men of Israel are after Absalom."

David said to all his servants who were with him at Jerusalem, "Arise, and let us flee; for else none of us shall escape from Absalom. Make speed to depart, lest he overtake us quickly, and bring down evil on us, and strike the city with the edge of the sword."

With Absalom seemingly capturing the hearts of the people, and advancing rapidly, David fled Jerusalem. Taking those fighting men who were loyal to him, David also took the ark of the covenant, carried by the Levite priests. David also wisely left behind a few trusted men who would report on the movements of Absalom. Absalom pursued David, hoping to defeat him while he was tired and on the run; soon the battle lines were drawn, and the forces of the king and his son fought for supremacy.

David numbered the people who were with him, and set captains of thousands and captains of hundreds over them. David sent forth the people, a third part under the hand of Joab, and a third part under the hand of Abishai the son of Zeruiah, Joab's brother, and a third part under the hand of Ittai the Gittite. The king said to the people, "I will surely go forth with you myself also."

But the people said, "You shall not go forth; for if we flee away, they will not care for us; neither if half of us die, will they care for us. But you are worth ten thousand of us. Therefore now it is better that you are ready to help us out of the city."

The king said to them, "I will do what seems best to you." The king stood beside the gate, and all the people went out by hundreds and by thousands. The king commanded Joab and Abishai and Ittai, saying, "Deal gently for my sake with the young man, even with Absalom." All the people heard when the king commanded all the captains concerning Absalom.

So the people went out into the field against Israel: and the battle was in the forest of Ephraim. The people of Israel were struck there before the servants of David, and there was a great slaughter there that day of twenty thousand men. For the battle was there spread over the surface of all the country; and the forest devoured more people that day than the sword devoured.

Absalom happened to meet the servants of David. Absalom was riding on his mule, and the mule went under the thick boughs of a great oak, and his head caught hold of the oak, and he was taken up between the sky and earth; and the mule that was under him went on. A certain man saw it, and told Joab, and said, "Behold, I saw Absalom hanging in an oak."

Joab said to the man who told him, "Behold, you saw it, and why didn't you strike him there to the ground? I would have given you ten pieces of silver, and a sash."

The man said to Joab, "Though I should receive a thousand pieces of silver in my hand, I still wouldn't put forth my hand against the king's son; for in our hearing the king commanded you and Abishai and Ittai, saying, 'Beware that none touch the young man Absalom.' Otherwise if I had dealt falsely against his life (and there is no matter hidden from the king), then you yourself would have set yourself against me."

Then Joab said, "I'm not going to wait like this with you." He took three darts in his hand, and thrust them through the heart of Absalom, while he was yet alive in the midst of the oak. Ten young men who bore Joab's armor surrounded and struck Absalom, and killed him. Joab blew the trumpet, and the people returned from pursuing after Israel; for Joab held back the people. They took Absalom, and cast him into the great pit in the forest, and raised over him a very great heap of stones. Then all Israel fled everyone to his tent. Now Absalom in his lifetime had taken and reared up for himself the pillar, which is in the king's dale; for he said, "I have no son to keep my name in memory." He called the pillar after his own name; and it is called Absalom's monument, to this day.

Then Joab said to the Cushite, "Go, tell the king what you have seen!" The Cushite bowed himself to Joab, and ran.

Behold, the Cushite came. The Cushite said, "News for my lord the king; for Yahweh has avenged you this day of all those who rose up against you."

The king said to the Cushite, "Is it well with the young man Absalom?"

The Cushite answered, "May the enemies of my lord the king, and all who rise up against you to do you harm, be as that young man is."

The king was much moved, and went up to the room over the gate, and wept. As he went, he said, "My son Absalom! My son, my son Absalom! I wish I had died for you, Absalom, my son, my son!"

It was told Joab, "Behold, the king weeps and mourns for Absalom." The victory that day was turned into mourning to all the people; for the people heard it said that day, "The king grieves for his son."

The people sneaked into the city that day, as people who are ashamed steal away when they flee in battle. The king covered his face, and the king cried with a loud voice, "My son Absalom, Absalom, my son, my son!"

David was protected by a band of "mighty men," who were given special fighting skills by God for the purpose of fighting for Israel and fully establishing the nation. These men performed many amazing feats on the battlefield.

These are the names of the mighty men whom David had: Josheb Basshebeth a Tahchemonite, chief of the captains; the same was Adino the Eznite, against eight hundred slain at one time. After him was Eleazar the son of Dodai the son of an Ahohite, one of the three mighty men with David, when they defied the Philistines who were there gathered together to battle, and the men of Israel were gone away. He arose, and struck the Philistines until his hand was weary, and his hand froze to the sword; and Yahweh worked a great victory that day; and the people returned after him only to take spoil. After him was Shammah the son of Agee a Hararite. The Philistines were gathered together into a troop, where there was a plot of ground full of lentils; and the people fled from the Philistines. But he stood in the midst of the plot, and defended it, and killed the Philistines; and Yahweh worked a great victory. Three of the thirty chief men went down, and came to David in the harvest time to the cave of Adullam; and the troop of the Philistines was encamped in the valley of Rephaim. David was then in the stronghold; and the garrison of the Philistines was then in Bethlehem. David longed, and said, "Oh that one would give me water to drink of the well of Bethlehem, which is by the gate!"

The three mighty men broke through the army of the Philistines, and drew water out of the well of Bethlehem, that was by the gate, and took it, and brought it to David: but he would not drink of it, but poured it out to Yahweh. He said, "Be it far from me, Yahweh, that I should do this! Isn't it the blood of the men who went in jeopardy of their lives?" Therefore he would not drink it. The three mighty men did these things. Abishai, the brother of Joab, the son of Zeruiah, was chief of the three. He lifted up his spear against three hundred and killed them, and had a name among the three. Wasn't he most honorable of the three? therefore he was made their captain: however he didn't attain to the three. Benaiah the son of Jehoiada, the son of a valiant man of Kabzeel, who had done mighty deeds, he killed the two sons of Ariel of Moab: he went down also and killed a lion in the midst of a pit in time of snow. He killed an Egyptian, a goodly man: and the Egyptian had a spear in his hand; but he went down to him with a staff, and plucked the spear out of the Egyptian's hand, and killed him with his own spear.

After the death of Absalom, David decided to number the fighting men of Israel (the northern kingdom) and Judah (the southern kingdom). Joab advised David against this, as this was a means of placing his trust in the number of fighting men under his command, instead of trusting God. The king, who as a young boy had killed the giant Goliath, and who had seen God's miraculous support in times of battle, had seemingly forgotten God's ability to protect and support his chosen people. The king's word prevailed, and after nearly 10 months, Joab came back with his report. But the people paid a high price for David's insolence.

Joab gave up the sum of the numbering of the people to the king: and there were in Israel eight hundred thousand valiant men who drew the sword; and the men of Judah were five hundred thousand men. David's heart struck him after that he had numbered the people. David said to Yahweh, "I have sinned greatly in that which I have done. But now, Yahweh, put away, I beg you, the iniquity of your servant; for I have done very foolishly."

When David rose up in the morning, the word of Yahweh came to the prophet Gad, David's seer, saying, "Go and speak to David, 'Thus says Yahweh, "I offer you three things. Choose one of them, that I may do it to you."

So Gad came to David, and told him, and said to him, "Shall seven years of famine come to you in your land? Or will you flee three months before your foes while they pursue you? Or shall there be three days' pestilence in your land? Now answer, and consider what answer I shall return to him who sent me."

David said to Gad, "I am in distress. Let us fall now into the hand of Yahweh; for his mercies are great. Let me not fall into the hand of man."

So Yahweh sent a pestilence on Israel from the morning even to the appointed time; and there died of the people from Dan even to Beersheba seventy thousand men. When the angel stretched out his hand toward Jerusalem to destroy it, Yahweh relented of the disaster, and said to the angel who destroyed the people, "It is enough. Now stay your hand." The angel of Yahweh was by the threshing floor of Araunah the Jebusite.

David spoke to Yahweh when he saw the angel who struck the people, and said, "Behold, I have sinned, and I have done perversely; but these sheep, what have they done? Please let your hand be against me, and against my father's house."

Gad came that day to David, and said to him, "Go up, build an altar to Yahweh on the threshing floor of Araunah the Jebusite."

David built an altar to Yahweh there, and offered burnt offerings and peace offerings. So Yahweh was entreated for the land, and the plague was stayed from Israel.

15 THE PSALMS

Poetic Beauty to Glorify God and Soothe the Soul

The psalms are a much beloved collection of songs and prayers, written in Old Testament times. Of the 150 psalms in the Bible, slightly more than half are ascribed to King David. The rest are written by a broad range of known and unknown writers, over a span of centuries.

The psalms cover the range of human emotion; from thanksgiving to lament, from happiness to sorrow, and from songs written to glorify God to those asking for forgiveness. These writers often seek help in understanding deep sorrow and at times even seem to question God on matters of concern. They are written from the concept of humans who struggle with emotion and faith, which is part of what makes them so relevant to believers today.

Many psalms of lament cry out to God for understanding. They often begin with the question "Why?" and end with an affirmation of faith in God even in the midst of pain and sorrow.

Another broad category of hymns are psalms of praise, glorifying God for his majesty and his love. And psalms of thanksgiving express thankfulness to God for his blessings, often in response to some situation or circumstance in which the working of God is evident. Thirteen of the psalms refer to a specific event in the life of David, for example.

A small group of key psalms has been selected, to give the reader a feel for the breadth and majesty of this inspired poetic literature. We encourage the reader to read and come to know all of the psalms in the Bible.

Psalm 1

The first psalm is a song of encouragement in righteousness. Here, blessings are predicted for the man or woman who chooses the path of righteousness, and the ultimate punishment of the wicked is forecast as is the blowing away of chaff by the wind. This is contrasted to the righteous, who are "planted" like a tree by streams of water.

Blessed is the man who doesn't walk in the counsel of the wicked, nor stand in the way of sinners, nor sit in the seat of scoffers;

but his delight is in Yahweh's law. On his law he meditates day and night.

He will be like a tree planted by the streams of water, that brings forth its fruit in its season, whose leaf also does not wither. Whatever he does shall prosper.

The wicked are not so, but are like the chaff which the wind drives away.

Therefore the wicked shall not stand in the judgment, nor sinners in the congregation of the righteous.

For Yahweh knows the way of the righteous, but the way of the wicked shall perish.

Psalm 2

Many of the psalms contain prophesies about the coming of the Messiah. Here, scholars point to "the Anointed" and "the Son" as referring to the Christ, who will be established "on Zion," despite the evil intentions of the rulers and kings of the earth.

Why do the nations rage, and the peoples plot a vain thing?

The kings of the earth take a stand, and the rulers take counsel together, against Yahweh, and against his Anointed, saying,

"Let's break their bonds apart, and cast their cords from us."

He who sits in the heavens will laugh. The Lord will have them in derision.

Then he will speak to them in his anger, and terrify them in his wrath:

"Yet I have set my King on my holy hill of Zion."

I will tell of the decree. Yahweh said to me, "You are my son. Today I have become your father.

Ask of me, and I will give the nations for your inheritance, the uttermost parts of the earth for your possession.

You shall break them with a rod of iron. You shall dash them in pieces like a potter's vessel."

Now therefore be wise, you kings. Be instructed, you judges of the earth.

Serve Yahweh with fear, and rejoice with trembling.

Give sincere homage to the Son, lest he be angry, and you perish in the way, for his wrath will soon be kindled. Blessed are all those who take refuge in him.

Psalm 19

For the Chief Musician. A Psalm by David.

The heavens declare the glory of God. The expanse shows his handiwork.

Day after day they pour forth speech, and night after night they display knowledge.

There is no speech nor language, where their voice is not heard.

Their voice has gone out through all the earth, their words to the end of the world. In them he has set a tent for the sun,

which is as a bridegroom coming out of his room, like a strong man rejoicing to run his course.

His going forth is from the end of the heavens, his circuit to its ends; There·is nothing hidden from its heat.

In poetic form, this psalm switches from a description of the glory of the creation to a discourse of the greatness of God's law. In the face of that greatness, the believer is inspired to be upright, blameless and·innocent. God becomes his rock and his redeemer.

Yahweh's law is perfect, restoring the soul. Yahweh's testimony is sure, making wise the simple.

Yahweh's precepts are right, rejoicing the heart. Yahweh's commandment is pure, enlightening the eyes.

The fear of Yahweh is clean, enduring forever. Yahweh's ordinances are true, and righteous altogether.

More to be desired are they than gold, yes, than much fine gold; sweeter also than honey and the extract of the honeycomb.

Moreover by them is your servant warned. In keeping them there is great reward.

Who can discern his errors? Forgive me from hidden errors.

Keep back your servant also from presumptuous sins. Let them not have dominion over me. Then I will be upright. I will be blameless and innocent of great transgression.

Let the words of my mouth and the meditation of my heart be acceptable in your sight, Yahweh, my rock, and my redeemer.

Psalm 22

Many of the psalms contain notations to help the musical directors in worship; this one gives the name of a song by which it was to be sung.

The first sentence of this psalm was quoted by Jesus, and were his last words on the cross. This psalm may have been on the Savior's mind at that time, due to prophesies it contained about the suffering of the Messiah. Among these amazing prophesies, which were fulfilled at the crucifixion of Jesus, were that he would be surrounded by enemies, that his clothing would be divided up by lots, that his hands and feet would be pierced, and that his bones would not be broken ("I can count all my bones...")

In the pattern of many psalms, it starts with phrases of deep lament, then transitions into great joy and trust in God.

For the Chief Musician; set to "The Doe of the Morning." A Psalm by David.

My God, my God, why have you forsaken me? Why are you so far from helping me, and from the words of my groaning?

My God, I cry in the daytime, but you don't answer; in the night season, and am not silent.

But you are holy, you who inhabit the praises of Israel.

Our fathers trusted in you. They trusted, and you delivered them.

They cried to you, and were delivered. They trusted in you, and were not disappointed.

But I am a worm, and no man; a reproach of men, and despised by the people.

All those who see me mock me. They insult me with their lips. They shake their heads, saying,

"He trusts in Yahweh; let him deliver him. Let him rescue him, since he delights in him."

But you brought me out of the womb. You made me trust at my mother's breasts.

I was thrown on you from my mother's womb. You are my God since my mother bore me.

Don't be far from me, for trouble is near. For there is none to help.

Many bulls have surrounded me. Strong bulls of Bashan have encircled me.

They open their mouths wide against me, lions tearing prey and roaring.

I am poured out like water. All my bones are out of joint. My heart is like wax; it is melted within me.

My strength is dried up like a potsherd. My tongue sticks to the roof of my mouth. You have brought me into the dust of death.

For dogs have surrounded me. A company of evildoers have enclosed me. They have pierced my hands and feet.

I can count all of my bones. They look and stare at me.

They divide my garments among them. They cast lots for my clothing.

But don't be far off, Yahweh. You are my help: hurry to help me.

Deliver my soul from the sword, my precious life from the power of the dog.

Save me from the lion's mouth! Yes, from the horns of the wild oxen, you have answered me.

I will declare your name to my brothers. In the midst of the assembly, I will praise you.

You who fear Yahweh, praise him! All you descendants of Jacob, glorify him! Stand in awe of him, all you descendants of Israel!

For he has not despised nor abhorred the affliction of the afflicted, Neither has he hidden his face from him; but when he cried to him, he heard.

Of you comes my praise in the great assembly. I will pay my vows before those who fear him.

The humble shall eat and be satisfied. They shall praise Yahweh who seek after him. Let your hearts live forever.

All the ends of the earth shall remember and turn to Yahweh. All the relatives of the nations shall worship before you.

For the kingdom is Yahweh's. He is the ruler over the nations.

All the rich ones of the earth shall eat and worship. All those who go down to the dust shall bow before him, even he who can't keep his soul alive.

Posterity shall serve him. Future generations shall be told about the Lord.

They shall come and shall declare his righteousness to a people that shall be born, for he has done it.

Psalm 23

The Twenty Third Psalm is perhaps the most popular and beloved of all of the psalms. Over thousands of years, countless people have been comforted by its words in times of sorrow, such as during the death of a loved one.

David, who as a young man worked as a shepherd, could relate to outdoor scenes and the trust of sheep in the care and love of the shepherd. Here, David likens God to our shepherd, who watches over us and cares for us even in the deep valleys of despair and death. Stay with God, and your table will be spread, your cup will run over, and you will dwell with God forever.

A Psalm by David.

Yahweh is my shepherd: I shall lack nothing.

He makes me lie down in green pastures. He leads me beside still waters.

He restores my soul. He guides me in the paths of righteousness for his name's sake.

Even though I walk through the valley of the shadow of death, I will fear no evil, for you are with me. Your rod and your staff, they comfort me.

You prepare a table before me in the presence of my enemies. You anoint my head with oil. My cup runs over.

Surely goodness and loving kindness shall follow me all the days of my life, and I will dwell in Yahweh's house forever.

Psalm 27

David was no stranger to distress. At many points in his life, he was pursued by armies, kings, and traitors, even among his own family. He knew what it felt like to have an army of superior force camped against him, with no hope of delivery except through faith in God.

Even in times like this, when most generals would be focusing on strategy and numbers, David focused on God. Ultimately, he had faith that God would protect and deliver him from his enemies, even if his own mother and father forsook him. In times like these, David advises us to wait for God.

By David.

Yahweh is my light and my salvation. Whom shall I fear? Yahweh is the strength of my life. Of whom shall I be afraid?

When evildoers came at me to eat up my flesh, even my adversaries and my foes, they stumbled and fell.

Though an army should encamp against me, my heart shall not fear. Though war should rise against me, even then I will be confident.

One thing I have asked of Yahweh, that I will seek after, that I may dwell in the house of Yahweh all the days of my life, to see Yahweh's beauty, and to inquire in his temple.

For in the day of trouble he will keep me secretly in his pavilion. In the covert of his tabernacle he will hide me. He will lift me up on a rock.

Now my head will be lifted up above my enemies around me.

I will offer sacrifices of joy in his tent. I will sing, yes, I will sing praises to Yahweh.

Hear, Yahweh, when I cry with my voice. Have mercy also on me, and answer me. When you said, "Seek my face," my heart said to you, "I will seek your face, Yahweh."

Don't hide your face from me. Don't put your servant away in anger. You have been my help. Don't abandon me, neither forsake me, God of my salvation.

When my father and my mother forsake me, then Yahweh will take me up.

Teach me your way, Yahweh. Lead me in a straight path, because of my enemies.

Don't deliver me over to the desire of my adversaries, for false witnesses have risen up against me, such as breathe out cruelty.

I am still confident of this: I will see the goodness of Yahweh in the land of the living.

Wait for Yahweh. Be strong, and let your heart take courage. Yes, wait for Yahweh.

Psalm 51

In today's society, politicians are very slow to admit guilt. But this psalm, written by David after his sinful adultery with Bathsheba and his arranged murder of her husband, shows King David in sincere repentance. Rather than hiding what he did, David brought it out into the open, even publishing this psalm of repentance publicly.

David acknowledges that he has sinned against God himself - and expresses confidence that despite the terrible nature of this sin, God would be able to cleanse him and forgive. In meditating on this psalm today, we can take comfort that God has the power to forgive us, no matter how deep our own transgressions.

In the end, David acknowledges what God really desires - "The sacrifices of God are a broken spirit. A broken and contrite heart..."

For the Chief Musician. A Psalm by David, when Nathan the prophet came to him, after he had gone in to Bathsheba.

Have mercy on me, God, according to your loving kindness. According to the multitude of your tender mercies, blot out my transgressions.

Wash me thoroughly from my iniquity. Cleanse me from my sin.

For I know my transgressions. My sin is constantly before me.

Against you, and you only, have I sinned, and done that which is evil in your sight; that you may be proved right when you speak, and justified when you judge.

Behold, I was brought forth in iniquity. In sin my mother conceived me.

Behold, you desire truth in the inward parts. You teach me wisdom in the inmost place.

Purify me with hyssop, and I will be clean. Wash me, and I will be whiter than snow.

Let me hear joy and gladness, That the bones which you have broken may rejoice.

Hide your face from my sins, and blot out all of my iniquities.

Create in me a clean heart, O God. Renew a right spirit within me.

Don't throw me from your presence, and don't take your holy Spirit from

me.

Restore to me the joy of your salvation. Uphold me with a willing spirit.

Then I will teach transgressors your ways. Sinners shall be converted to you.

Deliver me from bloodguiltiness, O God, the God of my salvation. My tongue shall sing aloud of your righteousness.

Lord, open my lips. My mouth shall declare your praise.

For you don't delight in sacrifice, or else I would give it. You have no pleasure in burnt offering.

The sacrifices of God are a broken spirit. A broken and contrite heart, O God, you will not despise.

Do well in your good pleasure to Zion. Build the walls of Jerusalem.

Then you will delight in the sacrifices of righteousness, in burnt offerings and in whole burnt offerings. Then they will offer bulls on your altar.

Psalm 84

This psalm begins by singing the praises of the temple. Recognized as the spiritual house of God on earth, and the center of Jewish religious identity, the psalmist expresses a deep appreciation of the time he can spend there, feeling close to God. Moving his prose away from the temple courts, the writer confirms the blessings to be found by all who have a relationship with God.

For the Chief Musician. On an instrument of Gath. A Psalm by the sons of Korah.

How lovely are your dwellings, Yahweh of Armies!

My soul longs, and even faints for the courts of Yahweh. My heart and my flesh cry out for the living God.

Yes, the sparrow has found a home, and the swallow a nest for herself, where she may have her young, near your altars, Yahweh of Armies, my King, and my God.

Blessed are those who dwell in your house. They are always praising you.

Selah.

Blessed are those whose strength is in you; who have set their hearts on a pilgrimage.

Passing through the valley of Weeping, they make it a place of springs. Yes, the autumn rain covers it with blessings.

They go from strength to strength. Everyone of them appears before God in Zion.

Yahweh, God of Armies, hear my prayer. Listen, God of Jacob. Selah.

Behold, God our shield, look at the face of your anointed.

For a day in your courts is better than a thousand.

I would rather be a doorkeeper in the house of my God, than to dwell in the tents of wickedness.

For Yahweh God is a sun and a shield. Yahweh will give grace and glory. He withholds no good thing from those who walk blamelessly.

Yahweh of Armies, blessed is the man who trusts in you.

Psalm 90

This psalm, written by Moses, asks for wisdom, compassion, and kindness from God, so that the work of our short days may be used wisely for great benefit.

A Prayer by Moses, the man of God.

Lord, you have been our dwelling place for all generations.

Before the mountains were brought forth, before you had formed the earth and the world, even from everlasting to everlasting, you are God.

You turn man to destruction, saying, "Return, you children of men."

For a thousand years in your sight are just like yesterday when it is past, like a watch in the night.

You sweep them away as they sleep. In the morning they sprout like new grass.

In the morning it sprouts and springs up. By evening, it is withered and dry.

For we are consumed in your anger. We are troubled in your wrath.

You have set our iniquities before you, our secret sins in the light of your presence.

For all our days have passed away in your wrath. We bring our years to an end as a sigh.

The days of our years are seventy, or even by reason of strength eighty years; yet their pride is but labor and sorrow, for it passes quickly, and we fly away.

Who knows the power of your anger, your wrath according to the fear that is due to you?

So teach us to number our days, that we may gain a heart of wisdom.

Relent, Yahweh! How long? Have compassion on your servants!

Satisfy us in the morning with your loving kindness, that we may rejoice and be glad all our days.

Make us glad for as many days as you have afflicted us, for as many years as we have seen evil.

Let your work appear to your servants; your glory to their children.

Let the favor of the Lord our God be on us; establish the work of our hands for us; yes, establish the work of our hands.

Psalm 103

This psalm praises the goodness of God. Despite their history of turning away from God, the Israelites received great benefits when they turned back to Him. This psalm goes over some of that tumultuous history, and, in the end, confirms the loving kindness of the everlasting Creator. The psalm concludes by confirming that God gives us much more than what we deserve.

By David.
Praise Yahweh, my soul! All that is within me, praise his holy name!
Praise Yahweh, my soul, and don't forget all his benefits;
who forgives all your sins; who heals all your diseases;
who redeems your life from destruction; who crowns you with loving kindness and tender mercies;
who satisfies your desire with good things, so that your youth is renewed like the eagle's.
Yahweh executes righteous acts, and justice for all who are oppressed.
He made known his ways to Moses, his deeds to the children of Israel.
Yahweh is merciful and gracious, slow to anger, and abundant in loving kindness.
He will not always accuse; neither will he stay angry forever.
He has not dealt with us according to our sins, nor repaid us for our iniquities.
For as the heavens are high above the earth, so great is his loving kindness toward those who fear him.
As far as the east is from the west, so far has he removed our transgressions from us.
Like a father has compassion on his children, so Yahweh has compassion on those who fear him.
For he knows how we are made. He remembers that we are dust.
As for man, his days are like grass. As a flower of the field, so he flourishes.
For the wind passes over it, and it is gone. Its place remembers it no more.
But Yahweh's loving kindness is from everlasting to everlasting with those who fear him, his righteousness to children's children;
to those who keep his covenant, to those who remember to obey his precepts.

Yahweh has established his throne in the heavens. His kingdom rules over all.

Praise Yahweh, you angels of his, who are mighty in strength, who fulfill his word, obeying the voice of his word.

Praise Yahweh, all you armies of his, you servants of his, who do his pleasure.

Praise Yahweh, all you works of his, in all places of his dominion. Praise Yahweh, my soul!

Psalm 139

This next psalm confirms that God knows us completely - our comings and goings, and our innermost thoughts. God was involved when we were "knit together" in our mother's womb, and there is no place we can go to escape his presence.

The psalmist confirms that compared to our ways, the ways of God are infinitely greater. He is to be praised for this greatness. Indeed, we are to seek after the God who knows our very hearts.

For the Chief Musician. A Psalm by David.

Yahweh, you have searched me, and you know me.

You know my sitting down and my rising up. You perceive my thoughts from afar. You search out my path and my lying down, and are acquainted with all my ways.

For there is not a word on my tongue, but, behold, Yahweh, you know it altogether.

You hem me in behind and before. You laid your hand on me.

This knowledge is beyond me. It's lofty. I can't attain it.

Where could I go from your Spirit? Or where could I flee from your presence?

If I ascend up into heaven, you are there. If I make my bed in Sheol, behold, you are there!

If I take the wings of the dawn, and settle in the uttermost parts of the sea;

Even there your hand will lead me, and your right hand will hold me.

If I say, "Surely the darkness will overwhelm me; the light around me will be night";

even the darkness doesn't hide from you, but the night shines as the day. The darkness is like light to you.

For you formed my inmost being. You knit me together in my mother's womb.

I will give thanks to you, for I am fearfully and wonderfully made. Your works are wonderful. My soul knows that very well.

My frame wasn't hidden from you, when I was made in secret, woven together in the depths of the earth.

Your eyes saw my body. In your book they were all written, the days that were ordained for me, when as yet there were none of them.

How precious to me are your thoughts, God! How vast is their sum!

If I would count them, they are more in number than the sand. When I wake up, I am still with you.

If only you, God, would kill the wicked. Get away from me, you bloodthirsty men! For they speak against you wickedly. Your enemies take your name in vain.

Yahweh, don't I hate those who hate you? Am I not grieved with those who rise up against you?

I hate them with perfect hatred. They have become my enemies.

Search me, God, and know my heart. Try me, and know my thoughts.

See if there is any wicked way in me, and lead me in the everlasting way.

16 WISDOM AND PROSPERITY

Prospering Under a New King

As David grew old in years, his oldest son, Adonijah, gathered supporters and announced himself to be king, even though David's intention was for his son Solomon to succeed his kingship. Thus, Adonijah rose up against David, an evil act against his still-living father.

Adonijah was supported by Joab, the captain of the army of Israel, and Abiathar the priest. These men had followed David from the beginning, so their defection was especially troubling. To counteract this, David was convinced to proclaim Solomon as his rightful heir, even before his death.

Now king David was old and stricken in years; and they covered him with clothes, but he couldn't keep warm.

Then Adonijah the son of Haggith exalted himself, saying, "I will be king." Then he prepared him chariots and horsemen, and fifty men to run before him. His father had not displeased him at any time in saying, "Why have you done so?" and he was also a very handsome man; and he was born after Absalom. He conferred with Joab the son of Zeruiah, and with Abiathar the priest: and they following Adonijah helped him.

Then Nathan spoke to Bathsheba the mother of Solomon, saying, "Haven't you heard that Adonijah the son of Haggith reigns, and David our lord doesn't know it? Now therefore come, please let me give you counsel, that you may save your own life, and the life of your son Solomon. Go in to king David, and tell him, 'Didn't you, my lord, king, swear to your handmaid, saying, Assuredly Solomon your son shall reign after me, and he shall sit on my throne? Why then does Adonijah reign?' Behold, while you yet talk there with the king, I also will come in after you, and confirm your words."

Bathsheba went in to the king into the room. The king was very old; and Abishag the Shunammite was ministering to the king. Bathsheba bowed, and showed respect to the king. The king said, "What would you like?" She said to him, "My lord, you swore by Yahweh your God to your handmaid, 'Assuredly Solomon your son shall reign after me, and he shall sit on my throne.'

The king swore, and said, "As Yahweh lives, who has redeemed my soul out of all adversity, most certainly as I swore to you by Yahweh, the God of Israel, saying, 'Assuredly Solomon your son shall reign after me, and he shall sit on my throne in my place;' most certainly so will I do this day."

Then Bathsheba bowed with her face to the earth, and showed respect to the king, and said, "Let my lord king David live forever!"

So Zadok the priest, and Nathan the prophet, and Benaiah the son of Jehoiada, and the Cherethites and the Pelethites, went down, and caused Solomon to ride on king David's mule, and brought him to Gihon. Zadok the priest took the horn of oil out of the Tent, and anointed Solomon. They blew the trumpet; and all the people said, "Long live king Solomon!"

All the people came up after him, and the people piped with pipes, and rejoiced with great joy, so that the earth shook with their sound.

Now the days of David drew near that he should die; and he commanded Solomon his son, saying, "I am going the way of all the earth. You be strong therefore, and show yourself a man; and keep the instruction of Yahweh your God, to walk in his ways, to keep his statutes, his commandments, his ordinances, and his testimonies, according to that which is written in the law of Moses, that you may prosper in all that you do, and wherever you turn yourself. That Yahweh may establish his word which he spoke concerning me, saying, 'If your children take heed to their way, to walk before me in truth with all their heart and with all their soul, there shall not fail you,' he said, 'a man on the throne of Israel.'

David slept with his fathers, and was buried in the city of David. The days that David reigned over Israel were forty years; he reigned seven years in Hebron, and he reigned thirty-three years in Jerusalem. Solomon sat on the throne of David his father; and his kingdom was firmly established.

David chose well in naming Solomon as his heir. Under the leadership of Solomon, the nation of Israel prospered. In terms of wisdom, stability, and wealth, he was one of the greatest kings who ever lived. He walked in the ways of God, and God blessed him greatly. As evidence of his wisdom, when he was offered anything he wanted by God, he asked for knowledge. Because he made this wise choice, God blessed him with both wisdom and wealth. This wisdom was evident in his judgment over his people, as well as in his teachings, such as the many proverbs that he wrote.

Solomon made affinity with Pharaoh king of Egypt, and took Pharaoh's daughter, and brought her into the city of David, until he had made an end of building his own house, and the house of Yahweh, and the wall of Jerusalem all around. Only the people sacrificed in the high places, because there was no house built for the name of Yahweh until those days. Solomon loved Yahweh, walking in the statutes of David his father: only he sacrificed and burnt incense in the high places. The king went to Gibeon to sacrifice there; for that was the great high place. Solomon offered a thousand burnt offerings on that altar. In Gibeon Yahweh appeared to Solomon in a dream by night; and God said, "Ask what I shall give you."

Solomon said, "You have shown to your servant David my father great loving kindness, according as he walked before you in truth, and in righteousness, and in uprightness of heart with you. You have kept for him this great loving kindness, that you have given him a son to sit on his throne, as it is this day. Now, Yahweh my God, you have made your servant king instead of David my father. I am but a little child. I don't know how to go out or come in. Your servant is in the midst of your people which you have chosen, a great people, that can't be numbered nor counted for multitude. Give your servant therefore an understanding heart to judge your people, that I may discern between good and evil; for who is able to judge this your great people?"

The speech pleased the Lord, that Solomon had asked this thing. God said to him, "Because you have asked this thing, and have not asked for yourself long life, neither have asked riches for yourself, nor have asked the life of your enemies, but have asked for yourself understanding to discern justice; behold, I have done according to your word. Behold, I have given you a wise and an understanding heart; so that there has been none like you before you, neither after you shall any arise like you. I have also given you that which you have not asked, both riches and honor, so that there shall not be any among the kings like you, all your days. If you will walk in my ways, to keep my statutes and my commandments, as your father David walked, then I will lengthen your days."

Solomon awoke; and behold, it was a dream. Then he came to Jerusalem, and stood before the ark of the covenant of Yahweh, and offered up burnt offerings, offered peace offerings, and made a feast to all his servants.

Then two women who were prostitutes came to the king, and stood before him. The one woman said, "Oh, my lord, I and this woman dwell in one house. I delivered a child with her in the house. It happened the third day after I delivered, that this woman delivered also. We were together. There was no stranger with us in the house, just us two in the house. This woman's child died in the night, because she lay on it. She arose at midnight, and took my son from beside me, while your handmaid slept, and laid it in her bosom, and laid her dead child in my bosom. When I rose in the morning to nurse my child, behold, it was dead; but when I had looked at it in the morning, behold, it was not my son, whom I bore."

The other woman said, "No; but the living is my son, and the dead is your son."

This said, "No; but the dead is your son, and the living is my son." Thus they spoke before the king.

Then the king said, "The one says, 'This is my son who lives, and your son is the dead;' and the other says, 'No; but your son is the dead one, and my son is the living one.'" The king said, "Get me a sword." They brought a sword before the king. The king said, "Divide the living child in two, and give half to the one, and half to the other."

Then the woman whose the living child was spoke to the king, for her heart yearned over her son, and she said, "Oh, my lord, give her the living child, and in no way kill it!"

But the other said, "It shall be neither mine nor yours. Divide it."

Then the king answered, "Give her the living child, and in no way kill it. She is its mother."

All Israel heard of the judgment which the king had judged; and they feared the king: for they saw that the wisdom of God was in him, to do justice.

Judah and Israel were many as the sand which is by the sea in multitude, eating and drinking and making merry. Solomon ruled over all the kingdoms from the River to the land of the Philistines, and to the border of Egypt: they brought tribute, and served Solomon all the days of his life. Solomon's provision for one day was thirty measures of fine flour, and sixty measures of meal, ten head of fat cattle, and twenty head of cattle out of the pastures, and one hundred sheep, besides harts, and gazelles, and roebucks, and fattened fowl. For he had dominion over all on this side the River, from Tiphsah even to Gaza, over all the kings on this side the River: and he had peace on all sides around him. Judah and Israel lived safely, every man under his vine and under his fig tree, from Dan even to Beersheba, all the days of Solomon. Solomon had forty thousand stalls of horses for his chariots, and twelve thousand horsemen. Those officers provided food for king Solomon, and for all who came to king Solomon's table, every man in his month; they let nothing be lacking. Barley also and straw for the horses and swift steeds brought they to the place where the officers were, every man according to his duty. God gave Solomon wisdom and understanding exceeding much, and very great understanding, even as the sand that is on the seashore. Solomon's wisdom excelled the wisdom of all the children of the east, and all the wisdom of Egypt. For he was wiser than all men; than Ethan the Ezrahite, and Heman, and Calcol, and Darda, the sons of Mahol: and his fame was in all the nations all around. He spoke three thousand proverbs; and his songs were one thousand five. He spoke of trees, from the cedar that is in Lebanon even to the hyssop that springs out of the wall; he spoke also of animals, and of birds, and of creeping things, and of fish. There came of all peoples to hear the wisdom of Solomon, from all kings of the earth, who had heard of his wisdom.

Hiram king of Tyre sent his servants to Solomon; for he had heard that they had anointed him king in the place of his father: for Hiram was ever a lover of David. Solomon sent to Hiram, saying, "You know how that David my father could not build a house for the name of Yahweh his God for the wars which were about him on every side, until Yahweh put them under the soles of his feet. But now Yahweh my God has given me rest on every side. There is neither adversary, nor evil occurrence. Behold, I purpose to build a house for the name of Yahweh my God, as Yahweh spoke to David my father, saying, 'Your son, whom I will set on your throne in your place, he shall build the house for my name.' Now therefore command that they cut me cedar trees out of Lebanon. My servants shall be with your servants; and I will give you wages for your servants according to all that you shall say. For you know that there is not among us any who knows how to cut timber like the Sidonians."

It happened, when Hiram heard the words of Solomon, that he rejoiced greatly, and said, "Blessed is Yahweh this day, who has given to David a wise son over this great people." Hiram sent to Solomon, saying, "I have heard the message which you have sent to me. I will do all your desire concerning timber of cedar, and concerning timber of fir. My servants shall bring them down from Lebanon to the sea. I will make them into rafts to go by sea to the place that you shall appoint me, and will cause them to be broken up there, and you shall receive them. You shall accomplish my desire, in giving food for my household."

So Hiram gave Solomon timber of cedar and timber of fir according to all his desire. Solomon gave Hiram twenty thousand measures of wheat for food to his household, and twenty measures of pure oil. Solomon gave this to Hiram year by year. Yahweh gave Solomon wisdom, as he promised him; and there was peace between Hiram and Solomon; and they two made a treaty together.

With peace on every side, and great wealth rolling into the country, Solomon decided the time was right to begin building the temple. His father, David, had longed to build a permanent house for God, but God denied him this right because he was a king of war. Before David's death, preparations had been made - now Solomon started the massive task of building

171

this great structure.

It happened in the four hundred and eightieth year after the children of Israel had come out of the land of Egypt, in the fourth year of Solomon's reign over Israel, in the month Ziv, which is the second month, that he began to build the house of Yahweh.

The word of Yahweh came to Solomon, saying, "Concerning this house which you are building, if you will walk in my statutes, and execute my ordinances, and keep all my commandments to walk in them; then will I establish my word with you, which I spoke to David your father. I will dwell among the children of Israel, and will not forsake my people Israel."

Thus all the work that king Solomon worked in the house of Yahweh was finished. Solomon brought in the things which David his father had dedicated, the silver, and the gold, and the vessels, and put them in the treasuries of the house of Yahweh.

No expense was spared in building the temple. Thousands upon thousands of laborers worked in stonework, gold work, and timbers. The best craftsmen and artists were summoned to dedicate their work to making the temple a marvelous home for God. When the temple was completed, a great ceremony was called to dedicate it to the Lord.

Then Solomon assembled the elders of Israel, and all the heads of the tribes, the princes of the fathers' households of the children of Israel, to king Solomon in Jerusalem, to bring up the ark of the covenant of Yahweh out of the city of David, which is Zion. All the men of Israel assembled themselves to king Solomon at the feast, in the month Ethanim, which is the seventh month. All the elders of Israel came, and the priests took up the ark. They brought up the ark of Yahweh, and the Tent of Meeting, and all the holy vessels that were in the Tent; even these the priests and the Levites brought up. King Solomon and all the congregation of Israel, who were assembled to him, were with him before the ark, sacrificing sheep and cattle, that could not be counted nor numbered for multitude. The priests brought in the ark of the covenant of Yahweh to its place, into the oracle of the house, to the most holy place, even under the wings of the cherubim.

It came to pass, when the priests had come out of the holy place, that the cloud filled the house of Yahweh, so that the priests could not stand to minister by reason of the cloud; for the glory of Yahweh filled the house of Yahweh. Then Solomon said, "Yahweh has said that he would dwell in the thick darkness.

I have surely built you a house of habitation, a place for you to dwell in forever."

Solomon stood before the altar of Yahweh in the presence of all the assembly of Israel, and spread forth his hands toward heaven; and he said, "Yahweh, the God of Israel, there is no God like you, in heaven above, or on earth beneath; who keep covenant and loving kindness with your servants, who walk before you with all their heart; who have kept with your servant David my father that which you promised him.

"Now therefore, God of Israel, please let your word be verified, which you spoke to your servant David my father. But will God in very deed dwell on the earth? Behold, heaven and the heaven of heavens can't contain you; how much less this house that I have built! Yet have respect for the prayer of your servant, and for his supplication, Yahweh my God, to listen to the cry and to the prayer which your servant prays before you this day; that your eyes may be open toward this house night and day, even toward the place of which you have said, 'My name shall be there;' to listen to the prayer which your servant shall pray toward this place. Listen to the supplication of your servant, and of your people Israel, when they shall pray toward this place. Yes, hear in heaven, your dwelling place; and when you hear, forgive.

It was so, that when Solomon had made an end of praying all this prayer and supplication to Yahweh, he arose from before the altar of Yahweh, from kneeling on his knees with his hands spread forth toward heaven. He stood, and blessed all the assembly of Israel with a loud voice, saying, "Blessed be Yahweh, who has given rest to his people Israel, according to all that he promised. There has not failed one word of all his good promise, which he promised by Moses his servant. May Yahweh our God be with us, as he was with our fathers. Let him not leave us, nor forsake us; that he may incline our hearts to him, to walk in all his ways, and to keep his commandments, and his statutes, and his ordinances, which he commanded our fathers. Let these my words, with which I have made supplication before Yahweh, be near to Yahweh our God day and night, that he may maintain the cause of his servant, and the cause of his people Israel, as every day shall require; that all the peoples of the earth may know that Yahweh, he is God. There is none else.

"Let your heart therefore be perfect with Yahweh our God, to walk in his statutes, and to keep his commandments, as at this day."

It happened, when Solomon had finished the building of the house of Yahweh, and the king's house, and all Solomon's desire which he was pleased to do, that Yahweh appeared to Solomon the second time, as he had appeared to him at Gibeon. Yahweh said to him, "I have heard your prayer and your supplication, that you have made before me. I have made this house holy, which you have built, to put my name there forever; and my eyes and my heart shall be there perpetually. As for you, if you will walk before me, as David your father walked, in integrity of heart, and in uprightness, to do according to all that I have commanded you, and will keep my statutes and my ordinances; then I will establish the throne of your kingdom over Israel forever, according as I promised to David your father, saying, 'There shall not fail you a man on the throne of Israel.' But if you turn away from following me, you or your children, and not keep my commandments and my statutes which I have set before you, but shall go and serve other gods, and worship them; then will I cut off Israel out of the land which I have given them; and this house, which I have made holy for my name, will I cast out of my sight; and Israel shall be a proverb and a byword among all peoples.

The wealth and wisdom of Solomon spread wide and far. The Queen of Sheba, likely from the region of what today are Ethiopia and Yemen, came to Solomon, bearing riches as a gift, to test his wisdom.

When the queen of Sheba heard of the fame of Solomon concerning the name of Yahweh, she came to prove him with hard questions. She came to Jerusalem with a very great train, with camels that bore spices, and very much gold, and precious stones; and when she had come to Solomon, she talked with him of all that was in her heart. Solomon told her all her questions: there was not anything hidden from the king which he didn't tell her. When the queen of Sheba had seen all the wisdom of Solomon, and the house that he had built, and the food of his table, and the sitting of his servants, and the attendance of his ministers, and their clothing, and his cup bearers, and his ascent by which he went up to the house of Yahweh; there was no more spirit in her.

She said to the king, "It was a true report that I heard in my own land of your acts, and of your wisdom. However I didn't believe the words, until I came, and my eyes had seen it. Behold, the half was not told me! Your wisdom and prosperity exceed the fame which I heard. Happy are your men, happy are these your servants, who stand continually before you, who hear your wisdom. Blessed is Yahweh your God, who delighted in you, to set you on the throne of Israel. Because Yahweh loved Israel forever, therefore made he you king, to do justice and righteousness."

She gave the king one hundred twenty talents of gold, and of spices very great store, and precious stones. There came no more such abundance of spices as these which the queen of Sheba gave to king Solomon.

King Solomon gave to the queen of Sheba all her desire, whatever she asked, besides that which Solomon gave her of his royal bounty. So she turned, and went to her own land, she and her servants.

Now the weight of gold that came to Solomon in one year was six hundred sixty-six talents of gold, besides that which the traders brought, and the traffic of the merchants, and of all the kings of the mixed people, and of the governors of the country. King Solomon made two hundred bucklers of beaten gold; six hundred shekels of gold went to one buckler. He made three hundred shields of beaten gold; three minas of gold went to one shield: and the king put them in the house of the forest of Lebanon. Moreover the king made a great throne of ivory, and overlaid it with the finest gold. There were six steps to the throne, and the top of the throne was round behind; and there were stays on either side by the place of the seat, and two lions standing beside the stays. Twelve lions stood there on the one side and on the other on the six steps: there was nothing like it made in any kingdom. All king Solomon's drinking vessels were of gold, and all the vessels of the house of the forest of Lebanon were of pure gold: none were of silver; it was nothing accounted of in the days of Solomon. For the king had at sea a navy of Tarshish with the navy of Hiram: once every three years came the navy of Tarshish, bringing gold, and silver, ivory, and apes, and peacocks. So king Solomon exceeded all the kings of the earth in riches and in wisdom.

All the earth sought the presence of Solomon, to hear his wisdom, which God had put in his heart. They brought every man his tribute, vessels of silver, and vessels of gold, and clothing, and armor, and spices, horses, and mules, a rate year by year. Solomon gathered together chariots and horsemen: and he had a thousand and four hundred chariots, and twelve thousand horsemen, that he bestowed in the chariot cities, and with the king at Jerusalem. The king made silver to be in Jerusalem as stones, and cedars made he to be as the sycamore trees that are in the lowland, for abundance. The horses which Solomon had were brought out of Egypt; and the king's merchants received them in droves, each drove at a price. A chariot came up and went out of Egypt for six hundred shekels of silver, and a horse for one hundred fifty; and so for all the kings of the Hittites, and for the kings of Syria, they brought them out by their means.

As we just read, "All the earth sought the presence of Solomon, to hear his wisdom, which God had put in his heart." Some of the wisdom of Solomon was captured in his many writings. In the Bible, these can be found in the books of Proverbs, Ecclesiastes, and the Song of Solomon. These books, written in poetic form, contain phrases and sayings that are still widely used today, thousands of years after they were first written down. The timeless and insightful knowledge of Solomon can still guide us today.

Following is a short selection of verses from the Proverbs.

175

The proverbs of Solomon, the son of David, king of Israel:

to know wisdom and instruction; to discern the words of understanding;

to receive instruction in wise dealing, in righteousness, justice, and equity;

to give prudence to the simple, knowledge and discretion to the young man:

that the wise man may hear, and increase in learning; that the man of understanding may attain to sound counsel:

to understand a proverb, and parables, the words and riddles of the wise.

The fear of Yahweh is the beginning of knowledge; but the foolish despise wisdom and instruction.

My son, if you will receive my words, and store up my commandments within you;

So as to turn your ear to wisdom, and apply your heart to understanding;

Yes, if you call out for discernment, and lift up your voice for understanding;

If you seek her as silver, and search for her as for hidden treasures:

then you will understand the fear of Yahweh, and find the knowledge of God.

For Yahweh gives wisdom. Out of his mouth comes knowledge and understanding.

He lays up sound wisdom for the upright. He is a shield to those who walk in integrity;

that he may guard the paths of justice, and preserve the way of his saints.

My son, don't forget my teaching; but let your heart keep my commandments:

for length of days, and years of life, and peace, will they add to you.

Don't let kindness and truth forsake you. Bind them around your neck. Write them on the tablet of your heart.

So you will find favor, and good understanding in the sight of God and man.

Trust in Yahweh with all your heart, and don't lean on your own understanding.

In all your ways acknowledge him, and he will make your paths straight.

Don't be wise in your own eyes. Fear Yahweh, and depart from evil.

It will be health to your body, and nourishment to your bones.

Honor Yahweh with your substance, with the first fruits of all your increase:

so your barns will be filled with plenty, and your vats will overflow with new wine.

My son, don't despise Yahweh's discipline, neither be weary of his reproof:

for whom Yahweh loves, he reproves; even as a father reproves the son in whom he delights.

There are six things which Yahweh hates; yes, seven which are an abomination to him:
haughty eyes, a lying tongue, hands that shed innocent blood;
a heart that devises wicked schemes, feet that are swift in running to mischief,
a false witness who utters lies, and he who sows discord among brothers.
Can a man scoop fire into his lap, and his clothes not be burned?
Or can one walk on hot coals, and his feet not be scorched?
So is he who goes in to his neighbor's wife. Whoever touches her will not be unpunished.

The fruit of the righteous is a tree of life. He who is wise wins souls.
Behold, the righteous shall be repaid in the earth; how much more the wicked and the sinner!
He who is slow to anger has great understanding, but he who has a quick temper displays folly.
Righteousness exalts a nation, but sin is a disgrace to any people.
A gentle answer turns away wrath, but a harsh word stirs up anger.
Pride goes before destruction, and a haughty spirit before a fall.
There is a way which seems right to a man, but in the end it leads to death.

A fool has no delight in understanding, but only in revealing his own opinion.
Whoever finds a wife finds a good thing, and obtains favor of Yahweh.
The poor plead for mercy, but the rich answer harshly.
A man of many companions may be ruined, but there is a friend who sticks closer than a brother.
Better is the poor who walks in his integrity than he who is perverse in his lips and is a fool.
It isn't good to have zeal without knowledge; nor being hasty with one's feet and missing the way.

A righteous man walks in integrity. Blessed are his children after him.
Don't love sleep, lest you come to poverty. Open your eyes, and you shall be satisfied with bread.
He who goes about as a tale-bearer reveals secrets; therefore don't keep company with him who opens wide his lips.
Whoever curses his father or his mother, his lamp shall be put out in

blackness of darkness.

An inheritance quickly gained at the beginning, won't be blessed in the end.

Don't say, "I will pay back evil." Wait for Yahweh, and he will save you.

The king's heart is in Yahweh's hand like the watercourses. He turns it wherever he desires.

Every way of a man is right in his own eyes, but Yahweh weighs the hearts.

To do righteousness and justice is more acceptable to Yahweh than sacrifice.

A high look, and a proud heart, the lamp of the wicked, is sin.

The plans of the diligent surely lead to profit; and everyone who is hasty surely rushes to poverty.

Getting treasures by a lying tongue is a fleeting vapor for those who seek death.

The violence of the wicked will drive them away, because they refuse to do what is right.

Whoever stops his ears at the cry of the poor, he will also cry out, but shall not be heard.

A gift in secret pacifies anger; and a bribe in the cloak, strong wrath.

It is joy to the righteous to do justice; but it is a destruction to the workers of iniquity.

It is better to dwell in a desert land, than with a contentious and fretful woman.

There is precious treasure and oil in the dwelling of the wise; but a foolish man swallows it up.

He who follows after righteousness and kindness finds life, righteousness, and honor.

The sacrifice of the wicked is an abomination: how much more, when he brings it with a wicked mind!

A false witness will perish, and a man who listens speaks to eternity.

A wicked man hardens his face; but as for the upright, he establishes his ways.

There is no wisdom nor understanding nor counsel against Yahweh.

The horse is prepared for the day of battle; but victory is with Yahweh.

A good name is more desirable than great riches, and loving favor is better than silver and gold.

Train up a child in the way he should go, and when he is old he will not depart from it.

Don't exploit the poor, because he is poor; and don't crush the needy in court;

for Yahweh will plead their case, and plunder the life of those who plunder them.

Don't befriend a hot-tempered man, and don't associate with one who harbors anger:

lest you learn his ways, and ensnare your soul.

Listen to your father who gave you life, and don't despise your mother when she is old.

Buy the truth, and don't sell it. Get wisdom, discipline, and understanding.

Who has woe? Who has sorrow? Who has strife? Who has complaints? Who has needless bruises? Who has bloodshot eyes?

Those who stay long at the wine; those who go to seek out mixed wine.

Don't look at the wine when it is red, when it sparkles in the cup, when it goes down smoothly.

In the end, it bites like a snake, and poisons like a viper.

Don't boast about tomorrow; for you don't know what a day may bring forth.

Iron sharpens iron; so a man sharpens his friend's countenance.

Better is the poor who walks in his integrity, than he who is perverse in his ways, and he is rich.

A fool vents all of his anger, but a wise man brings himself under control.

"What is the meaning of life?" This is a question that has been asked by men through the ages. The book of Ecclesiastes follows the journey of Solomon as he tries to find the meaning of life. As a king, Solomon had the time, money and wisdom to explore this question fully, and he tried to find fulfillment through wealth, work, pleasure, and other means. In the end, he found it all to be vanity, with one exception; the meaning of life is to fear God, and keep His commandments. This is the purpose for which we were created. Only with this life plan can we find meaning, fulfillment and ultimately, salvation.

The words of the Preacher, the son of David, king in Jerusalem:

"Vanity of vanities," says the Preacher; "Vanity of vanities, all is vanity." What does man gain from all his labor in which he labors under the sun? One generation goes, and another generation comes; but the earth remains forever. The sun also rises, and the sun goes down, and hurries to its place where it rises. The wind goes toward the south, and turns around to the north. It turns around continually as it goes, and the wind returns again to its courses. All the rivers run into the sea, yet the sea is not full. To the place where the rivers flow, there they flow again. All things are full of weariness beyond uttering. The eye is not satisfied with seeing, nor the ear filled with hearing. That which has been is that which shall be; and that which has been done is that which shall be done: and there is no new thing under the sun. Is there a thing of which it may be said, "Behold, this is new?" It has been long ago, in the ages which were before us.

I applied my heart to seek and to search out by wisdom concerning all that is done under the sky.

I have seen all the works that are done under the sun; and behold, all is vanity and a chasing after wind.

I said to myself, "Behold, I have obtained for myself great wisdom above all who were before me in Jerusalem. Yes, my heart has had great experience of wisdom and knowledge." I applied my heart to know wisdom, and to know madness and folly. I perceived that this also was a chasing after wind. For in much wisdom is much grief; and he who increases knowledge increases sorrow.

I said in my heart, "Come now, I will test you with mirth: therefore enjoy pleasure"; and behold, this also was vanity. I said of laughter, "It is foolishness"; and of mirth, "What does it accomplish?"

Whatever my eyes desired, I didn't keep from them. I didn't withhold my heart from any joy, for my heart rejoiced because of all my labor, and this was my portion from all my labor. Then I looked at all the works that my hands had worked, and at the labor that I had labored to do; and behold, all was vanity and a chasing after wind, and there was no profit under the sun.

For of the wise man, even as of the fool, there is no memory for ever, since in the days to come all will have been long forgotten. Indeed, the wise man must die just like the fool!

There is nothing better for a man than that he should eat and drink, and make his soul enjoy good in his labor. This also I saw, that it is from the hand of God. For who can eat, or who can have enjoyment, more than I?

For everything there is a season, and a time for every purpose under heaven.

A time to be born, and a time to die; a time to plant, and a time to pluck up that which is planted.

A time to kill, and a time to heal; a time to break down, and a time to build up.

A time to weep, and a time to laugh; a time to mourn, and a time to dance.

A time to cast away stones, and a time to gather stones together; a time to embrace, and a time to refrain from embracing.

A time to seek, and a time to lose; a time to keep, and a time to cast away,

A time to tear, and a time to sew; a time to keep silence, and a time to speak.

A time to love, and a time to hate; a time for war, and a time for peace.

This is the end of the matter. All has been heard. Fear God, and keep his commandments; for this is the whole duty of man. For God will bring every work into judgment, with every hidden thing, whether it is good, or whether it is evil.

17 A NATION DIVIDED

The Perils of Idolatry

Despite his great wisdom and love for God, King Solomon had one great weakness - women. In time his foreign wives, many of whom he may have married for political alliances, turned him away from God and toward idols. Because of this, God resolved to tear most of the kingdom away from Solomon and his heirs. After its peak of glory under the first part of Solomon's reign, the nation begins a downward slide which will ultimately lead to division and foreign captivity.

Now king Solomon loved many foreign women, together with the daughter of Pharaoh, women of the Moabites, Ammonites, Edomites, Sidonians, and Hittites; of the nations concerning which Yahweh said to the children of Israel, "You shall not go among them, neither shall they come among you; for surely they will turn away your heart after their gods." Solomon joined to these in love. He had seven hundred wives, princesses, and three hundred concubines; and his wives turned away his heart. For it happened, when Solomon was old, that his wives turned away his heart after other gods; and his heart was not perfect with Yahweh his God, as was the heart of David his father. For Solomon went after Ashtoreth the goddess of the Sidonians, and after Milcom the abomination of the Ammonites. Solomon did that which was evil in the sight of Yahweh, and didn't go fully after Yahweh, as did David his father. Then Solomon built a high place for Chemosh the abomination of Moab, on the mountain that is before Jerusalem, and for Molech the abomination of the children of Ammon. So he did for all his foreign wives, who burnt incense and sacrificed to their gods.

Yahweh was angry with Solomon, because his heart was turned away from Yahweh, the God of Israel, who had appeared to him twice, and had commanded him concerning this thing, that he should not go after other gods: but he didn't keep that which Yahweh commanded. Therefore Yahweh said to

Solomon, "Because this is done by you, and you have not kept my covenant and my statutes, which I have commanded you, I will surely tear the kingdom from you, and will give it to your servant. Notwithstanding I will not do it in your days, for David your father's sake; but I will tear it out of the hand of your son. However I will not tear away all the kingdom; but I will give one tribe to your son, for David my servant's sake, and for Jerusalem's sake which I have chosen."

The sin of Solomon in following idols was responsible for the division of Israel into two kingdoms; the northern kingdom, known as Israel, and the southern kingdom, known as Judah. For the next 325 years, these two kingdoms would not only be separate, but over most of this time would become adversaries and war against each other. The prophet Ahijah prophesied that Jeroboam, the son of one of Solomon's servants, would take over the ten tribes of Israel in the near future.

The man Jeroboam was a mighty man of valor; and Solomon saw the young man that he was industrious, and he put him in charge of all the labor of the house of Joseph. It happened at that time, when Jeroboam went out of Jerusalem, that the prophet Ahijah the Shilonite found him in the way; now Ahijah had clad himself with a new garment; and they two were alone in the field. Ahijah laid hold of the new garment that was on him, and tore it in twelve pieces.

He said to Jeroboam, "Take ten pieces; for thus says Yahweh, the God of Israel, 'Behold, I will tear the kingdom out of the hand of Solomon, and will give ten tribes to you.

"'However I will not take the whole kingdom out of his hand; but I will make him prince all the days of his life, for David my servant's sake whom I chose, who kept my commandments and my statutes; but I will take the kingdom out of his son's hand, and will give it to you, even ten tribes.

The time that Solomon reigned in Jerusalem over all Israel was forty years. Solomon slept with his fathers, and was buried in the city of David his father: and Rehoboam his son reigned in his place.

After the death of Solomon, his son Rehoboam became king. Young and inexperienced, he soon succumbed to poor counsel, which triggered the severing of the northern and southern kingdoms, as had been prophesied. Only the timely words of a prophet prevented immediate civil war.

Rehoboam went to Shechem: for all Israel had come to Shechem to make him king. It happened, when Jeroboam the son of Nebat heard of it (for he was yet in Egypt, where he had fled from the presence of king Solomon, and Jeroboam lived in Egypt, and they sent and called him), that Jeroboam and all the assembly of Israel came, and spoke to Rehoboam, saying, "Your father made our yoke grievous: now therefore make you the grievous service of your father, and his heavy yoke which he put on us, lighter, and we will serve you."

He said to them, "Depart for three days, then come back to me." The people departed. King Rehoboam took counsel with the old men, who had stood before Solomon his father while he yet lived, saying, "What counsel do you give me to return answer to this people?"

They spoke to him, saying, "If you will be a servant to this people this day, and will serve them, and answer them, and speak good words to them, then they will be your servants forever."

But he forsook the counsel of the old men which they had given him, and took counsel with the young men who had grown up with him, who stood before him. He said to them, "What counsel do you give, that we may return answer to this people, who have spoken to me, saying, 'Make the yoke that your father put on us lighter?'"

The young men who had grown up with him spoke to him, saying, "Thus you shall tell this people who spoke to you, saying, 'Your father made our yoke heavy, but make it lighter to us;' you shall say to them, 'My little finger is thicker than my father's waist. Now whereas my father burdened you with a heavy yoke, I will add to your yoke: my father chastised you with whips, but I will chastise you with scorpions.'"

So Jeroboam and all the people came to Rehoboam the third day, as the king asked, saying, "Come to me again the third day." The king answered the people roughly, and forsook the counsel of the old men which they had given him, and spoke to them according to the counsel of the young men, saying, "My father made your yoke heavy, but I will add to your yoke. My father chastised you with whips, but I will chastise you with scorpions."

When all Israel saw that the king didn't listen to them, the people answered the king, saying, "What portion have we in David? Neither do we have an inheritance in the son of Jesse. To your tents, Israel! Now see to your own house, David." So Israel departed to their tents.

But as for the children of Israel who lived in the cities of Judah, Rehoboam reigned over them. Then king Rehoboam sent Adoram, who was over the men subject to forced labor; and all Israel stoned him to death with stones. King Rehoboam made speed to get him up to his chariot, to flee to Jerusalem. So Israel rebelled against the house of David to this day. It happened, when all Israel heard that Jeroboam was returned, that they sent and called him to the congregation, and made him king over all Israel: there was none who followed the house of David, but the tribe of Judah only. When Rehoboam had come to Jerusalem, he assembled all the house of Judah, and the tribe of Benjamin, a hundred and eighty thousand chosen men, who were warriors, to fight against the house of Israel, to bring the kingdom again to Rehoboam the son of Solomon. But the word of God came to Shemaiah the man of God, saying, "Speak to Rehoboam the son of Solomon, king of Judah, and to all the house of Judah and Benjamin, and to the rest of the people, saying, 'Thus says Yahweh, "You shall not go up, nor fight against your brothers, the children of Israel. Everyone return to his house; for this thing is of me." So they listened to the word of Yahweh, and returned and went their way, according to the word of Yahweh.

Then Jeroboam built Shechem in the hill country of Ephraim, and lived in it; and he went out from there, and built Penuel. Jeroboam said in his heart, "Now the kingdom will return to the house of David. If this people goes up to offer sacrifices in the house of Yahweh at Jerusalem, then the heart of this people will turn again to their lord, even to Rehoboam king of Judah; and they will kill me, and return to Rehoboam king of Judah." Whereupon the king took counsel, and made two calves of gold; and he said to them, "It is too much for you to go up to Jerusalem. Look and see your gods, Israel, which brought you up out of the land of Egypt!" He set the one in Bethel, and the other put he in Dan. This thing became a sin; for the people went to worship before the one, even to Dan.

The glory days of the nation of Israel were soon over. The once proud nation split into two; the southern kingdom, now known as Judah, was comprised of the tribes of Judah and Benjamin. The northern kingdom, still known as Israel, was thus comprised of the other 10 tribes. Israel and Judah were weakened by fighting among themselves and against strong adversaries. Worse than that, over most of this time the kings that ruled were wicked, and cast God aside to follow after idols and pagan worship practices.

The riches collected during the time of David and Solomon were lost to invading armies and squandered to buy alliances with foreign kings in times of war.

From time to time, a good king would reign in Judah, but the good kings were few and far between. Meanwhile, the northern kingdom suffered under an endless string of evil, wicked kings. As Israel launched itself as a stand-alone nation, it did not take long for Jeroboam to fall deep into idolatry, starting a long pattern of wicked practices.

Behold, there came a man of God out of Judah by the word of Yahweh to Beth El: and Jeroboam was standing by the altar to burn incense. He cried against the altar by the word of Yahweh, and said, "Altar, altar, thus says

Yahweh: 'Behold, a son shall be born to the house of David, Josiah by name. On you he shall sacrifice the priests of the high places who burn incense on you, and they will burn men's bones on you.'" He gave a sign the same day, saying, "This is the sign which Yahweh has spoken: Behold, the altar will be split apart, and the ashes that are on it will be poured out."

It happened, when the king heard the saying of the man of God, which he cried against the altar in Bethel, that Jeroboam put out his hand from the altar, saying, "Seize him!" His hand, which he put out against him, dried up, so that he could not draw it back again to himself. The altar also was split apart, and the ashes poured out from the altar, according to the sign which the man of God had given by the word of Yahweh. The king answered the man of God, "Now entreat the favor of Yahweh your God, and pray for me, that my hand may be restored me again."

The man of God entreated Yahweh, and the king's hand was restored him again, and became as it was before.

After this thing Jeroboam didn't return from his evil way, but again made priests of the high places from among all the people. Whoever wanted to, he consecrated him, that there might be priests of the high places. This thing became sin to the house of Jeroboam, even to cut it off, and to destroy it from off the surface of the earth.

At that time Abijah the son of Jeroboam fell sick. Jeroboam said to his wife, "Please get up and disguise yourself, that you won't be recognized as the wife of Jeroboam. Go to Shiloh. Behold, there is Ahijah the prophet, who spoke concerning me that I should be king over this people. Take with you ten loaves, and cakes, and a jar of honey, and go to him. He will tell you what will become of the child."

Jeroboam's wife did so, and arose, and went to Shiloh, and came to the house of Ahijah. Now Ahijah could not see; for his eyes were set by reason of his age. Yahweh said to Ahijah, "Behold, the wife of Jeroboam comes to inquire of you concerning her son; for he is sick. Thus and thus you shall tell her; for it will be, when she comes in, that she will pretend to be another woman."

It was so, when Ahijah heard the sound of her feet, as she came in at the door, that he said, "Come in, you wife of Jeroboam! Why do you pretend to be another? For I am sent to you with heavy news. Go, tell Jeroboam, 'Thus says Yahweh, the God of Israel: "Because I exalted you from among the people, and made you prince over my people Israel, and tore the kingdom away from the house of David, and gave it you; and yet you have not been as my servant David, who kept my commandments, and who followed me with all his heart, to do that only which was right in my eyes, but have done evil above all who were before you, and have gone and made you other gods, and molten images, to provoke me to anger, and have cast me behind your back: therefore, behold, I will bring evil on the house of Jeroboam, and will cut off from Jeroboam everyone who urinates on a wall, he who is shut up and he who is left at large in Israel, and will utterly sweep away the house of Jeroboam, as a man sweeps away dung, until it is all gone. He who dies of Jeroboam in the city shall the dogs eat; and he who dies in the field shall the birds of the sky eat: for Yahweh has spoken it.'" Arise therefore, and go to your house. When your feet enter into the city, the child shall die. All Israel shall mourn for him, and bury him; for he only of Jeroboam shall come to the grave, because in him there is found some good thing toward Yahweh, the God of Israel, in the house of Jeroboam.

Moreover Yahweh will raise him up a king over Israel, who shall cut off the house of Jeroboam. This is day! What? Even now. For Yahweh will strike Israel, as a reed is shaken in the water; and he will root up Israel out of this good land which he gave to their fathers, and will scatter them beyond the River, because they have made their Asherim, provoking Yahweh to anger. He will give Israel up because of the sins of Jeroboam, which he has sinned, and with which he has made Israel to sin."

Jeroboam's wife arose, and departed, and came to Tirzah. As she came to the threshold of the house, the child died. All Israel buried him, and mourned for him, according to the word of Yahweh, which he spoke by his servant Ahijah the prophet.

The days which Jeroboam reigned were two and twenty years: and he slept with his fathers, and Nadab his son reigned in his place.

Rehoboam the son of Solomon reigned in Judah. Rehoboam was forty-one years old when he began to reign, and he reigned seventeen years in Jerusalem.

Following the example of King Jeroboam and Israel, the southern kingdom of Judah soon also slipped into idolatry and paganism. War erupted between the two kingdoms, and stretched out over the years.

Judah did that which was evil in the sight of Yahweh, and they provoked him to jealousy with their sins which they committed, above all that their fathers had done. For they also built them high places, and pillars, and Asherim, on every high hill, and under every green tree; and there were also sodomites in the land: they did according to all the abominations of the nations which Yahweh drove out before the children of Israel. It happened in the fifth year of king Rehoboam, that Shishak king of Egypt came up against Jerusalem; and he took away the treasures of the house of Yahweh, and the treasures of the king's house; he even took away all: and he took away all the shields of gold which Solomon had made. King Rehoboam made in their place shields of brass, and committed them to the hands of the captains of the guard, who kept the door of the king's house. It was so, that as often as the king went into the house of Yahweh, the guard bore them, and brought them back into the guard room.

There was war between Rehoboam and Jeroboam continually. Rehoboam slept with his fathers, and was buried with his fathers in the city of David: and his mother's name was Naamah the Ammonitess. Abijam his son reigned in his place.

Now in the eighteenth year of king Jeroboam the son of Nebat began Abijam to reign over Judah. He reigned three years in Jerusalem: and his mother's name was Maacah the daughter of Abishalom. He walked in all the sins of his father, which he had done before him; and his heart was not perfect with Yahweh his God, as the heart of David his father. Nevertheless for David's sake, Yahweh his God gave him a lamp in Jerusalem, to set up his son after him, and to establish Jerusalem;

Abijam slept with his fathers; and they buried him in the city of David: and Asa his son reigned in his place. In the twentieth year of Jeroboam king of Israel began Asa to reign over Judah. He reigned forty-one years in Jerusalem: and his mother's name was Maacah the daughter of Abishalom. Asa did that which was right in the eyes of Yahweh, as did David his father. He put away the sodomites out of the land, and removed all the idols that his fathers had made. Also Maacah his mother he removed from being queen, because she had made an abominable image for an Asherah; and Asa cut down her image, and burnt it at the brook Kidron. But the high places were not taken away: nevertheless the heart of Asa was perfect with Yahweh all his days. He brought into the house of Yahweh the things that his father had dedicated, and the things that himself had dedicated, silver, and gold, and vessels.

There was war between Asa and Baasha king of Israel all their days. Baasha king of Israel went up against Judah, and built Ramah, that he might not allow anyone to go out or come in to Asa king of Judah. Then Asa took all the silver and the gold that were left in the treasures of the house of Yahweh, and the treasures of the king's house, and delivered them into the hand of his servants; and king Asa sent them to Ben Hadad, the son of Tabrimmon, the son of Hezion, king of Syria, who lived at Damascus, saying, "There is a treaty between me and you, between my father and your father. Behold, I have sent to you a present of silver and gold. Go, break your treaty with Baasha king of Israel, that he may depart from me."

Ben Hadad listened to king Asa, and sent the captains of his armies against the cities of Israel, and struck Ijon, and Dan, and Abel Beth Maacah, and all Chinneroth, with all the land of Naphtali. It happened, when Baasha heard of it, that he left off building Ramah, and lived in Tirzah.

In the thirty-ninth year of his reign Asa was diseased in his feet; his disease was exceeding great: yet in his disease he didn't seek Yahweh, but to the physicians.

Asa slept with his fathers, and was buried with his fathers in the city of David his father; and Jehoshaphat his son reigned in his place.

After the reign of Asa, who walked in the ways of God, his successor, Ahab, along with his wife Jezebel, were among the most wicked leaders in the history of the Israelites. The names Ahab and Jezebel have become synonymous with wickedness. It was during their reign that Elijah, a great prophet of God, became prominent. As he spoke strongly against the wicked ways of Ahab, he was soon running for his life. But soon God would send him back to Ahab, bringing a great challenge against the prophets of Baal - one man and his God against 450 prophets of Baal and 400 prophets of Asherah, and their gods. The dramatic showdown was pivotal in turning the people back from idolatry to the worship of the one true and living God.

In the thirty-eighth year of Asa king of Judah began Ahab the son of Omri to reign over Israel: and Ahab the son of Omri reigned over Israel in Samaria twenty-two years. Ahab the son of Omri did that which was evil in the sight of Yahweh above all that were before him. It happened, as if it had been a light thing for him to walk in the sins of Jeroboam the son of Nebat, that he took as wife Jezebel the daughter of Ethbaal king of the Sidonians, and went and served Baal, and worshiped him. He reared up an altar for Baal in the house of Baal, which he had built in Samaria. Ahab made the Asherah; and Ahab did yet more to provoke Yahweh, the God of Israel, to anger than all the kings of Israel who were before him.

Elijah the Tishbite, who was of the foreigners of Gilead, said to Ahab, "As Yahweh, the God of Israel, lives, before whom I stand, there shall not be dew nor rain these years, but according to my word." The word of Yahweh came to him, saying, "Go away from here, turn eastward, and hide yourself by the brook Cherith, that is before the Jordan. It shall be, that you shall drink of the brook. I have commanded the ravens to feed you there." So he went and did according to the word of Yahweh; for he went and lived by the brook Cherith, that is before the Jordan. The ravens brought him bread and flesh in the morning, and bread and flesh in the evening; and he drank of the brook.

It happened after a while, that the brook dried up, because there was no rain in the land. The word of Yahweh came to him, saying, "Arise, go to Zarephath, which belongs to Sidon, and stay there. Behold, I have commanded a widow there to sustain you."

So he arose and went to Zarephath; and when he came to the gate of the city, behold, a widow was there gathering sticks: and he called to her, and said, "Please get me a little water in a vessel, that I may drink."

As she was going to get it, he called to her, and said, "Please bring me a morsel of bread in your hand."

She said, "As Yahweh your God lives, I don't have a cake, but a handful of meal in the jar, and a little oil in the jar. Behold, I am gathering two sticks, that I may go in and bake it for me and my son, that we may eat it, and die."

Elijah said to her, "Don't be afraid. Go and do as you have said; but make me of it a little cake first, and bring it out to me, and afterward make some for you and for your son. For thus says Yahweh, the God of Israel, 'The jar of meal shall not empty, neither shall the jar of oil fail, until the day that Yahweh sends rain on the earth.'"

She went and did according to the saying of Elijah: and she, and he, and her house, ate many days. The jar of meal didn't empty, neither did the jar of oil fail, according to the word of Yahweh, which he spoke by Elijah. It happened after these things, that the son of the woman, the mistress of the house, fell sick; and his sickness was so severe, that there was no breath left in him. She said to Elijah, "What have I to do with you, you man of God? You have come to me to bring my sin to memory, and to kill my son!"

He said to her, "Give me your son." He took him out of her bosom, and carried him up into the room where he stayed, and laid him on his own bed. He cried to Yahweh, and said, "Yahweh my God, have you also brought evil on the widow with whom I stay, by killing her son?"

He stretched himself on the child three times, and cried to Yahweh, and said, "Yahweh my God, please let this child's soul come into him again."

Yahweh listened to the voice of Elijah; and the soul of the child came into him again, and he revived. Elijah took the child, and brought him down out of the room into the house, and delivered him to his mother; and Elijah said, "Behold, your son lives."

The woman said to Elijah, "Now I know that you are a man of God, and that the word of Yahweh in your mouth is truth."

It happened after many days, that the word of Yahweh came to Elijah, in the third year, saying, "Go, show yourself to Ahab; and I will send rain on the earth."

Elijah went to show himself to Ahab. The famine was severe in Samaria.

It happened, when Ahab saw Elijah, that Ahab said to him, "Is that you, you troubler of Israel?"

He answered, "I have not troubled Israel; but you, and your father's house, in that you have forsaken the commandments of Yahweh, and you have followed the Baals. Now therefore send, and gather to me all Israel to Mount Carmel, and four hundred fifty of the prophets of Baal, and four hundred of the prophets of the Asherah, who eat at Jezebel's table."

So Ahab sent to all the children of Israel, and gathered the prophets together to Mount Carmel. Elijah came near to all the people, and said, "How long will you waver between the two sides? If Yahweh is God, follow him; but if Baal, then follow him." The people answered him not a word.

Then Elijah said to the people, "I, even I only, am left a prophet of Yahweh; but Baal's prophets are four hundred fifty men. Let them therefore give us two bulls; and let them choose one bull for themselves, and cut it in pieces, and lay it on the wood, and put no fire under; and I will dress the other bull, and lay it on the wood, and put no fire under it. You call on the name of your god, and I will call on the name of Yahweh. The God who answers by fire, let him be God."

All the people answered, "It is well said."

Elijah said to the prophets of Baal, "Choose one bull for yourselves, and dress it first; for you are many; and call on the name of your god, but put no fire under it."

They took the bull which was given them, and they dressed it, and called on the name of Baal from morning even until noon, saying, Baal, hear us. But there was no voice, nor any who answered. They leaped about the altar which was made. It happened at noon, that Elijah mocked them, and said, "Cry aloud; for he is a god. Either he is musing, or he has gone aside, or he is on a journey, or perhaps he sleeps and must be awakened."

They cried aloud, and cut themselves in their way with knives and lances, until the blood gushed out on them. It was so, when midday was past, that they prophesied until the time of the offering of the offering; but there was neither voice, nor any to answer, nor any who regarded.

Elijah said to all the people, "Come near to me"; and all the people came near to him. He repaired the altar of Yahweh that was thrown down. Elijah took twelve stones, according to the number of the tribes of the sons of Jacob, to whom the word of Yahweh came, saying, "Israel shall be your name." With the stones he built an altar in the name of Yahweh. He made a trench around the altar, large enough to contain two measures of seed. He put the wood in order, and cut the bull in pieces, and laid it on the wood. He said, "Fill four jars with water, and pour it on the burnt offering, and on the wood." He said, "Do it a second time"; and they did it the second time. He said, "Do it a third time"; and they did it the third time. The water ran around the altar; and he also filled the trench with water.

It happened at the time of the offering of the offering, that Elijah the prophet came near, and said, "Yahweh, the God of Abraham, of Isaac, and of Israel, let it be known this day that you are God in Israel, and that I am your servant, and that I have done all these things at your word. Hear me, Yahweh, hear me, that this people may know that you, Yahweh, are God, and that you have turned their heart back again."

Then the fire of Yahweh fell, and consumed the burnt offering, and the wood, and the stones, and the dust, and licked up the water that was in the trench. When all the people saw it, they fell on their faces. They said, "Yahweh, he is God! Yahweh, he is God!"

Elijah said to them, "Seize the prophets of Baal! Don't let one of them escape!"

They seized them. Elijah brought them down to the brook Kishon, and killed them there. Elijah said to Ahab, "Get up, eat and drink; for there is the sound of abundance of rain."

So Ahab went up to eat and to drink. Elijah went up to the top of Carmel; and he bowed himself down on the earth, and put his face between his knees.

He said to his servant, "Go up now, look toward the sea." He went up, and looked, and said, "There is nothing." He said, "Go again" seven times.

It happened at the seventh time, that he said, "Behold, a small cloud, like a man's hand, is rising out of the sea."

He said, "Go up, tell Ahab, 'Get ready and go down, so that the rain doesn't stop you.'"

It happened in a little while, that the sky grew black with clouds and wind, and there was a great rain. Ahab rode, and went to Jezreel. The hand of Yahweh was on Elijah; and he tucked his cloak into his belt and ran before Ahab to the entrance of Jezreel.

Ahab told Jezebel all that Elijah had done, and how he had killed all the prophets with the sword. Then Jezebel sent a messenger to Elijah, saying, "So let the gods do to me, and more also, if I don't make your life as the life of one of them by tomorrow about this time!"

Once again, Elijah is on the run for his life. Old and tired, he wishes for death. But in the wilderness he is cared for by angels, and later he has a direct and powerful encounter with God. There, God encourages Elijah that he is not alone, and that He had reserved 7,000 people who had not bowed their knees to Baal. With these words Elijah was given another mission; to anoint Jehu, the son of Nimshi, to be king over Israel; and to anoint Elisha to take his place as a prophet.

When he saw that, he arose, and went for his life, and came to Beersheba, which belongs to Judah, and left his servant there. But he himself went a day's journey into the wilderness, and came and sat down under a juniper tree: and he requested for himself that he might die, and said, "It is enough. Now, O Yahweh, take away my life; for I am not better than my fathers."

He lay down and slept under a juniper tree; and behold, an angel touched him, and said to him, "Arise and eat!"

He looked, and behold, there was at his head a cake baked on the coals, and a jar of water. He ate and drank, and lay down again. The angel of Yahweh came again the second time, and touched him, and said, "Arise and eat, because the journey is too great for you."

He arose, and ate and drank, and went in the strength of that food forty days and forty nights to Horeb the Mount of God. He came there to a cave, and lodged there; and behold, the word of Yahweh came to him, and he said to him, "What are you doing here, Elijah?"

He said, "I have been very jealous for Yahweh, the God of Armies; for the children of Israel have forsaken your covenant, thrown down your altars, and slain your prophets with the sword. I, even I only, am left; and they seek my life, to take it away."

He said, "Go out, and stand on the mountain before Yahweh."

Behold, Yahweh passed by, and a great and strong wind tore the mountains, and broke in pieces the rocks before Yahweh; but Yahweh was not in the wind. After the wind an earthquake; but Yahweh was not in the earthquake. After the earthquake a fire passed; but Yahweh was not in the fire: and after the fire a still small voice. It was so, when Elijah heard it, that he wrapped his face in his mantle, and went out, and stood in the entrance of the cave. Behold, a voice came to him, and said, "What are you doing here, Elijah?"

He said, "I have been very jealous for Yahweh, the God of Armies; for the children of Israel have forsaken your covenant, thrown down your altars, and slain your prophets with the sword. I, even I only, am left; and they seek my life, to take it away."

Yahweh said to him, "Go, return on your way to the wilderness of Damascus. When you arrive, you shall anoint Hazael to be king over Syria. You shall anoint Jehu the son of Nimshi to be king over Israel; and you shall anoint Elisha the son of Shaphat of Abel Meholah to be prophet in your place. It shall happen, that he who escapes from the sword of Hazael, Jehu will kill; and he who escapes from the sword of Jehu, Elisha will kill. Yet will I leave seven thousand in Israel, all the knees which have not bowed to Baal, and every mouth which has not kissed him."

So he departed there, and found Elisha the son of Shaphat, who was plowing, with twelve yoke of oxen before him, and he with the twelfth: and Elijah passed over to him, and cast his mantle on him. He left the oxen, and ran after Elijah, and said, "Let me please kiss my father and my mother, and then I will follow you."

He said to him, "Go back again; for what have I done to you?"

He returned from following him, and took the yoke of oxen, and killed them, and boiled their flesh with the instruments of the oxen, and gave to the people, and they ate. Then he arose, and went after Elijah, and served him.

The word of Yahweh came to Elijah the Tishbite, saying, "Arise, go down to meet Ahab king of Israel, who dwells in Samaria. Behold, he is in the vineyard of Naboth, where he has gone down to take possession of it. You shall speak to him, saying, 'Thus says Yahweh, "Have you killed and also taken possession?"' You shall speak to him, saying, 'Thus says Yahweh, "In the place where dogs licked the blood of Naboth, dogs will lick your blood, even yours."'

Yahweh also spoke of Jezebel, saying, "The dogs shall eat Jezebel by the rampart of Jezreel. The dogs will eat he who dies of Ahab in the city; and the birds of the sky will eat he who dies in the field."

But there was none like Ahab, who sold himself to do that which was evil in the sight of Yahweh, whom Jezebel his wife stirred up. He did very abominably in following idols, according to all that the Amorites did, whom Yahweh cast out before the children of Israel. It happened, when Ahab heard those words, that he tore his clothes, and put sackcloth on his flesh, and fasted, and lay in sackcloth, and went softly.

The word of Yahweh came to Elijah the Tishbite, saying, "See how Ahab humbles himself before me? Because he humbles himself before me, I will not bring the evil in his days; but in his son's days will I bring the evil on his house."

So [Ahab] the king of Israel and Jehoshaphat the king of Judah went up to Ramoth Gilead. The king of Israel said to Jehoshaphat, "I will disguise myself, and go into the battle; but you put on your robes." The king of Israel disguised himself, and went into the battle.

Now the king of Syria had commanded the thirty-two captains of his chariots, saying, Fight neither with small nor great, except only with the king of Israel. It happened, when the captains of the chariots saw Jehoshaphat, that they said, "Surely that is the king of Israel!" and they turned aside to fight against him. Jehoshaphat cried out. It happened, when the captains of the chariots saw that it was not the king of Israel, that they turned back from pursuing him. A certain man drew his bow at random, and struck the king of the joints of the armor. Therefore he said to the driver of his chariot, "Turn your Israel between hand, and carry me out of the battle; for I am severely wounded." The battle increased that day. The king was propped up in his chariot facing the Syrians, and died at evening. The blood ran out of the wound into the bottom of the chariot. A cry went throughout the army about the going down of the sun, saying, "Every man to his city, and every man to his country!"

So the king died, and was brought to Samaria; and they buried the king in Samaria. They washed the chariot by the pool of Samaria; and the dogs licked up his blood where the prostitutes washed themselves; according to the word of Yahweh which he spoke.

18 THE FINAL DOWNFALL

The Days of Kings are Numbered

After the death of Ahab, the nation of Moab continued to fight against the kingdom of Israel. Ahab was succeeded by two kings who were also wicked; Ahaziah (who reigned 2 years) and Jehoram, who reigned 12 years.

The devout prophet Elijah continued his work during their time on the throne of the northern kingdom. But the time came for Elijah to die, and Elisha would assume the position of the chief prophet of the northern kingdom of Israel.

It happened, when Yahweh would take up Elijah by a whirlwind into heaven, that Elijah went with Elisha from Gilgal. Elijah said to Elisha, "Please wait here, for Yahweh has sent me as far as Bethel."

Elisha said, "As Yahweh lives, and as your soul lives, I will not leave you." So they went down to Bethel.

Fifty men of the sons of the prophets went, and stood opposite them at a distance; and they both stood by the Jordan. Elijah took his mantle, and wrapped it together, and struck the waters, and they were divided here and there, so that they two went over on dry ground. It happened, when they had gone over, that Elijah said to Elisha, "Ask what I shall do for you, before I am taken from you."

Elisha said, "Please let a double portion of your spirit be on me."

He said, "You have asked a hard thing. If you see me when I am taken from you, it shall be so for you; but if not, it shall not be so."

It happened, as they still went on, and talked, that behold, a chariot of fire and horses of fire separated them; and Elijah went up by a whirlwind into heaven. Elisha saw it, and he cried, "My father, my father, the chariots of Israel and its horsemen!"

He saw him no more: and he took hold of his own clothes, and tore them in two pieces. He took up also the mantle of Elijah that fell from him, and went back, and stood by the bank of the Jordan. He took the mantle of Elijah that fell from him, and struck the waters, and said, "Where is Yahweh, the God of Elijah?" When he also had struck the waters, they were divided here and there; and Elisha went over. When the sons of the prophets who were at Jericho over against him saw him, they said, "The spirit of Elijah rests on Elisha." They came to meet him, and bowed themselves to the ground before him.

In the time of Elisha, Jehoram the king of Israel and Jehoshaphat the king of Judah joined forces to attack Moab. Elisha was called to prophesy about the outcome of the battle; he informed them that God would bring victory, out of respect for the righteousness of Jehoshaphat. And, as predicted, the Israelites won a great battle that day and Moab was utterly defeated.

Elisha was a great prophet, performing many miracles to validate God's power. Having inherited a double portion of the spirit of Elijah, his power to do miracles was unprecedented. Not since the plagues against Egypt had God worked so powerfully in one man. Meanwhile, the politics of the nations of Judah and Israel spiraled into an endless cycle of intrigue and bloody revolt.

Now there cried a certain woman of the wives of the sons of the prophets to Elisha, saying, "Your servant my husband is dead. You know that your servant feared Yahweh. Now the creditor has come to take for himself my two children to be slaves."

Elisha said to her, "What shall I do for you? Tell me: what do you have in the house?"

She said, "Your handmaid has nothing in the house, except a pot of oil."

Then he said, "Go, borrow containers from of all your neighbors, even empty containers. Don't borrow just a few. You shall go in, and shut the door on you and on your sons, and pour out into all those containers; and you shall set aside that which is full."

So she went from him, and shut the door on her and on her sons; they brought the containers to her, and she poured out. It happened, when the containers were full, that she said to her son, "Bring me another container."

He said to her, "There isn't another container." The oil stopped flowing.

Then she came and told the man of God. He said, "Go, sell the oil, and pay your debt; and you and your sons live on the rest."

It fell on a day, that Elisha passed to Shunem, where there was a prominent woman; and she persuaded him to eat bread. So it was, that as often as he passed by, he turned in there to eat bread. She said to her husband, "See now, I perceive that this is a holy man of God, that passes by us continually. Please let us make a little room on the wall. Let us set for him there a bed, a table, a chair, and a lamp stand. It shall be, when he comes to us, that he shall turn in there."

One day he came there, and he turned into the room and lay there. He said to Gehazi his servant, "Call this Shunammite." When he had called her, she stood before him. He said to him, "Say now to her, 'Behold, you have cared for us with all this care. What is to be done for you? Would you like to be spoken for to the king, or to the captain of the army?'"

She answered, "I dwell among my own people."

He said, "What then is to be done for her?"

Gehazi answered, "Most certainly she has no son, and her husband is old."

He said, "Call her." When he had called her, she stood in the door. He said, "At this season, when the time comes around, you will embrace a son."

She said, "No, my lord, you man of God, do not lie to your handmaid."

The woman conceived, and bore a son at that season, when the time came around, as Elisha had said to her. When the child was grown, it happened one day that he went out to his father to the reapers. He said to his father, "My head! My head!" He said to his servant, "Carry him to his mother."

When he had taken him, and brought him to his mother, he sat on her knees until noon, and then died.

So she went, and came to the man of God to Mount Carmel. It happened, when the man of God saw her afar off, that he said to Gehazi his servant, "Behold, there is the Shunammite."

When she came to the man of God to the hill, she caught hold of his feet. Gehazi came near to thrust her away; but the man of God said, "Leave her alone; for her soul is troubled within her; and Yahweh has hidden it from me, and has not told me."

Then she said, "Did I desire a son of my lord? Didn't I say, Do not deceive me?"

Then he said to Gehazi, "Tuck your cloak into your belt, take my staff in your hand, and go your way. If you meet any man, don't greet him; and if anyone greets you, don't answer him again. Then lay my staff on the face of the child."

The mother of the child said, "As Yahweh lives, and as your soul lives, I will not leave you."

He arose, and followed her.

Gehazi passed on before them, and laid the staff on the face of the child; but there was neither voice, nor hearing. Therefore he returned to meet him, and told him, saying, "The child has not awakened."

When Elisha had come into the house, behold, the child was dead, and laid on his bed. He went in therefore, and shut the door on them both, and prayed to Yahweh. He went up, and lay on the child, and put his mouth on his mouth, and his eyes on his eyes, and his hands on his hands. He stretched himself on him; and the flesh of the child grew warm. Then he returned, and walked in the house once back and forth; and went up, and stretched himself on him. Then the child sneezed seven times, and the child opened his eyes. He called Gehazi, and said, "Call this Shunammite!" So he called her.

When she had come in to him, he said, "Take up your son."

Then she went in, and fell at his feet, and bowed herself to the ground; and she took up her son, and went out.

Now Naaman, captain of the army of the king of Syria, was a great man with his master, and honorable, because by him Yahweh had given victory to Syria: he was also a mighty man of valor, but he was a leper. The Syrians had gone out in bands, and had brought away captive out of the land of Israel a little maiden; and she waited on Naaman's wife. She said to her mistress, "I wish that my lord were with the prophet who is in Samaria! Then he would heal him of his leprosy."

So Naaman came with his horses and with his chariots, and stood at the door of the house of Elisha. Elisha sent a messenger to him, saying, "Go and wash in the Jordan seven times, and your flesh shall come again to you, and you shall be clean."

But Naaman was angry, and went away, and said, "Behold, I thought, 'He will surely come out to me, and stand, and call on the name of Yahweh his God, and wave his hand over the place, and heal the leper.' Aren't Abanah and Pharpar, the rivers of Damascus, better than all the waters of Israel? Couldn't I wash in them, and be clean?" So he turned and went away in a rage.

His servants came near, and spoke to him, and said, "My father, if the prophet had asked you do some great thing, wouldn't you have done it? How much rather then, when he says to you, 'Wash, and be clean?'"

Then went he down, and dipped himself seven times in the Jordan, according to the saying of the man of God; and his flesh was restored like the flesh of a little child, and he was clean. He returned to the man of God, he and all his company, and came, and stood before him; and he said, "See now, I know that there is no God in all the earth, but in Israel.

The power of Elisha was known not just throughout Israel, but among neighboring countries as well. In one interesting occasion, Elisha allowed one of his servants to see the hidden army of God, and he struck an entire army with blindness.

Now the king of Syria was warring against Israel; and he took counsel with his servants, saying, "My camp will be in such and such a place."

The man of God sent to the king of Israel, saying, "Beware that you not pass such a place; for the Syrians are coming down there." The king of Israel sent to the place which the man of God told him and warned him of; and he saved himself there, not once nor twice. The heart of the king of Syria was very troubled about this. He called his servants, and said to them, "Won't you show me which of us is for the king of Israel?"

One of his servants said, "No, my lord, O king; but Elisha, the prophet who is in Israel, tells the king of Israel the words that you speak in your bedroom."

He said, "Go and see where he is, that I may send and get him."

It was told him, saying, "Behold, he is in Dothan."

Therefore he sent horses, chariots, and a great army there. They came by night, and surrounded the city. When the servant of the man of God had risen early, and gone out, behold, an army with horses and chariots was around the city. His servant said to him, "Alas, my master! What shall we do?"

He answered, "Don't be afraid; for those who are with us are more than those who are with them." Elisha prayed, and said, "Yahweh, please open his eyes, that he may see." Yahweh opened the eyes of the young man; and he saw: and behold, the mountain was full of horses and chariots of fire around Elisha. When they came down to him, Elisha prayed to Yahweh, and said, "Please strike this people with blindness."

He struck them with blindness according to the word of Elisha. Elisha said to them, "This is not the way, neither is this the city. Follow me, and I will bring you to the man whom you seek." He led them to Samaria. It happened, when they had come into Samaria, that Elisha said, "Yahweh, open the eyes of these men, that they may see."

Yahweh opened their eyes, and they saw; and behold, they were in the midst of Samaria. The king of Israel said to Elisha, when he saw them, "My father, shall I strike them? Shall I strike them?"

He answered, "You shall not strike them. Would you strike those whom you have taken captive with your sword and with your bow? Set bread and water before them, that they may eat and drink, and go to their master."

He prepared great feast for them. When they had eaten and drunk, he sent them away, and they went to their master. The bands of Syria stopped raiding the land of Israel.

God provided another miraculous deliverance to Israel. Benhadad, king of Syria, gathered all his army, and besieged Samaria. After some time, the hunger inside the city was so bad that people were even eating their own children. Four lepers, deciding it was better to put their fate in the hands of the Syrian army than to die of hunger, left the cit, and found the Syrian camp totally empty. For God had made the army of the Syrians to hear the noise of chariots, horses and a great army, and they fled in panic.

Jehoshaphat reigned 25 years. His son Jehoram reigned 8 years over Judah in Jerusalem, but was evil, influenced by his wife, a daughter of the wicked Ahab king of Israel.

Meanwhile, in the northern kingdom of Israel, Jehu rose to power after being anointed by one of the servants of Elisha. His reign started strong; he followed the command of God to wipe out all descendants of the evil king Ahab, including his wife, Jezebel. In his initial zeal, he even had the prophets of Baal put to death. But then Jehu turned to idolatry and did not walk in the ways of God, becoming part of a continuous string of evil kings in the northern kingdom.

Things also were not going well in the southern kingdom of Judah. After the death of Ahaziah, his mother, queen Athaliah, killed all the royal children and took the throne for herself. But one son, Joash, escaped, and after six years, was crowned the king of Judah in a successful plot by Jehoiada the priest. For 40 years, Joash, only 7 years old when crowned, walked in the ways of God. Under his rule, the temple was repaired. But after he reigned 40 years, he was killed in an evil plot by some of his servants, and Amaziah, his son, reigned in his place.

Time continued to march on, and the succession of kings continued. Judah continued to alternate between good and evil kings, but the northern kingdom of Israel suffered under a continual string of evil leaders. After the death of Elisha, the northern kingdom interacted with prophets such as Jonah, Amos, and Hosea. The southern kingdom of Judah interacted with the prophets Joel, Zechariah, Isaiah and Micah.

Finally, God had enough of the evil ways of Israel. For years the mighty Assyrian army had been chipping away at Israel's northern border, capturing towns and taking captives. But in the days of King Hezekiah, the Assyrians came in full force. After a siege of the capital city of Samaria, in which the people valiantly held out for three years, the Assyrians fully conquered Israel, and carried many of the people away as captives. Thus, the sad history of the northern kingdom was abruptly ended.

In the twelfth year of Ahaz king of Judah, Hoshea the son of Elah began to reign in Samaria over Israel for nine years. He did that which was evil in the sight of Yahweh, yet not as the kings of Israel who were before him. Against him came up Shalmaneser king of Assyria; and Hoshea became his servant, and brought him tribute. The king of Assyria found conspiracy in Hoshea; for he had sent messengers to So king of Egypt, and offered no tribute to the king of Assyria, as he had done year by year: therefore the king of Assyria shut him up, and bound him in prison. Then the king of Assyria came up throughout all the land, and went up to Samaria, and besieged it three years. In the ninth year of Hoshea the king of Assyria took Samaria, and carried Israel away to Assyria, and placed them in Halah, and on the Habor, the river of Gozan, and in the cities of the Medes.

It was so, because the children of Israel had sinned against Yahweh their God, who brought them up out of the land of Egypt from under the hand of Pharaoh king of Egypt, and had feared other gods, and walked in the statutes of the nations, whom Yahweh cast out from before the children of Israel, and of the kings of Israel, which they made. The children of Israel did secretly things that were not right against Yahweh their God: and they built them high places in all their cities, from the tower of the watchmen to the fortified city; and they set them up pillars and Asherim on every high hill, and under every green tree; and there they burnt incense in all the high places, as did the nations whom Yahweh carried away before them; and they worked wicked things to provoke Yahweh to anger; and they served idols, of which Yahweh had said to them, "You shall not do this thing."

They forsook all the commandments of Yahweh their God, and made them molten images, even two calves, and made an Asherah, and worshiped all the army of the sky, and served Baal. They caused their sons and their daughters to pass through the fire, and used divination and enchantments, and sold themselves to do that which was evil in the sight of Yahweh, to provoke him to anger. Therefore Yahweh was very angry with Israel, and removed them out of his sight: there was none left but the tribe of Judah only.

So Israel was carried away out of their own land to Assyria to this day. The king of Assyria brought men from Babylon, and from Cuthah, and from Avva, and from Hamath and Sepharvaim, and placed them in the cities of Samaria instead of the children of Israel; and they possessed Samaria, and lived in the cities of it.

While Israel was in captivity, the southern kingdom of Judah continued to alternate between good and evil kings. One bright spot was the reign of Hezekiah.

Now it happened in the third year of Hoshea son of Elah king of Israel, that Hezekiah the son of Ahaz king of Judah began to reign. He was twenty-five years old when he began to reign; and he reigned twenty-nine years in Jerusalem:

He did that which was right in the eyes of Yahweh, according to all that David his father had done. He removed the high places, and broke the pillars, and cut down the Asherah: and he broke in pieces the bronze serpent that Moses had made; for in those days the children of Israel burned incense to it; and he called it Nehushtan. He trusted in Yahweh, the God of Israel; so that after him was none like him among all the kings of Judah, nor among them that were before him. For he joined with Yahweh; he didn't depart from following him, but kept his commandments, which Yahweh commanded Moses. Yahweh was with him; wherever he went forth he prospered: and he rebelled against the king of Assyria, and didn't serve him.

The king of Assyria sent Tartan and Rabsaris and Rabshakeh from Lachish to king Hezekiah with a great army to Jerusalem. They went up and came to Jerusalem. When they had come up, they came and stood by the conduit of the upper pool, which is in the highway of the fuller's field. When they had called to the king, there came out to them Eliakim the son of Hilkiah, who was over the household, and Shebnah the scribe, and Joah the son of Asaph the recorder. Rabshakeh said to them, "Say now to Hezekiah, 'Thus says the great king, the king of Assyria, "What confidence is this in which you trust? You say (but they are but vain words), 'There is counsel and strength for war.' Now on whom do you trust, that you have rebelled against me? Now, behold, you trust in the staff of this bruised reed, even in Egypt. If a man leans on it, it will go into his hand, and pierce it. So is Pharaoh king of Egypt to all who trust on him. But if you tell me, 'We trust in Yahweh our God;' isn't that he whose high places and whose altars Hezekiah has taken away, and has said to Judah and to Jerusalem, 'You shall worship before this altar in Jerusalem?' Now therefore, please give pledges to my master the king of Assyria, and I will give you two thousand horses, if you are able on your part to set riders on them. How then can you turn away the face of one captain of the least of my master's servants, and put your trust on Egypt for chariots and for horsemen? Have I now come up without Yahweh against this place to destroy it? Yahweh said to me, 'Go up against this land, and destroy it.'"

Then Rabshakeh stood, and cried with a loud voice in the Jews' language, and spoke, saying, "Hear the word of the great king, the king of Assyria. Thus says the king, 'Don't let Hezekiah deceive you; for he will not be able to deliver you out of his hand. Neither let Hezekiah make you trust in Yahweh, saying, "Yahweh will surely deliver us, and this city shall not be given into the hand of the king of Assyria." Don't listen to Hezekiah.' For thus says the king of Assyria, 'Make your peace with me, and come out to me; and everyone of you eat of his vine, and everyone of his fig tree, and everyone drink the waters of his own cistern; until I come and take you away to a land like your own land, a land of grain and new wine, a land of bread and vineyards, a land of olive trees and of honey, that you may live, and not die. Don't listen to Hezekiah, when he persuades you, saying, "Yahweh will deliver us." Has any of the gods of the nations ever delivered his land out of the hand of the king of Assyria?

So the servants of king Hezekiah came to Isaiah. Isaiah said to them, "Thus you shall tell your master, 'Thus says Yahweh, "Don't be afraid of the words that you have heard, with which the servants of the king of Assyria have blasphemed me. Behold, I will put a spirit in him, and he will hear news, and will return to his own land. I will cause him to fall by the sword in his own land."

So Rabshakeh returned, and found the king of Assyria warring against Libnah; for he had heard that he had departed from Lachish. When he heard it said of Tirhakah king of Ethiopia, "Behold, he has come out to fight against you, he sent messengers again to Hezekiah, saying, 'Thus you shall speak to Hezekiah king of Judah, saying, "Don't let your God in whom you trust deceive you, saying, Jerusalem will not be given into the hand of the king of Assyria. Behold, you have heard what the kings of Assyria have done to all lands, by destroying them utterly. Will you be delivered? Have the gods of the nations delivered them, which my fathers have destroyed, Gozan, and Haran, and Rezeph, and the children of Eden that were in Telassar? Where is the king of Hamath, and the king of Arpad, and the king of the city of Sepharvaim, of Hena, and Ivvah?"

Hezekiah received the letter from the hand of the messengers, and read it. Then Hezekiah went up to the house of Yahweh, and spread it before Yahweh. Hezekiah prayed before Yahweh, and said, "Yahweh, the God of Israel, who sit above the cherubim, you are the God, even you alone, of all the kingdoms of the earth. You have made heaven and earth. Incline your ear, Yahweh, and hear. Open your eyes, Yahweh, and see. Hear the words of Sennacherib, with which he has sent to defy the living God. Truly, Yahweh, the kings of Assyria have laid waste the nations and their lands, and have cast their gods into the fire; for they were no gods, but the work of men's hands, wood and stone. Therefore they have destroyed them. Now therefore, Yahweh our God, save us, I beg you, out of his hand, that all the kingdoms of the earth may know that you, Yahweh, are God alone."

The situation seemed hopeless. The Assyrians surrounded Jerusalem, and the army was seemingly without number. King Hezekiah prayed fervently to God for deliverance. The prophet Isaiah assured Hezekiah that God would provide deliverance. And this deliverance came mightily, by the hand of the angel of God.

Then Isaiah the son of Amoz sent to Hezekiah, saying, "Thus says Yahweh, the God of Israel, 'Whereas you have prayed to me against Sennacherib king of Assyria, I have heard you. This is the word that Yahweh has spoken concerning him:

Whom have you defied and blasphemed? Against whom have you exalted your voice and lifted up your eyes on high? Against the Holy One of Israel.

But I know your sitting down, and your going out, and your coming in, and your raging against me. Because of your raging against me, and because your arrogance has come up into my ears, therefore will I put my hook in your nose, and my bridle in your lips, and I will turn you back by the way by which you came."

"Therefore thus says Yahweh concerning the king of Assyria, 'He shall not come to this city, nor shoot an arrow there, neither shall he come before it with shield, nor cast up a mound against it. By the way that he came, by the same shall he return, and he shall not come to this city,' says Yahweh. 'For I will defend this city to save it, for my own sake, and for my servant David's sake.'"

It happened that night, that the angel of Yahweh went out, and struck one hundred eighty-five thousand in the camp of the Assyrians. When men arose early in the morning, behold, these were all dead bodies. So Sennacherib king of Assyria departed, and went and returned, and lived at Nineveh. It happened, as he was worshiping in the house of Nisroch his god, that Adrammelech and Sharezer struck him with the sword; and they escaped into the land of Ararat. Esar Haddon his son reigned in his place.

Over his lifetime, Hezekiah remained faithful to God. Because of his enduring loyalty, God extended his life by 15 years. This story is a testimony of the power of the faithful in approaching God in prayer. Unfortunately, after his death, his son Manasseh did evil in the sight of God, serving idols, working with wizards, shedding much innocent blood, and even sacrificing his own son in fire. His evil was unprecedented in Israel, leading to the defeat and captivity of Israel by the Assyrians.

Yahweh spoke to Manasseh, and to his people; but they gave no heed. Therefore Yahweh brought on them the captains of the army of the king of Assyria, who took Manasseh in chains, and bound him with fetters, and carried him to Babylon. When he was in distress, he begged Yahweh his God, and humbled himself greatly before the God of his fathers. He prayed to him; and he was entreated by him, and heard his supplication, and brought him again to Jerusalem into his kingdom. Then Manasseh knew that Yahweh was God.

So Manasseh slept with his fathers, and they buried him in his own house: and Amon his son reigned in his place. Amon was twenty-two years old when he began to reign; and he reigned two years in Jerusalem. He did that which was evil in the sight of Yahweh, as did Manasseh his father; and Amon sacrificed to all the engraved images which Manasseh his father had made, and served them. He didn't humble himself before Yahweh, as Manasseh his father had humbled himself; but this same Amon trespassed more and more. His servants conspired against him, and put him to death in his own house. But the people of the land killed all those who had conspired against king Amon; and the people of the land made Josiah his son king in his place.

After Manasseh, his evil son, Amon, reigned for two years. Some of his servants conspired against him, and killed him; but the people put those men to death and raised his son Josiah to be king. It was during his reign that the nearly forgotten words of God were rediscovered.

Josiah was eight years old when he began to reign; and he reigned thirty-one years in Jerusalem: and his mother's name was Jedidah the daughter of Adaiah of Bozkath. He did that which was right in the eyes of Yahweh, and walked in all the way of David his father, and didn't turn aside to the right hand or to the left.

Hilkiah the high priest said to Shaphan the scribe, "I have found the book of the law in the house of Yahweh." Hilkiah delivered the book to Shaphan, and he read it. Shaphan the scribe came to the king, and brought the king word again, and said, "Your servants have emptied out the money that was found in the house, and have delivered it into the hand of the workmen who have the oversight of the house of Yahweh." Shaphan the scribe told the king, saying, "Hilkiah the priest has delivered a book to me." Shaphan read it before the king. It happened, when the king had heard the words of the book of the law, that he tore his clothes. The king commanded Hilkiah the priest, and Ahikam the son of Shaphan, and Achbor the son of Micaiah, and Shaphan the scribe, and Asaiah the king's servant, saying, "Go inquire of Yahweh for me, and for the people, and for all Judah, concerning the words of this book that is found; for great is the wrath of Yahweh that is kindled against us, because our fathers have not listened to the words of this book, to do according to all that which is written concerning us."

The king sent, and they gathered to him all the elders of Judah and of Jerusalem. The king went up to the house of Yahweh, and all the men of Judah and all the inhabitants of Jerusalem with him, and the priests, and the prophets, and all the people, both small and great: and he read in their ears all the words of the book of the covenant which was found in the house of Yahweh. The king stood by the pillar, and made a covenant before Yahweh, to walk after Yahweh, and to keep his commandments, and his testimonies, and his statutes, with all his heart, and all his soul, to confirm the words of this covenant that were written in this book: and all the people stood to the covenant.

The king commanded all the people, saying, "Keep the Passover to Yahweh your God, as it is written in this book of the covenant." Surely there was not kept such a Passover from the days of the judges who judged Israel, nor in all the days of the kings of Israel, nor of the kings of Judah; but in the eighteenth year of king Josiah was this Passover kept to Yahweh in Jerusalem. Moreover Josiah removed those who had familiar spirits, and the wizards, and the teraphim, and the idols, and all the abominations that were seen in the land of Judah and in Jerusalem, that he might confirm the words of the law which were written in the book that Hilkiah the priest found in the house of Yahweh. Like him was there no king before him, who turned to Yahweh with all his heart, and with all his soul, and with all his might, according to all the law of Moses; neither after him arose there any like him. Notwithstanding, Yahweh didn't turn from the fierceness of his great wrath, with which his anger was kindled against Judah, because of all the provocation with which Manasseh had provoked him. Yahweh said, "I will remove Judah also out of my sight, as I have removed Israel, and I will cast off this city which I have chosen, even Jerusalem, and the house of which I said, 'My name shall be there.'"

Josiah was killed in battle by Pharaoh Necoh, king of Egypt. His son Johoahaz reigned for only three months, and then he was carried away by the Pharaoh to Egypt, where he died. His son Johoiakim took his place.

Jehoiakim was twenty-five years old when he began to reign; and he reigned eleven years in Jerusalem:

He did that which was evil in the sight of Yahweh, according to all that his fathers had done. In his days Nebuchadnezzar king of Babylon came up, and Jehoiakim became his servant three years: then he turned and rebelled against him. Yahweh sent against him bands of the Chaldeans, and bands of the Syrians, and bands of the Moabites, and bands of the children of Ammon, and sent them against Judah to destroy it, according to the word of Yahweh, which he spoke by his servants the prophets.

So Jehoiakim slept with his fathers; and Jehoiachin his son reigned in his place.

Jehoiachin was eighteen years old when he began to reign; and he reigned in Jerusalem three months: and his mother's name was Nehushta the daughter of Elnathan of Jerusalem. He did that which was evil in the sight of Yahweh, according to all that his father had done. At that time the servants of Nebuchadnezzar king of Babylon came up to Jerusalem, and the city was besieged. Nebuchadnezzar king of Babylon came to the city, while his servants were besieging it; and Jehoiachin the king of Judah went out to the king of Babylon, he, and his mother, and his servants, and his princes, and his officers: and the king of Babylon took him in the eighth year of his reign. He carried out there all the treasures of the house of Yahweh, and the treasures of the king's house, and cut in pieces all the vessels of gold, which Solomon king of Israel had made in Yahweh's temple, as Yahweh had said. He carried away all Jerusalem, and all the princes, and all the mighty men of valor, even ten thousand captives, and all the craftsmen and the smiths; none remained, except the poorest sort of the people of the land. He carried away Jehoiachin to Babylon; and the king's mother, and the king's wives, and his officers, and the chief men of the land, carried he into captivity from Jerusalem to Babylon. All the men of might, even seven thousand, and the craftsmen and the smiths one thousand, all of them strong and apt for war, even them the king of Babylon brought captive to Babylon. The king of Babylon made Mattaniah, Jehoiachin's father's brother, king is his place, and changed his name to Zedekiah.

This defeat led to the first of three deportations of the Jews of Judah to Babylon. This initial deportation of the court of King Jehoiachin and the skilled people of the nation occurred in the eighth year of the reign of king Nebuchadnezzar of Babylon.

In the second deportation, Jeconiah's successor, Zedekiah, and many more people were carried away to Babylon in Nebuchadnezzar's eighteenth year; and a later deportation occurred in Nebuchadnezzar's twenty-third year.

Zedekiah was twenty-one years old when he began to reign; and he reigned eleven years in Jerusalem: and he did that which was evil in the sight of Yahweh his God; he didn't humble himself before Jeremiah the prophet speaking from the mouth of Yahweh. He also rebelled against king Nebuchadnezzar, who had made him swear by God: but he stiffened his neck, and hardened his heart against turning to Yahweh, the God of Israel. Moreover all the chiefs of the priests, and the people, trespassed very greatly after all the abominations of the nations; and they polluted the house of Yahweh which he had made holy in Jerusalem.

Yahweh, the God of their fathers, sent to them by his messengers, rising up early and sending, because he had compassion on his people, and on his dwelling place: but they mocked the messengers of God, and despised his words, and scoffed at his prophets, until the wrath of Yahweh arose against his people, until there was no remedy.

It happened in the ninth year of his reign, in the tenth month, in the tenth day of the month, that Nebuchadnezzar king of Babylon came, he and all his army, against Jerusalem, and encamped against it; and they built forts against it around it. So the city was besieged to the eleventh year of king Zedekiah. On the ninth day of the fourth month the famine was severe in the city, so that there was no bread for the people of the land.

Then a breach was made in the city, and all the men of war fled by night by the way of the gate between the two walls, which was by the king's garden (now the Chaldeans were against the city around it); and the king went by the way of the Arabah. But the army of the Chaldeans pursued after the king, and overtook him in the plains of Jericho; and all his army was scattered from him. Then they took the king, and carried him up to the king of Babylon to Riblah; and they gave judgment on him. They killed the sons of Zedekiah before his eyes, and put out the eyes of Zedekiah, and bound him in fetters, and carried him to Babylon. Now in the fifth month, on the seventh day of the month, which was the nineteenth year of king Nebuchadnezzar, king of Babylon, came Nebuzaradan the captain of the guard, a servant of the king of Babylon, to Jerusalem. He burnt the house of Yahweh, and the king's house; and all the houses of Jerusalem, even every great house, burnt he with fire. All the army of the Chaldeans, who were with the captain of the guard, broke down the walls around Jerusalem. Nebuzaradan the captain of the guard carried away captive the residue of the people who were left in the city, and those who fell away, who fell to the king of Babylon, and the residue of the multitude. But the captain of the guard left some of the poorest of the land to work the vineyards and fields.

All the vessels of God's house, great and small, and the treasures of the house of Yahweh, and the treasures of the king, and of his princes, all these he brought to Babylon. They burnt God's house, and broke down the wall of Jerusalem, and burnt all its palaces with fire, and destroyed all the goodly vessels of it. He carried those who had escaped from the sword away to Babylon; and they were servants to him and his sons until the reign of the kingdom of Persia: to fulfill the word of Yahweh by the mouth of Jeremiah, until the land had enjoyed its Sabbaths. As long as it lay desolate it kept Sabbath, to fulfill seventy years.

So Judah was carried away captive out of his land.

For the second time in their storied history, the Israelites found themselves in captivity. Just as during their time in Egypt, they were out of their homeland and under the rule of foreign leaders; Israel in Assyria and Judah in Babylon. God had prophesied that this captivity would happen, and that he would eventually deliver his people once again, as he had out of Egypt.

This was a pivotal and defining point in the history of the people of Israel. The people of Israel had been organized by tribes prior to exile; afterward, they were organized by clans, with only the tribe of Levi remaining intact for their work in the priesthood. Despite this unique separation of the Levites, the captivity led to the emergence of scribes (teachers learned in the scriptures) as key spiritual leaders of the nation.

19 THE TRIALS OF JOB

Patient Suffering in Time of Struggle

The testing of Job is an enduring example of how the righteous can endure and handle their situation with grace, even when they do not deserve what life throws at them. Job was a righteous and innocent man, but God allowed Satan to bring great suffering on Job in order to test his righteousness. In the span of a few days, Job experienced more suffering than most people endure in a lifetime. Despite poor counsel from friends and even being mocked by his own wife, Job never spoke evil of or turned his back on God.

Job asked many questions as he reflected on his trials, but the thing he most wanted was an answer from God. Like many of us do when we have trials, we ask, "Why am I suffering?" But in Job's case, he eventually does receive a direct response from God.

Job and his friends make many eloquent speeches about the situation; these discourses, especially God's replies, are regarded as some of the greatest poetic literature ever written.

There was a man in the land of Uz, whose name was Job. That man was blameless and upright, and one who feared God, and turned away from evil. There were born to him seven sons and three daughters. His possessions also were seven thousand sheep, three thousand camels, five hundred yoke of oxen, five hundred female donkeys, and a very great household; so that this man was the greatest of all the children of the east. His sons went and held a feast in the house of each one on his birthday; and they sent and called for their three sisters to eat and to drink with them. It was so, when the days of their feasting had run their course, that Job sent and sanctified them, and rose up early in the morning, and offered burnt offerings according to the number of them all. For Job said, "It may be that my sons have sinned, and renounced God in their hearts." Job did so continually.

Now it happened on the day when God's sons came to present themselves before Yahweh, that Satan also came among them. Yahweh said to Satan,

"Where have you come from?"

Then Satan answered Yahweh, and said, "From going back and forth in the earth, and from walking up and down in it."

Yahweh said to Satan, "Have you considered my servant, Job? For there is none like him in the earth, a blameless and an upright man, one who fears God, and turns away from evil."

Then Satan answered Yahweh, and said, "Does Job fear God for nothing? Haven't you made a hedge around him, and around his house, and around all that he has, on every side? You have blessed the work of his hands, and his substance is increased in the land. But put forth your hand now, and touch all that he has, and he will renounce you to your face."

Yahweh said to Satan, "Behold, all that he has is in your power. Only on himself don't put forth your hand."

So Satan went forth from the presence of Yahweh. It fell on a day when his sons and his daughters were eating and drinking wine in their eldest brother's house, that there came a messenger to Job, and said, "The oxen were plowing, and the donkeys feeding beside them, and the Sabeans attacked, and took them away. Yes, they have killed the servants with the edge of the sword, and I alone have escaped to tell you."

While he was still speaking, there also came another, and said, "The fire of God has fallen from the sky, and has burned up the sheep and the servants, and consumed them, and I alone have escaped to tell you."

While he was still speaking, there came also another, and said, "The Chaldeans made three bands, and swept down on the camels, and have taken them away, yes, and killed the servants with the edge of the sword; and I alone have escaped to tell you."

While he was still speaking, there came also another, and said, "Your sons and your daughters were eating and drinking wine in their eldest brother's house, and behold, there came a great wind from the wilderness, and struck the four corners of the house, and it fell on the young men, and they are dead. I alone have escaped to tell you."

Then Job arose, and tore his robe, and shaved his head, and fell down on the ground, and worshiped. He said, "Naked I came out of my mother's womb, and naked shall I return there. Yahweh gave, and Yahweh has taken away. Blessed be the name of Yahweh." In all this, Job did not sin, nor charge God with wrongdoing.

Job passed this early test, but Satan was not done with him. Again, Satan made an accusation that if Job's health was attacked, then he would turn away from God. God allowed

Satan to further test Job, but only with the condition that he not take his life.

So Satan went forth from the presence of Yahweh, and struck Job with painful sores from the sole of his foot to his head. He took for himself a potsherd to scrape himself with, and he sat among the ashes. Then his wife said to him, "Do you still maintain your integrity? Renounce God, and die."

But he said to her, "You speak as one of the foolish women would speak. What? Shall we receive good at the hand of God, and shall we not receive evil?"

In all this Job didn't sin with his lips.

Now when Job's three friends heard of all this evil that had come on him, they each came from his own place: Eliphaz the Temanite, Bildad the Shuhite, and Zophar the Naamathite, and they made an appointment together to come to sympathize with him and to comfort him. When they lifted up their eyes from a distance, and didn't recognize him, they raised their voices, and wept; and they each tore his robe, and sprinkled dust on their heads toward the sky. So they sat down with him on the ground seven days and seven nights, and none spoke a word to him, for they saw that his grief was very great.

After this Job opened his mouth, and cursed the day of his birth. Job answered:

"Let the day perish in which I was born, the night which said, 'There is a boy conceived.'

Let that day be darkness. Don't let God from above seek for it, neither let the light shine on it.

Let the stars of its twilight be dark. Let it look for light, but have none, neither let it see the eyelids of the morning,

because it didn't shut up the doors of my mother's womb, nor did it hide trouble from my eyes.

"Why didn't I die from the womb? Why didn't I give up the spirit when my mother bore me?

"Why is light given to him who is in misery, life to the bitter in soul,

Who long for death, but it doesn't come; and dig for it more than for hidden treasures,

who rejoice exceedingly, and are glad, when they can find the grave? My groanings are poured out like water.

For the thing which I fear comes on me, That which I am afraid of comes to me.

I am not at ease, neither am I quiet, neither have I rest; but trouble comes."

Then Eliphaz the Temanite answered,

"If someone ventures to talk with you, will you be grieved? But who can withhold himself from speaking?

Behold, you have instructed many, you have strengthened the weak hands.

Your words have supported him who was falling, You have made firm the feeble knees.

But now it has come to you, and you faint. It touches you, and you are troubled.

Isn't your piety your confidence? Isn't the integrity of your ways your hope?

"Remember, now, whoever perished, being innocent?

Or where were the upright cut off?

According to what I have seen, those who plow iniquity, and sow trouble, reap the same.

By the breath of God they perish. By the blast of his anger are they consumed.

For affliction doesn't come forth from the dust, neither does trouble spring out of the ground;

"Behold, happy is the man whom God corrects. Therefore do not despise the chastening of the Almighty.

Thus began a long back-and-forth discourse between Job and his friends. Although his friends sit with Job for days, in the end the words they offered up were not true words of wisdom. They placed the blame for Job's troubles on Job - claiming that it must be due to something that he had done. But Job refused to believe that God perverts justice, even though he wrestled with questions such as "why do the unrighteous flourish?"

Then Job answered,

"Oh that my anguish were weighed, and all my calamity laid in the balances!

"Oh that I might have my request, that God would grant the thing that I long for,

even that it would please God to crush me; that he would let loose his hand, and cut me off!

Be it still my consolation, yes, let me exult in pain that doesn't spare, that I have not denied the words of the Holy One.

"Therefore I will not keep silent. I will speak in the anguish of my spirit. I will complain in the bitterness of my soul.

I loathe my life. I don't want to live forever. Leave me alone, for my days are but a breath.

What is man, that you should magnify him, that you should set your mind on him,

213

that you should visit him every morning, and test him every moment?

How long will you not look away from me, nor leave me alone until I swallow down my spittle?

If I have sinned, what do I do to you, you watcher of men? Why have you set me as a mark for you, so that I am a burden to myself?

Why do you not pardon my disobedience, and take away my iniquity? For now shall I lie down in the dust. You will seek me diligently, but I shall not be."

Then Bildad the Shuhite answered,

"How long will you speak these things? Shall the words of your mouth be a mighty wind?

Does God pervert justice? Or does the Almighty pervert righteousness?

If your children have sinned against him, He has delivered them into the hand of their disobedience.

If you want to seek God diligently, make your supplication to the Almighty.

If you were pure and upright, surely now he would awaken for you, and make the habitation of your righteousness prosperous.

"Behold, God will not cast away a blameless man, neither will he uphold the evildoers.

He will still fill your mouth with laughter, your lips with shouting.

Those who hate you shall be clothed with shame. The tent of the wicked shall be no more."

Then Job answered,

"Truly I know that it is so, but how can man be just with God?

If he is pleased to contend with him, he can't answer him one time in a thousand.

He does great things past finding out; yes, marvelous things without number.

Behold, he goes by me, and I don't see him. He passes on also, but I don't perceive him.

Though I am righteous, my own mouth shall condemn me. Though I am blameless, it shall prove me perverse.

I am blameless. I don't respect myself. I despise my life.

"My soul is weary of my life. I will give free course to my complaint. I will speak in the bitterness of my soul.

I will tell God, 'Do not condemn me. Show me why you contend with me.

if I sin, then you mark me. You will not acquit me from my iniquity.

If I am wicked, woe to me. If I am righteous, I still shall not lift up my head, being filled with disgrace, and conscious of my affliction.

Then Zophar, the Naamathite, answered,

But oh that God would speak, and open his lips against you,

that he would show you the secrets of wisdom! For true wisdom has two sides. Know therefore that God exacts of you less than your iniquity deserves.

But the eyes of the wicked shall fail. They shall have no way to flee. Their hope shall be the giving up of the spirit."

Then Job answered,

"No doubt, but you are the people, and wisdom shall die with you.

But I have understanding as well as you; I am not inferior to you. Yes, who doesn't know such things as these?

What you know, I know also. I am not inferior to you.

"Surely I would speak to the Almighty. I desire to reason with God.

But you are forgers of lies. You are all physicians of no value.

Oh that you would be completely silent! Then you would be wise.

Hear now my reasoning. Listen to the pleadings of my lips.

Will you speak unrighteously for God, and talk deceitfully for him?

Will you show partiality to him? Will you contend for God?

Behold, he will kill me. I have no hope. Nevertheless, I will maintain my ways before him.

This also shall be my salvation, that a godless man shall not come before him.

Hear diligently my speech. Let my declaration be in your ears.

See now, I have set my cause in order. I know that I am righteous.

"Man, who is born of a woman, is of few days, and full of trouble.

He comes forth like a flower, and is cut down. He also flees like a shadow, and doesn't continue.

If a man dies, shall he live again? All the days of my warfare would I wait, until my release should come.

Then Bildad the Shuhite answered,

"How long will you hunt for words? Consider, and afterward we will speak.

"Yes, the light of the wicked shall be put out, The spark of his fire shall not shine.

The light shall be dark in his tent. His lamp above him shall be put out.

The steps of his strength shall be shortened. His own counsel shall cast him down.

Surely such are the dwellings of the unrighteous. This is the place of him who doesn't know God."

Then Job answered,

"How long will you torment me, and crush me with words?

You have reproached me ten times. You aren't ashamed that you attack me.

If it is true that I have erred, my error remains with myself.

"Have pity on me, have pity on me, you my friends; for the hand of God has touched me.

Why do you persecute me as God, and are not satisfied with my flesh?

"Oh that my words were now written! Oh that they were inscribed in a book!

That with an iron pen and lead they were engraved in the rock forever!

But as for me, I know that my Redeemer lives. In the end, he will stand upon the earth.

After my skin is destroyed, then in my flesh shall I see God,

"Why do the wicked live, become old, yes, and grow mighty in power?

Their child is established with them in their sight, their offspring before their eyes.

Their houses are safe from fear, neither is the rod of God upon them.

What is the Almighty, that we should serve him? What profit should we have, if we pray to him?'

Behold, their prosperity is not in their hand. The counsel of the wicked is far from me.

"How often is it that the lamp of the wicked is put out, that their calamity comes on them, that God distributes sorrows in his anger?

One dies in his full strength, being wholly at ease and quiet.

His pails are full of milk. The marrow of his bones is moistened.

Another dies in bitterness of soul, and never tastes of good.

They lie down alike in the dust. The worm covers them.

Job again took up his parable, and said,

"Oh that I were as in the months of old, as in the days when God watched over me;

when his lamp shone on my head, and by his light I walked through darkness,

as I was in the ripeness of my days, when the friendship of God was in my tent,

when the Almighty was yet with me, and my children were around me,

when my steps were washed with butter, and the rock poured out streams of oil for me,

when I went forth to the city gate, when I prepared my seat in the street.

"Now my soul is poured out within me. Days of affliction have taken hold on

me.

In the night season my bones are pierced in me, and the pains that gnaw me take no rest.

By great force is my garment disfigured. It binds me about as the collar of my coat.

He has cast me into the mire. I have become like dust and ashes.

I cry to you, and you do not answer me. I stand up, and you gaze at me.

You have turned to be cruel to me. With the might of your hand you persecute me.

You lift me up to the wind, and drive me with it. You dissolve me in the storm.

For I know that you will bring me to death, To the house appointed for all living.

if like Adam I have covered my transgressions, by hiding my iniquity in my heart,

because I feared the great multitude, and the contempt of families terrified me, so that I kept silence, and didn't go out of the door—

oh that I had one to hear me! (behold, here is my signature, let the Almighty answer me); let the accuser write my indictment!

Surely I would carry it on my shoulder; and I would bind it to me as a crown.

I would declare to him the number of my steps. as a prince would I go near to him.

If my land cries out against me, and its furrows weep together;

if I have eaten its fruits without money, or have caused its owners to lose their life,

let briars grow instead of wheat, and stinkweed instead of barley."

The words of Job are ended.

So these three men ceased to answer Job, because he was righteous in his own eyes. Then the wrath of Elihu the son of Barachel, the Buzite, of the family of Ram, was kindled against Job. His wrath was kindled because he justified himself rather than God. Also his wrath was kindled against his three friends, because they had found no answer, and yet had condemned Job. Now Elihu had waited to speak to Job, because they were elder than he. When Elihu saw that there was no answer in the mouth of these three men, his wrath was kindled.

Elihu the son of Barachel the Buzite answered,

"I am young, and you are very old; Therefore I held back, and didn't dare show you my opinion.

I said, 'Days should speak, and multitude of years should teach wisdom.'

But there is a spirit in man, and the breath of the Almighty gives them understanding.

"However, Job, please hear my speech, and listen to all my words.

Behold, I am toward God even as you are. I am also formed out of the clay.

Behold, my terror shall not make you afraid, neither shall my pressure be heavy on you.

"Surely you have spoken in my hearing, I have heard the voice of your words, saying,

'I am clean, without disobedience. I am innocent, neither is there iniquity in me.

"Behold, I will answer you. In this you are not just, for God is greater than man.

"Behold, God is mighty, and doesn't despise anyone. He is mighty in strength of understanding.

He doesn't preserve the life of the wicked, but gives to the afflicted their right.

He doesn't withdraw his eyes from the righteous, but with kings on the throne, he sets them forever, and they are exalted.

He also opens their ears to instruction, and commands that they return from iniquity.

If they listen and serve him, they shall spend their days in prosperity, and their years in pleasures.

But if they don't listen, they shall perish by the sword; they shall die without knowledge.

Now men don't see the light which is bright in the skies, but the wind passes, and clears them.

Out of the north comes golden splendor. With God is awesome majesty.

We can't reach the Almighty. He is exalted in power. In justice and great righteousness, he will not oppress.

Therefore men revere him. He doesn't regard any who are wise of heart."

It is interesting that immediately after Elihu made the claim that God was unreachable, and that God has no regard for men, that God finally spoke. After much pleading, Job finally received what he had wanted — a response from God. But in the majesty and eloquence of God's discourse, Job was left without response. In return for his faithfulness, God blessed Job, and he died old and full of days.

Then Yahweh answered Job out of the whirlwind,

"Who is this who darkens counsel by words without knowledge?

Brace yourself like a man, for I will question you, then you answer me!

"Where were you when I laid the foundations of the earth? Declare, if you have understanding.

Who determined its measures, if you know? Or who stretched the line on it?

Whereupon were its foundations fastened? Or who laid its cornerstone,

when the morning stars sang together, and all the sons of God shouted for joy?

"Or who shut up the sea with doors, when it broke forth from the womb,

when I made clouds its garment, and wrapped it in thick darkness,

marked out for it my bound, set bars and doors,

and said, 'Here you may come, but no further. Here your proud waves shall be stayed?'

"Have you commanded the morning in your days, and caused the dawn to know its place;

that it might take hold of the ends of the earth, and shake the wicked out of it?

It is changed as clay under the seal, and stands forth as a garment.

From the wicked, their light is withheld. The high arm is broken.

"Have you entered into the springs of the sea? Or have you walked in the recesses of the deep?

Have the gates of death been revealed to you? Or have you seen the gates of the shadow of death?

Have you comprehended the earth in its breadth? Declare, if you know it all.

"What is the way to the dwelling of light? As for darkness, where is its place,

that you should take it to its bound, that you should discern the paths to its house?

Surely you know, for you were born then, and the number of your days is great!

Have you entered the treasuries of the snow, or have you seen the treasures of the hail,

which I have reserved against the time of trouble, against the day of battle and war?

By what way is the lightning distributed, or the east wind scattered on the earth?

Who has cut a channel for the flood water, or the path for the thunderstorm;

To cause it to rain on a land where no man is; on the wilderness, in which there is no man;

to satisfy the waste and desolate ground, to cause the tender grass to spring forth?

Does the rain have a father? Or who fathers the drops of dew?

Out of whose womb came the ice? The gray frost of the sky, who has given birth to it?

The waters become hard like stone, when the surface of the deep is frozen.

"Can you bind the cluster of the Pleiades, or loosen the cords of Orion?

Can you lead forth the constellations in their season? Or can you guide the Bear with her cubs?

Do you know the laws of the heavens? Can you establish its dominion over the earth?

"Can you lift up your voice to the clouds, That abundance of waters may cover you?

Can you send forth lightnings, that they may go? Do they report to you, 'Here we are?'

Who has put wisdom in the inward parts? Or who has given understanding to the mind?

Who can number the clouds by wisdom? Or who can pour out the bottles of the sky,

when the dust runs into a mass, and the clods of earth stick together?

"Can you hunt the prey for the lioness, or satisfy the appetite of the young lions,

when they crouch in their dens, and lie in wait in the thicket?

Who provides for the raven his prey, when his young ones cry to God, and wander for lack of food?

"Do you know the time when the mountain goats give birth? Do you watch when the doe bears fawns?

Can you number the months that they fulfill? Or do you know the time when they give birth?

"Have you given the horse might? Have you clothed his neck with a quivering mane?

Have you made him to leap as a locust? The glory of his snorting is awesome.

He paws in the valley, and rejoices in his strength. He goes out to meet the armed men.

He mocks at fear, and is not dismayed, neither does he turn back from the sword.

The quiver rattles against him,

the flashing spear and the javelin. He eats up the ground with fierceness and rage,

neither does he stand still at the sound of the trumpet.

As often as the trumpet sounds he snorts, 'Aha!' He smells the battle afar off, the thunder of the captains, and the shouting.

"Is it by your wisdom that the hawk soars, and stretches her wings toward the south?

Is it at your command that the eagle mounts up, and makes his nest on high?

On the cliff he dwells, and makes his home, on the point of the cliff, and the stronghold.

From there he spies out the prey. His eyes see it afar off.

His young ones also suck up blood. Where the slain are, there he is."

Moreover Yahweh answered Job,

"Shall he who argues contend with the Almighty? He who argues with God, let him answer it."

Then Job answered Yahweh,

"Behold, I am of small account. What shall I answer you? I lay my hand on my mouth.

I have spoken once, and I will not answer; Yes, twice, but I will proceed no further."

Then Yahweh answered Job out of the whirlwind,

"Now brace yourself like a man. I will question you, and you will answer me.

Will you even annul my judgment? Will you condemn me, that you may be justified?

Or do you have an arm like God? Can you thunder with a voice like him?

"Now deck yourself with excellency and dignity. Array yourself with honor and majesty.

Pour out the fury of your anger. Look at everyone who is proud, and bring him low.

Look at everyone who is proud, and humble him. Crush the wicked in their place.

Hide them in the dust together. Bind their faces in the hidden place.

Then I will also admit to you that your own right hand can save you.

"See now, behemoth, which I made as well as you. He eats grass as an ox.

Look now, his strength is in his thighs. His force is in the muscles of his belly.

He moves his tail like a cedar. The sinews of his thighs are knit together.

His bones are like tubes of brass. His limbs are like bars of iron.

He is the chief of the ways of God. He who made him gives him his sword.

Surely the mountains produce food for him, where all the animals of the field play.

He lies under the lotus trees, in the covert of the reed, and the marsh.

The lotuses cover him with their shade. The willows of the brook surround him.

Behold, if a river overflows, he doesn't tremble. He is confident, though the Jordan swells even to his mouth.

Shall any take him when he is on the watch, or pierce through his nose with a snare?

"Can you draw out Leviathan with a fishhook, or press down his tongue with a cord?

Can you put a rope into his nose, or pierce his jaw through with a hook?

Will he make many petitions to you, or will he speak soft words to you?

Will he make a covenant with you, that you should take him for a servant forever?

Will you play with him as with a bird? Or will you bind him for your girls?

Will traders barter for him? Will they part him among the merchants?

Can you fill his skin with barbed irons, or his head with fish spears?

Lay your hand on him. Remember the battle, and do so no more.

Behold, the hope of him is in vain. Won't one be cast down even at the sight of him?

None is so fierce that he dare stir him up. Who then is he who can stand before me?

Who has first given to me, that I should repay him? Everything under the heavens is mine.

"I will not keep silence concerning his limbs, nor his mighty strength, nor his goodly frame.

Who can strip off his outer garment? Who shall come within his jaws?

Who can open the doors of his face? Around his teeth is terror.

Strong scales are his pride, shut up together with a close seal.

One is so near to another, that no air can come between them.

They are joined one to another. They stick together, so that they can't be pulled apart.

His sneezing flashes out light. His eyes are like the eyelids of the morning.

Out of his mouth go burning torches. Sparks of fire leap forth.

Out of his nostrils a smoke goes, as of a boiling pot over a fire of reeds.

His breath kindles coals. A flame goes forth from his mouth.

There is strength in his neck. Terror dances before him.

The flakes of his flesh are joined together. They are firm on him. They can't be moved.

His heart is as firm as a stone, yes, firm as the lower millstone.

When he raises himself up, the mighty are afraid. They retreat before his thrashing.

If one attacks him with the sword, it can't prevail; nor the spear, the dart, nor the pointed shaft.

He counts iron as straw; and brass as rotten wood.

The arrow can't make him flee. Sling stones are like chaff to him.

Clubs are counted as stubble. He laughs at the rushing of the javelin.

His undersides are like sharp potsherds, leaving a trail in the mud like a threshing sledge.

He makes the deep to boil like a pot. He makes the sea like a pot of ointment.

He makes a path shine after him. One would think the deep had white hair.

On earth there is not his equal, that is made without fear.

He sees everything that is high. He is king over all the sons of pride."

Then Job answered Yahweh,

"I know that you can do all things, and that no purpose of yours can be restrained.

You asked, 'Who is this who hides counsel without knowledge?' therefore I have uttered that which I did not understand, things too wonderful for me, which I didn't know.

You said, 'Listen, now, and I will speak; I will question you, and you will answer me.' I had heard of you by the hearing of the ear, but now my eye sees you.

Therefore I abhor myself, and repent in dust and ashes."

It was so, that after Yahweh had spoken these words to Job, Yahweh said to Eliphaz the Temanite, "My wrath is kindled against you, and against your two friends; for you have not spoken of me the thing that is right, as my servant Job has. Now therefore, take to yourselves seven bulls and seven rams, and go to my servant Job, and offer up for yourselves a burnt offering; and my servant Job shall pray for you, for I will accept him, that I not deal with you according to your folly. For you have not spoken of me the thing that is right, as my servant Job has."

So Eliphaz the Temanite and Bildad the Shuhite and Zophar the Naamathite went, and did what Yahweh commanded them, and Yahweh accepted Job.

Yahweh turned the captivity of Job, when he prayed for his friends. Yahweh gave Job twice as much as he had before. Then came there to him all his brothers, and all his sisters, and all those who had been of his acquaintance before, and ate bread with him in his house. They comforted him, and consoled him concerning all the evil that Yahweh had brought on him. Everyone also gave him a piece of money, and everyone a ring of gold.

So Yahweh blessed the latter end of Job more than his beginning. He had fourteen thousand sheep, six thousand camels, one thousand yoke of oxen, and a thousand female donkeys. He had also seven sons and three daughters.

He called the name of the first, Jemimah; and the name of the second, Keziah; and the name of the third, Keren Happuch. In all the land were no women found so beautiful as the daughters of Job. Their father gave them an inheritance among their brothers. After this Job lived one hundred forty years, and saw his sons, and his sons' sons, to four generations. So Job died, being old and full of days.

GOD'S LOVE STORY

20 I DESIRE MERCY

Major Lessons from Minor Prophets

The story of the reluctant prophet Jonah is one that is familiar to nearly everyone, even those who are not Christians. Called by God to preach in the mighty Assyrian city of Nineveh, Jonah instead fled from his responsibilities. The story of Jonah, who was swallowed by a great fish and was in its belly for three days, is a staple of childhood books and Bible classes. What is often overlooked is the fact that Jonah repented, went to Nineveh, and had amazing results there.

Now the word of Yahweh came to Jonah the son of Amittai, saying, "Arise, go to Nineveh, that great city, and preach against it, for their wickedness has come up before me."

But Jonah rose up to flee to Tarshish from the presence of Yahweh. He went down to Joppa, and found a ship going to Tarshish; so he paid its fare, and went down into it, to go with them to Tarshish from the presence of Yahweh. But Yahweh sent out a great wind on the sea, and there was a mighty storm on the sea, so that the ship was likely to break up. Then the mariners were afraid, and every man cried to his god. They threw the cargo that was in the ship into the sea to lighten the ship. But Jonah had gone down into the innermost parts of the ship, and he was laying down, and was fast asleep. So the shipmaster came to him, and said to him, "What do you mean, sleeper? Arise, call on your God! Maybe your God will notice us, so that we won't perish."

They all said to each other, "Come, let us cast lots, that we may know who is responsible for this evil that is on us." So they cast lots, and the lot fell on Jonah. Then they asked him, "Tell us, please, for whose cause this evil is on us. What is your occupation? Where do you come from? What is your country? Of what people are you?"

He said to them, "I am a Hebrew, and I fear Yahweh, the God of heaven,

225

who has made the sea and the dry land."

Then were the men exceedingly afraid, and said to him, "What is this that you have done?" For the men knew that he was fleeing from the presence of Yahweh, because he had told them. Then they said to him, "What shall we do to you, that the sea may be calm to us?" For the sea grew more and more stormy.

He said to them, "Take me up, and throw me into the sea. Then the sea will be calm for you; for I know that because of me this great storm is on you."

Nevertheless the men rowed hard to get them back to the land; but they could not, for the sea grew more and more stormy against them. Therefore they cried to Yahweh, and said, "We beg you, Yahweh, we beg you, don't let us die for this man's life, and don't lay on us innocent blood; for you, Yahweh, have done as it pleased you." So they took up Jonah, and threw him into the sea; and the sea ceased its raging. Then the men feared Yahweh exceedingly; and they offered a sacrifice to Yahweh, and made vows.

Yahweh prepared a great fish to swallow up Jonah, and Jonah was in the belly of the fish three days and three nights.

Then Jonah prayed to Yahweh, his God, out of the fish's belly.

Yahweh spoke to the fish, and it vomited out Jonah on the dry land.

The word of Yahweh came to Jonah the second time, saying, "Arise, go to Nineveh, that great city, and preach to it the message that I give you."

So Jonah arose, and went to Nineveh, according to the word of Yahweh. Now Nineveh was an exceedingly great city, three days' journey across. Jonah began to enter into the city a day's journey, and he cried out, and said, "In forty days, Nineveh will be overthrown!"

The people of Nineveh believed God; and they proclaimed a fast, and put on sackcloth, from their greatest even to their least. The news reached the king of Nineveh, and he arose from his throne, and took off his royal robe, covered himself with sackcloth, and sat in ashes.

God saw their works, that they turned from their evil way. God relented of the disaster which he said he would do to them, and he didn't do it.

Amazingly, Jonah was not pleased that Nineveh repented. They had a reputation as hardened warriors, using ruthless tactics. Jonah saw them as an enemy of God's people, not as precious souls that needed to be saved. And just as He had taught Jonah with the fish, God used nature to teach Jonah about his love for all of mankind, not just the nation of Israel. The lesson of Jonah is a lesson for all of us - God desires for all men to repent and be saved; we must demonstrate love and forgiveness, and not rebel against God's mercy.

But it displeased Jonah exceedingly, and he was angry.

Then Jonah went out of the city, and sat on the east side of the city, and there made himself a booth, and sat under it in the shade, until he might see what would become of the city. Yahweh God prepared a vine, and made it to come up over Jonah, that it might be a shade over his head, to deliver him from his discomfort. So Jonah was exceedingly glad because of the vine. But God prepared a worm at dawn the next day, and it chewed on the vine, so that it withered. It happened, when the sun arose, that God prepared a sultry east wind; and the sun beat on Jonah's head, so that he fainted, and requested for himself that he might die, and said, "It is better for me to die than to live."

God said to Jonah, "Is it right for you to be angry about the vine?"

He said, "I am right to be angry, even to death."

Yahweh said, "You have been concerned for the vine, for which you have not labored, neither made it grow; which came up in a night, and perished in a night. Shouldn't I be concerned for Nineveh, that great city, in which are more than one hundred twenty thousand persons who can't discern between their right hand and their left hand; and also much livestock?"

Amos was an outsider, a poor farmer from the southern kingdom of Judah who was called to prophesy to the northern kingdom, Israel. As an outsider, Amos was outraged at the injustices he saw - people who were dishonest, becoming rich at the expense of the poor, paying bribes, and using money to buy privilege. It was a time of prosperity in Israel, with no imminent military threats and with many people enjoying their wealth. But there was evil below the surface, and Hosea pointed out the injustice that often led to this prosperity in Israel and its surrounding countries.

The words of Amos, who was among the herdsmen of Tekoa, which he saw concerning Israel in the days of Uzziah king of Judah, and in the days of Jeroboam the son of Joash king of Israel, two years before the earthquake. He said:

"Yahweh will roar from Zion,
and utter his voice from Jerusalem;
and the pastures of the shepherds will mourn,
and the top of Carmel will wither."

Thus says Yahweh:

"For three transgressions of Israel, yes, for four,
I will not turn away its punishment;
because they have sold the righteous for silver,
and the needy for a pair of shoes;
They trample on the dust of the earth on the head of the poor,

and deny justice to the oppressed;

and a man and his father use the same maiden, to profane my holy name;

and they lay themselves down beside every altar on clothes taken in pledge;

and in the house of their God they drink the wine of those who have been fined.

Therefore thus says the Lord Yahweh:

"An adversary will overrun the land;

and he will pull down your strongholds,

and your fortresses will be plundered."

Listen to this word, you cows of Bashan, who are on the mountain of Samaria, who oppress the poor, who crush the needy, who tell their husbands, "Bring us drinks!"

The Lord Yahweh has sworn by his holiness that behold,

"The days shall come on you that they will take you away with hooks,

and the last of you with fish hooks.

Historians have found ancient paintings showing the Assyrian army leading captives who are strung together with large fish hooks through their cheeks.

For thus says the Lord Yahweh:

"The city that went forth a thousand shall have a hundred left,

and that which went forth one hundred shall have ten left to the house of Israel."

Seek good, and not evil,

that you may live;

and so Yahweh, the God of Armies, will be with you,

as you say.

I hate, I despise your feasts,

and I can't stand your solemn assemblies.

Yes, though you offer me your burnt offerings and meal offerings,

I will not accept them;

neither will I regard the peace offerings of your fat animals.

Take away from me the noise of your songs!

I will not listen to the music of your harps.

But let justice roll on like rivers,

and righteousness like a mighty stream.

Thus he showed me and behold, the Lord stood beside a wall made by a plumb line, with a plumb line in his hand. Yahweh said to me, "Amos, what do you see?"

I said, "A plumb line."

Then the Lord said, "Behold, I will set a plumb line in the midst of my people Israel. I will not again pass by them any more. The high places of Isaac will be desolate, the sanctuaries of Israel will be laid waste; and I will rise against the house of Jeroboam with the sword."

Then Amaziah the priest of Bethel sent to Jeroboam king of Israel, saying, "Amos has conspired against you in the midst of the house of Israel. The land is not able to bear all his words. For Amos says, 'Jeroboam will die by the sword, and Israel shall surely be led away captive out of his land.'"

Amaziah also said to Amos, "You seer, go, flee away into the land of Judah, and there eat bread, and prophesy there: but don't prophesy again any more at Bethel; for it is the king's sanctuary, and it is a royal house!"

Then Amos answered Amaziah, "I was no prophet, neither was I a prophet's son; but I was a herdsman, and a farmer of sycamore figs; and Yahweh took me from following the flock, and Yahweh said to me, 'Go, prophesy to my people Israel.'

Now therefore listen to the word of Yahweh: 'You say, Don't prophesy against Israel, and don't preach against the house of Isaac.' Therefore thus says Yahweh: 'Your wife shall be a prostitute in the city, and your sons and your daughters shall fall by the sword, and your land shall be divided by line; and you yourself shall die in a land that is unclean, and Israel shall surely be led away captive out of his land.'"

The prophet Hosea spoke to the northern kingdom of Israel, which he also referred to as Ephraim. Over the course of time, he spoke during the reigns of five kings, in what seemed to be times of prosperity. But Hosea had the task of warning that Israel's unfaithful worship of idols, which he called adultery, would lead God to bring about their destruction as a nation. Hosea most likely lived to see the Assyrian army conquer the capital city of Samaria and take the nation captive to other lands.

Hosea was called, not just to preach, but to act out Israel's predicament by marrying an unfaithful prostitute. Hosea's love for this unfaithful woman demonstrated God's love for Israel, despite the nations love of idolatry. Hosea showed that God desires to love, not to punish. But, like a parent disciplines a child, God will discipline his children out of love.

When Yahweh spoke at first by Hosea, Yahweh said to Hosea, "Go, take for yourself a wife of prostitution and children of unfaithfulness; for the land commits great adultery, forsaking Yahweh." So he went and took Gomer the daughter of Diblaim; and she conceived, and bore him a son.

Yahweh said to him, "Call his name Jezreel; for yet a little while, and I will avenge the blood of Jezreel on the house of Jehu, and will cause the kingdom of the house of Israel to cease. It will happen in that day that I will break the bow of Israel in the valley of Jezreel."

She conceived again, and bore a daughter.

Then he said to him, "Call her name Lo-Ruhamah; for I will no longer have mercy on the house of Israel, that I should in any way pardon them. But I will have mercy on the house of Judah, and will save them by Yahweh their God, and will not save them by bow, sword, battle, horses, or horsemen."

Now when she had weaned Lo-Ruhamah, she conceived, and bore a son.

He said, "Call his name Lo-Ammi; for you are not my people, and I will not be yours. Yet the number of the children of Israel will be as the sand of the sea, which can't be measured nor numbered; and it will come to pass that, in the place where it was said to them, 'You are not my people,' they will be called 'sons of the living God.' The children of Judah and the children of Israel will be gathered together, and they will appoint themselves one head, and will go up from the land; for great will be the day of Jezreel.

Yahweh said to me, "Go again, love a woman loved by another, and an adulteress, even as Yahweh loves the children of Israel, though they turn to other gods, and love cakes of raisins."

So I bought her for myself for fifteen pieces of silver and a homer and a half of barley. I said to her, "You shall stay with me many days. You shall not play the prostitute, and you shall not be with any other man. I will also be so toward you."

For the children of Israel shall live many days without king, and without prince, and without sacrifice, and without sacred stone, and without ephod or idols. Afterward the children of Israel shall return, and seek Yahweh their God, and David their king, and shall come with trembling to Yahweh and to his blessings in the last days.

Hear the word of Yahweh, you children of Israel;
for Yahweh has a charge against the inhabitants of the land:
"Indeed there is no truth,
nor goodness, nor knowledge of God in the land.
There is cursing, lying, murder, stealing, and committing adultery;
they break boundaries, and bloodshed causes bloodshed.
Therefore the land will mourn,
and everyone who dwells therein will waste away.
all living things in her,
even the animals of the field and the birds of the sky;
yes, the fish of the sea also die.

I know Ephraim, and Israel is not hidden from me;
for now, Ephraim, you have played the prostitute.
Israel is defiled.
Their deeds won't allow them to turn to their God;
for the spirit of prostitution is within them,
and they don't know Yahweh.
They are unfaithful to Yahweh;
for they have borne illegitimate children.
Now the new moon will devour them with their fields.
For I will be to Ephraim like a lion,
and like a young lion to the house of Judah.
I myself will tear in pieces and go away.
I will carry off, and there will be no one to deliver.
I will go and return to my place,
until they acknowledge their offense,
and seek my face.
In their affliction they will seek me earnestly."
"Ephraim, what shall I do to you?
Judah, what shall I do to you?
For your love is like a morning cloud,
and like the dew that disappears early.
For I desire mercy, and not sacrifice;
and the knowledge of God more than burnt offerings.
Because Ephraim has multiplied altars for sinning,
they became for him altars for sinning.
I wrote for him the many things of my law;
but they were regarded as a strange thing.
As for the sacrifices of my offerings,
they sacrifice flesh and eat it;
But Yahweh doesn't accept them.
Now he will remember their iniquity,
and punish their sins.
They will return to Egypt.
For Israel has forgotten his Maker and built palaces;
and Judah has multiplied fortified cities;
but I will send a fire on his cities,
and it will devour its fortresses."
The days of visitation have come.
The days of reckoning have come.

231

Israel will consider the prophet to be a fool,
and the man who is inspired to be insane,
because of the abundance of your sins,
and because your hostility is great.
My God will cast them away, because they did not listen to him;
and they will be wanderers among the nations.
"They won't return into the land of Egypt;
but the Assyrian will be their king,
because they refused to repent.
The sword will fall on their cities,
and will destroy the bars of their gates,
and will put an end to their plans.
My people are determined to turn from me.
Though they call to the Most High,
he certainly won't exalt them.
"How can I give you up, Ephraim?
How can I hand you over, Israel?
Samaria will bear her guilt;
for she has rebelled against her God.
They will fall by the sword.
Their infants will be dashed in pieces,
and their pregnant women will be ripped open."
Israel, return to Yahweh your God;
for you have fallen because of your sin.
Take words with you, and return to Yahweh.
Tell him, "Forgive all our sins,
and accept that which is good:
so we offer our lips like bulls.

21 WARNINGS IN PROSPERITY

The Early Prophets of Judah

Isaiah stands as a true giant among men, one of the most influential of the Old Testament prophets. He served in the southern kingdom of Judah, in a pivotal time for the nation. While the people were enjoying prosperity, trouble was brewing, as they had turned their backs on God. Both Assyria and Babylon were growing in power, and God was soon to use these nations to punish the Israelites for their lack of devotion.

Isaiah served four kings of Judah, advising them and having inside access to the halls of power. He was instrumental in bringing about some dramatic rescues of the nation, and helped them to hold off, for a time, the oncoming destruction. Isaiah spoke and wrote on many fronts, including:

- *Warnings against the nation for turning away from God.*
- *Messages to neighboring nations.*
- *Prophesies regarding both Assyria and Babylon.*
- *Words of hope about final deliverance by the Messiah, who Isaiah cast as a "suffering servant."*

Isaiah is quoted more than any other prophet in the New Testament. His influence was strong during his lifetime, and his words continue to give guidance and comfort to this day.

The vision of Isaiah the son of Amoz, which he saw concerning Judah and Jerusalem, in the days of Uzziah, Jotham, Ahaz, and Hezekiah, kings of Judah.

Hear, heavens, and listen, earth; for Yahweh has spoken: "I have nourished and brought up children, and they have rebelled against me.

"What are the multitude of your sacrifices to me?," says Yahweh. "I have had enough of the burnt offerings of rams, and the fat of fed animals. I don't delight in the blood of bulls, or of lambs, or of male goats.

Wash yourselves, make yourself clean. Put away the evil of your doings from before my eyes. Cease to do evil.

Learn to do well. Seek justice. Relieve the oppressed. Judge the fatherless. Plead for the widow."

"Come now, and let us reason together," says Yahweh: "Though your sins be as scarlet, they shall be as white as snow. Though they be red like crimson, they shall be as wool.

If you are willing and obedient, you shall eat the good of the land; but if you refuse and rebel, you shall be devoured with the sword; for the mouth of Yahweh has spoken it."

This is what Isaiah the son of Amoz saw concerning Judah and Jerusalem.

It shall happen in the latter days, that the mountain of Yahweh's house shall be established on the top of the mountains, and shall be raised above the hills; and all nations shall flow to it.

Many peoples shall go and say, "Come, let's go up to the mountain of Yahweh, to the house of the God of Jacob; and he will teach us of his ways, and we will walk in his paths." For out of Zion the law shall go forth, and the word of Yahweh from Jerusalem.

He will judge between the nations, and will decide concerning many peoples; and they shall beat their swords into plowshares, and their spears into pruning hooks. Nation shall not lift up sword against nation, neither shall they learn war any more.

For, behold, the Lord, Yahweh of Armies, takes away from Jerusalem and from Judah supply and support, the whole supply of bread, and the whole supply of water; the mighty man, the man of war, the judge, the prophet, the diviner, the elder, the captain of fifty, the honorable man, the counselor, the skilled craftsman, and the clever enchanter.

For Jerusalem is ruined, and Judah is fallen; because their tongue and their doings are against Yahweh, to provoke the eyes of his glory.

The look of their faces testify against them. They parade their sin like Sodom. They don't hide it. Woe to their soul! For they have brought disaster upon themselves. My people, those who lead you cause you to err, and destroy the way of your paths.

Yahweh stands up to contend, and stands to judge the peoples.

Therefore my people go into captivity for lack of knowledge.

In the year that king Uzziah died, I saw the Lord sitting on a throne, high and lifted up; and his train filled the temple. Above him stood the seraphim. Each one had six wings. With two he covered his face. With two he covered his feet. With two he flew. One called to another, and said, "Holy, holy, holy, is Yahweh of Armies! The whole earth is full of his glory!"

The foundations of the thresholds shook at the voice of him who called, and the house was filled with smoke. Then I said, "Woe is me! For I am undone, because I am a man of unclean lips, and I dwell in the midst of a people of unclean lips: for my eyes have seen the King, Yahweh of Armies!"

Then one of the seraphim flew to me, having a live coal in his hand, which he had taken with the tongs from off the altar. He touched my mouth with it, and said, "Behold, this has touched your lips; and your iniquity is taken away, and your sin forgiven."

I heard the Lord's voice, saying, "Whom shall I send, and who will go for us?"

Then I said, "Here I am. Send me!"

The noise of a multitude is in the mountains, as of a great people; the noise of an uproar of the kingdoms of the nations gathered together! Yahweh of Armies is mustering the army for the battle. They come from a far country, from the uttermost part of heaven, even Yahweh, and the weapons of his indignation, to destroy the whole land.

Wail; for the day of Yahweh is at hand! It will come as destruction from the Almighty.

For Yahweh will have compassion on Jacob, and will yet choose Israel, and set them in their own land. The foreigner will join himself with them, and they will unite with the house of Jacob. The peoples will take them, and bring them to their place. The house of Israel will possess them in Yahweh's land for servants and for handmaids. They will take as captives those whose captives they were; and they shall rule over their oppressors. It will happen in the day that Yahweh will give you rest from your sorrow, from your trouble, and from the hard service in which you were made to serve, that you will take up this parable against the king of Babylon, and say, "How the oppressor has ceased! The golden city has ceased!" Yahweh has broken the staff of the wicked, the scepter of the rulers.

Woe to those who go down to Egypt for help, and rely on horses, and trust in chariots because they are many, and in horsemen because they are very strong, but they don't look to the Holy One of Israel, and they don't seek Yahweh!

Thus says Yahweh, "In an acceptable time have I answered you, and in a day of salvation have I helped you; and I will preserve you, and give you for a covenant of the people, to raise up the land, to make them inherit the desolate heritage: saying to those who are bound, 'Come out!'; to those who are in darkness, 'Show yourselves!'

Sing, heavens; and be joyful, earth; and break forth into singing, mountains: for Yahweh has comforted his people, and will have compassion on his afflicted. But Zion said, "Yahweh has forsaken me, and the Lord has forgotten me."

"Can a woman forget her nursing child, that she should not have compassion on the son of her womb? Yes, these may forget, yet I will not forget you! Behold, I have engraved you on the palms of my hands; your walls are continually before me. Your children make haste; your destroyers and those who made you waste shall go forth from you. Lift up your eyes all around, and see: all these gather themselves together, and come to you. As I live," says Yahweh, "you shall surely clothe yourself with them all as with an ornament, and dress yourself with them, like a bride.

You shall know that I am Yahweh; and those who wait for me shall not be disappointed."

All flesh shall know that I, Yahweh, am your Savior, and your Redeemer, the Mighty One of Jacob."

The book of Isaiah contains prophesies about the coming life and death of the Messiah. The prophesies are remarkable in their detailed descriptions. When one reads about the life of Jesus in the gospel writings, the amazing accuracy of these prophesies becomes clear.

Who has believed our message? To whom has the arm of Yahweh been revealed?

For he grew up before him as a tender plant, and as a root out of dry ground.

He has no good looks or majesty. When we see him, there is no beauty that we should desire him.

He was despised, and rejected by men; a man of suffering, and acquainted with disease. He was despised as one from whom men hide their face; and we didn't respect him.

Surely he has borne our sickness, and carried our suffering; yet we considered him plagued, struck by God, and afflicted.

But he was pierced for our transgressions. He was crushed for our iniquities. The punishment that brought our peace was on him; and by his wounds we are healed.

All we like sheep have gone astray. Everyone has turned to his own way; and Yahweh has laid on him the iniquity of us all.

He was oppressed, yet when he was afflicted he didn't open his mouth. As a lamb that is led to the slaughter, and as a sheep that before its shearers is mute, so he didn't open his mouth.

He was taken away by oppression and judgment; and as for his generation, who considered that he was cut off out of the land of the living and stricken for the disobedience of my people?

They made his grave with the wicked, and with a rich man in his death;

although he had done no violence, neither was any deceit in his mouth.

Yet it pleased Yahweh to bruise him. He has caused him to suffer. When you make his soul an offering for sin, he shall see his seed. He shall prolong his days, and the pleasure of Yahweh shall prosper in his hand.

After the suffering of his soul, he will see the light and be satisfied. My righteous servant will justify many by the knowledge of himself; and he will bear their iniquities.

Therefore will I divide him a portion with the great, and he shall divide the spoil with the strong; because he poured out his soul to death, and was numbered with the transgressors; yet he bore the sin of many, and made intercession for the transgressors.

Seek Yahweh while he may be found; call you on him while he is near: let the wicked forsake his way, and the unrighteous man his thoughts; and let him return to Yahweh, and he will have mercy on him; and to our God, for he will abundantly pardon.

"For my thoughts are not your thoughts, neither are your ways my ways," says Yahweh.

"For as the heavens are higher than the earth, so are my ways higher than your ways, and my thoughts than your thoughts.

Behold, Yahweh's hand is not shortened, that it can't save; neither his ear heavy, that it can't hear: but your iniquities have separated between you and your God, and your sins have hidden his face from you, so that he will not hear.

Micah was a country prophet who was called by God in a time of brutal warfare between Israel, Judah and the surrounding countries. Speaking mainly to Judah, Micah was disturbed that the religious perversion of Israel was finding its way into the lives of the people of Judah. Along with perversion came the problems of bribery, injustice, corruption and distrust that were destroying family and neighborly relationships.

With this backdrop, Micah made very strong prophesies about impending destruction. He also gave clear predictions about the future Messiah, offsetting his dire predictions for Judah with a hopeful tone for the future. Despite the impending punishment, God was already preparing a way for his Son to open the doors of repentance and forgiveness to the world he so dearly loved.

The word of Yahweh that came to Micah the Morashtite in the days of Jotham, Ahaz, and Hezekiah, kings of Judah, which he saw concerning Samaria and Jerusalem.

Hear, you peoples, all of you.

Listen, O earth, and all that is therein:

and let the Lord Yahweh be witness against you,
the Lord from his holy temple.
For, behold, Yahweh comes forth out of his place,
and will come down and tread on the high places of the earth.
The mountains melt under him,
and the valleys split apart,
like wax before the fire,
like waters that are poured down a steep place.
"All this is for the disobedience of Jacob,
and for the sins of the house of Israel.
What is the disobedience of Jacob?
Isn't it Samaria?
And what are the high places of Judah?
Aren't they Jerusalem?
Therefore I will make Samaria like a rubble heap of the field,
like places for planting vineyards;
and I will pour down its stones into the valley,
and I will uncover its foundations.
Therefore Zion for your sake will be plowed like a field,
and Jerusalem will become heaps of rubble,
and the mountain of the temple like the high places of a forest.
But in the latter days,
it will happen that the mountain of Yahweh's temple will be established on
the top of the mountains,
and it will be exalted above the hills;
and peoples will stream to it.
Many nations will go and say,
"Come, and let us go up to the mountain of Yahweh,
and to the house of the God of Jacob;
and he will teach us of his ways,
and we will walk in his paths."
For out of Zion will go forth the law,
and the word of Yahweh from Jerusalem;
and he will judge between many peoples,
and will decide concerning strong nations afar off.
They will beat their swords into plowshares,
and their spears into pruning hooks.
Nation will not lift up sword against nation,
neither will they learn war any more.

But you, Bethlehem Ephrathah,
being small among the clans of Judah,
out of you one will come forth to me that is to be ruler in Israel;
whose goings forth are from of old, from everlasting.
He shall stand, and shall shepherd in the strength of Yahweh,
in the majesty of the name of Yahweh his God:
and they will live, for then he will be great to the ends of the earth.
Listen now to what Yahweh says:
"Arise, plead your case before the mountains,
and let the hills hear what you have to say.
Hear, you mountains, Yahweh's controversy,
and you enduring foundations of the earth;
for Yahweh has a controversy with his people,
and he will contend with Israel.
How shall I come before Yahweh,
and bow myself before the exalted God?
Shall I come before him with burnt offerings,
with calves a year old?
Will Yahweh be pleased with thousands of rams?
With tens of thousands of rivers of oil?
Shall I give my firstborn for my disobedience?
The fruit of my body for the sin of my soul?
He has shown you, O man, what is good.
What does Yahweh require of you, but to act justly,
to love mercy, and to walk humbly with your God?
But as for me, I will look to Yahweh.
I will wait for the God of my salvation.
My God will hear me.
Who is a God like you, who pardons iniquity,
and passes over the disobedience of the remnant of his heritage?
He doesn't retain his anger forever,
because he delights in loving kindness.
He will again have compassion on us.
He will tread our iniquities under foot;
and you will cast all their sins into the depths of the sea.

The prophet Habakkuk has questions for God; How long would he cry, and God not hear? Why do you tolerate those who deal treacherously? Would God deal with Judah without mercy? God answered Habakkuk - he would raise the Babylonians (Chaldeans) to punish

Judah, but ultimately they would be punished even more. The work of mighty nations is as vanity compared to the power and work of our God. God's response to Habakkuk is that he will judge as a loving God. It may take time, but ultimately justice will come - if not in our lifetime, then in eternity.

The oracle which Habakkuk the prophet saw. Yahweh, how long will I cry, and you will not hear? I cry out to you "Violence!" and will you not save? Why do you show me iniquity, and look at perversity? For destruction and violence are before me. There is strife, and contention rises up. Therefore the law is paralyzed, and justice never goes forth; for the wicked surround the righteous; therefore justice goes forth perverted.

"Look among the nations, watch, and wonder marvelously; for I am working a work in your days, which you will not believe though it is told you. For, behold, I raise up the Chaldeans, that bitter and hasty nation, that march through the breadth of the earth, to possess dwelling places that are not theirs.

Aren't you from everlasting, Yahweh my God, my Holy One? We will not die. Yahweh, you have appointed him for judgment. You, Rock, have established him to punish.

You who have purer eyes than to see evil, and who cannot look on perversity, why do you tolerate those who deal treacherously, and keep silent when the wicked swallows up the man who is more righteous than he?

Yahweh answered me, "Write the vision, and make it plain on tablets, that he who runs may read it. For the vision is yet for the appointed time, and it hurries toward the end, and won't prove false. Though it takes time, wait for it; because it will surely come. It won't delay. Behold, his soul is puffed up. It is not upright in him, but the righteous will live by his faith.

Behold, isn't it of Yahweh of Armies that the peoples labor for the fire, and the nations weary themselves for vanity? For the earth will be filled with the knowledge of the glory of Yahweh, as the waters cover the sea.

The reign of Manasseh was a low point - he was truly one of the worst kings in the history of Judah. It may be that the consistent warnings of the prophet Zephaniah played a role in leading Judah back toward righteousness as young king Josiah came to power.

Like other prophets, Zephaniah warned against impending punishment as a result of unfaithfulness. Using the term, "Day of the Lord," he predicted a major event that would impact the entire global stage. But he also saw hope that a small remnant of faithful people would trust in God, and that God would restore them to a new kingdom that would come after the judgment.

The word of Yahweh which came to Zephaniah, the son of Cushi, the son of Gedaliah, the son of Amariah, the son of Hezekiah, in the days of Josiah, the son of Amon, king of Judah. I will utterly sweep away everything off of the surface of the earth, says Yahweh. I will sweep away man and animal. I will sweep away the birds of the sky, the fish of the sea, and the heaps of rubble with the wicked. I will cut off man from the surface of the earth, says Yahweh.

Gather yourselves together, yes, gather together, you nation that has no shame, before the appointed time when the day passes as the chaff, before the fierce anger of Yahweh comes on you, before the day of Yahweh's anger comes on you. Seek Yahweh, all you humble of the land, who have kept his ordinances. Seek righteousness. Seek humility. It may be that you will be hidden in the day of Yahweh's anger.

I have cut off nations. Their battlements are desolate. I have made their streets waste, so that no one passes by. Their cities are destroyed, so that there is no man, so that there is no inhabitant. I said, "Just fear me. Receive correction, so that her dwelling won't be cut off, according to all that I have appointed concerning her." But they rose early and corrupted all their doings.

But I will leave in the midst of you an afflicted and poor people, and they will take refuge in the name of Yahweh. The remnant of Israel will not do iniquity, nor speak lies, neither will a deceitful tongue be found in their mouth, for they will feed and lie down, and no one will make them afraid."

Yahweh, your God, is in the midst of you, a mighty one who will save. He will rejoice over you with joy. He will calm you in his love. He will rejoice over you with singing.

At that time will I bring you in, and at that time will I gather you; for I will give you honor and praise among all the peoples of the earth, when I restore your fortunes before your eyes, says Yahweh.

Jeremiah is the story of a man chosen by God - a reluctant prophet. He was thrust into this important role while a young man, called to prophesy messages of warning to nations, kings and people who did not want to hear God's unwelcome news.

Jeremiah knew his life would be difficult if he carried out God's call, yet he did accept it. His only measure of comfort was that God promised him, "I have made you this day a fortified city, and an iron pillar, and bronze walls, against the whole land, against the kings of Judah, against its princes, against its priests, and against the people of the land."

Speaking a dire message in gloomy time, Jeremiah reminded the people and nations of his time that there was a steep price to be paid for disregarding God. About 100 years earlier, the northern kingdom of Israel had fallen to the Assyrians. Now, the Babylonians were knocking on Judah's door. Sadly, Jeremiah was not successful in convincing Judah to change its ways;

after prophesying during the reigns of five kings of Judah, he lived to see the nation fall to Babylon.

Now the word of Yahweh came to me, saying, "Before I formed you in the belly, I knew you. Before you came forth out of the womb, I sanctified you. I have appointed you a prophet to the nations." Then I said, "Ah, Lord Yahweh! Behold, I don't know how to speak; for I am a child."

But Yahweh said to me, "Don't say, 'I am a child;' for to whoever I shall send you, you shall go, and whatever I shall command you, you shall speak. Don't be afraid because of them; for I am with you to deliver you," says Yahweh. Then Yahweh put forth his hand, and touched my mouth; and Yahweh said to me, "Behold, I have put my words in your mouth. Behold, I have this day set you over the nations and over the kingdoms, to pluck up and to break down and to destroy and to overthrow, to build and to plant."

Then Yahweh said to me, "Out of the north evil will break out on all the inhabitants of the land. For, behold, I will call all the families of the kingdoms of the north," says Yahweh; "and they shall come, and they shall each set his throne at the entrance of the gates of Jerusalem, and against all its walls all around, and against all the cities of Judah. I will utter my judgments against them touching all their wickedness, in that they have forsaken me, and have burned incense to other gods, and worshiped the works of their own hands.

"You therefore put your belt on your waist, arise, and speak to them all that I command you. Don't be dismayed at them, lest I dismay you before them.

For, behold, I have made you this day a fortified city, and an iron pillar, and bronze walls, against the whole land, against the kings of Judah, against its princes, against its priests, and against the people of the land. They will fight against you; but they will not prevail against you; for I am with you," says Yahweh, "to deliver you."

Hear the word of Yahweh, O house of Jacob, and all the families of the house of Israel!

Has a nation changed its gods, which really are no gods? But my people have changed their glory for that which does not profit.

"Be astonished, you heavens, at this, and be horribly afraid. Be very desolate," says Yahweh. "For my people have committed two evils: they have forsaken me, the spring of living waters, and cut them out cisterns, broken cisterns, that can hold no water.

"For of old time I have broken your yoke, and burst your bonds; and you said, 'I will not serve;' for on every high hill and under every green tree you bowed yourself, playing the prostitute. Yet I had planted you a noble vine, wholly a right seed. How then have you turned into the degenerate branches of a foreign vine to me? For though you wash yourself with lye, and use much soap, yet your iniquity is marked before me," says the Lord Yahweh.

As the thief is ashamed when he is found, so is the house of Israel ashamed; they, their kings, their princes, and their priests, and their prophets; who tell wood, 'You are my father;' and a stone, 'You have brought me out:' for they have turned their back to me, and not their face; but in the time of their trouble they will say, 'Arise, and save us.'

"But where are your gods that you have made for yourselves? Let them arise, if they can save you in the time of your trouble: for according to the number of your cities are your gods, Judah.

Declare in Judah, and publish in Jerusalem; and say, 'Blow the trumpet in the land!' Cry aloud and say, 'Assemble yourselves! Let us go into the fortified cities!' Set up a standard toward Zion. Flee for safety! Don't wait; for I will bring evil from the north, and a great destruction."

A lion is gone up from his thicket, and a destroyer of nations; he is on his way, he is gone forth from his place, to make your land desolate, that your cities be laid waste, without inhabitant. For this clothe yourself with sackcloth, lament and wail; for the fierce anger of Yahweh hasn't turned back from us.

"Run back and forth through the streets of Jerusalem, and see now, and know, and seek in the broad places of it, if you can find a man, if there are any who does justly, who seeks truth; and I will pardon her. Though they say, 'As Yahweh lives;' surely they swear falsely."

"But even in those days," says Yahweh, "I will not make a full end with you. It will happen, when you say, 'Why has Yahweh our God done all these things to us?' Then you shall say to them, 'Just like you have forsaken me, and served foreign gods in your land, so you shall serve strangers in a land that is not yours.'

Thus says Yahweh, "Stand in the ways and see, and ask for the old paths, 'Where is the good way?' and walk in it, and you will find rest for your souls. But they said, 'We will not walk in it.'

Since the day that your fathers came forth out of the land of Egypt to this day, I have sent to you all my servants the prophets, daily rising up early and sending them: yet they didn't listen to me, nor inclined their ear, but made their neck stiff: they did worse than their fathers. You shall speak all these words to them; but they will not listen to you: you shall also call to them; but they will not answer you.

They have sown wheat, and have reaped thorns; they have put themselves to pain, and profit nothing: and you shall be ashamed of your fruits, because of the fierce anger of Yahweh. Thus says Yahweh against all my evil neighbors, who touch the inheritance which I have caused my people Israel to inherit: behold, I will pluck them up from off their land, and will pluck up the house of Judah from among them. It shall happen, after that I have plucked them up, I will return and have compassion on them; and I will bring them again, every man to his heritage, and every man to his land.

Hear, and give ear; don't be proud; for Yahweh has spoken.

But if you will not hear it, my soul shall weep in secret for your pride; and my eye shall weep bitterly, and run down with tears, because Yahweh's flock is taken captive. Say to the king and to the queen mother, Humble yourselves, sit down; for your headdresses have come down, even the crown of your glory. The cities of the South are shut up, and there is none to open them: Judah is carried away captive, all of it; it is wholly carried away captive.

Thus said Yahweh: Go down to the house of the king of Judah, and speak there this word, Say, Hear the word of Yahweh, king of Judah, who sits on the throne of David, you, and your servants, and your people who enter in by these gates. Thus says Yahweh: Execute justice and righteousness, and deliver him who is robbed out of the hand of the oppressor: and do no wrong, do no violence, to the foreigner, the fatherless, nor the widow; neither shed innocent blood in this place. For if you do this thing indeed, then shall there enter in by the gates of this house kings sitting on the throne of David, riding in chariots and on horses, he, and his servants, and his people. But if you will not hear these words, I swear by myself, says Yahweh, that this house shall become a desolation. For thus says Yahweh concerning the house of the king of Judah: You are Gilead to me, the head of Lebanon. Yet surely I will make you a wilderness, cities which are not inhabited. I will prepare destroyers against you, everyone with his weapons; and they shall cut down your choice cedars, and cast them into the fire. Many nations shall pass by this city, and they shall say every man to his neighbor, Why has Yahweh done thus to this great city? Then they shall answer, Because they forsook the covenant of Yahweh their God, and worshiped other gods, and served them. Don't weep for the dead, neither bemoan him; but weep bitterly for him who goes away; for he shall return no more, nor see his native country.

Behold, the days come, says Yahweh, that I will raise to David a righteous Branch, and he shall reign as king and deal wisely, and shall execute justice and righteousness in the land. In his days Judah shall be saved, and Israel shall dwell safely; and this is his name by which he shall be called: Yahweh our righteousness.

Jeremiah is traditionally thought to be the author of Lamentations, a poetic book which mourned the destruction of Jerusalem and the taking away in captivity of most of Judah's surviving peoples. The city of Jerusalem was destroyed by the marauding Babylonians after a long siege in 586 B.C. The writings of Jeremiah, although by nature grim, concludes with a hopeful prediction that God will restore his people in a time of healing, if they repent.

How the city sits solitary, that was full of people! She has become as a widow, who was great among the nations! She who was a princess among the provinces has become tributary!

She weeps bitterly in the night, and her tears are on her cheeks; among all her lovers she has none to comfort her: All her friends have dealt treacherously with her; they are become her enemies.

Judah is gone into captivity because of affliction, and because of great servitude; she dwells among the nations, she finds no rest: all her persecutors overtook her within the straits.

The ways of Zion do mourn, because none come to the solemn assembly; all her gates are desolate, her priests do sigh: her virgins are afflicted, and she herself is in bitterness.

Her adversaries are become the head, her enemies prosper; for Yahweh has afflicted her for the multitude of her transgressions: her young children are gone into captivity before the adversary.

Is it nothing to you, all you who pass by?

Look, and see if there is any sorrow like my sorrow, which is brought on me, With which Yahweh has afflicted me in the day of his fierce anger.

For these things I weep; my eye, my eye runs down with water; Because the comforter who should refresh my soul is far from me: My children are desolate, because the enemy has prevailed.

The Lord has become as an enemy, he has swallowed up Israel; He has swallowed up all her palaces, he has destroyed his strongholds; He has multiplied in the daughter of Judah mourning and lamentation.

Yahweh has done that which he purposed; he has fulfilled his word that he commanded in the days of old;

He has thrown down, and has not pitied:

He has caused the enemy to rejoice over you; he has exalted the horn of your adversaries.

I am the man that has seen affliction by the rod of his wrath.

This I recall to my mind; therefore have I hope.

It is because of Yahweh's loving kindnesses that we are not consumed, because his compassion doesn't fail.

They are new every morning; great is your faithfulness.

Yahweh is my portion, says my soul; therefore will I hope in him.

Yahweh is good to those who wait for him, to the soul that seeks him.

It is good that a man should hope and quietly wait for the salvation of Yahweh.

For the Lord will not cast off forever.

For though he cause grief, yet he will have compassion according to the multitude of his loving kindnesses.

Yahweh has accomplished his wrath, he has poured out his fierce anger; He has kindled a fire in Zion, which has devoured its foundations.

The kings of the earth didn't believe, neither all the inhabitants of the world, That the adversary and the enemy would enter into the gates of Jerusalem.

It is because of the sins of her prophets, and the iniquities of her priests, That have shed the blood of the just in the midst of her.

Remember, Yahweh, what has come on us: Look, and see our reproach.

The joy of our heart is ceased; Our dance is turned into mourning.

The crown is fallen from our head: Woe to us! for we have sinned.

You, Yahweh, remain forever; Your throne is from generation to generation.

Why do you forget us forever, And forsake us so long time?

Turn us to yourself, Yahweh, and we shall be turned. Renew our days as of old.

22 STRANGE PROPHESIES IN EXOTIC LANDS

Messengers During Captivity

.

As a young man, Daniel was carried away into captivity when the Babylonian empire overran Jerusalem. It would seem that would be the end of a promising life path for Daniel and many other bright young Jewish men. But Daniel and three of his close friends excelled despite their circumstances, by carefully controlling their food and behavior, and by never losing sight of God.

Daniel served God for nearly 70 years while in Babylon. In this capacity he rose to the rank of prime minister and showed his value under different kings in two different empires. During this time, he and his loyal friends overcame severe trials and persecutions. Their steadfastness in the face of trials, even while facing death, serves as a motivation to us today.

In the third year of the reign of Jehoiakim king of Judah came Nebuchadnezzar king of Babylon to Jerusalem, and besieged it. The Lord gave Jehoiakim king of Judah into his hand, with part of the vessels of the house of God; and he carried them into the land of Shinar to the house of his god: and he brought the vessels into the treasure house of his god.

The king spoke to Ashpenaz the master of his eunuchs, that he should bring in certain of the children of Israel, even of the seed royal and of the nobles; youths in whom was no blemish, but well-favored, and skillful in all wisdom, and endowed with knowledge, and understanding science, and such as had ability to stand in the king's palace; and that he should teach them the learning and the language of the Chaldeans. The king appointed for them a daily portion of the king's dainties, and of the wine which he drank, and that they should be nourished three years; that at its end they should stand before the king. Now among these were, of the children of Judah, Daniel, Hananiah, Mishael, and Azariah. The prince of the eunuchs gave names to them: to Daniel he gave the name of Belteshazzar; and to Hananiah, of Shadrach; and to Mishael, of Meshach; and to Azariah, of Abednego.

But Daniel purposed in his heart that he would not defile himself with the king's food, nor with the wine which he drank: therefore he requested of the prince of the eunuchs that he might not defile himself. Now God made Daniel to find kindness and compassion in the sight of the prince of the eunuchs. The prince of the eunuchs said to Daniel, I fear my Lord the king, who has appointed your food and your drink: for why should he see your faces worse looking than the youths who are of your own age? so would you endanger my head with the king. Then Daniel said to the steward whom the prince of the eunuchs had appointed over Daniel, Hananiah, Mishael, and Azariah: Test your servants, I beg you, ten days; and let them give us vegetables to eat, and water to drink. Then let our faces be looked on before you, and the face of the youths who eat of the king's dainties; and as you see, deal with your servants. So he listened to them in this matter, and proved them ten days.

At the end of ten days their faces appeared fairer, and they were fatter in flesh, than all the youths who ate of the king's food. So the steward took away their food, and the wine that they should drink, and gave them vegetables. Now as for these four youths, God gave them knowledge and skill in all learning and wisdom: and Daniel had understanding in all visions and dreams. At the end of the days which the king had appointed for bringing them in, the prince of the eunuchs brought them in before Nebuchadnezzar. The king talked with them; and among them all was found none like Daniel, Hananiah, Mishael, and Azariah: therefore stood they before the king. In every matter of wisdom and understanding, concerning which the king inquired of them, he found them ten times better than all the magicians and enchanters who were in all his realm. Daniel continued even to the first year of king Cyrus.

When the king had a troubling dream, Daniel was able to interpret the dream with the help of God. Just as God had used the ability to interpret dreams to set aside Joseph in Egypt, he now used this capability to establish Daniel in Babylon.

Normally the king would tell the plot of his dream to the sorcerers, and they would interpret some meaning to the dream. But in this case the king asked them to prove if their magic was true by asking them to tell him what he dreamed, not just the interpretation. Perhaps the king had learned that the so-called magic of his magicians was not real.

Daniel was able to inform the king of this dream, and the interpretation. The dream prophesied about the coming of the spiritual kingdom, the church, which would influence the entire world and, unlike earthly kingdoms, would never be destroyed. This event launched Daniel from being just another bright man serving the king to an elevated position as his trusted adviser and positioned God to have great influence in the Babylonian and Persian empires.

In the second year of the reign of Nebuchadnezzar, Nebuchadnezzar dreamed dreams; and his spirit was troubled, and his sleep went from him. Then the king commanded to call the magicians, and the enchanters, and the sorcerers, and the Chaldeans, to tell the king his dreams. So they came in and stood before the king. The king said to them, I have dreamed a dream, and my spirit is troubled to know the dream.

Then spoke the Chaldeans to the king in the Syrian language, O king, live forever: tell your servants the dream, and we will show the interpretation. The king answered the Chaldeans, The thing is gone from me: if you don't make known to me the dream and its interpretation, you shall be cut in pieces, and your houses shall be made a dunghill. But if you show the dream and its interpretation, you shall receive of me gifts and rewards and great honor: therefore show me the dream and its interpretation.

They answered the second time and said, Let the king tell his servants the dream, and we will show the interpretation. The king answered, I know of a certainty that you would gain time, because you see the thing is gone from me. But if you don't make known to me the dream, there is but one law for you; for you have prepared lying and corrupt words to speak before me, until the time be changed: therefore tell me the dream, and I shall know that you can show me its interpretation.

The Chaldeans answered before the king, and said, There is not a man on the earth who can show the king's matter, because no king, Lord, or ruler, has asked such a thing of any magician, or enchanter, or Chaldean. It is a rare thing that the king requires, and there is no other who can show it before the king, except the gods, whose dwelling is not with flesh.

For this cause the king was angry and very furious, and commanded to destroy all the wise men of Babylon. So the decree went forth, and the wise men were to be slain; and they sought Daniel and his companions to be slain.

Then Daniel returned answer with counsel and prudence to Arioch the captain of the king's guard, who was gone forth to kill the wise men of Babylon; he answered Arioch the king's captain, Why is the decree so urgent from the king? Then Arioch made the thing known to Daniel. Daniel went in, and desired of the king that he would appoint him a time, and he would show the king the interpretation.

Then Daniel went to his house, and made the thing known to Hananiah, Mishael, and Azariah, his companions: that they would desire mercies of the

God of heaven concerning this secret; that Daniel and his companions should not perish with the rest of the wise men of Babylon. Then was the secret revealed to Daniel in a vision of the night. Then Daniel blessed the God of heaven. Daniel answered, Blessed be the name of God forever and ever; for wisdom and might are his. He changes the times and the seasons; he removes kings, and sets up kings; he gives wisdom to the wise, and knowledge to those who have understanding; he reveals the deep and secret things; he knows what is in the darkness, and the light dwells with him. I thank you, and praise you, you God of my fathers, who have given me wisdom and might, and have now made known to me what we desired of you; for you have made known to us the king's matter.

Therefore Daniel went in to Arioch, whom the king had appointed to destroy the wise men of Babylon; he went and said thus to him: Don't destroy the wise men of Babylon; bring me in before the king, and I will show to the king the interpretation. Then Arioch brought in Daniel before the king in haste, and said thus to him, I have found a man of the children of the captivity of Judah, who will make known to the king the interpretation. The king answered Daniel, whose name was Belteshazzar, Are you able to make known to me the dream which I have seen, and its interpretation?

Daniel answered before the king, and said, The secret which the king has demanded can neither wise men, enchanters, magicians, nor soothsayers, show to the king; but there is a God in heaven who reveals secrets, and he has made known to the king Nebuchadnezzar what shall be in the latter days. Your dream, and the visions of your head on your bed, are these: as for you, O king, your thoughts came into your mind on your bed, what should happen hereafter; and he who reveals secrets has made known to you what shall happen. But as for me, this secret is not revealed to me for any wisdom that I have more than any living, but to the intent that the interpretation may be made known to the king, and that you may know the thoughts of your heart.

You, O king, saw, and behold, a great image. This image, which was mighty, and whose brightness was excellent, stood before you; and its aspect was awesome. As for this image, its head was of fine gold, its breast and its arms of silver, its belly and its thighs of brass, its legs of iron, its feet part of iron, and part of clay. You saw until a stone was cut out without hands, which struck the image on its feet that were of iron and clay, and broke them in pieces. Then was the iron, the clay, the brass, the silver, and the gold, broken in pieces together, and became like the chaff of the summer threshing floors; and the wind carried them away, so that no place was found for them: and the stone that struck the image became a great mountain, and filled the whole earth.

This is the dream; and we will tell its interpretation before the king. You, O king, are king of kings, to whom the God of heaven has given the kingdom, the power, and the strength, and the glory; and wherever the children of men dwell, the animals of the field and the birds of the sky has he given into your hand, and has made you to rule over them all: you are the head of gold.

After you shall arise another kingdom inferior to you; and another third kingdom of brass, which shall bear rule over all the earth. The fourth kingdom shall be strong as iron, because iron breaks in pieces and subdues all things; and as iron that crushes all these, shall it break in pieces and crush. Whereas you saw the feet and toes, part of potters' clay, and part of iron, it shall be a divided kingdom; but there shall be in it of the strength of the iron, because you saw the iron mixed with miry clay. As the toes of the feet were part of iron, and part of clay, so the kingdom shall be partly strong, and partly broken. Whereas you saw the iron mixed with miry clay, they shall mingle themselves with the seed of men; but they shall not cling to one another, even as iron does not mingle with clay.

In the days of those kings shall the God of heaven set up a kingdom which shall never be destroyed, nor shall its sovereignty be left to another people; but it shall break in pieces and consume all these kingdoms, and it shall stand forever. Because you saw that a stone was cut out of the mountain without hands, and that it broke in pieces the iron, the brass, the clay, the silver, and the gold; the great God has made known to the king what shall happen hereafter: and the dream is certain, and its interpretation sure.

Then the king Nebuchadnezzar fell on his face, and worshiped Daniel, and commanded that they should offer an offering and sweet odors to him. The king answered to Daniel, and said, Of a truth your God is the God of gods, and the Lord of kings, and a revealer of secrets, since you have been able to reveal this secret. Then the king made Daniel great, and gave him many great gifts, and made him to rule over the whole province of Babylon, and to be chief governor over all the wise men of Babylon. Daniel requested of the king, and he appointed Shadrach, Meshach, and Abednego, over the affairs of the province of Babylon: but Daniel was in the gate of the king.

Over time, king Nebuchadnezzar seemed to forget the working of God in revealing his dream, and his proclamation that God was "the God of gods, and the Lord of kings." The king set up a large golden statue, and every person was commanded to bow in worship to this idol. Shadrach, Meshach, and Abednego were sentenced to death in a furnace when they refused the king's command. In the face of certain death, their faith was unwavering, as they boldly told the king, "...our God whom we serve is able to deliver us from the burning fiery furnace; and he will deliver us out of your hand, O king." After God provided an amazing

251

deliverance from the furnace, the men were promoted, and Nebuchadnezzar issued a decree
forbidding any evil to be spoken of God. We see how the righteous faith of a few men can have
great effect, even in the pagan culture of Babylon. This story clearly shows how our loving God
has the ability to influence events, and deliver us from evil.

Nebuchadnezzar the king made an image of gold, whose height was sixty cubits, and its breadth six cubits: he set it up in the plain of Dura, in the province of Babylon.

Then the satraps, the deputies, and the governors, the judges, the treasurers, the counselors, the sheriffs, and all the rulers of the provinces, were gathered together to the dedication of the image that Nebuchadnezzar the king had set up.

Therefore at that time certain Chaldeans came near, and brought accusation against the Jews. They answered Nebuchadnezzar the king, O king, live forever. You, O king, have made a decree, that every man that shall hear the sound of the horn, flute, zither, lyre, harp, pipe, and all kinds of music, shall fall down and worship the golden image; and whoever doesn't fall down and worship shall be cast into the midst of a burning fiery furnace. There are certain Jews whom you have appointed over the affairs of the province of Babylon: Shadrach, Meshach, and Abednego; these men, O king, have not respected you. They don't serve your gods, nor worship the golden image which you have set up.

Then Nebuchadnezzar in his rage and fury commanded to bring Shadrach, Meshach, and Abednego. Then they brought these men before the king. Nebuchadnezzar answered them, Is it on purpose, Shadrach, Meshach, and Abednego, that you don't serve my god, nor worship the golden image which I have set up? Now if you are ready whenever you hear the sound of the horn, flute, zither, lyre, harp, pipe, and all kinds of music to fall down and worship the image which I have made, well: but if you don't worship, you shall be cast the same hour into the midst of a burning fiery furnace; and who is that god that shall deliver you out of my hands?

Shadrach, Meshach, and Abednego answered the king, Nebuchadnezzar, we have no need to answer you in this matter. If it be so, our God whom we serve is able to deliver us from the burning fiery furnace; and he will deliver us out of your hand, O king. But if not, be it known to you, O king, that we will not serve your gods, nor worship the golden image which you have set up.

Then was Nebuchadnezzar full of fury, and the form of his appearance was changed against Shadrach, Meshach, and Abednego: therefore he spoke, and commanded that they should heat the furnace seven times more than it was usually heated. He commanded certain mighty men who were in his army to bind Shadrach, Meshach, and Abednego, and to cast them into the burning fiery furnace. Then these men were bound in their pants, their tunics, and their mantles, and their other garments, and were cast into the midst of the burning fiery furnace. Therefore because the king's commandment was urgent, and the furnace exceeding hot, the flame of the fire killed those men who took up Shadrach, Meshach, and Abednego. These three men, Shadrach, Meshach, and Abednego, fell down bound into the midst of the burning fiery furnace.

Then Nebuchadnezzar the king was astonished, and rose up in haste: he spoke and said to his counselors, Didn't we cast three men bound into the midst of the fire? They answered the king, True, O king. He answered, Look, I see four men loose, walking in the midst of the fire, and they are unharmed; and the aspect of the fourth is like a son of the gods. Then Nebuchadnezzar came near to the mouth of the burning fiery furnace: he spoke and said, Shadrach, Meshach, and Abednego, you servants of the Most High God, come forth, and come here. Then Shadrach, Meshach, and Abednego came forth out of the midst of the fire.

The satraps, the deputies, and the governors, and the king's counselors, being gathered together, saw these men, that the fire had no power on their bodies, nor was the hair of their head singed, neither were their pants changed, nor had the smell of fire passed on them. Nebuchadnezzar spoke and said, Blessed be the God of Shadrach, Meshach, and Abednego, who has sent his angel, and delivered his servants who trusted in him, and have changed the king's word, and have yielded their bodies, that they might not serve nor worship any god, except their own God. Therefore I make a decree, that every people, nation, and language, which speak anything evil against the God of Shadrach, Meshach, and Abednego, shall be cut in pieces, and their houses shall be made a dunghill; because there is no other god who is able to deliver after this sort. Then the king promoted Shadrach, Meshach, and Abednego in the province of Babylon.

King Nebuchadnezzar went through an amazing transformation during his reign, seemingly going crazy for several years, living in the fields, eating grass with oxen and becoming a wild man. After seven years God brought him back to full consciousness, and he returned to the throne. The following statement, a written letter from Nebuchadnezzar describing this story, is amazing in the glory that he ascribes to God. This letter seems to be written by a prophet of God, not a foreign monarch. God showed his ability to bring a pagan king, leader of the most powerful country in the world, into submission. These events were crucial for protecting the Jews who were living under the command of this foreign empire.

Nebuchadnezzar the king, to all the peoples, nations, and languages, who dwell in all the earth: Peace be multiplied to you. It has seemed good to me to show the signs and wonders that the Most High God has worked toward me. How great are his signs! and how mighty are his wonders! his kingdom is an everlasting kingdom, and his dominion is from generation to generation.

I, Nebuchadnezzar, was at rest in my house, and flourishing in my palace. I saw a dream which made me afraid; and the thoughts on my bed and the visions of my head troubled me. Therefore made I a decree to bring in all the wise men of Babylon before me, that they might make known to me the interpretation of the dream. Then came in the magicians, the enchanters, the Chaldeans, and the soothsayers; and I told the dream before them; but they did not make known to me its interpretation. But at the last Daniel came in before me, whose name was Belteshazzar, according to the name of my god, and in whom is the spirit of the holy gods: and I told the dream before him, saying, Belteshazzar, master of the magicians, because I know that the spirit of the holy gods is in you, and no secret troubles you, tell me the visions of my dream that I have seen, and its interpretation.

Nebuchadnezzar then described the dream, in which a beautiful and strong tree which reached the sky was cut down, leaving only a stump in the earth. Daniel interpreted this dream, predicting that the king would become insane for seven years, living among the animals of the field, then being restored to his position of power after learning that God rules over all the kingdoms of men.

All this came on the king Nebuchadnezzar. At the end of twelve months he was walking in the royal palace of Babylon. The king spoke and said, Is not this great Babylon, which I have built for the royal dwelling place, by the might of my power and for the glory of my majesty? While the word was in the king's mouth, there fell a voice from the sky, saying, O king Nebuchadnezzar, to you it is spoken: The kingdom has departed from you: and you shall be driven from men; and your dwelling shall be with the animals of the field; you shall be made to eat grass as oxen; and seven times shall pass over you; until you know that the Most High rules in the kingdom of men, and gives it to whomever he will. The same hour was the thing fulfilled on Nebuchadnezzar: and he was driven from men, and ate grass as oxen, and his body was wet with the dew of the sky, until his hair was grown like eagles' feathers, and his nails like birds' claws.

At the end of the days I, Nebuchadnezzar, lifted up my eyes to heaven, and my understanding returned to me, and I blessed the Most High, and I praised and honored him who lives forever; for his dominion is an everlasting dominion, and his kingdom from generation to generation. All the inhabitants of the earth are reputed as nothing; and he does according to his will in the army of heaven, and among the inhabitants of the earth; and none can stay his hand, or ask him, What are you doing? At the same time my understanding returned to me; and for the glory of my kingdom, my majesty and brightness returned to me; and my counselors and my Lords sought to me; and I was established in my kingdom, and excellent greatness was added to me. Now I, Nebuchadnezzar, praise and extol and honor the King of heaven; for all his works are truth, and his ways justice; and those who walk in pride he is able to abase.

The son of King Nebuchadnezzar was Belshazzar. This son, though he grew up in the times of the miracles involving Daniel and his friends, had no regard for God. He was more focused on living the high life of a king and earthly pleasures. In fact, he even threw a lavish party as the Persian Empire army approached Babylon. During this drunken feast they brought out and defiled the golden articles they had taken from the temple in Jerusalem. It was during this feast that God wrote on the wall with what appeared to be the "fingers of a man's hand." Once again, Daniel is called to interpret the writing, which spelled out doom for the king and Babylon. That very night the king was slain by the Mede and Persian armies.

Daniel, now advanced in age, became a top adviser to the conquering king Darius, distinguishing himself by his wise decisions. The other advisers, jealous of Daniel's good fortune, attempted to trap him by initiating a proclamation forbidding the worship of anyone other than the king himself. When Daniel was spotted worshiping God in the face of this decree, Darius reluctantly agreed to throw his favorite adviser into a den of lions, a certain death sentence. The deliverance of Daniel from the lion's den is a favorite story of Christians around the world, as it shows God's ability to deliver from evil those he so dearly loves.

It pleased Darius to set over the kingdom one hundred twenty satraps, who should be throughout the whole kingdom; and over them three presidents, of whom Daniel was one; that these satraps might give account to them, and that the king should have no damage. Then this Daniel was distinguished above the presidents and the satraps, because an excellent spirit was in him; and the king thought to set him over the whole realm.

Then the presidents and the satraps sought to find occasion against Daniel as touching the kingdom; but they could find no occasion nor fault, because he was faithful, neither was there any error or fault found in him. Then these men said, We shall not find any occasion against this Daniel, except we find it against him concerning the law of his God.

Then these presidents and satraps assembled together to the king, and said thus to him, King Darius, live forever. All the presidents of the kingdom, the deputies and the satraps, the counselors and the governors, have consulted together to establish a royal statute, and to make a strong decree, that whoever shall ask a petition of any god or man for thirty days, except of you, O king, he shall be cast into the den of lions. Now, O king, establish the decree, and sign the writing, that it not be changed, according to the law of the Medes and Persians, which doesn't alter. Therefore king Darius signed the writing and the decree.

When Daniel knew that the writing was signed, he went into his house (now his windows were open in his room toward Jerusalem) and he kneeled on his knees three times a day, and prayed, and gave thanks before his God, as he did before. Then these men assembled together, and found Daniel making petition and supplication before his God. Then they came near, and spoke before the king concerning the king's decree: Haven't you signed a decree, that every man who shall make petition to any god or man within thirty days, except to you, O king, shall be cast into the den of lions? The king answered, The thing is true, according to the law of the Medes and Persians, which doesn't alter. Then answered they and said before the king, That Daniel, who is of the children of the captivity of Judah, doesn't respect you, O king, nor the decree that you have signed, but makes his petition three times a day. Then the king, when he heard these words, was very displeased, and set his heart on Daniel to deliver him; and he labored until the going down of the sun to rescue him.

Then these men assembled together to the king, and said to the king, Know, O king, that it is a law of the Medes and Persians, that no decree nor statute which the king establishes may be changed. Then the king commanded, and they brought Daniel, and cast him into the den of lions. Now the king spoke and said to Daniel, Your God whom you serve continually, he will deliver you. A stone was brought, and laid on the mouth of the den; and the king sealed it with his own signet, and with the signet of his Lords; that nothing might be changed concerning Daniel.

Then the king went to his palace, and passed the night fasting; neither were instruments of music brought before him: and his sleep fled from him. Then the king arose very early in the morning, and went in haste to the den of lions. When he came near to the den to Daniel, he cried with a lamentable voice; the king spoke and said to Daniel, Daniel, servant of the living God, is your God, whom you serve continually, able to deliver you from the lions? Then Daniel said to the king, O king, live forever. My God has sent his angel, and has shut the lions' mouths, and they have not hurt me; because as before him innocence was found in me; and also before you, O king, have I done no hurt. Then was the king exceeding glad, and commanded that they should take Daniel up out of the den. So Daniel was taken up out of the den, and no kind of harm was found on him, because he had trusted in his God.

The king commanded, and they brought those men who had accused Daniel, and they cast them into the den of lions, them, their children, and their wives; and the lions mauled them, and broke all their bones in pieces, before they came to the bottom of the den. Then king Darius wrote to all the peoples, nations, and languages, who dwell in all the earth: Peace be multiplied to you. I make a decree, that in all the dominion of my kingdom men tremble and fear before the God of Daniel; for he is the living God, and steadfast forever, His kingdom that which shall not be destroyed; and his dominion shall be even to the end. He delivers and rescues, and he works signs and wonders in heaven and in earth, who has delivered Daniel from the power of the lions. So this Daniel prospered in the reign of Darius, and in the reign of Cyrus the Persian.

In addition to being a wise adviser and interpreter of dreams, Daniel was also a prophet. His prophesies are highly symbolic, containing distinct images of amazing beasts, angelic messengers, cruel kings, plagues and warfare. Like those in the book of Revelation, his prophesies are difficult to interpret, and even today, men disagree on the meaning of many of his visions. But behind the sometimes confusing visions is a clear message; battles will rage, kingdoms will rise and fall, but God and his kingdom will endure forever. God controls history and destiny, and His ultimate power and authority will be given to "one like a son of man," a name Jesus Christ later took for himself.

The life and visions of Daniel give hope to followers of God that despite the turmoil in which they may live, in the end God will save those who love him and worship him.

Ezekiel was carried away to Babylon at the age of 25, along with Daniel, as part of the "first wave" of exiles from Judah. Five years later, he had a remarkable encounter with God, in which he was called to be a prophet. During the same time that Jeremiah was prophesying in Jerusalem, Ezekiel was also warning the nation of Judah of a long captivity and the imminent destruction of Jerusalem. Both Ezekiel and Jeremiah lived to witness the destruction of Jerusalem and the temple by the Babylonians.

Now it happened in the thirtieth year, in the fourth month, in the fifth of the month, as I was among the captives by the river Chebar, that the heavens were opened, and I saw visions of God.

I looked, and behold, a stormy wind came out of the north, a great cloud, with flashing lightning, and a brightness around it, and out of its midst as it were glowing metal, out of the midst of the fire. Out of its midst came the likeness of four living creatures. This was their appearance: they had the likeness of a man. Everyone had four faces, and each one of them had four wings.

As for the likeness of their faces, they had the face of a man; and the four of them had the face of a lion on the right side; and the four of them had the face of an ox on the left side; the four of them also had the face of an eagle.

As for the likeness of the living creatures, their appearance was like burning coals of fire, like the appearance of torches: the fire went up and down among the living creatures; and the fire was bright, and out of the fire went forth lightning.

The living creatures ran and returned as the appearance of a flash of lightning. Now as I saw the living creatures, behold, one wheel on the earth beside the living creatures, for each of the four faces of it. The appearance of the wheels and their work was like a beryl: and the four of them had one likeness; and their appearance and their work was as it were a wheel within a wheel. When they went, they went in their four directions: they didn't turn when they went. As for their rims, they were high and dreadful; and the four of them had their rims full of eyes all around. When the living creatures went, the wheels went beside them; and when the living creatures were lifted up from the earth, the wheels were lifted up. Wherever the spirit was to go, they went; there was the spirit to go: and the wheels were lifted up beside them; for the spirit of the living creature was in the wheels. When those went, these went; and when those stood, these stood; and when those were lifted up from the earth, the wheels were lifted up beside them: for the spirit of the living creature was in the wheels. Over the head of the living creature there was the likeness of an expanse, like the awesome crystal to look on, stretched forth over their heads above. Under the expanse were their wings straight, the one toward the other: each one had two which covered on this side, and every one had two which covered on that side, their bodies. When they went, I heard the noise of their wings like the noise of great waters, like the voice of the Almighty, a noise of tumult like the noise of an army: when they stood, they let down their wings. There was a voice above the expanse that was over their heads: when they stood, they let down their wings. Above the expanse that was over their heads was the likeness of a throne, as the appearance of a sapphire stone; and on the likeness of the throne was a likeness as the appearance of a man on it above. I saw as it were glowing metal, as the appearance of fire within it all around, from the appearance of his waist and upward; and from the appearance of his waist and downward I saw as it were the appearance of fire, and there was brightness around him. As the appearance of the rainbow that is in the cloud in the day of rain, so was the appearance of the brightness all around. This was the appearance of the likeness of the glory of Yahweh. When I saw it, I fell on my face, and I heard a voice of one that spoke.

He said to me, Son of man, stand on your feet, and I will speak with you. The

Spirit entered into me when he spoke to me, and set me on my feet; and I heard him who spoke to me. He said to me, Son of man, I send you to the children of Israel, to a nation of rebels who have rebelled against me. They and their fathers have transgressed against me even to this very day. The children are impudent and stiff-hearted: I am sending you to them; and you shall tell them, Thus says the Lord Yahweh.

They, whether they will hear, or whether they will forbear, (for they are a rebellious house), yet shall know that there has been a prophet among them.

You, son of man, don't be afraid of them, neither be afraid of their words, though briers and thorns are with you, and you do dwell among scorpions: don't be afraid of their words, nor be dismayed at their looks, though they are a rebellious house. You shall speak my words to them, whether they will hear, or whether they will forbear; for they are most rebellious.

When I looked, behold, a hand was put forth to me; and, behold, a scroll of a book was therein; He spread it before me: and it was written within and without; and there were written therein lamentations, and mourning, and woe.

Go to them of the captivity, to the children of your people, and speak to them, and tell them, Thus says the Lord Yahweh; whether they will hear, or whether they will forbear.

The word of Yahweh came to me, saying, Son of man, set your face toward the mountains of Israel, and prophesy to them, and say, You mountains of Israel, hear the word of the Lord Yahweh: Thus says the Lord Yahweh to the mountains and to the hills, to the watercourses and to the valleys: Behold, I, even I, will bring a sword on you, and I will destroy your high places. Your altars shall become desolate, and your incense altars shall be broken; and I will cast down your slain men before your idols. I will lay the dead bodies of the children of Israel before their idols; and I will scatter your bones around your altars. In all your dwelling places the cities shall be laid waste, and the high places shall be desolate; that your altars may be laid waste and made desolate, and your idols may be broken and cease, and your incense altars may be cut down, and your works may be abolished. The slain shall fall in the midst of you, and you shall know that I am Yahweh. Yet will I leave a remnant, in that you shall have some that escape the sword among the nations, when you shall be scattered through the countries. Those of you that escape shall remember me among the nations where they shall be carried captive, how that I have been broken with their lewd heart, which has departed from me, and with their eyes, which play the prostitute after their idols: and they shall loathe themselves in their own sight for the evils which they have committed in all their abominations. They shall know that I am Yahweh: I have not said in vain that I would do this evil to them.

My eye shall not spare you, neither will I have pity; but I will bring your ways on you, and your abominations shall be in the midst of you: and you shall know that I am Yahweh. Thus says the Lord Yahweh: An evil, an only evil; behold, it comes. An end has come, the end has come; it awakes against you; behold, it comes. Your doom has come to you, inhabitant of the land: the time has come, the day is near, a day of tumult, and not of joyful shouting, on the mountains. Now will I shortly pour out my wrath on you, and accomplish my anger against you, and will judge you according to your ways; and I will bring on you all your abominations.

Despite its dire overtones, the prophesies of Ezekiel end on a hopeful note. Ezekiel predicted the eventual return of the people to the Promised Land, with a renewing from God, in which, "you shall be my (God's) people, and I will be your God." He also prophesied of a "New Jerusalem," and described the city as he saw in his vision, with the most important characteristic being "the name of the city from that day shall be, Yahweh is there."

Better times would come. The nation, under captivity, was feeling isolated from God. But God had a plan to return his people home. The ultimate master plan is that after we leave this earth, God's people can dwell in heaven, the new Jerusalem, and He will be there with us.

Therefore tell the house of Israel, Thus says the Lord Yahweh: I don't do *this* for your sake, house of Israel, but for my holy name, which you have profaned among the nations, where you went. I will sanctify my great name, which has been profaned among the nations, which you have profaned in their midst; and the nations shall know that I am Yahweh, says the Lord Yahweh, when I shall be sanctified in you before their eyes. For I will take you from among the nations, and gather you out of all the countries, and will bring you into your own land. I will sprinkle clean water on you, and you shall be clean: from all your filthiness, and from all your idols, will I cleanse you. I will also give you a new heart, and I will put a new spirit within you; and I will take away the stony heart out of your flesh, and I will give you a heart of flesh. I will put my Spirit within you, and cause you to walk in my statutes, and you shall keep my ordinances, and do them. You shall dwell in the land that I gave to your fathers; and you shall be my people, and I will be your God.

Thus says the Lord Yahweh: In the day that I cleanse you from all your iniquities, I will cause the cities to be inhabited, and the waste places shall be built. The land that was desolate shall be tilled, whereas it was a desolation in the sight of all who passed by. They shall say, This land that was desolate has become like the garden of Eden; and the waste and desolate and ruined cities are fortified and inhabited. Then the nations that are left around you shall know that

I, Yahweh, have built the ruined places, and planted that which was desolate: I, Yahweh, have spoken it, and I will do it.

In another strange event, God worked through Ezekiel to bring the bones of a large group of dead people back to life. Scholars debate whether this was an actual event or a vision; in either event, the purpose was to confirm the future restoration of Israel.

The hand of Yahweh was on me, and he brought me out in the Spirit of Yahweh, and set me down in the midst of the valley; and it was full of bones. He caused me to pass by them all around: and behold, there were very many in the open valley; and behold, they were very dry. He said to me, Son of man, can these bones live? I answered, Lord Yahweh, you know. Again he said to me, Prophesy over these bones, and tell them, you dry bones, hear the word of Yahweh. Thus says the Lord Yahweh to these bones: Behold, I will cause breath to enter into you, and you shall live. I will lay sinews on you, and will bring up flesh on you, and cover you with skin, and put breath in you, and you shall live; and you shall know that I am Yahweh. So I prophesied as I was commanded: and as I prophesied, there was a noise, and behold, an earthquake; and the bones came together, bone to its bone. I saw, and, behold, there were sinews on them, and flesh came up, and skin covered them above; but there was no breath in them. Then he said to me, Prophesy to the wind, prophesy, son of man, and tell the wind, Thus says the Lord Yahweh: Come from the four winds, breath, and breathe on these slain, that they may live. So I prophesied as he commanded me, and the breath came into them, and they lived, and stood up on their feet, an exceedingly great army. Then he said to me, Son of man, these bones are the whole house of Israel: behold, they say, Our bones are dried up, and our hope is lost; we are clean cut off. Therefore prophesy, and tell them, Thus says the Lord Yahweh: Behold, I will open your graves, and cause you to come up out of your graves, my people; and I will bring you into the land of Israel. You shall know that I am Yahweh, when I have opened your graves, and caused you to come up out of your graves, my people.

I will put my Spirit in you, and you shall live, and I will place you in your own land: and you shall know that I, Yahweh, have spoken it and performed it, says Yahweh.

Living in Judah, the prophet Nahum was given the task of preaching against Nineveh, the mighty Assyrian city. Already Assyria had carried Israel into captivity, and now the nation of Judah was paying tribute to Nineveh while their king, Manasseh, was held there in prison. Despite the prominence of this world power, Nahum confidently predicted their demise. Within about 80 years of his predictions, these events came true when Nineveh was utterly destroyed by the Babylonians and Persians. God's force is continually at work in controlling world destiny and setting the stage for the return of his people.

An oracle about Nineveh. The book of the vision of Nahum the Elkoshite. Yahweh is a jealous God and avenges. Yahweh avenges and is full of wrath. Yahweh takes vengeance on his adversaries, and he maintains wrath against his enemies. Yahweh is slow to anger, and great in power, and will by no means leave the guilty unpunished. Yahweh has his way in the whirlwind and in the storm, and the clouds are the dust of his feet.

He rebukes the sea, and makes it dry, and dries up all the rivers. Bashan languishes, and Carmel; and the flower of Lebanon languishes. The mountains quake before him, and the hills melt away. The earth trembles at his presence, yes, the world, and all who dwell in it. Who can stand before his indignation? Who can endure the fierceness of his anger? His wrath is poured out like fire, and the rocks are broken apart by him. Yahweh is good, a stronghold in the day of trouble; and he knows those who take refuge in him. But with an overflowing flood, he will make a full end of her place, and will pursue his enemies into darkness.

Yahweh has commanded concerning you: "No more descendants will bear your name. Out of the house of your gods, will I cut off the engraved image and the molten image. I will make your grave, for you are vile."

It will happen that all those who look at you will flee from you, and say, 'Nineveh is laid waste! Who will mourn for her?' Where will I seek comforters for you?"

Along with Ezra, the prophet Haggai helped to stir Israel to rebuild the temple. Some 20 years after their return from Babylon, the temple rebuilding was stalled. People were focusing on their own houses instead of God's. Because of this, Haggai said, their crops were not successful and their wealth was not increasing. He told the people to put their attention on the loving God, and God would in turn put his attention on blessing them. Unlike most prophets, Haggai was wildly successful. Some four years after his plea, the temple was finally finished.

Then the Word of Yahweh came by Haggai, the prophet, saying, "Is it a time for you yourselves to dwell in your paneled houses, while this house lies waste? Now therefore this is what Yahweh of Armies says: Consider your ways. You have sown much, and bring in little. You eat, but you don't have enough. You drink, but you aren't filled with drink. You clothe yourselves, but no one is warm, and he who earns wages earns wages to put them into a bag with holes in it."

This is what Yahweh of Armies says: "Consider your ways.

Then Zerubbabel, the son of Shealtiel, and Joshua, the son of Jehozadak, the high priest, with all the remnant of the people, obeyed the voice of Yahweh, their God, and the words of Haggai, the prophet, as Yahweh, their God, had sent him; and the people feared Yahweh.

Then Haggai, Yahweh's messenger, spoke Yahweh's message to the people, saying, "I am with you," says Yahweh.

Yahweh stirred up the spirit of Zerubbabel, the son of Shealtiel, governor of Judah, and the spirit of Joshua, the son of Jehozadak, the high priest, and the spirit of all the remnant of the people; and they came and worked on the house of Yahweh of Armies, their God,

In the twenty-fourth day of the ninth month, in the second year of Darius, the Word of Yahweh came by Haggai the prophet, saying,

'Consider, please, from this day and backward, from the twenty-fourth day of the ninth month, since the day that the foundation of Yahweh's temple was laid, consider it. Is the seed yet in the barn? Yes, the vine, the fig tree, the pomegranate, and the olive tree haven't brought forth. From this day will I bless you.'"

Along with Haggai, Zechariah also helped to stir the Israelite people to rebuild the temple. More importantly, he showed them that their hearts must first be in the right place. They must first return to God - not physically, but spiritually.

In the eighth month, in the second year of Darius, the word of Yahweh came to Zechariah the son of Berechiah, the son of Iddo, the prophet, saying, "Yahweh was very displeased with your fathers. Therefore tell them: Thus says Yahweh of Armies: 'Return to me,' says Yahweh of Armies, 'and I will return to you,' says Yahweh of Armies. Don't you be like your fathers, to whom the former prophets proclaimed, saying: Thus says Yahweh of Armies, 'Return now from your evil ways, and from your evil doings;' but they did not hear, nor listen to me, says Yahweh.

Therefore thus says Yahweh: "I have returned to Jerusalem with mercy. My house shall be built in it," says Yahweh of Armies, "and a line shall be stretched forth over Jerusalem.'"

"Proclaim further, saying, 'Thus says Yahweh of Armies: "My cities will again overflow with prosperity, and Yahweh will again comfort Zion, and will again choose Jerusalem."

The word of Yahweh came to Zechariah, saying, "Thus has Yahweh of

Armies spoken, saying, 'Execute true judgment, and show kindness and compassion every man to his brother. Don't oppress the widow, nor the fatherless, the foreigner, nor the poor; and let none of you devise evil against his brother in your heart.'

Thus says Yahweh of Armies: "Behold, I will save my people from the east country, and from the west country; and I will bring them, and they will dwell in the midst of Jerusalem; and they will be my people, and I will be their God, in truth and in righteousness."

The prophet Joel recorded a short history of a natural disaster - an invasion of locusts that utterly ravaged the land. We do not know much about Joel - when he lived, or whether he prophesied in the Northern or Southern kingdom is not revealed. But his message is typical of the prophets — he described a calamity, informed the people that this was due to their lack of obedience, called them to repent, and promised brighter days if they would return back to God.

The Word of Yahweh that came to Joel, the son of Pethuel.
Hear this, you elders,
And listen, all you inhabitants of the land.
Has this ever happened in your days,
or in the days of your fathers?
Tell your children about it,
and have your children tell their children,
and their children, another generation.
What the swarming locust has left, the great locust has eaten.
What the great locust has left, the grasshopper has eaten.
What the grasshopper has left, the caterpillar has eaten.
A day of darkness and gloominess,
a day of clouds and thick darkness.
As the dawn spreading on the mountains,
a great and strong people;
there has never been the like,
neither will there be any more after them,
even to the years of many generations.
Yahweh thunders his voice before his army;
for his forces are very great;
for he is strong who obeys his command;
for the day of Yahweh is great and very awesome,
and who can endure it?
"Yet even now," says Yahweh, "turn to me with all your heart,

and with fasting, and with weeping, and with mourning."
Tear your heart, and not your garments,
and turn to Yahweh, your God;
for he is gracious and merciful,
slow to anger, and abundant in loving kindness,
and relents from sending calamity.
"Be glad then, you children of Zion,
and rejoice in Yahweh, your God;
for he gives you the former rain in just measure,
and he causes the rain to come down for you,
the former rain and the latter rain,
as before.
The threshing floors will be full of wheat,
and the vats will overflow with new wine and oil.
I will restore to you the years that the swarming locust has eaten,
the great locust, the grasshopper, and the caterpillar,
my great army, which I sent among you.

Obadiah prophesied against the nation of Edom. Edomites were the descendants of Esau, the brother of Jacob. Although related, the nations became bitter enemies. The Edomites even helped to plunder Israel during their defeat by Babylon. Their capital city, Sela, was on a high plateau and protected from raiders. The Edomites rested confidently in their belief that this city could not be conquered. But Obadiah correctly predicted their demise. By A.D. 70, when Jerusalem was sacked by Rome, the Edomites were completely wiped out.

The vision of Obadiah. This is what the Lord Yahweh says about Edom. We have heard news from Yahweh, and an ambassador is sent among the nations, saying, "Arise, and let's rise up against her in battle. Behold, I have made you small among the nations. You are greatly despised. The pride of your heart has deceived you, you who dwell in the clefts of the rock, whose habitation is high, who says in his heart, 'Who will bring me down to the ground?' Though you mount on high as the eagle, and though your nest is set among the stars, I will bring you down from there," says Yahweh.

How Esau will be ransacked! How his hidden treasures are sought out!

But in Mount Zion, there will be those who escape, and it will be holy. The house of Jacob will possess their possessions. The house of Jacob will be a fire, the house of Joseph a flame, and the house of Esau for stubble. They will burn among them, and devour them. There will not be any remaining to the house of Esau." Indeed, Yahweh has spoken.

Malachi, sometimes called "The Last Prophet," labored in Judah, trying to convince Jerusalem to turn back to God. The people of Judah were lukewarm - calling themselves "children of God," but not being truly serious about their worship. This apathetic attitude in worship was also evident in their lives, with divorce, dishonesty and other problems being evident. In a time when Judah seemed to be fading in glory, Malachi tried to teach them that going through the spiritual motions was not good enough for a demanding God. This same message is true for us today – God demands our total loyalty, but in return the rewards of eternity will vastly outweigh any tribulation in this life.

An oracle: the word of Yahweh to Israel by Malachi.

"A son honors his father, and a servant his master. If I am a father, then where is my honor? And if I am a master, where is the respect due me? Says Yahweh of Armies to you, priests, who despise my name. You say, 'How have we despised your name?' You offer polluted bread on my altar. You say, 'How have we polluted you?' In that you say, 'Yahweh's table contemptible.' When you offer the blind for sacrifice, isn't that evil? And when you offer the lame and sick, isn't that evil? Present it now to your governor! Will he be pleased with you? Or will he accept your person?" says Yahweh of Armies.

"Now, please entreat the favor of God, that he may be gracious to us. With this, will he accept any of you?" says Yahweh of Armies.

"Oh that there were one among you who would shut the doors, that you might not kindle fire on my altar in vain! I have no pleasure in you," says Yahweh of Armies, "neither will I accept an offering at your hand. For from the rising of the sun even to the going down of the same, my name is great among the nations, and in every place incense will be offered to my name, and a pure offering: for my name is great among the nations," says Yahweh of Armies.

"But the deceiver is cursed, who has in his flock a male, and vows, and sacrifices to the Lord a blemished thing; for I am a great King," says Yahweh of Armies, "and my name is awesome among the nations."

"Behold, I send my messenger, and he will prepare the way before me; and the Lord, whom you seek, will suddenly come to his temple; and the messenger of the covenant, whom you desire, behold, he comes!" says Yahweh of Armies. "But who can endure the day of his coming? And who will stand when he appears?

I will come near to you to judgment; and I will be a swift witness against the sorcerers, and against the adulterers, and against the perjurers, and against those who oppress the hireling in his wages, the widow, and the fatherless, and who deprive the foreigner of justice, and don't fear me," says Yahweh of Armies.

"For I, Yahweh, don't change; therefore you, sons of Jacob, are not consumed.

From the days of your fathers you have turned aside from my ordinances, and have not kept them. Return to me, and I will return to you," says Yahweh of Armies. "But you say, 'How shall we return?' Will a man rob God? Yet you rob me! But you say, 'How have we robbed you?' In tithes and offerings. You are cursed with the curse; for you rob me, even this whole nation. Bring the whole tithe into the storehouse, that there may be food in my house, and test me now in this," says Yahweh of Armies, "if I will not open you the windows of heaven, and pour you out a blessing, that there shall not be room enough for.

23 RETURN FROM CAPTIVITY

A Sweet Homecoming

After Judah had spent 70 years in Babylonian captivity, the Persian empire conquered Babylon, and the fortunes of the Israelites took a turn for the better. The Persian emperor Cyrus, who had an official policy of encouraging local religions to flourish among his conquered peoples, allowed the Jews to return to their homeland. It was almost too good for the Jews to believe.

God was working through the Persians to fulfill his promise to the Jews - that he would not forget them or the promise He had made to them. Jeremiah had prophesied that the captivity would last 70 years - and this was finally fulfilled.

Now in the first year of Cyrus king of Persia, that the word of Yahweh by the mouth of Jeremiah might be accomplished, Yahweh stirred up the spirit of Cyrus king of Persia, so that he made a proclamation throughout all his kingdom, and put it also in writing, saying, "Thus says Cyrus king of Persia, 'Yahweh, the God of heaven, has given me all the kingdoms of the earth; and he has commanded me to build him a house in Jerusalem, which is in Judah. Whoever there is among you of all his people, may his God be with him, and let him go up to Jerusalem, which is in Judah, and build the house of Yahweh, the God of Israel (he is God), which is in Jerusalem. Whoever is left, in any place where he lives, let the men of his place help him with silver, with gold, with goods, and with animals, besides the freewill offering for God's house which is in Jerusalem.'"

Then the heads of fathers' households of Judah and Benjamin, and the priests, and the Levites, even all whose spirit God had stirred to go up rose up to build the house of Yahweh which is in Jerusalem. All those who were around them strengthened their hands with vessels of silver, with gold, with goods, and with animals, and with precious things, besides all that was willingly offered. Also Cyrus the king brought forth the vessels of the house of Yahweh, which

268

Nebuchadnezzar had brought out of Jerusalem, and had put in the house of his gods; even those, Cyrus king of Persia brought out by the hand of Mithredath the treasurer, and numbered them to Sheshbazzar, the prince of Judah. This is the number of them: thirty platters of gold, one thousand platters of silver, twenty-nine knives, thirty bowls of gold, silver bowls of a second sort four hundred and ten, and other vessels one thousand. All the vessels of gold and of silver were five thousand and four hundred. Sheshbazzar brought all these up, when the captives were brought up from Babylon to Jerusalem.

Now these are the children of the province, who went up out of the captivity of those who had been carried away, whom Nebuchadnezzar the king of Babylon had carried away to Babylon, and who returned to Jerusalem and Judah, everyone to his city;

The whole assembly together was forty-two thousand three hundred sixty, besides their male servants and their female servants, of whom there were seven thousand three hundred thirty-seven: and they had two hundred singing men and singing women. Their horses were seven hundred thirty-six; their mules, two hundred forty-five; their camels, four hundred thirty-five; their donkeys, six thousand seven hundred and twenty.

When the seventh month had come, and the children of Israel were in the cities, the people gathered themselves together as one man to Jerusalem. Then Jeshua the son of Jozadak stood up with his brothers the priests, and Zerubbabel the son of Shealtiel and his brothers, and built the altar of the God of Israel, to offer burnt offerings thereon, as it is written in the law of Moses the man of God. In spite of their fear because of the peoples of the surrounding lands, they set the altar on its base; and they offered burnt offerings on it to Yahweh, even burnt offerings morning and evening. They kept the feast of tents, as it is written, and offered the daily burnt offerings by number, according to the ordinance, as the duty of every day required;

When the builders laid the foundation of Yahweh's temple, they set the priests in their clothing with trumpets, with the Levites the sons of Asaph with cymbals, to praise Yahweh, according to the directions of David king of Israel. They sang to one another in praising and giving thanks to Yahweh, "For he is good, for his loving kindness endures forever toward Israel." All the people shouted with a great shout, when they praised Yahweh, because the foundation of the house of Yahweh had been laid.

But many of the priests and Levites and heads of fathers' households, the old men who had seen the first house, when the foundation of this house was laid before their eyes, wept with a loud voice. Many also shouted aloud for joy, so that the people could not discern the noise of the shout of joy from the noise of the weeping of the people; for the people shouted with a loud shout, and the noise was heard far away.

The return to Israel and the worship rituals was a sweet homecoming to Judah. Unfortunately, the exiles of the northern kingdom of Israel were never formally released from Assyria, and they were spread throughout much of the region and integrated into local societies, largely losing their identity as a Jewish nation.

Upon their return to Jerusalem, the Israelites found themselves the target of local officials, who did not want them to rebuild the temple. They saw the return of the Jews as a threat to their own power. After their deceptive "offer of help" was wisely turned down, they used every means possible to stop the work on the temple.

Now when the adversaries of Judah and Benjamin heard that the children of the captivity were building a temple to Yahweh, the God of Israel; then they drew near to Zerubbabel, and to the heads of fathers' households, and said to them, "Let us build with you; for we seek your God, as you do; and we sacrifice to him since the days of Esar Haddon king of Assyria, who brought us up here."

But Zerubbabel, and Jeshua, and the rest of the heads of fathers' households of Israel, said to them, "You have nothing to do with us in building a house to our God; but we ourselves together will build to Yahweh, the God of Israel, as king Cyrus the king of Persia has commanded us."

Then the people of the land weakened the hands of the people of Judah, and troubled them in building, and hired counselors against them, to frustrate their purpose, all the days of Cyrus king of Persia, even until the reign of Darius king of Persia. In the reign of Ahasuerus, in the beginning of his reign, wrote they an accusation against the inhabitants of Judah and Jerusalem.

Then ceased the work of God's house which is at Jerusalem; and it ceased until the second year of the reign of Darius king of Persia.

The surrounding neighbors were successful in stopping progress on the temple for 20 years. But the prophets Haggai and Zechariah renewed the interest of the people in rebuilding the temple. When resistance arose again, they were able to overcome it - this time, through the assistance of the Persian king Darius. The plans of the local officials to stop the temple building were not only denied, but these same officials were ordered to support the work, under severe penalty for not complying. Once again, God's providence in supporting his people was evident.

Now the prophets, Haggai the prophet, and Zechariah the son of Iddo, prophesied to the Jews who were in Judah and Jerusalem; in the name of the

God of Israel they prophesied to them. Then rose up Zerubbabel the son of Shealtiel, and Jeshua the son of Jozadak, and began to build God's house which is at Jerusalem; and with them were the prophets of God, helping them. At the same time came to them Tattenai, the governor beyond the River, and Shetharbozenai, and their companions, and said thus to them, "Who gave you a decree to build this house, and to finish this wall?" Then we told them in this way, what the names of the men were who were making this building. But the eye of their God was on the elders of the Jews, and they did not make them cease, until the matter should come to Darius, and then answer should be returned by letter concerning it.

They sent a letter to him, in which was written thus: To Darius the king, all peace. Be it known to the king, that we went into the province of Judah, to the house of the great God, which is built with great stones, and timber is laid in the walls; and this work goes on with diligence and prospers in their hands. Then we asked those elders, and said to them thus, "Who gave you a decree to build this house, and to finish this wall?" We asked them their names also, to inform you that we might write the names of the men who were at their head. Thus they returned us answer, saying, "We are the servants of the God of heaven and earth, and are building the house that was built these many years ago, which a great king of Israel built and finished. But after that our fathers had provoked the God of heaven to wrath, he gave them into the hand of Nebuchadnezzar king of Babylon, the Chaldean, who destroyed this house, and carried the people away into Babylon. But in the first year of Cyrus king of Babylon, Cyrus the king made a decree to build this house of God. The gold and silver vessels also of God's house, which Nebuchadnezzar took out of the temple that was in Jerusalem, and brought into the temple of Babylon, those Cyrus the king took out of the temple of Babylon, and they were delivered to one whose name was Sheshbazzar, whom he had made governor; and he said to him, 'Take these vessels, go, put them in the temple that is in Jerusalem, and let God's house be built in its place.' Then the same Sheshbazzar came, and laid the foundations of God's house which is in Jerusalem: and since that time even until now has it been in building, and yet it is not completed. Now therefore, if it seem good to the king, let a search be made in the king's treasure house, which is there at Babylon, whether it be so, that a decree was made of Cyrus the king to build this house of God at Jerusalem; and let the king send his pleasure to us concerning this matter."

Then Darius the king made a decree, and search was made in the house of the archives, where the treasures were laid up in Babylon. There was found at Achmetha, in the palace that is in the province of Media, a scroll, and therein was thus written for a record: In the first year of Cyrus the king, Cyrus the king made a decree: Concerning God's house at Jerusalem, let the house be built, the place where they offer sacrifices, and let its foundations be strongly laid; its height sixty cubits, and its breadth sixty cubits; with three courses of great stones, and a course of new timber: and let the expenses be given out of the king's house. Also let the gold and silver vessels of God's house, which Nebuchadnezzar took forth out of the temple which is at Jerusalem, and brought to Babylon, be restored, and brought again to the temple which is at Jerusalem, everyone to its place; and you shall put them in God's house.

Now therefore, Tattenai, governor beyond the River, Shetharbozenai, and your companions the Apharsachites, who are beyond the River, you must stay far from there. Leave the work of this house of God alone; let the governor of the Jews and the elders of the Jews build this house of God in its place. Moreover I make a decree what you shall do to these elders of the Jews for the building of this house of God: that of the king's goods, even of the tribute beyond the River, expenses be given with all diligence to these men, that they be not hindered. That which they have need of, both young bulls, and rams, and lambs, for burnt offerings to the God of heaven; also wheat, salt, wine, and oil, according to the word of the priests who are at Jerusalem, let it be given them day by day without fail;

I Darius have made a decree; let it be done with all diligence. Then Tattenai, the governor beyond the River, Shetharbozenai, and their companions, because Darius the king had sent a decree, did accordingly with all diligence. The elders of the Jews built and prospered, through the prophesying of Haggai the prophet and Zechariah the son of Iddo. They built and finished it, according to the commandment of the God of Israel, and according to the decree of Cyrus, and Darius, and Artaxerxes king of Persia.

This house was finished on the third day of the month Adar, which was in the sixth year of the reign of Darius the king. The children of Israel, the priests, and the Levites, and the rest of the children of the captivity, kept the dedication of this house of God with joy. They offered at the dedication of this house of God one hundred bulls, two hundred rams, four hundred lambs; and for a sin offering for all Israel, twelve male goats, according to the number of the tribes of Israel. They set the priests in their divisions, and the Levites in their courses, for the service of God, which is at Jerusalem; as it is written in the book of Moses.

Another key moment in the re-establishment of the nation of Israel was the return of Ezra to Jerusalem. Ezra came bearing written approval, gold and precious gifts, and strong support from King Artaxerxes of Persia for the rebuilding of Jerusalem.

There went up some of the children of Israel, and of the priests, and the Levites, and the singers, and the porters, and the Nethinim, to Jerusalem, in the seventh year of Artaxerxes the king. He came to Jerusalem in the fifth month, which was in the seventh year of the king. For on the first day of the first month began he to go up from Babylon; and on the first day of the fifth month came he to Jerusalem, according to the good hand of his God on him. For Ezra had set his heart to seek the law of Yahweh, and to do it, and to teach in Israel statutes and ordinances.

Now this is the copy of the letter that the king Artaxerxes gave to Ezra the priest, the scribe, even the scribe of the words of the commandments of Yahweh, and of his statutes to Israel: Artaxerxes, king of kings, to Ezra the priest, the scribe of the law of the God of heaven, perfect and so forth. I make a decree, that all those of the people of Israel, and their priests and the Levites, in my realm, who are minded of their own free will to go to Jerusalem, go with you. Because you are sent of the king and his seven counselors, to inquire concerning Judah and Jerusalem, according to the law of your God which is in your hand, and to carry the silver and gold, which the king and his counselors have freely offered to the God of Israel, whose habitation is in Jerusalem, and all the silver and gold that you shall find in all the province of Babylon, with the freewill offering of the people, and of the priests, offering willingly for the house of their God which is in Jerusalem; therefore you shall with all diligence buy with this money bulls, rams, lambs, with their meal offerings and their drink offerings, and shall offer them on the altar of the house of your God which is in Jerusalem. Whatever shall seem good to you and to your brothers to do with the rest of the silver and the gold, do that after the will of your God. The vessels that are given to you for the service of the house of your God, deliver before the God of Jerusalem. Whatever more shall be needful for the house of your God, which you shall have occasion to bestow, bestow it out of the king's treasure house. I, even I Artaxerxes the king, do make a decree to all the treasurers who are beyond the River, that whatever Ezra the priest, the scribe of the law of the God of heaven, shall require of you, it be done with all diligence, to one hundred talents of silver, and to one hundred measures of wheat, and to one hundred baths of wine, and to one hundred baths of oil, and salt without prescribing how much. Whatever is commanded by the God of heaven, let it be done exactly for the house of the God of heaven; for why should there be wrath against the realm of the king and his sons? Also we inform you, that touching any of the priests and Levites, the singers, porters, Nethinim, or servants of this house of God, it shall not be lawful to impose tribute, custom, or toll, on them. You, Ezra, after the wisdom of your God who is in your hand, appoint magistrates and judges, who may judge all the people who are beyond the River, all such as know the laws of your God; and teach him who doesn't know them. Whoever will not do the law of your God, and the law of the king, let judgment be executed on him with all diligence, whether it be to death, or to banishment, or to confiscation of goods, or to imprisonment.

Blessed be Yahweh, the God of our fathers, who has put such a thing as this in the king's heart, to beautify the house of Yahweh which is in Jerusalem; and has extended loving kindness to me before the king, and his counselors, and before all the king's mighty princes. I was strengthened according to the hand of Yahweh my God on me, and I gathered together out of Israel chief men to go up with me.

In addition to attention on rebuilding Jerusalem, Ezra also had to pay attention to the spiritual purity and practices of the nation. Under his watch, the synagogues and scribes grew in importance. When he found out that many Israelites had married pagan wives, he was distraught. The people agreed to right this wrong, in an effort to ensure that idolatry would not again spread its way into the nation. It finally seemed that the nation had learned from its mistakes and their exile.

The children of the captivity, who had come out of exile, offered burnt offerings to the God of Israel, twelve bulls for all Israel, ninety-six rams, seventy-seven lambs, and twelve male goats for a sin offering: all this was a burnt offering to Yahweh. They delivered the king's commissions to the king's satraps, and to the governors beyond the River: and they furthered the people and God's house.

Now when these things were done, the princes drew near to me, saying, "The people of Israel, and the priests and the Levites, have not separated themselves from the peoples of the lands, following their abominations, even those of the Canaanites, the Hittites, the Perizzites, the Jebusites, the Ammonites, the Moabites, the Egyptians, and the Amorites. For they have taken of their daughters for themselves and for their sons, so that the holy seed have mixed themselves with the peoples of the lands. Yes, the hand of the princes and rulers has been chief in this trespass."

When I heard this thing, I tore my garment and my robe, and plucked off the hair of my head and of my beard, and sat down confounded. Then were assembled to me everyone who trembled at the words of the God of Israel, because of their trespass of the captivity; and I sat confounded until the evening offering. At the evening offering I arose up from my humiliation, even with my garment and my robe torn; and I fell on my knees, and spread out my hands to Yahweh my God; and I said, "My God, I am ashamed and blush to lift up my face to you, my God; for our iniquities have increased over our head, and our guiltiness has grown up to the heavens.

"Now, our God, what shall we say after this? For we have forsaken your commandments."

Now while Ezra prayed and made confession, weeping and casting himself down before God's house, there was gathered together to him out of Israel a very great assembly of men and women and children; for the people wept very bitterly. Shecaniah the son of Jehiel, one of the sons of Elam, answered Ezra, "We have trespassed against our God, and have married foreign women of the peoples of the land. Yet now there is hope for Israel concerning this thing. Now therefore let us make a covenant with our God to put away all the wives, and such as are born of them, according to the counsel of my lord, and of those who tremble at the commandment of our God. Let it be done according to the law. Arise; for the matter belongs to you, and we are with you. Be courageous, and do it."

Then Ezra arose, and made the chiefs of the priests, the Levites, and all Israel, to swear that they would do according to this word. So they swore.

Ezra the priest stood up, and said to them, "You have trespassed, and have married foreign women, to increase the guilt of Israel. Now therefore make confession to Yahweh, the God of your fathers, and do his pleasure; and separate yourselves from the peoples of the land, and from the foreign women."

Then all the assembly answered with a loud voice, "As you have said concerning us, so must we do.

They gave their hand that they would put away their wives; and being guilty, they offered a ram of the flock for their guilt.

Although nearly 100 years had passed since the exiles of Judah returned to Israel from Babylon, the nation was struggling. Although the temple had been completed some 70 years earlier, the city was still largely in ruins and not well occupied - most people lived in the outskirts. The wall around Jerusalem had not been rebuilt - and with no wall, there was no security., and no place where the nation could concentrate its political and spiritual focus.

Into this picture came Nehemiah, a Jew who had risen to a position of prominence in the Babylonian palace, through his leadership abilities. Although living a good life in Babylon, his heart was elsewhere - among his Jewish people in Israel. Using his influence with the king, Nehemiah secured permission to return to Jerusalem to rebuild the wall and thus strengthen the city and his nation. Applying the leadership skills he had honed in Babylon - organization, speaking, the will to overcome resistance, and, most importantly, prayer, he overcame great odds

GOD'S LOVE STORY MINISTRIES

and demonstrated how great spiritual leaders should conduct themselves.

The words of Nehemiah the son of Hacaliah. Now it happened in the month Chislev, in the twentieth year, as I was in Shushan the palace, that Hanani, one of my brothers, came, he and certain men out of Judah; and I asked them concerning the Jews who had escaped, who were left of the captivity, and concerning Jerusalem. They said to me, "The remnant who are left of the captivity there in the province are in great affliction and reproach. The wall of Jerusalem also is broken down, and its gates are burned with fire." It happened, when I heard these words, that I sat down and wept, and mourned certain days; and I fasted and prayed before the God of heaven, and said, "I beg you, Yahweh, the God of heaven, the great and awesome God, who keeps covenant and loving kindness with those who love him and keep his commandments: Let your ear now be attentive, and your eyes open, that you may listen to the prayer of your servant, which I pray before you at this time, day and night, for the children of Israel your servants while I confess the sins of the children of Israel, which we have sinned against you. Yes, I and my father's house have sinned.

"Now these are your servants and your people, whom you have redeemed by your great power, and by your strong hand. Lord, I beg you, let your ear be attentive now to the prayer of your servant, and to the prayer of your servants, who delight to fear your name; and please prosper your servant this day, and grant him mercy in the sight of this man."

Now I was cup bearer to the king.

It happened in the month Nisan, in the twentieth year of Artaxerxes the king, when wine was before him, that I took up the wine, and gave it to the king. Now I had not been sad before in his presence. The king said to me, "Why is your face sad, since you are not sick? This is nothing else but sorrow of heart."

Then I was very much afraid. I said to the king, "Let the king live forever! Why shouldn't my face be sad, when the city, the place of my fathers' tombs, lies waste, and its gates have been consumed with fire?"

Then the king said to me, "For what do you make request?"

So I prayed to the God of heaven. I said to the king, "If it pleases the king, and if your servant has found favor in your sight, that you would send me to Judah, to the city of my fathers' tombs, that I may build it."

The king said to me (the queen was also sitting by him), "For how long shall your journey be? And when will you return?"

So it pleased the king to send me; and I set him a time. Moreover I said to the king, "If it pleases the king, let letters be given me to the governors beyond the River, that they may let me pass through until I come to Judah; and a letter to

276

Asaph the keeper of the king's forest, that he may give me timber to make beams for the gates of the citadel by the temple, for the wall of the city, and for the house that I shall enter into."

The king granted my requests, because of the good hand of my God on me. Then I came to the governors beyond the River, and gave them the king's letters. Now the king had sent with me captains of the army and horsemen.

Through prayer and trust in God, Nehemiah was successful in securing the permission and support of king Artaxerxes in returning to Jerusalem to rebuild the wall. But it did not take long for opposition to appear. As happened 100 years ago in the rebuilding of the temple, other leaders saw the emergence of Jerusalem as a challenge to their own base of power. The task would not be easy. In a wise move, Nehemiah decided to keep the news of his task a secret for as long as possible.

When Sanballat the Horonite, and Tobiah the servant, the Ammonite, heard of it, it grieved them exceedingly, because a man had come to seek the welfare of the children of Israel. So I came to Jerusalem, and was there three days. I arose in the night, I and some few men with me; neither told I any man what my God put into my heart to do for Jerusalem; neither was there any animal with me, except the animal that I rode on. I went out by night by the valley gate, even toward the jackal's well, and to the dung gate, and viewed the walls of Jerusalem, which were broken down, and its gates were consumed with fire. Then I went on to the spring gate and to the king's pool: but there was no place for the animal that was under me to pass. Then went I up in the night by the brook, and viewed the wall; and I turned back, and entered by the valley gate, and so returned. The rulers didn't know where I went, or what I did; neither had I as yet told it to the Jews, nor to the priests, nor to the nobles, nor to the rulers, nor to the rest who did the work. Then I said to them, "You see the evil case that we are in, how Jerusalem lies waste, and its gates are burned with fire. Come, let us build up the wall of Jerusalem, that we won't be disgraced." I told them of the hand of my God which was good on me, as also of the king's words that he had spoken to me.

They said, "Let's rise up and build." So they strengthened their hands for the good work.

Nehemiah immediately began organizing the Israelites, by family, into working units. Each extended family took on a section of the wall, or a set of gates. A diverse group of men and women, from priests to farmers, from goldsmiths to perfumers, and from rulers to merchants, joined together in the task. On the gates, they laid its beams, and set up its doors,

277

bolts, and bars. They began repairs to the walls and towers. And the opposition strengthened.

So we built the wall; and all the wall was joined together to half its height: for the people had a mind to work. But it happened that when Sanballat, Tobiah, the Arabians, the Ammonites, and the Ashdodites heard that the repairing of the walls of Jerusalem went forward, and that the breaches began to be filled, then they were very angry; and they conspired all of them together to come and fight against Jerusalem, and to cause confusion therein. But we made our prayer to our God, and set a watch against them day and night, because of them. Judah said, "The strength of the bearers of burdens is fading, and there is much rubbish; so that we are not able to build the wall." Our adversaries said, "They shall not know, neither see, until we come into their midst, and kill them, and cause the work to cease."

It happened that when the Jews who lived by them came, they said to us ten times from all places, "Wherever you turn, they will attack us." Therefore set I in the lowest parts of the space behind the wall, in the open places, I set the people after their families with their swords, their spears, and their bows. I looked, and rose up, and said to the nobles, and to the rulers, and to the rest of the people, "Don't be afraid of them! Remember the Lord, who is great and awesome, and fight for your brothers, your sons, and your daughters, your wives, and your houses."

It happened, when our enemies heard that it was known to us, and God had brought their counsel to nothing, that we returned all of us to the wall, everyone to his work. It happened from that time forth, that half of my servants worked in the work, and half of them held the spears, the shields, and the bows, and the coats of mail; and the rulers were behind all the house of Judah. They all built the wall and those who bore burdens loaded themselves; everyone with one of his hands worked in the work, and with the other held his weapon; and the builders, everyone wore his sword at his side, and so built. He who sounded the trumpet was by me. I said to the nobles, and to the rulers and to the rest of the people, "The work is great and large, and we are separated on the wall, one far from another. Wherever you hear the sound of the trumpet, rally there to us. Our God will fight for us."

So we worked in the work: and half of them held the spears from the rising of the morning until the stars appeared. Likewise at the same time said I to the people, "Let everyone with his servant lodge within Jerusalem, that in the night they may be a guard to us, and may labor in the day." So neither I, nor my brothers, nor my servants, nor the men of the guard who followed me, none of us took off our clothes. Everyone took his weapon to the water.

Then there arose a great cry of the people and of their wives against their brothers the Jews. For there were that said, "We, our sons and our daughters, are many. Let us get grain, that we may eat and live." Some also there were that said, "We are mortgaging our fields, and our vineyards, and our houses. Let us get grain, because of the famine." There were also some who said, "We have borrowed money for the king's tribute using our fields and our vineyards as collateral. Yet now our flesh is as the flesh of our brothers, our children as their children. Behold, we bring into bondage our sons and our daughters to be servants, and some of our daughters have been brought into bondage. Neither is it in our power to help it; for other men have our fields and our vineyards."

As the work to rebuild the wall of Jerusalem continued, a severe famine was underway. The poor people of Israel cried out to Nehemiah, complaining that the few families that controlled the land were subjecting them to severe taxes. In desperation, some were even selling their property, and selling their children into slavery to buy food and pay taxes. These practices would have to stop for Israel to be successful, so Nehemiah again exerted his leadership.

I was very angry when I heard their cry and these words. Then I consulted with myself, and contended with the nobles and the rulers, and said to them, "You exact usury, everyone of his brother." I held a great assembly against them. I said to them, "We, after our ability, have redeemed our brothers the Jews that were sold to the nations; and would you even sell your brothers, and should they be sold to us?" Then they held their peace, and found never a word. Also I said, "The thing that you do is not good. Ought you not to walk in the fear of our God, because of the reproach of the nations our enemies? I likewise, my brothers and my servants, lend them money and grain. Please let us stop this usury. Please restore to them, even this day, their fields, their vineyards, their olive groves, and their houses, also the hundredth part of the money, and of the grain, the new wine, and the oil, that you are charging them."

Then they said, "We will restore them, and will require nothing of them; so will we do, even as you say."

As work progressed on the wall, the opposition became more entrenched. When their attempts to lure Nehemiah away from the city to harm him did not work, they resorted to intimidation. They sent an "unsealed" or open letter, spreading harmful rumors that Nehemiah was setting himself up as the king of Judah. They also hired a man to give poor counsel to Nehemiah, advising him to flee to the temple, hoping to create a situation in which they could give an evil report about him. Again, Nehemiah did not give in to their tactics.

Now it happened, when it was reported to Sanballat and Tobiah, and to Geshem the Arabian, and to the rest of our enemies, that I had built the wall, and that there was no breach left therein; (though even to that time I had not set up the doors in the gates;) that Sanballat and Geshem sent to me, saying, "Come, let us meet together in the villages in the plain of Ono." But they intended to harm me.

I sent messengers to them, saying, "I am doing a great work, so that I can't come down. Why should the work cease, while I leave it, and come down to you?" They sent to me four times after this sort; and I answered them the same way. Then Sanballat sent his servant to me the same way the fifth time with an open letter in his hand, in which was written, "It is reported among the nations, and Gashmu says it, that you and the Jews intend to rebel. Because of that, you are building the wall. You would be their king, according to these words. You have also appointed prophets to preach of you at Jerusalem, saying, 'There is a king in Judah!' Now it will be reported to the king according to these words. Come now therefore, and let us take counsel together."

Then I sent to him, saying, "There are no such things done as you say, but you imagine them out of your own heart." For they all would have made us afraid, saying, "Their hands will be weakened from the work, that it not be done. But now, strengthen my hands."

I went to the house of Shemaiah the son of Delaiah the son of Mehetabel, who was shut in at his home; and he said, "Let us meet together in God's house, within the temple, and let us shut the doors of the temple; for they will come to kill you; yes, in the night will they come to kill you."

I said, "Should such a man as I flee? Who is there that, being such as I, would go into the temple to save his life? I will not go in." I discerned, and behold, God had not sent him; but he pronounced this prophecy against me. Tobiah and Sanballat had hired him. He hired so that I would be afraid, do so, and sin, and that they might have material for an evil report, that they might reproach me. "Remember, my God, Tobiah and Sanballat according to these their works, and also the prophetess Noadiah, and the rest of the prophets, that would have put me in fear."

So the wall was finished in the twenty-fifth day of Elul, in fifty-two days. It happened, when all our enemies heard of it, that all the nations that were about us were afraid, and were much cast down in their own eyes; for they perceived that this work was worked of our God.

Now it happened, when the wall was built, and I had set up the doors, and the porters and the singers and the Levites were appointed, that I put my brother Hanani, and Hananiah the governor of the castle, in charge of Jerusalem; for he was a faithful man, and feared God above many. I said to them, "Don't let the gates of Jerusalem be opened until the sun is hot; and while they stand guard, let them shut the doors, and you bar them: and appoint watches of the inhabitants of Jerusalem, everyone in his watch, with everyone near his house."

The wall was completed; but the work of Nehemiah was not yet done. He now set his sights on populating the city, and ensuring spiritual purity among the people. The first steps were to take a census, counting the people by families, and to take a collection to fund the work ahead.

Now the city was wide and large; but the people were few therein, and the houses were not built. My God put into my heart to gather together the nobles, and the rulers, and the people, that they might be reckoned by genealogy. I found the book of the genealogy of those who came up at the first, and I found written therein: These are the children of the province, who went up out of the captivity of those who had been carried away, whom Nebuchadnezzar the king of Babylon had carried away, and who returned to Jerusalem and to Judah, everyone to his city;

The whole assembly together was forty-two thousand three hundred sixty, besides their male servants and their female servants, of whom there were seven thousand three hundred thirty-seven: and they had two hundred forty-five singing men and singing women.

Assemblies were held in which the Law of God was read, and the people confessed their sins and committed to follow God with purity. Nehemiah also had lots cast, and one of ten families were selected to populate the city.

All the people gathered themselves together as one man into the broad place that was before the water gate; and they spoke to Ezra the scribe to bring the book of the law of Moses, which Yahweh had commanded to Israel. Ezra the priest brought the law before the assembly, both men and women, and all who could hear with understanding, on the first day of the seventh month. He read therein before the broad place that was before the water gate from early morning until midday, in the presence of the men and the women, and of those who could understand; and the ears of all the people were attentive to the book of the law.

Ezra the scribe stood on a pulpit of wood, which they had made for the purpose.

Ezra opened the book in the sight of all the people; (for he was above all the people;) and when he opened it, all the people stood up: and Ezra blessed Yahweh, the great God. All the people answered, "Amen, Amen," with the lifting up of their hands. They bowed their heads, and worshiped Yahweh with their faces to the ground. Also Jeshua, and Bani, and Sherebiah, Jamin, Akkub, Shabbethai, Hodiah, Maaseiah, Kelita, Azariah, Jozabad, Hanan, Pelaiah, and the Levites, caused the people to understand the law: and the people stayed in their place. They read in the book, in the law of God, distinctly; and they gave the sense, so that they understood the reading. Nehemiah, who was the governor, and Ezra the priest the scribe, and the Levites who taught the people, said to all the people, "This day is holy to Yahweh your God. Don't mourn, nor weep." For all the people wept, when they heard the words of the law. Then he said to them, "Go your way. Eat the fat, drink the sweet, and send portions to him for whom nothing is prepared; for this day is holy to our Lord. Don't be grieved; for the joy of Yahweh is your strength."

So the Levites stilled all the people, saying, "Hold your peace, for the day is holy; neither be grieved."

All the people went their way to eat, and to drink, and to send portions, and to make great mirth, because they had understood the words that were declared to them. On the second day were gathered together the heads of fathers' households of all the people, the priests, and the Levites, to Ezra the scribe, even to give attention to the words of the law. They found written in the law, how that Yahweh had commanded by Moses, that the children of Israel should dwell in booths in the feast of the seventh month; and that they should publish and proclaim in all their cities, and in Jerusalem, saying, "Go out to the mountain, and get olive branches, and branches of wild olive, and myrtle branches, and palm branches, and branches of thick trees, to make booths, as it is written."

So the people went out, and brought them, and made themselves booths, everyone on the roof of his house, and in their courts, and in the courts of God's house, and in the broad place of the water gate, and in the broad place of the gate of Ephraim. All the assembly of those who had come again out of the captivity made booths, and lived in the booths; for since the days of Jeshua the son of Nun to that day the children of Israel had not done so. There was very great gladness. Also day by day, from the first day to the last day, he read in the book of the law of God. They kept the feast seven days; and on the eighth day was a solemn assembly, according to the ordinance.

Now in the twenty-fourth day of this month the children of Israel were assembled with fasting, and with sackcloth, and earth on them. The seed of Israel separated themselves from all foreigners, and stood and confessed their sins, and the iniquities of their fathers. They stood up in their place, and read in the book of the law of Yahweh their God a fourth part of the day; and a fourth part they confessed, and worshiped Yahweh their God.

The rest of the people, the priests, the Levites, the porters, the singers, the Nethinim, and all those who had separated themselves from the peoples of the lands to the law of God, their wives, their sons, and their daughters, everyone who had knowledge, and understanding— they joined with their brothers, their nobles, and entered into a curse, and into an oath, to walk in God's law, which was given by Moses the servant of God, and to observe and do all the commandments of Yahweh our Lord, and his ordinances and his statutes;

The princes of the people lived in Jerusalem: the rest of the people also cast lots, to bring one of ten to dwell in Jerusalem the holy city, and nine parts in the other cities. The people blessed all the men who willingly offered themselves to dwell in Jerusalem.

Finally, some 100 years after the captives left Babylon, the city of Jerusalem was again the center of Jewish identity. With the temple and city walls in place, the Jews had protection from their enemies and a defined place of worship.

24 A QUEEN'S DELIVERANCE

The Story of Esther

The unlikely story of Ester shows how God cares for his followers, even if achieved through indirect means. The beautiful Jewish girl Esther found herself chosen to be the queen of Ahasuerus, the ruler of Persia, one of the great world powers at that time. Influential Persians, jealous of the Jews who were living among them, devised a plot to have the king order the death of all Jews.

Esther, who had kept her nationality a closely guarded secret, found herself thrust into a position where she could intervene on her people's part, although at great risk to herself. A series of unlikely coincidences aided her in this task. The king, unable to sleep, read an account of a good deed that Esther's cousin Mordecai had done; he then sought to honor Mordecai just as the evil man Haman happened to come into his presence. These unlikely coincidences show the power of God, working behind the scenes to protect his beloved people even as they lived in pagan, idol worshiping countries.

Esther's story is an inspiring chapter in the narrative of God's love story.

Now it happened in the days of Ahasuerus (this is Ahasuerus who reigned from India even to Ethiopia, over one hundred twenty-seven provinces), that in those days, when the King Ahasuerus sat on the throne of his kingdom, which was in Shushan the palace, in the third year of his reign, he made a feast for all his princes and his servants; the power of Persia and Media, the nobles and princes of the provinces, being before him. He displayed the riches of his glorious kingdom and the honor of his excellent majesty many days, even one hundred eighty days. When these days were fulfilled, the king made a seven day feast for all the people who were present in Shushan the palace, both great and small, in the court of the garden of the king's palace.

On the seventh day, when the heart of the king was merry with wine, he commanded Mehuman, Biztha, Harbona, Bigtha, and Abagtha, Zethar, and

Carcass, the seven eunuchs who served in the presence of Ahasuerus the king, to bring Vashti the queen before the king with the royal crown, to show the people and the princes her beauty; for she was beautiful. But the queen Vashti refused to come at the king's commandment by the eunuchs. Therefore the king was very angry, and his anger burned in him. Then the king said to the wise men, who knew the times, (for it was the king's custom to consult those who knew law and judgment; and the next to him were Carshena, Shethar, Admatha, Tarshish, Meres, Marsena, and Memucan, the seven princes of Persia and Media, who saw the king's face, and sat first in the kingdom), "What shall we do to the queen Vashti according to law, because she has not done the bidding of the King Ahasuerus by the eunuchs?"

Memucan answered before the king and the princes, "Vashti the queen has not done wrong to just the king, but also to all the princes, and to all the people who are in all the provinces of the King Ahasuerus. For this deed of the queen will become known to all women, causing them to show contempt for their husbands, when it is reported, 'King Ahasuerus commanded Vashti the queen to be brought in before him, but she didn't come.' Today, the princesses of Persia and Media who have heard of the queen's deed will tell all the king's princes. This will cause much contempt and wrath.

"If it please the king, let a royal commandment go from him, and let it be written among the laws of the Persians and the Medes, so that it cannot be altered, that Vashti may never again come before King Ahasuerus; and let the king give her royal estate to another who is better than she. When the king's decree which he shall make is published throughout all his kingdom (for it is great), all the wives will give their husbands honor, both great and small."

This advice pleased the king and the princes, and the king did according to the word of Memucan:

After these things, when the wrath of King Ahasuerus was pacified, he remembered Vashti, and what she had done, and what was decreed against her. Then the king's servants who served him said, "Let beautiful young virgins be sought for the king. Let the king appoint officers in all the provinces of his kingdom, that they may gather together all the beautiful young virgins to the citadel of Susa, to the women's house, to the custody of Hegai the king's eunuch, keeper of the women. Let cosmetics be given them; and let the maiden who pleases the king be queen instead of Vashti." The thing pleased the king, and he did so.

There was a certain Jew in the citadel of Susa, whose name was Mordecai, the son of Jair, the son of Shimei, the son of Kish, a Benjamite, who had been carried away from Jerusalem with the captives who had been carried away with

Jeconiah king of Judah, whom Nebuchadnezzar the king of Babylon had carried away. He brought up Hadassah, that is, Esther, his uncle's daughter; for she had neither father nor mother. The maiden was fair and beautiful; and when her father and mother were dead, Mordecai took her for his own daughter. So it happened, when the king's commandment and his decree was heard, and when many maidens were gathered together to the citadel of Susa, to the custody of Hegai, that Esther was taken into the king's house, to the custody of Hegai, keeper of the women. The maiden pleased him, and she obtained kindness from him. He quickly gave her cosmetics and her portions of food, and the seven choice maidens who were to be given her out of the king's house. He moved her and her maidens to the best place in the women's house. Esther had not made known her people nor her relatives, because Mordecai had instructed her that she should not make it known. Mordecai walked every day in front of the court of the women's house, to find out how Esther was doing, and what would become of her.

Now when the turn of Esther, the daughter of Abihail the uncle of Mordecai, who had taken her for his daughter, came to go in to the king, she required nothing but what Hegai the king's eunuch, the keeper of the women, advised. Esther obtained favor in the sight of all those who looked at her. So Esther was taken to King Ahasuerus into his royal house in the tenth month, which is the month Tebeth, in the seventh year of his reign. The king loved Esther more than all the women, and she obtained favor and kindness in his sight more than all the virgins; so that he set the royal crown on her head, and made her queen instead of Vashti.

In those days, while Mordecai was sitting in the king's gate, two of the king's eunuchs, Bigthan and Teresh, who were doorkeepers, were angry, and sought to lay hands on the King Ahasuerus. This thing became known to Mordecai, who informed Esther the queen; and Esther informed the king in Mordecai's name. When this matter was investigated, and it was found to be so, they were both hanged on a tree; and it was written in the book of the chronicles in the king's presence.

After these things King Ahasuerus promoted Haman the son of Hammedatha the Agagite, and advanced him, and set his seat above all the princes who were with him. All the king's servants who were in the king's gate bowed down, and paid homage to Haman; for the king had so commanded concerning him. But Mordecai didn't bow down or pay him homage. Then the king's servants, who were in the king's gate, said to Mordecai, "Why do you disobey the king's commandment?" Now it came to pass, when they spoke daily to him, and he didn't listen to them, that they told Haman, to see whether

Mordecai's reason would stand; for he had told them that he was a Jew. When Haman saw that Mordecai didn't bow down, nor pay him homage, Haman was full of wrath. But he scorned the thought of laying hands on Mordecai alone, for they had made known to him Mordecai's people. Therefore Haman sought to destroy all the Jews who were throughout the whole kingdom of Ahasuerus, even Mordecai's people.

Haman, consumed by rage and pride, developed a plan to destroy the Jews. Soon, Esther, being Jewish, found herself in the middle of this controversy.

Haman said to King Ahasuerus, "There is a certain people scattered abroad and dispersed among the peoples in all the provinces of your kingdom, and their laws are different than other people's. They don't keep the king's laws. Therefore it is not for the king's profit to allow them to remain. If it pleases the king, let it be written that they be destroyed; and I will pay ten thousand talents of silver into the hands of those who are in charge of the king's business, to bring it into the king's treasuries."

The king took his ring from his hand, and gave it to Haman the son of Hammedatha the Agagite, the Jews' enemy. The king said to Haman, "The silver is given to you, the people also, to do with them as it seems good to you." Then the king's scribes were called in on the first month, on the thirteenth day of the month; and all that Haman commanded was written to the king's satraps, and to the governors who were over every province, and to the princes of every people, to every province according its writing, and to every people in their language. It was written in the name of King Ahasuerus, and it was sealed with the king's ring. Letters were sent by couriers into all the king's provinces, to destroy, to kill, and to cause to perish, all Jews, both young and old, little children and women, in one day, even on the thirteenth day of the twelfth month, which is the month Adar, and to plunder their possessions.

Now when Mordecai found out all that was done, Mordecai tore his clothes, and put on sackcloth with ashes, and went out into the midst of the city, and wailed loudly and a bitterly. He came even before the king's gate, for no one is allowed inside the king's gate clothed with sackcloth. In every province, wherever the king's commandment and his decree came, there was great mourning among the Jews, and fasting, and weeping, and wailing; and many lay in sackcloth and ashes. Esther's maidens and her eunuchs came and told her this, and the queen was exceedingly grieved. She sent clothing to Mordecai, to replace his sackcloth; but he didn't receive it. Then Esther called for Hathach, one of the king's eunuchs, whom he had appointed to attend her, and commanded him to go to Mordecai, to find out what this was, and why it was. So Hathach went out to Mordecai, to city square which was before the king's gate. Mordecai told him of all that had happened to him, and the exact sum of the money that Haman had promised to pay to the king's treasuries for the destruction of the Jews. He also gave him the copy of the writing of the decree that was given out in Shushan to destroy them, to show it to Esther, and to declare it to her, and to urge her to go in to the king, to make supplication to him, and to make request before him, for her people.

Hathach came and told Esther the words of Mordecai. Then Esther spoke to Hathach, and gave him a message to Mordecai: "All the king's servants, and the people of the king's provinces, know, that whoever, whether man or woman, comes to the king into the inner court without being called, there is one law for him, that he be put to death, except those to whom the king might hold out the golden scepter, that he may live. I have not been called to come in to the king these thirty days."

Esther was in a precarious position. Even though she was the queen, if she approached the king without being invited, she did so at the risk of death. The response given to her by Mordecai was a powerful reminder of our obligations to use our position in life for the purposes of God.

They told to Mordecai Esther's words. Then Mordecai asked them return answer to Esther, "Don't think to yourself that you will escape in the king's house any more than all the Jews. For if you remain silent now, then relief and deliverance will come to the Jews from another place, but you and your father's house will perish. Who knows if you haven't come to the kingdom for such a time as this?"

Then Esther asked them to answer Mordecai, "Go, gather together all the Jews who are present in Shushan, and fast for me, and neither eat nor drink three days, night or day. I and my maidens will also fast the same way. Then I will go in to the king, which is against the law; and if I perish, I perish." So Mordecai went his way, and did according to all that Esther had commanded him.

Now it happened on the third day that Esther put on her royal clothing, and stood in the inner court of the king's house, next to the king's house. The king sat on his royal throne in the royal house, next to the entrance of the house. When the king saw Esther the queen standing in the court, she obtained favor in his sight; and the king held out to Esther the golden scepter that was in his hand. So Esther came near, and touched the top of the scepter. Then the king asked her, "What would you like, queen Esther? What is your request? It shall be given you even to the half of the kingdom."

Esther said, "If it seems good to the king, let the king and Haman come today to the banquet that I have prepared for him."

Then the king said, "Bring Haman quickly, so that it may be done as Esther has said." So the king and Haman came to the banquet that Esther had prepared.

The king said to Esther at the banquet of wine, "What is your petition? It shall be granted you. What is your request? Even to the half of the kingdom it shall be performed."

Then Esther answered and said, "My petition and my request is this. If I have found favor in the sight of the king, and if it please the king to grant my petition and to perform my request, let the king and Haman come to the banquet that I will prepare for them, and I will do tomorrow as the king has said."

Even though she was granted immediate rights to make a request, Esther twice delayed stating her reason for approaching the king. The divine providence of God can be seen in this delay, as it allows for a remarkable series of events to bring a most dramatic conclusion.

Then Haman went out that day joyful and glad of heart, but when Haman saw Mordecai in the king's gate, that he didn't stand up nor move for him, he was filled with wrath against Mordecai. Nevertheless Haman restrained himself, and went home. There, he sent and called for his friends and Zeresh his wife. Haman recounted to them the glory of his riches, the multitude of his children, all the things in which the king had promoted him, and how he had advanced him above the princes and servants of the king. Haman also said, "Yes, Esther the queen let no man come in with the king to the banquet that she had prepared but myself; and tomorrow I am also invited by her together with the king. Yet all this avails me nothing, so long as I see Mordecai the Jew sitting at the king's gate."

Then Zeresh his wife and all his friends said to him, "Let a gallows be made fifty cubits high, and in the morning speak to the king about hanging Mordecai on it. Then go in merrily with the king to the banquet." This pleased Haman, so he had the gallows made.

On that night, the king couldn't sleep. He commanded the book of records of the chronicles to be brought, and they were read to the king. It was found written that Mordecai had told of Bigthana and Teresh, two of the king's eunuchs, who were doorkeepers, who had tried to lay hands on the King Ahasuerus. The king said, "What honor and dignity has been bestowed on Mordecai for this?"

Then the king's servants who attended him said, "Nothing has been done for him."

The king said, "Who is in the court?" Now Haman had come into the outer court of the king's house, to speak to the king about hanging Mordecai on the gallows that he had prepared for him.

The king's servants said to him, "Behold, Haman stands in the court."

The king said, "Let him come in." So Haman came in. The king said to him, "What shall be done to the man whom the king delights to honor?"

Now Haman said in his heart, "Who would the king delight to honor more than myself?" Haman said to the king, "For the man whom the king delights to honor, let royal clothing be brought which the king uses to wear, and the horse that the king rides on, and on the head of which a crown royal is set. Let the clothing and the horse be delivered to the hand of one of the king's most noble princes, that they may array the man whom the king delights to honor with them, and have him ride on horseback through the city square, and proclaim before him, 'Thus shall it be done to the man whom the king delights to honor!'"

Then the king said to Haman, "Hurry and take the clothing and the horse, as you have said, and do this for Mordecai the Jew, who sits at the king's gate. Let nothing fail of all that you have spoken."

Then Haman took the clothing and the horse, and arrayed Mordecai, and had him ride through the city square, and proclaimed before him, "Thus shall it be done to the man whom the king delights to honor!"

Mordecai came back to the king's gate, but Haman hurried to his house, mourning and having his head covered. Haman recounted to Zeresh his wife and all his friends everything that had happened to him. Then his wise men and Zeresh his wife said to him, "If Mordecai, before whom you have begun to fall, is of Jewish descent, you will not prevail against him, but you will surely fall before him." While they were yet talking with him, the king's eunuchs came, and hurried to bring Haman to the banquet that Esther had prepared.

So the king and Haman came to banquet with Esther the queen. The king said again to Esther on the second day at the banquet of wine, "What is your petition, queen Esther? It shall be granted you. What is your request? Even to the half of the kingdom it shall be performed."

Then Esther the queen answered, "If I have found favor in your sight, O king, and if it please the king, let my life be given me at my petition, and my people at my request. For we are sold, I and my people, to be destroyed, to be slain, and to perish. But if we had been sold for bondservants and bondmaids, I would have held my peace, although the adversary could not have compensated for the king's loss."

Then King Ahasuerus said to Esther the queen, "Who is he, and where is he who dared presume in his heart to do so?"

Esther said, "An adversary and an enemy, even this wicked Haman!"

Then Haman was afraid before the king and the queen. The king arose in his wrath from the banquet of wine and went into the palace garden. Haman stood up to make request for his life to Esther the queen; for he saw that there was evil determined against him by the king. Then the king returned out of the palace garden into the place of the banquet of wine; and Haman had fallen on the couch where Esther was. Then the king said, "Will he even assault the queen in front of me in the house?" As the word went out of the king's mouth, they covered Haman's face.

Then Harbonah, one of the eunuchs who were with the king said, "Behold, the gallows fifty cubits high, which Haman has made for Mordecai, who spoke good for the king, is standing at Haman's house."

The king said, "Hang him on it!"

So they hanged Haman on the gallows that he had prepared for Mordecai. Then was the king's wrath pacified.

On that day, King Ahasuerus gave the house of Haman, the Jews' enemy, to Esther the queen. Mordecai came before the king; for Esther had told what he was to her. The king took off his ring, which he had taken from Haman, and gave it to Mordecai. Esther set Mordecai over the house of Haman.

The fortunes of both Mordecai and Haman were reversed, but Esther's work was not done. She next had to convince the king to retract his decree, to make safe the plight of the Jewish people. In a dramatic twist, the Jews were not just spared, but granted the right to kill all of their enemies with the blessing of the king.

Esther spoke yet again before the king, and fell down at his feet, and begged him with tears to put away the mischief of Haman the Agagite, and his device that he had devised against the Jews. Then the king held out to Esther the golden scepter. So Esther arose, and stood before the king. She said, "If it pleases the king, and if I have found favor in his sight, and the thing seem right to the king, and I am pleasing in his eyes, let it be written to reverse the letters devised by Haman, the son of Hammedatha the Agagite, which he wrote to destroy the Jews who are in all the king's provinces. For how can I endure to see the evil that would come to my people? How can I endure to see the destruction of my relatives?"

Then King Ahasuerus said to Esther the queen and to Mordecai the Jew, "See, I have given Esther the house of Haman, and him they have hanged on the gallows, because he laid his hand on the Jews. Write also to the Jews, as it pleases you, in the king's name, and seal it with the king's ring; for the writing which is written in the king's name, and sealed with the king's ring, may not be reversed by any man."

Then the king's scribes were called at that time, in the third month Sivan, on the twenty-third day of the month; and it was written according to all that Mordecai commanded to the Jews, and to the satraps, and the governors and princes of the provinces which are from India to Ethiopia, one hundred twenty-seven provinces, to every province according to its writing, and to every people in their language, and to the Jews in their writing, and in their language. He wrote in the name of King Ahasuerus, and sealed it with the king's ring, and sent letters by courier on horseback, riding on royal horses that were bread from swift steeds.

In those letters, the king granted the Jews who were in every city to gather themselves together, and to defend their life, to destroy, to kill, and to cause to perish, all the power of the people and province that would assault them, their little ones and women, and to plunder their possessions, on one day in all the provinces of King Ahasuerus, on the thirteenth day of the twelfth month, which is the month Adar. A copy of the letter, that the decree should be given out in every province, was published to all the peoples, that the Jews should be ready for that day to avenge themselves on their enemies. So the couriers who rode on royal horses went out, hastened and pressed on by the king's commandment. The decree was given out in the citadel of Susa.

Mordecai went out of the presence of the king in royal clothing of blue and white, and with a great crown of gold, and with a robe of fine linen and purple; and the city of Susa shouted and was glad. The Jews had light, gladness, joy, and honor. In every province, and in every city, wherever the king's commandment and his decree came, the Jews had gladness, joy, a feast, and a good day. Many from among the peoples of the land became Jews; for the fear of the Jews was fallen on them.

Now in the twelfth month, which is the month Adar, on the thirteenth day of the month, when the king's commandment and his decree drew near to be put in execution, on the day that the enemies of the Jews hoped to conquer them, (but it was turned out the opposite happened, that the Jews conquered those who hated them), the Jews gathered themselves together in their cities throughout all the provinces of the King Ahasuerus, to lay hands on those who wanted to harm them. No one could withstand them, because the fear of them had fallen on all the people. All the princes of the provinces, the satraps, the governors, and those who did the king's business helped the Jews, because the fear of Mordecai had fallen on them. For Mordecai was great in the king's house, and his fame went out throughout all the provinces; for the man Mordecai grew greater and greater. The Jews struck all their enemies with the stroke of the sword, and with slaughter and destruction, and did what they wanted to those who hated them.

In the citadel of Susa, the Jews killed and destroyed five hundred men. They killed Parshandatha, Dalphon, Aspatha, Poratha, Adalia, Aridatha, Parmashta, Arisai, Aridai, and Vaizatha, the ten sons of Haman the son of Hammedatha, the Jew's enemy, but they didn't lay their hand on the plunder. On that day, the number of those who were slain in the citadel of Susa was brought before the king. The king said to Esther the queen, "The Jews have slain and destroyed five hundred men in the citadel of Susa, including the ten sons of Haman; what then have they done in the rest of the king's provinces! Now what is your petition? It shall be granted you. What is your further request? It shall be done."

Then Esther said, "If it pleases the king, let it be granted to the Jews who are in Shushan to do tomorrow also according to this day's decree, and let Haman's ten sons be hanged on the gallows."

The king commanded this to be done. A decree was given out in Shushan; and they hanged Haman's ten sons. The Jews who were in Shushan gathered themselves together on the fourteenth day also of the month Adar, and killed three hundred men in Shushan; but they didn't lay their hand on the spoil. The other Jews who were in the king's provinces gathered themselves together, defended their lives, had rest from their enemies, and killed seventy-five thousand of those who hated them; but they didn't lay their hand on the plunder. This was done on the thirteenth day of the month Adar; and on the fourteenth day of that month they rested and made it a day of feasting and gladness.

The story of Esther shows how ordinary people may be thrust into unique circumstances, and rise to the occasion to serve the purposes of God.

25 BIRTH OF A SAVIOR

Beginning of a New Era for God's People

After the Old Testament portion of the Bible ends, the prophets of God go silent for around 400 years. The Jews who had returned from captivity, although ruled politically by other powers, were generally given religious freedom and lived in relative stability. During this period, the Jewish synagogues and teachers (scribes) became influential in guiding the worship of the nation. As this 400 year period ended, in the time when the New Testament began, Judea was ruled by the Roman empire.

Having learned from their past captivity, the nation remained faithful to God, and continued to look steadfastly toward the coming of the promised Messiah. But most people awaited what they believed would be a political leader, who would restore the nation to the prominence it had enjoyed under David and Solomon by the means of military power.

Into this scene unfolds the "greatest story ever told" - the amazing birth and life of Jesus Christ. His mother Mary was told by the angel Gabriel, "He will be great, and will be called the Son of the Most High. The Lord God will give him the throne of his father, David, and he will reign over the house of Jacob forever. There will be no end to his Kingdom."

Entering the world by means of a miraculous virgin birth, the Messiah was celebrated and heralded by both common shepherds and heavenly angels. He was sought after by wise men and by the evil ruler King Herod, from whom his family had to flee for a time to save his life. As a child, we are told that "Jesus increased in wisdom and stature, and in favor with God and men." As he became a man and prepared to begin his ministry, his way was prepared by his cousin, John the Baptist, who began baptizing people for repentance, stating "I indeed baptize you with water, but he comes who is mightier than I, the latchet of whose sandals I am not worthy to loosen. He will baptize you in the Holy Spirit and fire."

God, due to His love for mankind, had prepared the way perfectly for the emergence of Jesus, his only son, to be our Savior. The sacrificial practices of the Old Law paved the way for a perfect sacrifice, which would allow our sins to be forgiven. This perfect sacrifice was Jesus himself, who gave himself for us. As was written by the disciple Timothy, "For there is one

God, and one mediator between God and men, the man Christ Jesus, who gave himself as a ransom for all."

In the beginning was the Word, and the Word was with God, and the Word was God. The same was in the beginning with God. All things were made through him. Without him was not anything made that has been made. In him was life, and the life was the light of men. The light shines in the darkness, and the darkness hasn't overcome it.

He was in the world, and the world was made through him, and the world didn't recognize him. He came to his own, and those who were his own didn't receive him. But as many as received him, to them he gave the right to become God's children, to those who believe in his name: who were born not of blood, nor of the will of the flesh, nor of the will of man, but of God. The Word became flesh, and lived among us. We saw his glory, such glory as of the one and only Son of the Father, full of grace and truth.

There was in the days of Herod, the king of Judea, a certain priest named Zacharias, of the priestly division of Abijah. He had a wife of the daughters of Aaron, and her name was Elizabeth. They were both righteous before God, walking blamelessly in all the commandments and ordinances of the Lord. But they had no child, because Elizabeth was barren, and they both were well advanced in years. Now it happened, while he executed the priest's office before God in the order of his division, according to the custom of the priest's office, his lot was to enter into the temple of the Lord and burn incense. The whole multitude of the people were praying outside at the hour of incense.

An angel of the Lord appeared to him, standing on the right side of the altar of incense. Zacharias was troubled when he saw him, and fear fell upon him. But the angel said to him, "Don't be afraid, Zacharias, because your request has been heard, and your wife, Elizabeth, will bear you a son, and you shall call his name John. You will have joy and gladness; and many will rejoice at his birth. For he will be great in the sight of the Lord, and he will drink no wine nor strong drink. He will be filled with the Holy Spirit, even from his mother's womb. He will turn many of the children of Israel to the Lord, their God. He will go before him in the spirit and power of Elijah, 'to turn the hearts of the fathers to the children,' and the disobedient to the wisdom of the just; to prepare a people prepared for the Lord."

Now in the sixth month, the angel Gabriel was sent from God to a city of Galilee, named Nazareth, to a virgin pledged to be married to a man whose name was Joseph, of the house of David. The virgin's name was Mary. Having come in, the angel said to her, "Rejoice, you highly favored one! The Lord is with you. Blessed are you among women!"

But when she saw him, she was greatly troubled at the saying, and considered what kind of salutation this might be. The angel said to her, "Don't be afraid, Mary, for you have found favor with God. Behold, you will conceive in your womb, and bring forth a son, and will call his name 'Jesus.' He will be great, and will be called the Son of the Most High. The Lord God will give him the throne of his father, David, and he will reign over the house of Jacob forever. There will be no end to his Kingdom."

Mary said to the angel, "How can this be, seeing I am a virgin?"

The angel answered her, "The Holy Spirit will come on you, and the power of the Most High will overshadow you. Therefore also the holy one who is born from you will be called the Son of God.

Mary said, "Behold, the handmaid of the Lord; be it to me according to your word."

Mary arose in those days and went into the hill country with haste, into a city of Judah, and entered into the house of Zacharias and greeted Elizabeth. It happened, when Elizabeth heard Mary's greeting, that the baby leaped in her womb, and Elizabeth was filled with the Holy Spirit. She called out with a loud voice, and said, "Blessed are you among women, and blessed is the fruit of your womb! Why am I so favored, that the mother of my Lord should come to me? For behold, when the voice of your greeting came into my ears, the baby leaped in my womb for joy! Blessed is she who believed, for there will be a fulfillment of the things which have been spoken to her from the Lord!"

Mary said,

"My soul magnifies the Lord.

My spirit has rejoiced in God my Savior,

for he has looked at the humble state of his handmaid.

For behold, from now on, all generations will call me blessed.

For he who is mighty has done great things for me.

Holy is his name.

Mary stayed with her about three months, and then returned to her house.

Joseph, her husband, being a righteous man, and not willing to make her a public example, intended to put her away secretly. But when he thought about these things, behold, an angel of the Lord appeared to him in a dream, saying, "Joseph, son of David, don't be afraid to take to yourself Mary, your wife, for that which is conceived in her is of the Holy Spirit. She shall bring forth a son. You shall call his name Jesus, for it is he who shall save his people from their sins."

Now all this has happened, that it might be fulfilled which was spoken by the

Lord through the prophet, saying,

"Behold, the virgin shall be with child,

and shall bring forth a son.

They shall call his name Immanuel";

which is, being interpreted, "God with us."

Joseph arose from his sleep, and did as the angel of the Lord commanded him, and took his wife to himself; and didn't know her sexually until she had brought forth her firstborn son.

Now it happened in those days, that a decree went out from Caesar Augustus that all the world should be enrolled. This was the first enrollment made when Quirinius was governor of Syria. All went to enroll themselves, everyone to his own city. Joseph also went up from Galilee, out of the city of Nazareth, into Judea, to the city of David, which is called Bethlehem, because he was of the house and family of David; to enroll himself with Mary, who was pledged to be married to him as wife, being pregnant.

It happened, while they were there, that the day had come that she should give birth. She brought forth her firstborn son, and she wrapped him in bands of cloth, and laid him in a feeding trough, because there was no room for them in the inn.

There were shepherds in the same country staying in the field, and keeping watch by night over their flock. Behold, an angel of the Lord stood by them, and the glory of the Lord shone around them, and they were terrified. The angel said to them, "Don't be afraid, for behold, I bring you good news of great joy which will be to all the people. For there is born to you, this day, in the city of David, a Savior, who is Christ the Lord. This is the sign to you: you will find a baby wrapped in strips of cloth, lying in a feeding trough." Suddenly, there was with the angel a multitude of the heavenly army praising God, and saying,

"Glory to God in the highest,

on earth peace, good will toward men."

It happened, when the angels went away from them into the sky, that the shepherds said one to another, "Let's go to Bethlehem, now, and see this thing that has happened, which the Lord has made known to us." They came with haste, and found both Mary and Joseph, and the baby was lying in the feeding trough. When they saw it, they publicized widely the saying which was spoken to them about this child. All who heard it wondered at the things which were spoken to them by the shepherds. But Mary kept all these sayings, pondering them in her heart. The shepherds returned, glorifying and praising God for all the things that they had heard and seen, just as it was told them.

When eight days were fulfilled for the circumcision of the child, his name was called Jesus, which was given by the angel before he was conceived in the womb.

Although the birth of Jesus was greatly rejoiced by many, King Herod, worried about his throne, was not pleased to hear of the birth of a future "King of the Jews." He would stop at nothing to preserve his power, and Joseph and Mary were forced to flee Judea to save the life of Jesus.

Now when Jesus was born in Bethlehem of Judea in the days of King Herod, behold, wise men from the east came to Jerusalem, saying, "Where is he who is born King of the Jews? For we saw his star in the east, and have come to worship him." When King Herod heard it, he was troubled, and all Jerusalem with him. Gathering together all the chief priests and scribes of the people, he asked them where the Christ would be born. They said to him, "In Bethlehem of Judea, for this is written through the prophet,

'You Bethlehem, land of Judah,

are in no way least among the princes of Judah:

for out of you shall come forth a governor,

who shall shepherd my people, Israel.'"

Then Herod secretly called the wise men, and learned from them exactly what time the star appeared. He sent them to Bethlehem, and said, "Go and search diligently for the young child. When you have found him, bring me word, so that I also may come and worship him."

They, having heard the king, went their way; and behold, the star, which they saw in the east, went before them, until it came and stood over where the young child was. When they saw the star, they rejoiced with exceedingly great joy. They came into the house and saw the young child with Mary, his mother, and they fell down and worshiped him. Opening their treasures, they offered to him gifts: gold, frankincense, and myrrh. Being warned in a dream that they shouldn't return to Herod, they went back to their own country another way.

Now when they had departed, behold, an angel of the Lord appeared to Joseph in a dream, saying, "Arise and take the young child and his mother, and flee into Egypt, and stay there until I tell you, for Herod will seek the young child to destroy him."

He arose and took the young child and his mother by night, and departed into Egypt, and was there until the death of Herod; that it might be fulfilled which was spoken by the Lord through the prophet, saying, "Out of Egypt I called my son."

Then Herod, when he saw that he was mocked by the wise men, was exceedingly angry, and sent out, and killed all the male children who were in

Bethlehem and in all the surrounding countryside, from two years old and under, according to the exact time which he had learned from the wise men. Then that which was spoken by Jeremiah the prophet was fulfilled, saying,

"A voice was heard in Ramah,
lamentation, weeping and great mourning,
Rachel weeping for her children;
she wouldn't be comforted,
because they are no more."

After the death of Herod, Joseph brought his family back to Nazareth, in the region of Galilee. Here, Jesus continued to grow, learning the work of Joseph, who was a carpenter. Even at a young age, the spiritual wisdom of Jesus was evident.

The child was growing, and was becoming strong in spirit, being filled with wisdom, and the grace of God was upon him.

His parents went every year to Jerusalem at the feast of the Passover. When he was twelve years old, they went up to Jerusalem according to the custom of the feast, and when they had fulfilled the days, as they were returning, the boy Jesus stayed behind in Jerusalem. Joseph and his mother didn't know it, but supposing him to be in the company, they went a day's journey, and they looked for him among their relatives and acquaintances. When they didn't find him, they returned to Jerusalem, looking for him. It happened after three days they found him in the temple, sitting in the midst of the teachers, both listening to them, and asking them questions. All who heard him were amazed at his understanding and his answers. When they saw him, they were astonished, and his mother said to him, "Son, why have you treated us this way? Behold, your father and I were anxiously looking for you."

He said to them, "Why were you looking for me? Didn't you know that I must be in my Father's house?" They didn't understand the saying which he spoke to them.

And he went down with them, and came to Nazareth. He was subject to them, and his mother kept all these sayings in her heart. And Jesus increased in wisdom and stature, and in favor with God and men.

26 EVERLASTING TRUTHS, CHANGED LIVES

Christ's Public Ministry Begins

Now John himself wore clothing made of camel's hair, with a leather belt around his waist. His food was locusts and wild honey.

He came into all the region around the Jordan, preaching the baptism of repentance for remission of sins.

As the people were in expectation, and all men reasoned in their hearts concerning John, whether perhaps he was the Christ, John answered them all, "I indeed baptize you with water, but he comes who is mightier than I, the latchet of whose sandals I am not worthy to loosen. He will baptize you in the Holy Spirit and fire, whose fan is in his hand, and he will thoroughly cleanse his threshing floor, and will gather the wheat into his barn; but he will burn up the chaff with unquenchable fire."

Then with many other exhortations he preached good news to the people.

Then Jesus came from Galilee to the Jordan to John, to be baptized by him. But John would have hindered him, saying, "I need to be baptized by you, and you come to me?"

But Jesus, answering, said to him, "Allow it now, for this is the fitting way for us to fulfill all righteousness." Then he allowed him. Jesus, when he was baptized, went up directly from the water: and behold, the heavens were opened to him. He saw the Spirit of God descending as a dove, and coming on him. Behold, a voice out of the heavens said, "This is my beloved Son, with whom I am well pleased."

Jesus himself, when he began to teach, was about thirty years old.

Jesus, full of the Holy Spirit, returned from the Jordan, and was led by the Spirit into the wilderness for forty days, being tempted by the devil. He ate nothing in those days. Afterward, when they were completed, he was hungry. The devil said to him, "If you are the Son of God, command this stone to become bread."

Jesus answered him, saying, "It is written, 'Man shall not live by bread alone, but by every word of God.'"

The devil, leading him up on a high mountain, showed him all the kingdoms of the world in a moment of time. The devil said to him, "I will give you all this authority, and their glory, for it has been delivered to me; and I give it to whomever I want. If you therefore will worship before me, it will all be yours."

Jesus answered him, "Get behind me Satan! For it is written, 'You shall worship the Lord your God, and you shall serve him only.'"

He led him to Jerusalem, and set him on the pinnacle of the temple, and said to him, "If you are the Son of God, cast yourself down from here, for it is written,

'He will put his angels in charge of you, to guard you;'

and, 'On their hands they will bear you up,

lest perhaps you dash your foot against a stone.'"

Jesus answering, said to him, "It has been said, 'You shall not tempt the Lord your God.'"

When the devil had completed every temptation, he departed from him until another time.

This is John's testimony, when the Jews sent priests and Levites from Jerusalem to ask him, "Who are you?"

He declared, and didn't deny, but he declared, "I am not the Christ."

They asked him, "What then? Are you Elijah?"

He said, "I am not."

"Are you the prophet?"

He answered, "No."

They said therefore to him, "Who are you? Give us an answer to take back to those who sent us. What do you say about yourself?"

He said, "I am the voice of one crying in the wilderness, 'Make straight the way of the Lord,' as Isaiah the prophet said."

The ones who had been sent were from the Pharisees. They asked him, "Why then do you baptize, if you are not the Christ, nor Elijah, nor the prophet?"

John answered them, "I baptize in water, but among you stands one whom you don't know. He is the one who comes after me, who is preferred before me, whose sandal strap I'm not worthy to loosen." These things were done in Bethany beyond the Jordan, where John was baptizing.

Shortly after Jesus began preaching, he selected certain men to be his disciples. These twelve men would walk and live with Jesus continually, sitting at his feet, observing his ministry, and continually learning. This intense training was important, because the time of the public ministry of Jesus would be short. Soon after Jesus began selecting his disciples, he performed his first recorded miracle, at a wedding ceremony in Cana.

It was not long after this that Jesus raised attention by violently throwing moneychangers out of the temple. These men were abusing their position in the temple to make profits rather than aiding the people who needed to buy items for their worship. This surely angered the religious leaders who had approved of this activity.

One of the two who heard John, and followed him, was Andrew, Simon Peter's brother. He first found his own brother, Simon, and said to him, "We have found the Messiah!" (which is, being interpreted, Christ). He brought him to Jesus. Jesus looked at him, and said, "You are Simon the son of Jonah. You shall be called Cephas" (which is by interpretation, Peter). On the next day, he was determined to go out into Galilee, and he found Philip. Jesus said to him, "Follow me." Now Philip was from Bethsaida, of the city of Andrew and Peter. Philip found Nathanael, and said to him, "We have found him, of whom Moses in the law, and the prophets, wrote: Jesus of Nazareth, the son of Joseph."

There was a marriage in Cana of Galilee. Jesus' mother was there. Jesus also was invited, with his disciples, to the marriage. When the wine ran out, Jesus' mother said to him, "They have no wine."

Jesus said to her, "Woman, what does that have to do with you and me? My hour has not yet come."

His mother said to the servants, "Whatever he says to you, do it." Now there were six water pots of stone set there after the Jews' way of purifying, containing twenty to thirty gallons apiece. Jesus said to them, "Fill the water pots with water." They filled them up to the brim. He said to them, "Now draw some out, and take it to the ruler of the feast." So they took it. When the ruler of the feast tasted the water now become wine, and didn't know where it came from (but the servants who had drawn the water knew), the ruler of the feast called the bridegroom, and said to him, "Everyone serves the good wine first, and when the guests have drunk freely, then that which is worse. You have kept the good wine until now!" This beginning of his signs Jesus did in Cana of Galilee, and revealed his glory; and his disciples believed in him.

After this, he went down to Capernaum, he, and his mother, his brothers, and his disciples; and they stayed there a few days.

The Passover of the Jews was at hand, and Jesus went up to Jerusalem. He found in the temple those who sold oxen, sheep, and doves, and the changers of money sitting. He made a whip of cords, and threw all out of the temple, both the sheep and the oxen; and he poured out the changers' money, and overthrew their tables. To those who sold the doves, he said, "Take these things out of here! Don't make my Father's house a marketplace!" His disciples remembered that it was written, "Zeal for your house will eat me up."

The Jews therefore answered him, "What sign do you show us, seeing that you do these things?"

Jesus answered them, "Destroy this temple, and in three days I will raise it up."

The Jews therefore said, "It took forty-six years to build this temple! Will you raise it up in three days?" But he spoke of the temple of his body. When therefore he was raised from the dead, his disciples remembered that he said this, and they believed the Scripture, and the word which Jesus had said.

Nicodemus, a member of the Jewish Sanhedrin court and a Pharisee, came secretly to Jesus by night, asking him to explain his teachings. In his response, Jesus outlined the concept of being "born again," a now common expression of Christianity. In their discourse, Jesus spoke what is now one of the most popular of all Bible passages, a concise summary of God's love and plan for mankind: "For God so loved the world, that he gave his one and only Son, that whoever believes in him should not perish, but have eternal life."

Nicodemus was apparently greatly affected by his discourse with Jesus. Later he spoke up on the behalf of Jesus in front of the entire Sanhedrin court, and he assisted Joseph of Arimathea in preparing the body of Jesus for burial. The man who came to Jesus at night later drew strength to aid Jesus publicly. Such was the effect that Jesus had on many people.

Now there was a man of the Pharisees named Nicodemus, a ruler of the Jews. The same came to him by night, and said to him, "Rabbi, we know that you are a teacher come from God, for no one can do these signs that you do, unless God is with him."

Jesus answered him, "Most certainly, I tell you, unless one is born anew, he can't see the Kingdom of God."

Nicodemus said to him, "How can a man be born when he is old? Can he enter a second time into his mother's womb, and be born?"

Jesus answered, "Most certainly I tell you, unless one is born of water and spirit, he can't enter into the Kingdom of God! That which is born of the flesh is flesh. That which is born of the Spirit is spirit. Don't marvel that I said to you, 'You must be born anew.' The wind blows where it wants to, and you hear its sound, but don't know where it comes from and where it is going. So is everyone who is born of the Spirit."

Nicodemus answered him, "How can these things be?"

Jesus answered him, "Are you the teacher of Israel, and don't understand these things? Most certainly I tell you, we speak that which we know, and testify of that which we have seen, and you don't receive our witness. If I told you earthly things and you don't believe, how will you believe if I tell you heavenly things? No one has ascended into heaven, but he who descended out of heaven, the Son of Man, who is in heaven. As Moses lifted up the serpent in the wilderness, even so must the Son of Man be lifted up, that whoever believes in him should not perish, but have eternal life. For God so loved the world, that he gave his one and only Son, that whoever believes in him should not perish, but have eternal life. For God didn't send his Son into the world to judge the world, but that the world should be saved through him. He who believes in him is not judged. He who doesn't believe has been judged already, because he has not believed in the name of the one and only Son of God."

Jesus returned in the power of the Spirit into Galilee, and news about him spread through all the surrounding area.

In another famous encounter, Jesus spoke to a Samaritan woman at a well. In a time when most Jews hated Samaritans so much that they often avoided even traveling through their neighborhoods, Jesus showed his love for all people by speaking not only to a Samaritan, but to a Samaritan woman. This brief encounter had a lasting effect on the woman and the entire town. Later, in his teachings he would paint a word picture of a Samaritan man kindly, making him out to be the loving neighbor in his beloved parable of the "Good Samaritan."

So he came to a city of Samaria, called Sychar, near the parcel of ground that Jacob gave to his son, Joseph. Jacob's well was there. Jesus therefore, being tired from his journey, sat down by the well. It was about the sixth hour. A woman of Samaria came to draw water. Jesus said to her, "Give me a drink." For his disciples had gone away into the city to buy food.

The Samaritan woman therefore said to him, "How is it that you, being a Jew, ask for a drink from me, a Samaritan woman?" (For Jews have no dealings with Samaritans.)

Jesus answered her, "If you knew the gift of God, and who it is who says to you, 'Give me a drink,' you would have asked him, and he would have given you living water."

The woman said to him, "Sir, you have nothing to draw with, and the well is deep. From where then have you that living water? Are you greater than our father, Jacob, who gave us the well, and drank of it himself, as did his children, and his livestock?"

Jesus answered her, "Everyone who drinks of this water will thirst again, but whoever drinks of the water that I will give him will never thirst again; but the water that I will give him will become in him a well of water springing up to eternal life."

The woman said to him, "Sir, give me this water, so that I don't get thirsty, neither come all the way here to draw."

Jesus said to her, "Go, call your husband, and come here."

The woman answered, "I have no husband."

Jesus said to her, "You said well, 'I have no husband,' for you have had five husbands; and he whom you now have is not your husband. This you have said truly."

The woman said to him, "Sir, I perceive that you are a prophet. Our fathers worshiped in this mountain, and you Jews say that in Jerusalem is the place where people ought to worship."

Jesus said to her, "Woman, believe me, the hour comes, when neither in this mountain, nor in Jerusalem, will you worship the Father. You worship that which you don't know. We worship that which we know; for salvation is from the Jews. But the hour comes, and now is, when the true worshipers will worship the Father in spirit and truth, for the Father seeks such to be his worshipers. God is spirit, and those who worship him must worship in spirit and truth."

The woman said to him, "I know that Messiah comes," (he who is called Christ). "When he has come, he will declare to us all things."

Jesus said to her, "I am he, the one who speaks to you." At this, his disciples came. They marveled that he was speaking with a woman; yet no one said, "What are you looking for?" or, "Why do you speak with her?" So the woman left her water pot, and went away into the city, and said to the people, "Come, see a man who told me everything that I did. Can this be the Christ?"

From that city many of the Samaritans believed in him because of the word of the woman, who testified, "He told me everything that I did." So when the Samaritans came to him, they begged him to stay with them. He stayed there two days. Many more believed because of his word. They said to the woman, "Now we believe, not because of your speaking; for we have heard for ourselves, and know that this is indeed the Christ, the Savior of the world."

From that time, Jesus began to preach, and to say, "Repent! For the Kingdom of Heaven is at hand."

Jesus came therefore again to Cana of Galilee, where he made the water into wine. There was a certain nobleman whose son was sick at Capernaum. When he heard that Jesus had come out of Judea into Galilee, he went to him, and begged him that he would come down and heal his son, for he was at the point of death. Jesus said to him, "Unless you see signs and wonders, you will in no way believe."

The nobleman said to him, "Sir, come down before my child dies." Jesus said to him, "Go your way. Your son lives." The man believed the word that Jesus spoke to him, and he went his way. As he was now going down, his servants met him and reported, saying "Your child lives!" So he inquired of them the hour when he began to get better. They said therefore to him, "Yesterday at the seventh hour, the fever left him." So the father knew that it was at that hour in which Jesus said to him, "Your son lives." He believed, as did his whole house. This is again the second sign that Jesus did, having come out of Judea into Galilee.

Leaving Nazareth, he came and lived in Capernaum, which is by the sea, in the region of Zebulun and Naphtali.

Now it happened, while the multitude pressed on him and heard the word of God, that he was standing by the lake of Gennesaret. He saw two boats standing by the lake, but the fishermen had gone out of them, and were washing their nets. He entered into one of the boats, which was Simon's, and asked him to put out a little from the land. He sat down and taught the multitudes from the boat. When he had finished speaking, he said to Simon, "Put out into the deep, and let down your nets for a catch."

Simon answered him, "Master, we worked all night, and took nothing; but at your word I will let down the net." When they had done this, they caught a great multitude of fish, and their net was breaking. They beckoned to their partners in the other boat, that they should come and help them. They came, and filled both boats, so that they began to sink. But Simon Peter, when he saw it, fell down at Jesus' knees, saying, "Depart from me, for I am a sinful man, Lord." For he was amazed, and all who were with him, at the catch of fish which they had caught; and so also were James and John, sons of Zebedee, who were partners with Simon. Jesus said to Simon, "Don't be afraid. From now on you will be catching people alive." When they had brought their boats to land, they left everything, and followed him.

They went into Capernaum, and immediately on the Sabbath day he entered into the synagogue and taught. They were astonished at his teaching, for he taught them as having authority, and not as the scribes.

Immediately there was in their synagogue a man with an unclean spirit, and he cried out, saying, "Ha! What do we have to do with you, Jesus, you Nazarene? Have you come to destroy us? I know you who you are: the Holy One of God!"

Jesus rebuked him, saying, "Be quiet, and come out of him!"

The unclean spirit, convulsing him and crying with a loud voice, came out of him. They were all amazed, so that they questioned among themselves, saying, "What is this? A new teaching? For with authority he commands even the unclean spirits, and they obey him!" The report of him went out immediately everywhere into all the region of Galilee and its surrounding area.

Immediately, when they had come out of the synagogue, they came into the house of Simon and Andrew, with James and John. Now Simon's wife's mother lay sick with a fever, and immediately they told him about her. He came and took her by the hand, and raised her up. The fever left her, and she served them. At evening, when the sun had set, they brought to him all who were sick, and those who were possessed by demons. All the city was gathered together at the door. He healed many who were sick with various diseases, and cast out many demons. He didn't allow the demons to speak, because they knew him.

He went into their synagogues throughout all Galilee, preaching and casting out demons. A leper came to him, begging him, kneeling down to him, and saying to him, "If you want to, you can make me clean."

Being moved with compassion, he stretched out his hand, and touched him, and said to him, "I want to. Be made clean." When he had said this, immediately the leprosy departed from him, and he was made clean. He strictly warned him, and immediately sent him out, and said to him, "See you say nothing to anybody, but go show yourself to the priest, and offer for your cleansing the things which Moses commanded, for a testimony to them."

But he went out, and began to proclaim it much, and to spread about the matter, so that Jesus could no more openly enter into a city, but was outside in desert places: and they came to him from everywhere.

When he entered again into Capernaum after some days, it was heard that he was in the house. Immediately many were gathered together, so that there was no more room, not even around the door; and he spoke the word to them. Four people came, carrying a paralytic to him. When they could not come near to him for the crowd, they removed the roof where he was. When they had broken it up, they let down the mat that the paralytic was lying on. Jesus, seeing their faith, said to the paralytic, "Son, your sins are forgiven you."

But there were some of the scribes sitting there, and reasoning in their hearts, "Why does this man speak blasphemies like that? Who can forgive sins but God alone?"

Immediately Jesus, perceiving in his spirit that they so reasoned within themselves, said to them, "Why do you reason these things in your hearts? Which is easier, to tell the paralytic, 'Your sins are forgiven;' or to say, 'Arise, and take up your bed, and walk?' But that you may know that the Son of Man has authority on earth to forgive sins"—he said to the paralytic— "I tell you, arise, take up your mat, and go to your house." He arose, and immediately took up the mat, and went out in front of them all; so that they were all amazed, and glorified God, saying, "We never saw anything like this!"

He went out again by the seaside. All the multitude came to him, and he taught them. As he passed by, he saw Levi, the son of Alphaeus, sitting at the tax office, and he said to him, "Follow me." And he arose and followed him.

Levi made a great feast for him in his house. There was a great crowd of tax collectors and others who were reclining with them. Their scribes and the Pharisees murmured against his disciples, saying, "Why do you eat and drink with the tax collectors and sinners?" Jesus answered them, "Those who are healthy have no need for a physician, but those who are sick do. I have not come to call the righteous, but sinners to repentance."

After some time, Jesus went up to Jerusalem to participate in the feasts. While there, he healed a man who had been lame for 38 years. But the Jewish religious leaders spoke against this, because Jesus healed the man on the Sabbath. They were further infuriated when Jesus claimed that God was his own Father. Jesus rebuked them for their unbelief.

Jesus was continually criticized by the religious leaders. On one occasion, as his hungry disciples walked through the grain fields, they plucked a few handfuls of grain and ate them. They were criticized for doing "work" on the Sabbath. On another occasion, Jesus healed a man with a withered hand on the Sabbath, in the synagogue. When this happened, the Pharisees went out, and conspired against him, planning how they might destroy him. But great multitudes followed Jesus, clinging to his words and hoping for miraculous healing.

It happened in these days, that he went out to the mountain to pray, and he continued all night in prayer to God. When it was day, he called his disciples, and from them he chose twelve, whom he also named apostles: Simon, whom he also named Peter; Andrew, his brother; James; John; Philip; Bartholomew; Matthew; Thomas; James, the son of Alphaeus; Simon, who was called the Zealot; Judas the son of James; and Judas Iscariot, who also became a traitor.

He came down with them, and stood on a level place, with a crowd of his disciples, and a great number of the people from all Judea and Jerusalem, and the sea coast of Tyre and Sidon, who came to hear him and to be healed of their diseases; as well as those who were troubled by unclean spirits, and they were being healed. All the multitude sought to touch him, for power came out from him and healed them all.

27 THE MASTER TEACHER

The Sermon On The Mount and Parables of Jesus

Jesus is known as "the Master Teacher," and for good reason. Throughout the Bible, men were profoundly affected by the words of Jesus. On one occasion, guards were sent to bring Jesus in for questioning. They returned empty handed, and when asked why, they said, "No one ever spoke the way this man does."

We now come to what many feel is the greatest sermon ever told - the "Sermon on the Mount." Spoken in plain, yet striking phrases, the teachings of Jesus here are simple, yet profound. Jesus spoke in a manner which the everyday people of the time could understand, while laying out new principles for Godly living that shook the religious establishment to its core. Starting with what are known as the beatitudes, ("Blessed are the...) most people, even those who are not deeply religious, will find familiar phrases and principles that have passed the test of time and are familiar to mankind some 2.000 years after Jesus spoke these phrases. At the end of his speaking, the Bible says "The multitudes were astonished at his teaching, for he taught them with authority, and not like the scribes."

Jesus connected with people on a deep, personal level. Yet he did not shy away from controversy, and at times seemed to welcome the wrath of those he opposed. He could, with a simple statement or parable, outline a new way of thinking about morality. He emphasized the condition of the heart over rote religious traditions.

Even the skeptical philosopher Ernest Renan (1823-92), who opposed Christian tradition on almost all points, stated: "Jesus will ever be the creator of the pure spirit of religion; the Sermon on the Mount will never be surpassed."

Seeing the multitudes, he went up onto the mountain. When he had sat down, his disciples came to him. He opened his mouth and taught them, saying,

"Blessed are the poor in spirit,
for theirs is the Kingdom of Heaven.
Blessed are those who mourn,

for they shall be comforted.
Blessed are the gentle,
for they shall inherit the earth.
Blessed are those who hunger and thirst after righteousness,
for they shall be filled.
Blessed are the merciful,
for they shall obtain mercy.
Blessed are the pure in heart,
for they shall see God.
Blessed are the peacemakers,
for they shall be called children of God.
Blessed are those who have been persecuted for righteousness' sake,
for theirs is the Kingdom of Heaven.

"Blessed are you when people reproach you, persecute you, and say all kinds of evil against you falsely, for my sake. Rejoice, and be exceedingly glad, for great is your reward in heaven. For that is how they persecuted the prophets who were before you.

"You are the salt of the earth, but if the salt has lost its flavor, with what will it be salted? It is then good for nothing, but to be cast out and trodden under the feet of men. You are the light of the world. A city located on a hill can't be hidden. Neither do you light a lamp, and put it under a measuring basket, but on a stand; and it shines to all who are in the house. Even so, let your light shine before men; that they may see your good works, and glorify your Father who is in heaven.

"Don't think that I came to destroy the law or the prophets. I didn't come to destroy, but to fulfill. For most certainly, I tell you, until heaven and earth pass away, not even one smallest letter or one tiny pen stroke shall in any way pass away from the law, until all things are accomplished. Whoever, therefore, shall break one of these least commandments, and teach others to do so, shall be called least in the Kingdom of Heaven; but whoever shall do and teach them shall be called great in the Kingdom of Heaven. For I tell you that unless your righteousness exceeds that of the scribes and Pharisees, there is no way you will enter into the Kingdom of Heaven.

"You have heard that it was said to the ancient ones, 'You shall not murder;' and 'Whoever shall murder shall be in danger of the judgment.' But I tell you, that everyone who is angry with his brother without a cause shall be in danger of the judgment; and whoever shall say to his brother, 'Raca!' shall be in danger of the council; and whoever shall say, 'You fool!' shall be in danger of the fire of Hell.

"If therefore you are offering your gift at the altar, and there remember that your brother has anything against you, leave your gift there before the altar, and go your way. First be reconciled to your brother, and then come and offer your gift. Agree with your adversary quickly, while you are with him in the way; lest perhaps the prosecutor deliver you to the judge, and the judge deliver you to the officer, and you be cast into prison. Most certainly I tell you, you shall by no means get out of there, until you have paid the last penny.

"You have heard that it was said, 'You shall not commit adultery;' but I tell you that everyone who gazes at a woman to lust after her has committed adultery with her already in his heart. If your right eye causes you to stumble, pluck it out and throw it away from you. For it is more profitable for you that one of your members should perish, than for your whole body to be cast into Hell. If your right hand causes you to stumble, cut it off, and throw it away from you. For it is more profitable for you that one of your members should perish, than for your whole body to be cast into Hell.

"It was also said, 'Whoever shall put away his wife, let him give her a writing of divorce,' but I tell you that whoever puts away his wife, except for the cause of sexual immorality, makes her an adulteress; and whoever marries her when she is put away commits adultery.

"You have heard that it was said, 'An eye for an eye, and a tooth for a tooth.' But I tell you, don't resist him who is evil; but whoever strikes you on your right cheek, turn to him the other also. If anyone sues you to take away your coat, let him have your cloak also. Whoever compels you to go one mile, go with him two. Give to him who asks you, and don't turn away him who desires to borrow from you.

"You have heard that it was said, 'You shall love your neighbor, and hate your enemy.' But I tell you, love your enemies, bless those who curse you, do good to those who hate you, and pray for those who mistreat you and persecute you, that you may be children of your Father who is in heaven. For he makes his sun to rise on the evil and the good, and sends rain on the just and the unjust. For if you love those who love you, what reward do you have? Don't even the tax collectors do the same? If you only greet your friends, what more do you do than others? Don't even the tax collectors do the same? Therefore you shall be perfect, just as your Father in heaven is perfect.

"Be careful that you don't do your charitable giving before men, to be seen by them, or else you have no reward from your Father who is in heaven. Therefore when you do merciful deeds, don't sound a trumpet before yourself, as the hypocrites do in the synagogues and in the streets, that they may get glory from men. Most certainly I tell you, they have received their reward. But when you do merciful deeds, don't let your left hand know what your right hand does, so that your merciful deeds may be in secret, then your Father who sees in secret will reward you openly.

"When you pray, you shall not be as the hypocrites, for they love to stand and pray in the synagogues and in the corners of the streets, that they may be seen by men. Most certainly, I tell you, they have received their reward. But you, when you pray, enter into your inner room, and having shut your door, pray to your Father who is in secret, and your Father who sees in secret will reward you openly. In praying, don't use vain repetitions, as the Gentiles do; for they think that they will be heard for their much speaking. Therefore don't be like them, for your Father knows what things you need, before you ask him. Pray like this: 'Our Father in heaven, may your name be kept holy. Let your Kingdom come. Let your will be done, as in heaven, so on earth. Give us today our daily bread. Forgive us our debts, as we also forgive our debtors. Bring us not into temptation, but deliver us from the evil one. For yours is the Kingdom, the power, and the glory forever. Amen.'

"For if you forgive men their trespasses, your heavenly Father will also forgive you. But if you don't forgive men their trespasses, neither will your Father forgive your trespasses.

"Don't lay up treasures for yourselves on the earth, where moth and rust consume, and where thieves break through and steal; but lay up for yourselves treasures in heaven, where neither moth nor rust consume, and where thieves don't break through and steal; for where your treasure is, there your heart will be also.

"No one can serve two masters, for either he will hate the one and love the other; or else he will be devoted to one and despise the other. You can't serve both God and Mammon. Therefore I tell you, don't be anxious for your life: what you will eat, or what you will drink; nor yet for your body, what you will wear. Isn't life more than food, and the body more than clothing? See the birds of the sky, that they don't sow, neither do they reap, nor gather into barns. Your heavenly Father feeds them. Aren't you of much more value than they?

"Which of you, by being anxious, can add one moment to his lifespan? Why are you anxious about clothing? Consider the lilies of the field, how they grow. They don't toil, neither do they spin, yet I tell you that even Solomon in all his glory was not dressed like one of these. But if God so clothes the grass of the field, which today exists, and tomorrow is thrown into the oven, won't he much more clothe you, you of little faith?

"Therefore don't be anxious, saying, 'What will we eat?', 'What will we drink?' or, 'With what will we be clothed?' For the Gentiles seek after all these things;

for your heavenly Father knows that you need all these things. But seek first God's Kingdom, and his righteousness; and all these things will be given to you as well. Therefore don't be anxious for tomorrow, for tomorrow will be anxious for itself. Each day's own evil is sufficient.

"Ask, and it will be given you. Seek, and you will find. Knock, and it will be opened for you. For everyone who asks receives. He who seeks finds. To him who knocks it will be opened.

"Enter in by the narrow gate; for wide is the gate and broad is the way that leads to destruction, and many are those who enter in by it. How narrow is the gate, and restricted is the way that leads to life! Few are those who find it.

"Beware of false prophets, who come to you in sheep's clothing, but inwardly are ravening wolves. By their fruits you will know them.

Not everyone who says to me, 'Lord, Lord,' will enter into the Kingdom of Heaven; but he who does the will of my Father who is in heaven. Many will tell me in that day, 'Lord, Lord, didn't we prophesy in your name, in your name cast out demons, and in your name do many mighty works?' Then I will tell them, 'I never knew you. Depart from me, you who work iniquity.'

"Everyone therefore who hears these words of mine, and does them, I will liken him to a wise man, who built his house on a rock. The rain came down, the floods came, and the winds blew, and beat on that house; and it didn't fall, for it was founded on the rock. Everyone who hears these words of mine, and doesn't do them will be like a foolish man, who built his house on the sand. The rain came down, the floods came, and the winds blew, and beat on that house; and it fell—and great was its fall."

It happened, when Jesus had finished saying these things, that the multitudes were astonished at his teaching, for he taught them with authority, and not like the scribes. When he came down from the mountain, great multitudes followed him.

It happened soon afterward, that he went to a city called Nain. Many of his disciples, along with a great multitude, went with him. Now when he drew near to the gate of the city, behold, one who was dead was carried out, the only son of his mother, and she was a widow. Many people of the city were with her. When the Lord saw her, he had compassion on her, and said to her, "Don't cry." He came near and touched the coffin, and the bearers stood still. He said, "Young man, I tell you, arise!" He who was dead sat up, and began to speak. And he gave him to his mother

Fear took hold of all, and they glorified God, saying, "A great prophet has arisen among us!" and, "God has visited his people!" This report went out concerning him in the whole of Judea, and in all the surrounding region.

313

The disciples of John told him about all these things. John, calling to himself two of his disciples, sent them to Jesus, saying, "Are you the one who is coming, or should we look for another?"

In that hour he cured many of diseases and plagues and evil spirits; and to many who were blind he gave sight. Jesus answered them, "Go and tell John the things which you have seen and heard: that the blind receive their sight, the lame walk, the lepers are cleansed, the deaf hear, the dead are raised up, and the poor have good news preached to them. Blessed is he who finds no occasion for stumbling in me."

"Come to me, all you who labor and are heavily burdened, and I will give you rest. Take my yoke upon you, and learn from me, for I am gentle and lowly in heart; and you will find rest for your souls. For my yoke is easy, and my burden is light."

One of the Pharisees invited him to eat with him. He entered into the Pharisee's house, and sat at the table. Behold, a woman in the city who was a sinner, when she knew that he was reclining in the Pharisee's house, she brought an alabaster jar of ointment. Standing behind at his feet weeping, she began to wet his feet with her tears, and she wiped them with the hair of her head, kissed his feet, and anointed them with the ointment. Now when the Pharisee who had invited him saw it, he said to himself, "This man, if he were a prophet, would have perceived who and what kind of woman this is who touches him, that she is a sinner."

Jesus answered him, "Simon, I have something to tell you."

He said, "Teacher, say on."

"A certain lender had two debtors. The one owed five hundred denarii, and the other fifty. When they couldn't pay, he forgave them both. Which of them therefore will love him most?"

Simon answered, "He, I suppose, to whom he forgave the most."

He said to him, "You have judged correctly." Turning to the woman, he said to Simon, "Do you see this woman? I entered into your house, and you gave me no water for my feet, but she has wet my feet with her tears, and wiped them with the hair of her head. You gave me no kiss, but she, since the time I came in, has not ceased to kiss my feet. You didn't anoint my head with oil, but she has anointed my feet with ointment. Therefore I tell you, her sins, which are many, are forgiven, for she loved much. But to whom little is forgiven, the same loves little." He said to her, "Your sins are forgiven."

Those who sat at the table with him began to say to themselves, "Who is this who even forgives sins?"

He said to the woman, "Your faith has saved you. Go in peace."

The parables of Jesus are among the most beloved of all stories in the Bible. Unique in approach, these simple and colorful stories were effective because they related to the everyday experiences of people, with poignant endings that brought the messages home powerfully.

In his parables, Jesus drew interesting verbal word pictures of the world around his listeners. These colorful stories, taken from everyday life, were used to teach simple, yet powerful lessons. In his parables, the emphasis is usually placed at the end of the story – making a strong conclusion that led the listener to accept the message. The messages were so plain that only the most hardened could refuse or reject the teaching.

Jesus spoke in the language of the people – he taught at their level. Listeners of any background or educational level could understand the messages of the parables. Jesus taught this way to convey the message of salvation and the kingdom in a clear, straightforward and simple manner.

On that day Jesus went out of the house, and sat by the seaside. Great multitudes gathered to him, so that he entered into a boat, and sat, and all the multitude stood on the beach. He spoke to them many things in parables, saying, "Behold, a farmer went out to sow. As he sowed, some seeds fell by the roadside, and the birds came and devoured them. Others fell on rocky ground, where they didn't have much soil, and immediately they sprang up, because they had no depth of earth. When the sun had risen, they were scorched. Because they had no root, they withered away. Others fell among thorns. The thorns grew up and choked them. Others fell on good soil, and yielded fruit: some one hundred times as much, some sixty, and some thirty. He who has ears to hear, let him hear."

The disciples came, and said to him, "Why do you speak to them in parables?"

He answered them, "To you it is given to know the mysteries of the Kingdom of Heaven, but it is not given to them. For whoever has, to him will be given, and he will have abundance, but whoever doesn't have, from him will be taken away even that which he has. Therefore I speak to them in parables, because seeing they don't see, and hearing, they don't hear, neither do they understand.

"Hear, then, the parable of the farmer. When anyone hears the word of the Kingdom, and doesn't understand it, the evil one comes, and snatches away that which has been sown in his heart. This is what was sown by the roadside. What was sown on the rocky places, this is he who hears the word, and immediately with joy receives it; yet he has no root in himself, but endures for a while. When oppression or persecution arises because of the word, immediately he stumbles.

What was sown among the thorns, this is he who hears the word, but the cares of this age and the deceitfulness of riches choke the word, and he becomes unfruitful. What was sown on the good ground, this is he who hears the word, and understands it, who most certainly bears fruit, and brings forth, some one hundred times as much, some sixty, and some thirty."

He said to them, "Is the lamp brought to be put under a basket or under a bed? Isn't it put on a stand? For there is nothing hidden, except that it should be made known; neither was anything made secret, but that it should come to light. If any man has ears to hear, let him hear."

He said to them, "Take heed what you hear. With whatever measure you measure, it will be measured to you, and more will be given to you who hear. For whoever has, to him will more be given, and he who doesn't have, even that which he has will be taken away from him."

He said, "The Kingdom of God is as if a man should cast seed on the earth, and should sleep and rise night and day, and the seed should spring up and grow, he doesn't know how. For the earth bears fruit: first the blade, then the ear, then the full grain in the ear. But when the fruit is ripe, immediately he puts forth the sickle, because the harvest has come."

He set another parable before them, saying, "The Kingdom of Heaven is like a man who sowed good seed in his field, but while people slept, his enemy came and sowed darnel weeds also among the wheat, and went away. But when the blade sprang up and brought forth fruit, then the darnel weeds appeared also. The servants of the householder came and said to him, 'Sir, didn't you sow good seed in your field? Where did this darnel come from?'

"He said to them, 'An enemy has done this.'

"The servants asked him, 'Do you want us to go and gather them up?'

"But he said, 'No, lest perhaps while you gather up the darnel weeds, you root up the wheat with them. Let both grow together until the harvest, and in the harvest time I will tell the reapers, "First, gather up the darnel weeds, and bind them in bundles to burn them; but gather the wheat into my barn."

He set another parable before them, saying, "The Kingdom of Heaven is like a grain of mustard seed, which a man took, and sowed in his field; which indeed is smaller than all seeds. But when it is grown, it is greater than the herbs, and becomes a tree, so that the birds of the air come and lodge in its branches."

He spoke another parable to them. "The Kingdom of Heaven is like yeast, which a woman took, and hid in three measures of meal, until it was all leavened."

Jesus spoke all these things in parables to the multitudes; and without a parable, he didn't speak to them, that it might be fulfilled which was spoken through the prophet, saying, "I will open my mouth in parables; I will utter things hidden from the foundation of the world."

Then Jesus sent the multitudes away, and went into the house. His disciples came to him, saying, "Explain to us the parable of the darnel weeds of the field."

He answered them, "He who sows the good seed is the Son of Man, the field is the world; and the good seed, these are the children of the Kingdom; and the darnel weeds are the children of the evil one. The enemy who sowed them is the devil. The harvest is the end of the age, and the reapers are angels. As therefore the darnel weeds are gathered up and burned with fire; so will it be at the end of this age. The Son of Man will send out his angels, and they will gather out of his Kingdom all things that cause stumbling, and those who do iniquity, and will cast them into the furnace of fire. There will be weeping and the gnashing of teeth. Then the righteous will shine forth like the sun in the Kingdom of their Father. He who has ears to hear, let him hear.

"Again, the Kingdom of Heaven is like a treasure hidden in the field, which a man found, and hid. In his joy, he goes and sells all that he has, and buys that field.

"Again, the Kingdom of Heaven is like a man who is a merchant seeking fine pearls, who having found one pearl of great price, he went and sold all that he had, and bought it.

"Again, the Kingdom of Heaven is like a dragnet, that was cast into the sea, and gathered some fish of every kind, which, when it was filled, they drew up on the beach. They sat down, and gathered the good into containers, but the bad they threw away. So will it be in the end of the world. The angels will come forth, and separate the wicked from among the righteous, and will cast them into the furnace of fire. There will be the weeping and the gnashing of teeth."

With many such parables he spoke the word to them, as they were able to hear it. Without a parable he didn't speak to them; but privately to his own disciples he explained everything.

On that day, when evening had come, he said to them, "Let's go over to the other side." Leaving the multitude, they took him with them, even as he was, in the boat. Other small boats were also with him. A big wind storm arose, and the waves beat into the boat, so much that the boat was already filled. He himself was in the stern, asleep on the cushion, and they woke him up, and told him, "Teacher, don't you care that we are dying?"

He awoke, and rebuked the wind, and said to the sea, "Peace! Be still!" The wind ceased, and there was a great calm. He said to them, "Why are you so afraid? How is it that you have no faith?"

They were greatly afraid, and said to one another, "Who then is this, that even the wind and the sea obey him?"

They came to the other side of the sea, into the country of the Gadarenes. When he had come out of the boat, immediately a man with an unclean spirit met him out of the tombs. He lived in the tombs. Nobody could bind him any more, not even with chains, because he had been often bound with fetters and chains, and the chains had been torn apart by him, and the fetters broken in pieces. Nobody had the strength to tame him. Always, night and day, in the tombs and in the mountains, he was crying out, and cutting himself with stones. When he saw Jesus from afar, he ran and bowed down to him, and crying out with a loud voice, he said, "What have I to do with you, Jesus, you Son of the Most High God? I adjure you by God, don't torment me." For he said to him, "Come out of the man, you unclean spirit!"

He asked him, "What is your name?"

He said to him, "My name is Legion, for we are many." He begged him much that he would not send them away out of the country. Now on the mountainside there was a great herd of pigs feeding. All the demons begged him, saying, "Send us into the pigs, that we may enter into them."

At once Jesus gave them permission. The unclean spirits came out and entered into the pigs. The herd of about two thousand rushed down the steep bank into the sea, and they were drowned in the sea. Those who fed them fled, and told it in the city and in the country. The people came to see what it was that had happened. They came to Jesus, and saw him who had been possessed by demons sitting, clothed, and in his right mind, even him who had the legion; and they were afraid.

When Jesus had crossed back over in the boat to the other side, a great multitude was gathered to him; and he was by the sea. Behold, one of the rulers of the synagogue, Jairus by name, came; and seeing him, he fell at his feet, and begged him much, saying, "My little daughter is at the point of death. Please come and lay your hands on her, that she may be made healthy, and live."

He went with him, and a great multitude followed him, and they pressed upon him on all sides.

A certain woman, who had an issue of blood for twelve years, and had suffered many things by many physicians, and had spent all that she had, and was no better, but rather grew worse, having heard the things concerning Jesus, came up behind him in the crowd, and touched his clothes. For she said, "If I just touch his clothes, I will be made well." Immediately the flow of her blood was dried up, and she felt in her body that she was healed of her affliction.

Immediately Jesus, perceiving in himself that the power had gone out from him, turned around in the crowd, and asked, "Who touched my clothes?"

His disciples said to him, "You see the multitude pressing against you, and you say, 'Who touched me?'"

He looked around to see her who had done this thing. But the woman, fearing and trembling, knowing what had been done to her, came and fell down before him, and told him all the truth.

He said to her, "Daughter, your faith has made you well. Go in peace, and be cured of your disease."

While he was still speaking, people came from the synagogue ruler's house saying, "Your daughter is dead. Why bother the Teacher any more?"

But Jesus, when he heard the message spoken, immediately said to the ruler of the synagogue, "Don't be afraid, only believe." He allowed no one to follow him, except Peter, James, and John the brother of James. He came to the synagogue ruler's house, and he saw an uproar, weeping, and great wailing. When he had entered in, he said to them, "Why do you make an uproar and weep? The child is not dead, but is asleep."

They ridiculed him. But he, having put them all out, took the father of the child, her mother, and those who were with him, and went in where the child was lying. Taking the child by the hand, he said to her, "Talitha cumi!" which means, being interpreted, "Girl, I tell you, get up!" Immediately the girl rose up and walked, for she was twelve years old. They were amazed with great amazement. He strictly ordered them that no one should know this, and commanded that something should be given to her to eat.

Coming into his own country, he taught them in their synagogue, so that they were astonished, and said, "Where did this man get this wisdom, and these mighty works? Isn't this the carpenter's son? Isn't his mother called Mary, and his brothers, James, Joses (Joseph), Simon, and Judas? Aren't all of his sisters with us? Where then did this man get all of these things?" They were offended by him.

But Jesus said to them, "A prophet is not without honor, except in his own country, and in his own house." He didn't do many mighty works there because of their unbelief.

Jesus went about all the cities and the villages, teaching in their synagogues, and preaching the Good News of the Kingdom, and healing every disease and every sickness among the people. But when he saw the multitudes, he was moved with compassion for them, because they were harassed and scattered, like sheep without a shepherd. Then he said to his disciples, "The harvest indeed is plentiful, but the laborers are few. Pray therefore that the Lord of the harvest will send out laborers into his harvest."

Jesus was having a great impact with his teaching, yet he desired to spread his message even faster. So he sent his disciples out with specific instructions on how to be his ambassadors.

He called to himself his twelve disciples, and gave them authority over unclean spirits, to cast them out, and to heal every disease and every sickness.

Jesus sent these twelve out, and commanded them, saying, "Don't go among the Gentiles, and don't enter into any city of the Samaritans. Rather, go to the lost sheep of the house of Israel. As you go, preach, saying, 'The Kingdom of Heaven is at hand!' Heal the sick, cleanse the lepers, and cast out demons. Freely you received, so freely give. Don't take any gold, nor silver, nor brass in your money belts. Take no bag for your journey, neither two coats, nor shoes, nor staff: for the laborer is worthy of his food. Into whatever city or village you enter, find out who in it is worthy; and stay there until you go on. As you enter into the household, greet it. If the household is worthy, let your peace come on it, but if it isn't worthy, let your peace return to you. Whoever doesn't receive you, nor hear your words, as you go out of that house or that city, shake off the dust from your feet. Most certainly I tell you, it will be more tolerable for the land of Sodom and Gomorrah in the day of judgment than for that city.

"Behold, I send you out as sheep in the midst of wolves. Therefore be wise as serpents, and harmless as doves. But beware of men: for they will deliver you up to councils, and in their synagogues they will scourge you. Yes, and you will be brought before governors and kings for my sake, for a testimony to them and to the nations. But when they deliver you up, don't be anxious how or what you will say, for it will be given you in that hour what you will say. For it is not you who speak, but the Spirit of your Father who speaks in you.

He who doesn't take his cross and follow after me, isn't worthy of me. He who seeks his life will lose it; and he who loses his life for my sake will find it. He who receives you receives me, and he who receives me receives him who sent me. He who receives a prophet in the name of a prophet will receive a prophet's reward. He who receives a righteous man in the name of a righteous man will receive a righteous man's reward. Whoever gives one of these little ones just a cup of cold water to drink in the name of a disciple, most certainly I tell you he will in no way lose his reward."

It happened that when Jesus had finished directing his twelve disciples, he departed from there to teach and preach in their cities.

Now Herod the tetrarch heard of all that was done by him; and he was very perplexed, because it was said by some that John had risen from the dead, and by some that Elijah had appeared, and by others that one of the old prophets had risen again. Herod said, "John I beheaded, but who is this, about whom I hear such things?" He sought to see him.

For Herod himself had sent out and arrested John, and bound him in prison for the sake of Herodias, his brother Philip's wife, for he had married her. For John said to Herod, "It is not lawful for you to have your brother's wife." Herodias set herself against him, and desired to kill him, but she couldn't, for Herod feared John, knowing that he was a righteous and holy man, and kept him safe. When he heard him, he did many things, and he heard him gladly.

Then a convenient day came, that Herod on his birthday made a supper for his nobles, the high officers, and the chief men of Galilee. When the daughter of Herodias herself came in and danced, she pleased Herod and those sitting with him. The king said to the young lady, "Ask me whatever you want, and I will give it to you." He swore to her, "Whatever you shall ask of me, I will give you, up to half of my kingdom."

She went out, and said to her mother, "What shall I ask?"

She said, "The head of John the Baptizer."

She came in immediately with haste to the king, and asked, "I want you to give me right now the head of John the Baptizer on a platter."

The king was exceedingly sorry, but for the sake of his oaths, and of his dinner guests, he didn't wish to refuse her. Immediately the king sent out a soldier of his guard, and commanded to bring John's head, and he went and beheaded him in the prison, and brought his head on a platter, and gave it to the young lady; and the young lady gave it to her mother.

When his disciples heard this, they came and took up his corpse, and laid it in a tomb.

28 TRAINING AND SCOLDING

Jesus Makes an Impact

As Jesus progressed in his ministry, he began spending more time focusing on training his apostles - the 12 close disciples he had selected. In addition to being with him night and day, Jesus also used many opportunities to explain the purpose and nature of his mission. Still, the apostles would not fully understand the nature of his ministry until after his death. Jesus also found himself in more struggles against the Pharisees and Scribes, who were becoming bolder in their moves to try to trap him into saying something that they could hold against him.

The apostles gathered themselves together to Jesus, and they told him all things, whatever they had done, and whatever they had taught.

Jesus came out, saw a great multitude, and he had compassion on them, because they were like sheep without a shepherd, and he began to teach them many things. When it was late in the day, his disciples came to him, and said, "This place is deserted, and it is late in the day. Send them away, that they may go into the surrounding country and villages, and buy themselves bread, for they have nothing to eat."

But he answered them, "You give them something to eat."

They asked him, "Shall we go and buy two hundred denarii worth of bread, and give them something to eat?"

He said to them, "How many loaves do you have? Go see."

When they knew, they said, "Five, and two fish."

He commanded them that everyone should sit down in groups on the green grass. They sat down in ranks, by hundreds and by fifties. He took the five loaves and the two fish, and looking up to heaven, he blessed and broke the loaves, and he gave to his disciples to set before them, and he divided the two fish among them all. They all ate, and were filled. They took up twelve baskets full of broken pieces and also of the fish. Those who ate the loaves were five thousand men.

Immediately he made his disciples get into the boat, and to go ahead to the other side, to Bethsaida, while he himself sent the multitude away. After he had taken leave of them, he went up the mountain to pray.

When evening had come, the boat was in the midst of the sea, and he was alone on the land. Seeing them distressed in rowing, for the wind was contrary to them, about the fourth watch of the night he came to them, walking on the sea, and he would have passed by them, but they, when they saw him walking on the sea, supposed that it was a ghost, and cried out; for they all saw him, and were troubled. But he immediately spoke with them, and said to them, "Cheer up! It is I! Don't be afraid." He got into the boat with them; and the wind ceased, and they were very amazed among themselves, and marveled.

When they had crossed over, they came to land at Gennesaret, and moored to the shore. When they had come out of the boat, immediately the people recognized him, and ran around that whole region, and began to bring those who were sick, on their mats, to where they heard he was. Wherever he entered, into villages, or into cities, or into the country, they laid the sick in the marketplaces, and begged him that they might touch just the fringe of his garment; and as many as touched him were made well.

Many of his disciples went back, and walked no more with him. Jesus said therefore to the twelve, "You don't also want to go away, do you?"

Simon Peter answered him, "Lord, to whom would we go? You have the words of eternal life. We have come to believe and know that you are the Christ, the Son of the living God."

The Pharisees and the scribes asked him, "Why don't your disciples walk according to the tradition of the elders, but eat their bread with unwashed hands?"

He answered them, "Well did Isaiah prophesy of you hypocrites, as it is written,

'This people honors me with their lips,
but their heart is far from me.
But in vain do they worship me,
teaching as doctrines the commandments of men.'

"For you set aside the commandment of God, and hold tightly to the tradition of men—the washing of pitchers and cups, and you do many other such things." He said to them, "Full well do you reject the commandment of God, that you may keep your tradition. For Moses said, 'Honor your father and your mother;' and, 'He who speaks evil of father or mother, let him be put to death.' But you say, 'If a man tells his father or his mother, "Whatever profit you

323

might have received from me is Corban, that is to say, given to God";' then you no longer allow him to do anything for his father or his mother, making void the word of God by your tradition, which you have handed down. You do many things like this."

He called all the multitude to himself, and said to them, "Hear me, all of you, and understand. There is nothing from outside of the man, that going into him can defile him; but the things which proceed out of the man are those that defile the man.

For from within, out of the hearts of men, proceed evil thoughts, adulteries, sexual sins, murders, thefts, covetings, wickedness, deceit, lustful desires, an evil eye, blasphemy, pride, and foolishness. All these evil things come from within, and defile the man."

Jesus continued his work among the people. On one occasion, he cast a demon from the daughter of a Greek woman, based on her demonstration of faith. When in Decapolis, he healed a deaf and mute man who was brought to him, resulting in great astonishment among the people. On another occasion, he again performed a miracle of feeding a large crowd containing four thousand men (thus even larger when including women and children), with only seven loaves and a few small fish. When traveling through Bethsaida, he healed a man who was blind. Many such miracles were witnessed and recorded.

Now when Jesus came into the parts of Caesarea Philippi, he asked his disciples, saying, "Who do men say that I, the Son of Man, am?"

They said, "Some say John the Baptizer, some, Elijah, and others, Jeremiah, or one of the prophets."

He said to them, "But who do you say that I am?"

Simon Peter answered, "You are the Christ, the Son of the living God."

Jesus answered him, "Blessed are you, Simon Bar Jonah, for flesh and blood has not revealed this to you, but my Father who is in heaven. I also tell you that you are Peter, and on this rock I will build my assembly, and the gates of Hades will not prevail against it. I will give to you the keys of the Kingdom of Heaven, and whatever you bind on earth will have been bound in heaven; and whatever you release on earth will have been released in heaven." Then he commanded the disciples that they should tell no one that he was Jesus the Christ.

From that time, Jesus began to show his disciples that he must go to Jerusalem and suffer many things from the elders, chief priests, and scribes, and be killed, and the third day be raised up.

Peter took him aside, and began to rebuke him, saying, "Far be it from you, Lord! This will never be done to you."

But he turned, and said to Peter, "Get behind me, Satan! You are a stumbling block to me, for you are not setting your mind on the things of God, but on the things of men."

Then Jesus said to his disciples, "If anyone desires to come after me, let him deny himself, and take up his cross, and follow me. For whoever desires to save his life will lose it, and whoever will lose his life for my sake will find it. For what will it profit a man, if he gains the whole world, and forfeits his life? Or what will a man give in exchange for his life?

For the Son of Man will come in the glory of his Father with his angels, and then he will render to everyone according to his deeds. Most certainly I tell you, there are some standing here who will in no way taste of death, until they see the Son of Man coming in his Kingdom."

After six days, Jesus took with him Peter, James, and John his brother, and brought them up into a high mountain by themselves. He was transfigured before them. His face shone like the sun, and his garments became as white as the light. Behold, Moses and Elijah appeared to them talking with him.

Peter answered, and said to Jesus, "Lord, it is good for us to be here. If you want, let's make three tents here: one for you, one for Moses, and one for Elijah."

While he was still speaking, behold, a bright cloud overshadowed them. Behold, a voice came out of the cloud, saying, "This is my beloved Son, in whom I am well pleased. Listen to him."

When the disciples heard it, they fell on their faces, and were very afraid. Jesus came and touched them and said, "Get up, and don't be afraid." Lifting up their eyes, they saw no one, except Jesus alone.

While they were staying in Galilee, Jesus said to them, "The Son of Man is about to be delivered up into the hands of men, and they will kill him, and the third day he will be raised up." They were exceedingly sorry.

The disciples came to Jesus, saying, "Who then is greatest in the Kingdom of Heaven?"

Jesus called a little child to himself, and set him in their midst, and said, "Most certainly I tell you, unless you turn, and become as little children, you will in no way enter into the Kingdom of Heaven. Whoever therefore humbles himself as this little child, the same is the greatest in the Kingdom of Heaven.

Whoever receives one such little child in my name receives me, but whoever causes one of these little ones who believe in me to stumble, it would be better for him that a huge millstone should be hung around his neck, and that he should be sunk in the depths of the sea.

John said to him, "Teacher, we saw someone who doesn't follow us casting out demons in your name; and we forbade him, because he doesn't follow us."

But Jesus said, "Don't forbid him, for there is no one who will do a mighty work in my name, and be able quickly to speak evil of me. For whoever is not against us is on our side. For whoever will give you a cup of water to drink in my name, because you are Christ's, most certainly I tell you, he will in no way lose his reward.

"What do you think? If a man has one hundred sheep, and one of them goes astray, doesn't he leave the ninety-nine, go to the mountains, and seek that which has gone astray? If he finds it, most certainly I tell you, he rejoices over it more than over the ninety-nine which have not gone astray. Even so it is not the will of your Father who is in heaven that one of these little ones should perish.

"If your brother sins against you, go, show him his fault between you and him alone. If he listens to you, you have gained back your brother. But if he doesn't listen, take one or two more with you, that at the mouth of two or three witnesses every word may be established. If he refuses to listen to them, tell it to the assembly. If he refuses to hear the assembly also, let him be to you as a Gentile or a tax collector.

Then Peter came and said to him, "Lord, how often shall my brother sin against me, and I forgive him? Until seven times?" Jesus said to him, "I don't tell you until seven times, but, until seventy times seven.

Therefore the Kingdom of Heaven is like a certain king, who wanted to reconcile accounts with his servants. When he had begun to reconcile, one was brought to him who owed him ten thousand talents. But because he couldn't pay, his lord commanded him to be sold, with his wife, his children, and all that he had, and payment to be made. The servant therefore fell down and kneeled before him, saying, 'Lord, have patience with me, and I will repay you all!' The lord of that servant, being moved with compassion, released him, and forgave him the debt.

"But that servant went out, and found one of his fellow servants, who owed him one hundred denarii, and he grabbed him, and took him by the throat, saying, 'Pay me what you owe!'

"So his fellow servant fell down at his feet and begged him, saying, 'Have patience with me, and I will repay you!' He would not, but went and cast him into prison, until he should pay back that which was due. So when his fellow servants saw what was done, they were exceedingly sorry, and came and told to their lord all that was done. Then his lord called him in, and said to him, 'You wicked servant! I forgave you all that debt, because you begged me. Shouldn't you also have had mercy on your fellow servant, even as I had mercy on you?' His lord was angry, and delivered him to the tormentors, until he should pay all that was due to him. So my heavenly Father will also do to you, if you don't each forgive your brother from your hearts for his misdeeds."

It came to pass, when the days were near that he should be taken up, he intently set his face to go to Jerusalem.

Despite his predictions that he would be captured and killed in Jerusalem, Jesus was still determined to go there. Although not looking forward to what was about to unfold, Jesus submitted to the will of God in following through with this plan.

The Jews therefore sought him at the feast, and said, "Where is he?" There was much murmuring among the multitudes concerning him. Some said, "He is a good man." Others said, "Not so, but he leads the multitude astray." Yet no one spoke openly of him for fear of the Jews. But when it was now the midst of the feast, Jesus went up into the temple and taught. The Jews therefore marveled, saying, "How does this man know letters, having never been educated?"

Jesus therefore answered them, "My teaching is not mine, but his who sent me. If anyone desires to do his will, he will know about the teaching, whether it is from God, or if I am speaking from myself. He who speaks from himself seeks his own glory, but he who seeks the glory of him who sent him is true, and no unrighteousness is in him.

Jesus therefore cried out in the temple, teaching and saying, "You both know me, and know where I am from. I have not come of myself, but he who sent me is true, whom you don't know. I know him, because I am from him, and he sent me."

They sought therefore to take him; but no one laid a hand on him, because his hour had not yet come. But of the multitude, many believed in him.

Now on the last and greatest day of the feast, Jesus stood and cried out, "If anyone is thirsty, let him come to me and drink! He who believes in me, as the Scripture has said, from within him will flow rivers of living water." But he said this about the Spirit, which those believing in him were to receive. For the Holy Spirit was not yet given, because Jesus wasn't yet glorified.

Many of the multitude therefore, when they heard these words, said, "This is truly the prophet." Others said, "This is the Christ." But some said, "What, does the Christ come out of Galilee? Hasn't the Scripture said that the Christ comes of the seed of David, and from Bethlehem, the village where David was?" So there arose a division in the multitude because of him. Some of them would have arrested him, but no one laid hands on him. The officers therefore came to the chief priests and Pharisees, and they said to them, "Why didn't you bring him?"

The officers answered, "No man ever spoke like this man! "The Pharisees therefore answered them, "You aren't also led astray, are you? Have any of the rulers believed in him, or of the Pharisees? But this multitude that doesn't know the law is accursed."

Nicodemus (he who came to him by night, being one of them) said to them, "Does our law judge a man, unless it first hears from him personally and knows what he does?"

They answered him, "Are you also from Galilee? Search, and see that no prophet has arisen out of Galilee."

Early the next day, Jesus was again tested. As he had done so many times before, Jesus turned the tables on the scribes and Pharisees. But they remained absolute in their evil desire to find something about Jesus that they could use against him.

Now very early in the morning, he came again into the temple, and all the people came to him. He sat down, and taught them. The scribes and the Pharisees brought a woman taken in adultery. Having set her in the midst, they told him, "Teacher, we found this woman in adultery, in the very act. Now in our law, Moses commanded us to stone such. What then do you say about her?" They said this testing him, that they might have something to accuse him of.

But Jesus stooped down, and wrote on the ground with his finger. But when they continued asking him, he looked up and said to them, "He who is without sin among you, let him throw the first stone at her." Again he stooped down, and with his finger wrote on the ground.

They, when they heard it, being convicted by their conscience, went out one by one, beginning from the oldest, even to the last. Jesus was left alone with the woman where she was, in the middle. Jesus, standing up, saw her and said, "Woman, where are your accusers? Did no one condemn you?"

She said, "No one, Lord."

Jesus said, "Neither do I condemn you. Go your way. From now on, sin no more."

Now after these things, the Lord also appointed seventy others, and sent them two by two ahead of him into every city and place, where he was about to come. Then he said to them, "The harvest is indeed plentiful, but the laborers are few. Pray therefore to the Lord of the harvest, that he may send out laborers into his harvest. Go your ways. Behold, I send you out as lambs among wolves. Carry no purse, nor wallet, nor sandals. Greet no one on the way."

The seventy returned with joy, saying, "Lord, even the demons are subject to us in your name!"

He said to them, "I saw Satan having fallen like lightning from heaven. Behold, I give you authority to tread on serpents and scorpions, and over all the power of the enemy. Nothing will in any way hurt you. Nevertheless, don't rejoice in this, that the spirits are subject to you, but rejoice that your names are written in heaven."

Behold, a certain lawyer stood up and tested him, saying, "Teacher, what shall I do to inherit eternal life?"

He said to him, "What is written in the law? How do you read it?"

He answered, "You shall love the Lord your God with all your heart, with all your soul, with all your strength, and with all your mind; and your neighbor as yourself."

He said to him, "You have answered correctly. Do this, and you will live."

But he, desiring to justify himself, asked Jesus, "Who is my neighbor?"

Jesus answered, "A certain man was going down from Jerusalem to Jericho, and he fell among robbers, who both stripped him and beat him, and departed, leaving him half dead. By chance a certain priest was going down that way. When he saw him, he passed by on the other side. In the same way a Levite also, when he came to the place, and saw him, passed by on the other side. But a certain Samaritan, as he traveled, came where he was. When he saw him, he was moved with compassion, came to him, and bound up his wounds, pouring on oil and wine. He set him on his own animal, and brought him to an inn, and took care of him. On the next day, when he departed, he took out two denarii, and gave them to the host, and said to him, 'Take care of him. Whatever you spend beyond that, I will repay you when I return.' Now which of these three do you think seemed to be a neighbor to him who fell among the robbers?"

He said, "He who showed mercy on him."

Then Jesus said to him, "Go and do likewise."

It happened, that when he finished praying in a certain place, one of his disciples said to him, "Lord, teach us to pray, just as John also taught his disciples."

He said to them, "When you pray, say,
'Our Father in heaven,
may your name be kept holy.
May your Kingdom come.
May your will be done on earth, as it is in heaven.
Give us day by day our daily bread.
Forgive us our sins,
for we ourselves also forgive everyone who is indebted to us.
Bring us not into temptation,

but deliver us from the evil one.'"

"I tell you, keep asking, and it will be given you. Keep seeking, and you will find. Keep knocking, and it will be opened to you. For everyone who asks receives. He who seeks finds. To him who knocks it will be opened.

He was casting out a demon, and it was mute. It happened, when the demon had gone out, the mute man spoke; and the multitudes marveled. But some of them said, "He casts out demons by Beelzebul, the prince of the demons." Others, testing him, sought from him a sign from heaven. But he, knowing their thoughts, said to them, "Every kingdom divided against itself is brought to desolation. A house divided against itself falls. If Satan also is divided against himself, how will his kingdom stand? For you say that I cast out demons by Beelzebul. But if I cast out demons by Beelzebul, by whom do your children cast them out? Therefore will they be your judges. But if I by the finger of God cast out demons, then the Kingdom of God has come to you.

Now as he spoke, a certain Pharisee asked him to dine with him. He went in, and sat at the table. When the Pharisee saw it, he marveled that he had not first washed himself before dinner. The Lord said to him, "Now you Pharisees cleanse the outside of the cup and of the platter, but your inward part is full of extortion and wickedness. You foolish ones, didn't he who made the outside make the inside also? But give for gifts to the needy those things which are within, and behold, all things will be clean to you. But woe to you Pharisees! For you tithe mint and rue and every herb, but you bypass justice and the love of God. You ought to have done these, and not to have left the other undone. Woe to you Pharisees! For you love the best seats in the synagogues, and the greetings in the marketplaces.

As he said these things to them, the scribes and the Pharisees began to be terribly angry, and to draw many things out of him; lying in wait for him, and seeking to catch him in something he might say, that they might accuse him.

He spoke a parable to them, saying, "The ground of a certain rich man brought forth abundantly. He reasoned within himself, saying, 'What will I do, because I don't have room to store my crops?' He said, 'This is what I will do. I will pull down my barns, and build bigger ones, and there I will store all my grain and my goods. I will tell my soul, "Soul, you have many goods laid up for many years. Take your ease, eat, drink, be merry."'

"But God said to him, 'You foolish one, tonight your soul is required of you. The things which you have prepared—whose will they be?' So is he who lays up treasure for himself, and is not rich toward God."

He said to his disciples, "Therefore I tell you, don't be anxious for your life, what you will eat, nor yet for your body, what you will wear. Life is more than food, and the body is more than clothing. Consider the ravens: they don't sow, they don't reap, they have no warehouse or barn, and God feeds them. How much more valuable are you than birds! Which of you by being anxious can add a cubit to his height? If then you aren't able to do even the least things, why are you anxious about the rest? Consider the lilies, how they grow. They don't toil, neither do they spin; yet I tell you, even Solomon in all his glory was not arrayed like one of these. But if this is how God clothes the grass in the field, which today exists, and tomorrow is cast into the oven, how much more will he clothe you, O you of little faith? Don't seek what you will eat or what you will drink; neither be anxious. For the nations of the world seek after all of these things, but your Father knows that you need these things. But seek God's Kingdom, and all these things will be added to you.

He was teaching in one of the synagogues on the Sabbath day. Behold, there was a woman who had a spirit of infirmity eighteen years, and she was bent over, and could in no way straighten herself up. When Jesus saw her, he called her, and said to her, "Woman, you are freed from your infirmity." He laid his hands on her, and immediately she stood up straight, and glorified God.

The ruler of the synagogue, being indignant because Jesus had healed on the Sabbath, said to the multitude, "There are six days in which men ought to work. Therefore come on those days and be healed, and not on the Sabbath day!"

Therefore the Lord answered him, "You hypocrites! Doesn't each one of you free his ox or his donkey from the stall on the Sabbath, and lead him away to water? Ought not this woman, being a daughter of Abraham, whom Satan had bound eighteen long years, be freed from this bondage on the Sabbath day?"

As he said these things, all his adversaries were disappointed, and all the multitude rejoiced for all the glorious things that were done by him.

He said, "What is the Kingdom of God like? To what shall I compare it? It is like a grain of mustard seed, which a man took, and put in his own garden. It grew, and became a large tree, and the birds of the sky lodged in its branches."
Again he said, "To what shall I compare the Kingdom of God? It is like yeast, which a woman took and hid in three measures of flour, until it was all leavened."

29 BOLDNESS AND POWER

Nearing the End of His Ministry

He went away again beyond the Jordan into the place where John was baptizing at first, and there he stayed. Many came to him. They said, "John indeed did no sign, but everything that John said about this man is true." Many believed in him there.

Some Pharisees came, saying to him, "Get out of here, and go away, for Herod wants to kill you."

He said to them, "Go and tell that fox, 'Behold, I cast out demons and perform cures today and tomorrow, and the third day I complete my mission. Nevertheless I must go on my way today and tomorrow and the next day, for it can't be that a prophet perish outside of Jerusalem.'

"Jerusalem, Jerusalem, that kills the prophets, and stones those who are sent to her! How often I wanted to gather your children together, like a hen gathers her own brood under her wings, and you refused! Behold, your house is left to you desolate. I tell you, you will not see me, until you say, 'Blessed is he who comes in the name of the Lord!'"

Now all the tax collectors and sinners were coming close to him to hear him. The Pharisees and the scribes murmured, saying, "This man welcomes sinners, and eats with them."

He told them this parable. "Which of you men, if you had one hundred sheep, and lost one of them, wouldn't leave the ninety-nine in the wilderness, and go after the one that was lost, until he found it? When he has found it, he carries it on his shoulders, rejoicing. When he comes home, he calls together his friends and his neighbors, saying to them, 'Rejoice with me, for I have found my sheep which was lost!' I tell you that even so there will be more joy in heaven over one sinner who repents, than over ninety-nine righteous people who need no repentance. Or what woman, if she had ten drachma coins, if she lost one drachma coin, wouldn't light a lamp, sweep the house, and seek diligently until she found it? When she has found it, she calls together her friends and neighbors, saying, 'Rejoice with me, for I have found the drachma which I had lost.' Even so, I tell you, there is joy in the presence of the angels of God over one sinner repenting."

Jesus told the beloved parable of the "Prodigal Son." Shortly after that time, he told another story that is much beloved by Christians, the story of the beggar Lazarus and a rich man. Stories like these, while infuriating the spiritual ruling class, were much beloved by the common people.

He said, "A certain man had two sons. The younger of them said to his father, 'Father, give me my share of your property.' He divided his livelihood between them. Not many days after, the younger son gathered all of this together and traveled into a far country. There he wasted his property with riotous living. When he had spent all of it, there arose a severe famine in that country, and he began to be in need. He went and joined himself to one of the citizens of that country, and he sent him into his fields to feed pigs. He wanted to fill his belly with the husks that the pigs ate, but no one gave him any. But when he came to himself he said, 'How many hired servants of my father have bread enough to spare, and I'm dying with hunger! I will get up and go to my father, and will tell him, "Father, I have sinned against heaven, and in your sight. I am no more worthy to be called your son. Make me as one of your hired servants."'

"He arose, and came to his father. But while he was still far off, his father saw him, and was moved with compassion, and ran, and fell on his neck, and kissed him. The son said to him, 'Father, I have sinned against heaven, and in your sight. I am no longer worthy to be called your son.'

"But the father said to his servants, 'Bring out the best robe, and put it on him. Put a ring on his hand, and shoes on his feet. Bring the fattened calf, kill it, and let us eat, and celebrate; for this, my son, was dead, and is alive again. He was lost, and is found.' They began to celebrate.

"Now his elder son was in the field. As he came near to the house, he heard music and dancing. He called one of the servants to him, and asked what was going on. He said to him, 'Your brother has come, and your father has killed the fattened calf, because he has received him back safe and healthy.' But he was angry, and would not go in. Therefore his father came out, and begged him. But he answered his father, 'Behold, these many years I have served you, and I never disobeyed a commandment of yours, but you never gave me a goat, that I might celebrate with my friends. But when this, your son, came, who has devoured your living with prostitutes, you killed the fattened calf for him.'

"He said to him, 'Son, you are always with me, and all that is mine is yours. But it was appropriate to celebrate and be glad, for this, your brother, was dead, and is alive again. He was lost, and is found.'"

"Now there was a certain rich man, and he was clothed in purple and fine linen, living in luxury every day. A certain beggar, named Lazarus, was laid at his gate, full of sores, and desiring to be fed with the crumbs that fell from the rich man's table. Yes, even the dogs came and licked his sores. It happened that the beggar died, and that he was carried away by the angels to Abraham's bosom. The rich man also died, and was buried. In Hades, he lifted up his eyes, being in torment, and saw Abraham far off, and Lazarus at his bosom. He cried and said, 'Father Abraham, have mercy on me, and send Lazarus, that he may dip the tip of his finger in water, and cool my tongue! For I am in anguish in this flame.'

"But Abraham said, 'Son, remember that you, in your lifetime, received your good things, and Lazarus, in the same way, bad things. But now here he is comforted and you are in anguish. Besides all this, between us and you there is a great gulf fixed, that those who want to pass from here to you are not able, and that none may cross over from there to us.'

"He said, 'I ask you therefore, father, that you would send him to my father's house; for I have five brothers, that he may testify to them, so they won't also come into this place of torment.'

"But Abraham said to him, 'They have Moses and the prophets. Let them listen to them.'

"He said, 'No, father Abraham, but if one goes to them from the dead, they will repent.'

"He said to him, 'If they don't listen to Moses and the prophets, neither will they be persuaded if one rises from the dead.'"

Jesus showed the amazing glory of God by performing his greatest miracle, the bringing back to life of his dear friend Lazarus, who had been dead for four days. This powerful demonstration of supernatural power resulted in the newfound belief of many Jews, and in the renewed commitment of the Jewish council to have Jesus killed.

Now a certain man was sick, Lazarus from Bethany, of the village of Mary and her sister, Martha. It was that Mary who had anointed the Lord with ointment, and wiped his feet with her hair, whose brother, Lazarus, was sick. The sisters therefore sent to him, saying, "Lord, behold, he for whom you have great affection is sick." But when Jesus heard it, he said, "This sickness is not to death, but for the glory of God, that God's Son may be glorified by it."

Now Jesus loved Martha, and her sister, and Lazarus. When therefore he heard that he was sick, he stayed two days in the place where he was. Then after this he said to the disciples, "Let's go into Judea again."

The disciples told him, "Rabbi, the Jews were just trying to stone you, and are you going there again?"

Jesus answered, "Aren't there twelve hours of daylight? If a man walks in the day, he doesn't stumble, because he sees the light of this world. But if a man walks in the night, he stumbles, because the light isn't in him." He said these things, and after that, he said to them, "Our friend, Lazarus, has fallen asleep, but I am going so that I may awake him out of sleep."

The disciples therefore said, "Lord, if he has fallen asleep, he will recover."

Now Jesus had spoken of his death, but they thought that he spoke of taking rest in sleep. So Jesus said to them plainly then, "Lazarus is dead. I am glad for your sakes that I was not there, so that you may believe. Nevertheless, let's go to him."

Thomas therefore, who is called Didymus, said to his fellow disciples, "Let's go also, that we may die with him."

So when Jesus came, he found that he had been in the tomb four days already. Now Bethany was near Jerusalem, about fifteen stadia away. Many of the Jews had joined the women around Martha and Mary, to console them concerning their brother. Then when Martha heard that Jesus was coming, she went and met him, but Mary stayed in the house. Therefore Martha said to Jesus, "Lord, if you would have been here, my brother wouldn't have died. Even now I know that, whatever you ask of God, God will give you." Jesus said to her, "Your brother will rise again."

Martha said to him, "I know that he will rise again in the resurrection at the last day."

Jesus said to her, "I am the resurrection and the life. He who believes in me will still live, even if he dies. Whoever lives and believes in me will never die. Do you believe this?"

She said to him, "Yes, Lord. I have come to believe that you are the Christ, God's Son, he who comes into the world."

When she had said this, she went away, and called Mary, her sister, secretly, saying, "The Teacher is here, and is calling you."

When she heard this, she arose quickly, and went to him. Now Jesus had not yet come into the village, but was in the place where Martha met him. Then the Jews who were with her in the house, and were consoling her, when they saw Mary, that she rose up quickly and went out, followed her, saying, "She is going to the tomb to weep there." Therefore when Mary came to where Jesus was, and

335

saw him, she fell down at his feet, saying to him, "Lord, if you would have been here, my brother wouldn't have died."

When Jesus therefore saw her weeping, and the Jews weeping who came with her, he groaned in the spirit, and was troubled, and said, "Where have you laid him?"

They told him, "Lord, come and see."

Jesus wept.

The Jews therefore said, "See how much affection he had for him!" Some of them said, "Couldn't this man, who opened the eyes of him who was blind, have also kept this man from dying?"

Jesus therefore, again groaning in himself, came to the tomb. Now it was a cave, and a stone lay against it. Jesus said, "Take away the stone."

Martha, the sister of him who was dead, said to him, "Lord, by this time there is a stench, for he has been dead four days."

Jesus said to her, "Didn't I tell you that if you believed, you would see God's glory?"

So they took away the stone from the place where the dead man was lying. Jesus lifted up his eyes, and said, "Father, I thank you that you listened to me. I know that you always listen to me, but because of the multitude that stands around I said this, that they may believe that you sent me." When he had said this, he cried with a loud voice, "Lazarus, come out!"

He who was dead came out, bound hand and foot with wrappings, and his face was wrapped around with a cloth.

Jesus said to them, "Free him, and let him go."

Therefore many of the Jews, who came to Mary and saw what Jesus did, believed in him. But some of them went away to the Pharisees, and told them the things which Jesus had done. The chief priests therefore and the Pharisees gathered a council, and said, "What are we doing? For this man does many signs. If we leave him alone like this, everyone will believe in him, and the Romans will come and take away both our place and our nation."

But a certain one of them, Caiaphas, being high priest that year, said to them, "You know nothing at all, nor do you consider that it is advantageous for us that one man should die for the people, and that the whole nation not perish." Now he didn't say this of himself, but being high priest that year, he prophesied that Jesus would die for the nation, and not for the nation only, but that he might also gather together into one the children of God who are scattered abroad. So from that day forward they took counsel that they might put him to death. Jesus therefore walked no more openly among the Jews, but departed from there into the country near the wilderness, to a city called Ephraim. He stayed there with his disciples.

He spoke also this parable to certain people who were convinced of their own righteousness, and who despised all others. "Two men went up into the temple to pray; one was a Pharisee, and the other was a tax collector. The Pharisee stood and prayed to himself like this: 'God, I thank you, that I am not like the rest of men, extortioners, unrighteous, adulterers, or even like this tax collector. I fast twice a week. I give tithes of all that I get.' But the tax collector, standing far away, wouldn't even lift up his eyes to heaven, but beat his breast, saying, 'God, be merciful to me, a sinner!' I tell you, this man went down to his house justified rather than the other; for everyone who exalts himself will be humbled, but he who humbles himself will be exalted."

It happened when Jesus had finished these words, he departed from Galilee, and came into the borders of Judea beyond the Jordan. Great multitudes followed him, and he healed them there.

Pharisees came to him, testing him, and saying, "Is it lawful for a man to divorce his wife for any reason?"

He answered, "Haven't you read that he who made them from the beginning made them male and female, and said, 'For this cause a man shall leave his father and mother, and shall join to his wife; and the two shall become one flesh?' So that they are no more two, but one flesh. What therefore God has joined together, don't let man tear apart."

They asked him, "Why then did Moses command us to give her a bill of divorce, and divorce her?"

He said to them, "Moses, because of the hardness of your hearts, allowed you to divorce your wives, but from the beginning it has not been so. I tell you that whoever divorces his wife, except for sexual immorality, and marries another, commits adultery; and he who marries her when she is divorced commits adultery."

His disciples said to him, "If this is the case of the man with his wife, it is not expedient to marry."

But he said to them, "Not all men can receive this saying, but those to whom it is given. For there are eunuchs who were born that way from their mother's womb, and there are eunuchs who were made eunuchs by men; and there are eunuchs who made themselves eunuchs for the Kingdom of Heaven's sake. He who is able to receive it, let him receive it."

They were bringing to him little children, that he should touch them, but the disciples rebuked those who were bringing them. But when Jesus saw it, he was moved with indignation, and said to them, "Allow the little children to come to me! Don't forbid them, for the Kingdom of God belongs to such as these. Most certainly I tell you, whoever will not receive the Kingdom of God like a little child, he will in no way enter into it." He took them in his arms, and blessed them, laying his hands on them.

As he was going out into the way, one ran to him, knelt before him, and asked him, "Good Teacher, what shall I do that I may inherit eternal life?"

Jesus said to him, "Why do you call me good? No one is good except one—God. You know the commandments: 'Do not murder,' 'Do not commit adultery,' 'Do not steal,' 'Do not give false testimony,' 'Do not defraud,' 'Honor your father and mother.'"

He said to him, "Teacher, I have observed all these things from my youth."

Jesus looking at him loved him, and said to him, "One thing you lack. Go, sell whatever you have, and give to the poor, and you will have treasure in heaven; and come, follow me, taking up the cross."

But his face fell at that saying, and he went away sorrowful, for he was one who had great possessions. Jesus looked around, and said to his disciples, "How difficult it is for those who have riches to enter into the Kingdom of God!"

They were on the way, going up to Jerusalem; and Jesus was going in front of them, and they were amazed; and those who followed were afraid. He again took the twelve, and began to tell them the things that were going to happen to him. "Behold, we are going up to Jerusalem. The Son of Man will be delivered to the chief priests and the scribes. They will condemn him to death, and will deliver him to the Gentiles. They will mock him, spit on him, scourge him, and kill him. On the third day he will rise again."

He entered and was passing through Jericho. There was a man named Zacchaeus. He was a chief tax collector, and he was rich. He was trying to see who Jesus was, and couldn't because of the crowd, because he was short. He ran on ahead, and climbed up into a sycamore tree to see him, for he was to pass that way. When Jesus came to the place, he looked up and saw him, and said to him, "Zacchaeus, hurry and come down, for today I must stay at your house." He hurried, came down, and received him joyfully. When they saw it, they all murmured, saying, "He has gone in to lodge with a man who is a sinner."

Zacchaeus stood and said to the Lord, "Behold, Lord, half of my goods I give to the poor. If I have wrongfully exacted anything of anyone, I restore four times as much."

Jesus said to him, "Today, salvation has come to this house, because he also is a son of Abraham. For the Son of Man came to seek and to save that which was lost."

Having said these things, he went on ahead, going up to Jerusalem.

Though only he knew it, Jesus was nearing the end of his life and his ministry. The short duration of the rest of his life would be dramatic, with periods of adulation followed by his capture and trial. Although it appeared that things were spiraling out of control, Jesus was fully aware of what was about to happen, and he allowed it to unfold to fulfill God's plan for mankind.

Now the Passover of the Jews was at hand. Many went up from the country to Jerusalem before the Passover, to purify themselves. Then they sought for Jesus and spoke one with another, as they stood in the temple, "What do you think—that he isn't coming to the feast at all?" Now the chief priests and the Pharisees had commanded that if anyone knew where he was, he should report it, that they might seize him.

Then six days before the Passover, Jesus came to Bethany, where Lazarus was, who had been dead, whom he raised from the dead.

A large crowd therefore of the Jews learned that he was there, and they came, not for Jesus' sake only, but that they might see Lazarus also, whom he had raised from the dead. But the chief priests conspired to put Lazarus to death also, because on account of him many of the Jews went away and believed in Jesus.

It happened, when he drew near to Bethsphage and Bethany, at the mountain that is called Olivet, he sent two of his disciples, saying, "Go your way into the village on the other side, in which, as you enter, you will find a colt tied, whereon no man ever yet sat. Untie it, and bring it. If anyone asks you, 'Why are you untying it?' say to him: 'The Lord needs it.'"

Those who were sent went away, and found things just as he had told them. As they were untying the colt, its owners said to them, "Why are you untying the colt?" They said, "The Lord needs it." They brought it to Jesus. They threw their cloaks on the colt, and set Jesus on them.

As he went, they spread their cloaks in the way. As he was now getting near, at the descent of the Mount of Olives, the whole multitude of the disciples began to rejoice and praise God with a loud voice for all the mighty works which they had seen, saying, "Blessed is the King who comes in the name of the Lord! Peace in heaven, and glory in the highest!"

The multitude therefore that was with him when he called Lazarus out of the tomb, and raised him from the dead, was testifying about it. For this cause also the multitude went and met him, because they heard that he had done this sign. The Pharisees therefore said among themselves, "See how you accomplish nothing. Behold, the world has gone after him."

When he had come into Jerusalem, all the city was stirred up, saying, "Who is this?" The multitudes said, "This is the prophet, Jesus, from Nazareth of Galilee."

Jesus entered into the temple in Jerusalem. When he had looked around at everything, it being now evening, he went out to Bethany with the twelve. The next day, when they had come out from Bethany, he was hungry. Seeing a fig tree afar off having leaves, he came to see if perhaps he might find anything on it. When he came to it, he found nothing but leaves, for it was not the season for figs. Jesus told it, "May no one ever eat fruit from you again!" and his disciples heard it.

Despite being closely monitored, Jesus did not hold back. He continued to heal on the Sabbath, and he threw the money changers out of the temple for a second time. With strong words, he condemned and argued against the religious leaders for their hypocrisy.

They came to Jerusalem, and Jesus entered into the temple, and began to throw out those who sold and those who bought in the temple, and overthrew the tables of the money changers, and the seats of those who sold the doves. He would not allow anyone to carry a container through the temple. He taught, saying to them, "Isn't it written, 'My house will be called a house of prayer for all the nations?' But you have made it a den of robbers!"

The chief priests and the scribes heard it, and sought how they might destroy him. For they feared him, because all the multitude was astonished at his teaching.

Every day Jesus was teaching in the temple, and every night he would go out and spend the night on the mountain that is called Olivet. All the people came early in the morning to him in the temple to hear him.

When evening came, he went out of the city.

As they passed by in the morning, they saw the fig tree withered away from the roots. Peter, remembering, said to him, "Rabbi, look! The fig tree which you cursed has withered away."

Jesus answered them, "Have faith in God. For most certainly I tell you, whoever may tell this mountain, 'Be taken up and cast into the sea,' and doesn't doubt in his heart, but believes that what he says is happening; he shall have whatever he says. Therefore I tell you, all things whatever you pray and ask for, believe that you have received them, and you shall have them. Whenever you stand praying, forgive, if you have anything against anyone; so that your Father, who is in heaven, may also forgive you your transgressions. But if you do not forgive, neither will your Father in heaven forgive your transgressions."

He began to speak to them in parables. "A man planted a vineyard, put a hedge around it, dug a pit for the wine press, built a tower, rented it out to a farmer, and went into another country. When it was time, he sent a servant to the farmer to get from the farmer his share of the fruit of the vineyard. They took him, beat him, and sent him away empty. Again, he sent another servant to them; and they threw stones at him, wounded him in the head, and sent him away shamefully treated. Again he sent another; and they killed him; and many others, beating some, and killing some. Therefore still having one, his beloved son, he sent him last to them, saying, 'They will respect my son.' But those farmers said among themselves, 'This is the heir. Come, let's kill him, and the inheritance will be ours.' They took him, killed him, and cast him out of the vineyard. What therefore will the lord of the vineyard do? He will come and destroy the farmers, and will give the vineyard to others.

But what do you think? A man had two sons, and he came to the first, and said, 'Son, go work today in my vineyard.' He answered, 'I will not,' but afterward he changed his mind, and went. He came to the second, and said the same thing. He answered, 'I go, sir,' but he didn't go. Which of the two did the will of his father?"

They said to him, "The first."

Jesus said to them, "Most certainly I tell you that the tax collectors and the prostitutes are entering into the Kingdom of God before you. For John came to you in the way of righteousness, and you didn't believe him, but the tax collectors and the prostitutes believed him. When you saw it, you didn't even repent afterward, that you might believe him.

When the chief priests and the Pharisees heard his parables, they perceived that he spoke about them. When they sought to seize him, they feared the multitudes, because they considered him to be a prophet.

Then the Pharisees went and took counsel how they might entrap him in his talk. They sent their disciples to him, along with the Herodians, saying, "Teacher, we know that you are honest, and teach the way of God in truth, no matter whom you teach, for you aren't partial to anyone. Tell us therefore, what do you think? Is it lawful to pay taxes to Caesar, or not?"

But Jesus perceived their wickedness, and said, "Why do you test me, you hypocrites? Show me the tax money."

They brought to him a denarius.

He asked them, "Whose is this image and inscription?"

They said to him, "Caesar's."

Then he said to them, "Give therefore to Caesar the things that are Caesar's, and to God the things that are God's."

When they heard it, they marveled, and left him, and went away.

One of them, a lawyer, asked him a question, testing him. "Teacher, which is the greatest commandment in the law?"

Jesus said to him, "'You shall love the Lord your God with all your heart, with all your soul, and with all your mind.' This is the first and great commandment. A second likewise is this, 'You shall love your neighbor as yourself.' The whole law and the prophets depend on these two commandments."

Then Jesus spoke to the multitudes and to his disciples, saying, "The scribes and the Pharisees sat on Moses' seat. All things therefore whatever they tell you to observe, observe and do, but don't do their works; for they say, and don't do. For they bind heavy burdens that are grievous to be borne, and lay them on mens' shoulders; but they themselves will not lift a finger to help them. But all their works they do to be seen by men. They make their phylacteries broad, enlarge the fringes of their garments, and love the place of honor at feasts, the best seats in the synagogues, the salutations in the marketplaces, and to be called 'Rabbi, Rabbi' by men. But don't you be called 'Rabbi,' for one is your teacher, the Christ, and all of you are brothers. Call no man on the earth your father, for one is your Father, he who is in heaven. Neither be called masters, for one is your master, the Christ. But he who is greatest among you will be your servant. Whoever exalts himself will be humbled, and whoever humbles himself will be exalted.

Jesus sat down opposite the treasury, and saw how the multitude cast money into the treasury. Many who were rich cast in much. A poor widow came, and she cast in two small brass coins, which equal a quadrans coin. He called his disciples to himself, and said to them, "Most certainly I tell you, this poor widow gave more than all those who are giving into the treasury, for they all gave out of their abundance, but she, out of her poverty, gave all that she had to live on."

30 IN THE SHADOWS

The Arrest and Trials

Jesus went out from the temple, and was going on his way. His disciples came to him to show him the buildings of the temple. But he answered them, "You see all of these things, don't you? Most certainly I tell you, there will not be left here one stone on another, that will not be thrown down."

"Then the Kingdom of Heaven will be like ten virgins, who took their lamps, and went out to meet the bridegroom. Five of them were foolish, and five were wise. Those who were foolish, when they took their lamps, took no oil with them, but the wise took oil in their vessels with their lamps. Now while the bridegroom delayed, they all slumbered and slept. But at midnight there was a cry, 'Behold! The bridegroom is coming! Come out to meet him!' Then all those virgins arose, and trimmed their lamps. The foolish said to the wise, 'Give us some of your oil, for our lamps are going out.' But the wise answered, saying, 'What if there isn't enough for us and you? You go rather to those who sell, and buy for yourselves.' While they went away to buy, the bridegroom came, and those who were ready went in with him to the marriage feast, and the door was shut. Afterward the other virgins also came, saying, 'Lord, Lord, open to us.' But he answered, 'Most certainly I tell you, I don't know you.' Watch therefore, for you don't know the day nor the hour in which the Son of Man is coming.

"But when the Son of Man comes in his glory, and all the holy angels with him, then he will sit on the throne of his glory. Before him all the nations will be gathered, and he will separate them one from another, as a shepherd separates the sheep from the goats. He will set the sheep on his right hand, but the goats on the left. Then the King will tell those on his right hand, 'Come, blessed of my Father, inherit the Kingdom prepared for you from the foundation of the world; for I was hungry, and you gave me food to eat. I was thirsty, and you gave me drink. I was a stranger, and you took me in. I was naked, and you clothed me. I was sick, and you visited me. I was in prison, and you came to me.'

"Then the righteous will answer him, saying, 'Lord, when did we see you hungry, and feed you; or thirsty, and give you a drink? When did we see you as a stranger, and take you in; or naked, and clothe you? When did we see you sick, or in prison, and come to you?'

"The King will answer them, 'Most certainly I tell you, inasmuch as you did it to one of the least of these my brothers, you did it to me.' Then he will say also to those on the left hand, 'Depart from me, you cursed, into the eternal fire which is prepared for the devil and his angels; for I was hungry, and you didn't give me food to eat; I was thirsty, and you gave me no drink; I was a stranger, and you didn't take me in; naked, and you didn't clothe me; sick, and in prison, and you didn't visit me.'

"Then they will also answer, saying, 'Lord, when did we see you hungry, or thirsty, or a stranger, or naked, or sick, or in prison, and didn't help you?'

"Then he will answer them, saying, 'Most certainly I tell you, inasmuch as you didn't do it to one of the least of these, you didn't do it to me.' These will go away into eternal punishment, but the righteous into eternal life."

It happened, when Jesus had finished all these words, that he said to his disciples, "You know that after two days the Passover is coming, and the Son of Man will be delivered up to be crucified."

Then the chief priests, the scribes, and the elders of the people were gathered together in the court of the high priest, who was called Caiaphas. They took counsel together that they might take Jesus by deceit, and kill him. But they said, "Not during the feast, lest a riot occur among the people."

Judas Iscariot, one of the apostles, decided to betray Jesus to the chief priests for money. He went secretly to the council and, after setting a price, waited for the right opportunity. In the meantime, Jesus asked his apostles to make arrangements for the Passover feast. This dinner with his closest disciples is known as "the Last Supper." It was at this occasion that Jesus washed the feet of his apostles, showing them the meaning of true servanthood. He also used this occasion to establish the Lord's Supper, which is still followed by Christians to this day. Finally, he gave some last teaching and instructions to his apostles.

Then one of the twelve, who was called Judas Iscariot, went to the chief priests, and said, "What are you willing to give me, that I should deliver him to you?" They weighed out for him thirty pieces of silver. From that time he sought opportunity to betray him.

The day of unleavened bread came, on which the Passover must be sacrificed. He sent Peter and John, saying, "Go and prepare the Passover for us, that we may eat."

They said to him, "Where do you want us to prepare?"

He said to them, "Behold, when you have entered into the city, a man carrying a pitcher of water will meet you. Follow him into the house which he enters.

Tell the master of the house, 'The Teacher says to you, "Where is the guest room, where I may eat the Passover with my disciples?"' He will show you a large, furnished upper room. Make preparations there."

They went, found things as he had told them, and they prepared the Passover.

When the hour had come, he sat down with the twelve apostles. He said to them, "I have earnestly desired to eat this Passover with you before I suffer, for I tell you, I will no longer by any means eat of it until it is fulfilled in the Kingdom of God."

Now before the feast of the Passover, Jesus, knowing that his time had come that he would depart from this world to the Father, having loved his own who were in the world, he loved them to the end. During supper, the devil having already put into the heart of Judas Iscariot, Simon's son, to betray him, Jesus, knowing that the Father had given all things into his hands, and that he came forth from God, and was going to God, arose from supper, and laid aside his outer garments. He took a towel, and wrapped a towel around his waist. Then he poured water into the basin, and began to wash the disciples' feet, and to wipe them with the towel that was wrapped around him. Then he came to Simon Peter. He said to him, "Lord, do you wash my feet?

Jesus answered him, "You don't know what I am doing now, but you will understand later."

Peter said to him, "You will never wash my feet!"

Jesus answered him, "If I don't wash you, you have no part with me."

Simon Peter said to him, "Lord, not my feet only, but also my hands and my head!"

Jesus said to him, "Someone who has bathed only needs to have his feet washed, but is completely clean. You are clean, but not all of you." For he knew him who would betray him, therefore he said, "You are not all clean." So when he had washed their feet, put his outer garment back on, and sat down again, he said to them, "Do you know what I have done to you? You call me, 'Teacher' and 'Lord.' You say so correctly, for so I am. If I then, the Lord and the Teacher, have washed your feet, you also ought to wash one another's feet. For I have given you an example, that you also should do as I have done to you.

When Jesus had said this, he was troubled in spirit, and testified, "Most certainly I tell you that one of you will betray me."

The disciples looked at one another, perplexed about whom he spoke. One of his disciples, whom Jesus loved, was at the table, leaning against Jesus' breast. Simon Peter therefore beckoned to him, and said to him, "Tell us who it is of whom he speaks."

He, leaning back, as he was, on Jesus' breast, asked him, "Lord, who is it?"

Jesus therefore answered, "It is he to whom I will give this piece of bread when I have dipped it." So when he had dipped the piece of bread, he gave it to Judas, the son of Simon Iscariot. After the piece of bread, then Satan entered into him.

Then Jesus said to him, "What you do, do quickly."

Now no man at the table knew why he said this to him. For some thought, because Judas had the money box, that Jesus said to him, "Buy what things we need for the feast," or that he should give something to the poor. Therefore having received that morsel, he went out immediately. It was night.

When he had gone out, Jesus said, "Now the Son of Man has been glorified, and God has been glorified in him. If God has been glorified in him, God will also glorify him in himself, and he will glorify him immediately. Little children, I will be with you a little while longer. You will seek me, and as I said to the Jews, 'Where I am going, you can't come,' so now I tell you. A new commandment I give to you, that you love one another, just like I have loved you; that you also love one another. By this everyone will know that you are my disciples, if you have love for one another."

Simon Peter said to him, "Lord, where are you going?"

Jesus answered, "Where I am going, you can't follow now, but you will follow afterwards."

Peter said to him, "Lord, why can't I follow you now? I will lay down my life for you."

Jesus answered him, "Will you lay down your life for me? Most certainly I tell you, the rooster won't crow until you have denied me three times.

He received a cup, and when he had given thanks, he said, "Take this, and share it among yourselves, for I tell you, I will not drink at all again from the fruit of the vine, until the Kingdom of God comes."

He took bread, and when he had given thanks, he broke it, and gave to them, saying, "This is my body which is given for you. Do this in memory of me." Likewise, he took the cup after supper, saying, "This cup is the new covenant in my blood, which is poured out for you.

"Don't let your heart be troubled. Believe in God. Believe also in me. In my Father's house are many homes. If it weren't so, I would have told you. I am going to prepare a place for you. If I go and prepare a place for you, I will come again, and will receive you to myself; that where I am, you may be there also. Where I go, you know, and you know the way."

Thomas said to him, "Lord, we don't know where you are going. How can we know the way?"

Jesus said to him, "I am the way, the truth, and the life. No one comes to the Father, except through me. If you had known me, you would have known my Father also. From now on, you know him, and have seen him."

"I command these things to you, that you may love one another. If the world hates you, you know that it has hated me before it hated you. If you were of the world, the world would love its own. But because you are not of the world, since I chose you out of the world, therefore the world hates you.

"When the Counselor has come, whom I will send to you from the Father, the Spirit of truth, who proceeds from the Father, he will testify about me. You will also testify, because you have been with me from the beginning.

"I have yet many things to tell you, but you can't bear them now. However when he, the Spirit of truth, has come, he will guide you into all truth, for he will not speak from himself; but whatever he hears, he will speak. He will declare to you things that are coming. He will glorify me, for he will take from what is mine, and will declare it to you. All things whatever the Father has are mine; therefore I said that he takes of mine, and will declare it to you. A little while, and you will not see me. Again a little while, and you will see me."

Jesus said these things, and lifting up his eyes to heaven, he said, "Father, the time has come. Glorify your Son, that your Son may also glorify you; even as you gave him authority over all flesh, he will give eternal life to all whom you have given him. This is eternal life, that they should know you, the only true God, and him whom you sent, Jesus Christ. I glorified you on the earth. I have accomplished the work which you have given me to do.

When they had sung a hymn, they went out to the Mount of Olives.

Leaving the place of the Passover feast, Jesus took his disciples to Gethsemane, and he went into the garden there to pray. It was in this location that the chief priests made their move, capturing Jesus with the help of the traitor, Judas.

They came to a place which was named Gethsemane. He said to his disciples, "Sit here, while I pray." He took with him Peter, James, and John, and began to be greatly troubled and distressed. He said to them, "My soul is exceedingly sorrowful, even to death. Stay here, and watch."

He went forward a little, and fell on the ground, and prayed that, if it were possible, the hour might pass away from him. He said, "Abba, Father, all things are possible to you. Please remove this cup from me. However, not what I desire, but what you desire."

An angel from heaven appeared to him, strengthening him. Being in agony he prayed more earnestly. His sweat became like great drops of blood falling down on the ground.

He came and found them sleeping, and said to Peter, "Simon, are you sleeping? Couldn't you watch one hour? Watch and pray, that you may not enter into temptation. The spirit indeed is willing, but the flesh is weak."

Again he went away, and prayed, saying the same words. Again he returned, and found them sleeping, for their eyes were very heavy, and they didn't know what to answer him. He came the third time, and said to them, "Sleep on now, and take your rest. It is enough. The hour has come. Behold, the Son of Man is betrayed into the hands of sinners. Arise, let us be going. Behold, he who betrays me is at hand."

Immediately, while he was still speaking, Judas, one of the twelve, came—and with him a multitude with swords and clubs, from the chief priests, the scribes, and the elders. Now he who betrayed him had given them a sign, saying, "Whomever I will kiss, that is he. Seize him, and lead him away safely." When he had come, immediately he came to him, and said, "Rabbi! Rabbi!" and kissed him.

Jesus therefore, knowing all the things that were happening to him, went forth, and said to them, "Who are you looking for?"

They answered him, "Jesus of Nazareth."

Jesus said to them, "I am he."

Judas also, who betrayed him, was standing with them. When therefore he said to them, "I am he," they went backward, and fell to the ground.

Then they came and laid hands on Jesus, and took him. Behold, one of those who were with Jesus stretched out his hand, and drew his sword, and struck the servant of the high priest, and struck off his ear. Then Jesus said to him, "Put your sword back into its place, for all those who take the sword will die by the sword. Or do you think that I couldn't ask my Father, and he would even now send me more than twelve legions of angels? How then would the Scriptures be fulfilled that it must be so?"

In that hour Jesus said to the multitudes, "Have you come out as against a robber with swords and clubs to seize me? I sat daily in the temple teaching, and you didn't arrest me. But all this has happened, that the Scriptures of the prophets might be fulfilled."

Then all the disciples left him, and fled.

They led Jesus away to the high priest. All the chief priests, the elders, and the scribes came together with him.

The high priest therefore asked Jesus about his disciples, and about his teaching. Jesus answered him, "I spoke openly to the world. I always taught in synagogues, and in the temple, where the Jews always meet. I said nothing in secret. Why do you ask me? Ask those who have heard me what I said to them. Behold, these know the things which I said."

When he had said this, one of the officers standing by slapped Jesus with his hand, saying, "Do you answer the high priest like that?"

Jesus answered him, "If I have spoken evil, testify of the evil; but if well, why do you beat me?"

Now the chief priests and the whole council sought witnesses against Jesus to put him to death, and found none. For many gave false testimony against him, and their testimony didn't agree with each other. Some stood up, and gave false testimony against him, saying, "We heard him say, 'I will destroy this temple that is made with hands, and in three days I will build another made without hands.'" Even so, their testimony did not agree.

The high priest stood up in the midst, and asked Jesus, "Have you no answer? What is it which these testify against you?" But he stayed quiet, and answered nothing. Again the high priest asked him, "Are you the Christ, the Son of the Blessed?"

Jesus said, "I am. You will see the Son of Man sitting at the right hand of Power, and coming with the clouds of the sky."

The high priest tore his clothes, and said, "What further need have we of witnesses? You have heard the blasphemy! What do you think?" They all condemned him to be worthy of death.

The men who held Jesus mocked him and beat him. Having blindfolded him, they struck him on the face and asked him, "Prophesy! Who is the one who struck you?" They spoke many other things against him, insulting him.

Simon Peter followed Jesus, as did another disciple. Now that disciple was known to the high priest, and entered in with Jesus into the court of the high priest; but Peter was standing at the door outside. So the other disciple, who was known to the high priest, went out and spoke to her who kept the door, and brought in Peter. Then the maid who kept the door said to Peter, "Are you also one of this man's disciples?"

He said, "I am not."

As Peter was in the courtyard below, one of the maids of the high priest came, and seeing Peter warming himself, she looked at him, and said, "You were also with the Nazarene, Jesus!"

But he denied it, saying, "I neither know, nor understand what you are saying."

He went out on the porch, and the rooster crowed.

The maid saw him, and began again to tell those who stood by, "This is one of them." But he again denied it.

After about one hour passed, another confidently affirmed, saying, "Truly this man also was with him, for he is a Galilean!"

But Peter said, "Man, I don't know what you are talking about!"

Immediately, while he was still speaking, a rooster crowed. The Lord turned, and looked at Peter. Then Peter remembered the Lord's word, how he said to him, "Before the rooster crows you will deny me three times." He went out, and wept bitterly.

As soon as it was day, the assembly of the elders of the people was gathered together, both chief priests and scribes, and they led him away into their council, saying, "If you are the Christ, tell us."

But he said to them, "If I tell you, you won't believe, and if I ask, you will in no way answer me or let me go. From now on, the Son of Man will be seated at the right hand of the power of God."

They all said, "Are you then the Son of God?"

He said to them, "You say it, because I am."

They said, "Why do we need any more witness? For we ourselves have heard from his own mouth!"

The Jewish court had found Jesus guilty of false charges. However, they did not have the ability to condemn any man to death; this power was reserved by the Romans, and only a Roman official could order death to any prisoner. Therefore, the Jewish court delivered Jesus to Pontius Pilate, the local governor, asking that Jesus be found deserving of execution. In the meantime Judas, feeling guilt and remorse over his betrayal of the Master, returned the money to the chief priests and elders; he threw it on the ground at their feet, he went away and hung himself. The money was used to buy the field where he died, as a place to bury the poor and strangers - a "potter's field."

They bound him, and led him away, and delivered him up to Pontius Pilate, the governor. They led Jesus therefore from Caiaphas into the Praetorium. It was early, and they themselves didn't enter into the Praetorium, that they might not be defiled, but might eat the Passover. Pilate therefore went out to them, and said, "What accusation do you bring against this man?"

They answered him, "If this man weren't an evildoer, we wouldn't have delivered him up to you."

Pilate therefore said to them, "Take him yourselves, and judge him according to your law."

Therefore the Jews said to him, "It is not lawful for us to put anyone to death," that the word of Jesus might be fulfilled, which he spoke, signifying by what kind of death he should die.

Pilate therefore entered again into the Praetorium, called Jesus, and said to him, "Are you the King of the Jews?"

Jesus answered him, "Do you say this by yourself, or did others tell you about me?"

Pilate answered, "I'm not a Jew, am I? Your own nation and the chief priests delivered you to me. What have you done?"

Jesus answered, "My Kingdom is not of this world. If my Kingdom were of this world, then my servants would fight, that I wouldn't be delivered to the Jews. But now my Kingdom is not from here."

Pilate therefore said to him, "Are you a king then?"

Jesus answered, "You say that I am a king. For this reason I have been born, and for this reason I have come into the world, that I should testify to the truth. Everyone who is of the truth listens to my voice."

Pilate said to him, "What is truth?"

When he had said this, he went out again to the Jews, and said to them, "I find no basis for a charge against him.

But they insisted, saying, "He stirs up the people, teaching throughout all Judea, beginning from Galilee even to this place." But when Pilate heard Galilee mentioned, he asked if the man was a Galilean. When he found out that he was in Herod's jurisdiction, he sent him to Herod, who was also in Jerusalem during those days.

Now when Herod saw Jesus, he was exceedingly glad, for he had wanted to see him for a long time, because he had heard many things about him. He hoped to see some miracle done by him. He questioned him with many words, but he gave no answers. The chief priests and the scribes stood, vehemently accusing him. Herod with his soldiers humiliated him and mocked him. Dressing him in luxurious clothing, they sent him back to Pilate. Herod and Pilate became friends with each other that very day, for before that they were enemies with each other.

Now at the feast he used to release to them one prisoner, whom they asked of him. There was one called Barabbas, bound with those who had made insurrection, men who in the insurrection had committed murder. The multitude, crying aloud, began to ask him to do as he always did for them. Pilate answered them, saying, "Do you want me to release to you the King of the Jews?" For he perceived that for envy the chief priests had delivered him up.

351

While he was sitting on the judgment seat, his wife sent to him, saying, "Have nothing to do with that righteous man, for I have suffered many things this day in a dream because of him."

Then they all shouted again, saying, "Not this man, but Barabbas!" Now Barabbas was a robber.

So Pilate then took Jesus, and flogged him. The soldiers twisted thorns into a crown, and put it on his head, and dressed him in a purple garment. They kept saying, "Hail, King of the Jews!" and they kept slapping him.

Then Pilate went out again, and said to them, "Behold, I bring him out to you, that you may know that I find no basis for a charge against him."

Jesus therefore came out, wearing the crown of thorns and the purple garment. Pilate said to them, "Behold, the man!"

Pilate called together the chief priests and the rulers and the people, and said to them, "You brought this man to me as one that perverts the people, and see, I have examined him before you, and found no basis for a charge against this man concerning those things of which you accuse him. Neither has Herod, for I sent you to him, and see, nothing worthy of death has been done by him. I will therefore chastise him and release him."

The Jews answered him, "We have a law, and by our law he ought to die, because he made himself the Son of God."

When therefore Pilate heard this saying, he was more afraid. He entered into the Praetorium again, and said to Jesus, "Where are you from?" But Jesus gave him no answer. Pilate therefore said to him, "Aren't you speaking to me? Don't you know that I have power to release you, and have power to crucify you?"

Jesus answered, "You would have no power at all against me, unless it were given to you from above. Therefore he who delivered me to you has greater sin."

At this, Pilate was seeking to release him, but the Jews cried out, saying, "If you release this man, you aren't Caesar's friend! Everyone who makes himself a king speaks against Caesar!"

When Pilate therefore heard these words, he brought Jesus out, and sat down on the judgment seat at a place called "The Pavement," but in Hebrew, "Gabbatha." Now it was the Preparation Day of the Passover, at about the sixth hour. He said to the Jews, "Behold, your King!"

They cried out, "Away with him! Away with him! Crucify him!"

Pilate said to them, "Shall I crucify your King?"

The chief priests answered, "We have no king but Caesar!"

Pilate said to them, "What then shall I do to Jesus, who is called Christ?"

They all said to him, "Let him be crucified!"

But the governor said, "Why? What evil has he done?"

But they cried out exceedingly, saying, "Let him be crucified!"

So when Pilate saw that nothing was being gained, but rather that a disturbance was starting, he took water, and washed his hands before the multitude, saying, "I am innocent of the blood of this righteous person. You see to it."

All the people answered, "May his blood be on us, and on our children!"

31 THE EMPTY TOMB

Jesus' Crucifixion and Resurrection

Pilate, giving in to the will of the mob, released Jesus to his soldiers to be killed by crucifixion. Although he could have spoken up in his own defense, Jesus remained silent, allowing these events to unfold. In doing so He fulfilled his very purpose for coming to earth in the form of a man – to become a perfect sacrifice for mankind. It seemed as though the enemies of Jesus had won the day. But the violent death of Jesus was just a precursor to a glorious miracle that would forever establish Jesus as our Messiah and Deliverer.

Pilate, wishing to please the multitude, released Barabbas to them, and handed over Jesus, when he had flogged him, to be crucified.

The soldiers led him away within the court, which is the Praetorium; and they called together the whole cohort. They clothed him with purple, and weaving a crown of thorns, they put it on him. They began to salute him, "Hail, King of the Jews!" They struck his head with a reed, and spat on him, and bowing their knees, did homage to him.

When they had mocked him, they took the purple off of him, and put his own garments on him. They led him out to crucify him. They compelled one passing by, coming from the country, Simon of Cyrene, the father of Alexander and Rufus, to go with them, that he might bear his cross.

They brought him to the place called Golgotha, which is, being interpreted, "The place of a skull."

They offered him wine mixed with myrrh to drink, but he didn't take it.

There were also others, two criminals, led with him to be put to death. When they came to the place that is called The Skull, they crucified him there with the criminals, one on the right and the other on the left.

Jesus said, "Father, forgive them, for they don't know what they are doing."

Pilate wrote a title also, and put it on the cross. There was written, "Jesus OF

NAZARETH, THE KING OF THE JEWS." Therefore many of the Jews read this title, for the place where Jesus was crucified was near the city; and it was written in Hebrew, in Latin, and in Greek. The chief priests of the Jews therefore said to Pilate, "Don't write, 'The King of the Jews,' but, 'he said, I am King of the Jews.'"

Pilate answered, "What I have written, I have written."

Then the soldiers, when they had crucified Jesus, took his garments and made four parts, to every soldier a part; and also the coat. Now the coat was without seam, woven from the top throughout. Then they said to one another, "Let's not tear it, but cast lots for it to decide whose it will be," that the Scripture might be fulfilled, which says,

"They parted my garments among them. For my cloak they cast lots."

Therefore the soldiers did these things.

But there were standing by the cross of Jesus his mother, and his mother's sister, Mary the wife of Clopas, and Mary Magdalene. Therefore when Jesus saw his mother, and the disciple whom he loved standing there, he said to his mother, "Woman, behold your son!" Then he said to the disciple, "Behold, your mother!" From that hour, the disciple took her to his own home.

One of the criminals who was hanged insulted him, saying, "If you are the Christ, save yourself and us!"

But the other answered, and rebuking him said, "Don't you even fear God, seeing you are under the same condemnation? And we indeed justly, for we receive the due reward for our deeds, but this man has done nothing wrong." He said to Jesus, "Lord, remember me when you come into your Kingdom."

Jesus said to him, "Assuredly I tell you, today you will be with me in Paradise."

Those who passed by blasphemed him, wagging their heads, and saying, "You who destroy the temple, and build it in three days, save yourself! If you are the Son of God, come down from the cross!"

Likewise the chief priests also mocking, with the scribes, the Pharisees, and the elders, said, "He saved others, but he can't save himself. If he is the King of Israel, let him come down from the cross now, and we will believe in him. He trusts in God. Let God deliver him now, if he wants him; for he said, 'I am the Son of God.'" The robbers also who were crucified with him cast on him the same reproach.

Now from the sixth hour there was darkness over all the land until the ninth hour. About the ninth hour Jesus cried with a loud voice, saying, "Eli, Eli, lima sabachthani?" That is, "My God, my God, why have you forsaken me?"

Some of them who stood there, when they heard it, said, "This man is calling

Elijah."

Immediately one of them ran, and took a sponge, and filled it with vinegar, and put it on a reed, and gave him a drink. The rest said, "Let him be. Let's see whether Elijah comes to save him."

Jesus cried again with a loud voice, and yielded up his spirit. Behold, the veil of the temple was torn in two from the top to the bottom. The earth quaked and the rocks were split. The tombs were opened, and many bodies of the saints who had fallen asleep were raised; and coming out of the tombs after his resurrection, they entered into the holy city and appeared to many. Now the centurion, and those who were with him watching Jesus, when they saw the earthquake, and the things that were done, feared exceedingly, saying, "Truly this was the Son of God."

Many women were there watching from afar, who had followed Jesus from Galilee, serving him. Among them were Mary Magdalene, Mary the mother of James and Joses (Joseph), and the mother of the sons of Zebedee.

Therefore the Jews, because it was the Preparation Day, so that the bodies wouldn't remain on the cross on the Sabbath, asked of Pilate that their legs might be broken, and that they might be taken away. Therefore the soldiers came, and broke the legs of the first, and of the other who was crucified with him; but when they came to Jesus, and saw that he was already dead, they didn't break his legs. However one of the soldiers pierced his side with a spear, and immediately blood and water came out. He who has seen has testified, and his testimony is true. He knows that he tells the truth, that you may believe. For these things happened, that the Scripture might be fulfilled, "A bone of him will not be broken." Again another Scripture says, "They will look on him whom they pierced."

When evening had now come, because it was the Preparation Day, that is, the day before the Sabbath, Joseph of Arimathaea, a prominent council member who also himself was looking for the Kingdom of God, came. He boldly went in to Pilate, and asked for Jesus' body. Pilate marveled if he were already dead; and summoning the centurion, he asked him whether he had been dead long. When he found out from the centurion, he granted the body to Joseph.

Pilate gave him permission. He came therefore and took away his body. Nicodemus, who at first came to Jesus by night, also came bringing a mixture of myrrh and aloes, about a hundred Roman pounds. So they took Jesus' body, and bound it in linen cloths with the spices, as the custom of the Jews is to bury. Now in the place where he was crucified there was a garden. In the garden was a new tomb in which no man had ever yet been laid. Then because of the Jews' Preparation Day (for the tomb was near at hand) they laid Jesus there.

The women, who had come with him out of Galilee, followed after, and saw the tomb, and how his body was laid. They returned, and prepared spices and ointments. On the Sabbath they rested according to the commandment.

Now on the next day, which was the day after the Preparation Day, the chief priests and the Pharisees were gathered together to Pilate, saying, "Sir, we remember what that deceiver said while he was still alive: 'After three days I will rise again.' Command therefore that the tomb be made secure until the third day, lest perhaps his disciples come at night and steal him away, and tell the people, 'He is risen from the dead;' and the last deception will be worse than the first."

Pilate said to them, "You have a guard. Go, make it as secure as you can." So they went with the guard and made the tomb secure, sealing the stone.

When the Sabbath was past, Mary Magdalene, and Mary the mother of James, and Salome, bought spices, that they might come and anoint him.

Behold, there was a great earthquake, for an angel of the Lord descended from the sky, and came and rolled away the stone from the door, and sat on it. His appearance was like lightning, and his clothing white as snow. For fear of him, the guards shook, and became like dead men.

Very early on the first day of the week, they came to the tomb when the sun had risen. They were saying among themselves, "Who will roll away the stone from the door of the tomb for us?" for it was very big. Looking up, they saw that the stone was rolled back.

Entering into the tomb, they saw a young man sitting on the right side, dressed in a white robe, and they were amazed. He said to them, "Don't be amazed. You seek Jesus, the Nazarene, who has been crucified. He has risen. He is not here. Behold, the place where they laid him! But go, tell his disciples and Peter, 'He goes before you into Galilee. There you will see him, as he said to you.'"

They went out, and fled from the tomb, for trembling and astonishment had come on them. They said nothing to anyone; for they were afraid.

Therefore Mary ran and came to Simon Peter, and to the other disciple whom Jesus loved, and said to them, "They have taken away the Lord out of the tomb, and we don't know where they have laid him!"

Therefore Peter and the other disciple went out, and they went toward the tomb. They both ran together. The other disciple outran Peter, and came to the tomb first. Stooping and looking in, he saw the linen cloths lying, yet he didn't enter in. Then Simon Peter came, following him, and entered into the tomb. He saw the linen cloths lying, and the cloth that had been on his head, not lying with the linen cloths, but rolled up in a place by itself. So then the other disciple who came first to the tomb also entered in, and he saw and believed. For as yet they didn't know the Scripture, that he must rise from the dead. So the disciples went away again to their own homes.

But Mary was standing outside at the tomb weeping. So, as she wept, she stooped and looked into the tomb, and she saw two angels in white sitting, one at the head, and one at the feet, where the body of Jesus had lain. They told her, "Woman, why are you weeping?"

She said to them, "Because they have taken away my Lord, and I don't know where they have laid him." When she had said this, she turned around and saw Jesus standing, and didn't know that it was Jesus.

Jesus said to her, "Woman, why are you weeping? Who are you looking for?"

She, supposing him to be the gardener, said to him, "Sir, if you have carried him away, tell me where you have laid him, and I will take him away."

Jesus said to her, "Mary."

She turned and said to him, "Rabboni!" which is to say, "Teacher!"

Jesus said to her, "Don't hold me, for I haven't yet ascended to my Father; but go to my brothers, and tell them, 'I am ascending to my Father and your Father, to my God and your God.' Mary Magdalene came and told the disciples that she had seen the Lord, and that he had said these things to her.

As they went to tell his disciples, behold, Jesus met them, saying, "Rejoice!"

They came and took hold of his feet, and worshiped him.

Then Jesus said to them, "Don't be afraid. Go tell my brothers that they should go into Galilee, and there they will see me."

Now while they were going, behold, some of the guards came into the city, and told the chief priests all the things that had happened. When they were assembled with the elders, and had taken counsel, they gave a large amount of silver to the soldiers, saying, "Say that his disciples came by night, and stole him away while we slept. If this comes to the governor's ears, we will persuade him and make you free of worry." So they took the money and did as they were told.

The key event in God's plan for mankind had unfolded. With the empty tomb, Jesus conquered death, and rose triumphantly over Satan and all the enemies of God. In his life trials, crucifixion and resurrection, Jesus fulfilled over 300 prophesies that had made hundreds of years before these events by the prophets.

Jesus began to show himself to his disciples after his resurrection. On one occasion, He appeared to Cleopas and another disciple as they walked along the road to a village called Emmaus. After Jesus ate a meal with them, he vanished out of sight. They immediately returned to report what they saw to the remaining 11 apostles.

Behold, two of them were going that very day to a village named Emmaus, which was sixty stadia from Jerusalem. They talked with each other about all of these things which had happened. It happened, while they talked and questioned together, that Jesus himself came near, and went with them. But their eyes were kept from recognizing him. He said to them, "What are you talking about as you walk, and are sad?"

One of them, named Cleopas, answered him, "Are you the only stranger in Jerusalem who doesn't know the things which have happened there in these days?"

He said to them, "What things?"

They said to him, "The things concerning Jesus, the Nazarene, who was a prophet mighty in deed and word before God and all the people; and how the chief priests and our rulers delivered him up to be condemned to death, and crucified him. But we were hoping that it was he who would redeem Israel. Yes, and besides all this, it is now the third day since these things happened. Also, certain women of our company amazed us, having arrived early at the tomb; and when they didn't find his body, they came saying that they had also seen a vision of angels, who said that he was alive. Some of us went to the tomb, and found it just like the women had said, but they didn't see him."

He said to them, "Foolish men, and slow of heart to believe in all that the prophets have spoken! Didn't the Christ have to suffer these things and to enter into his glory?" Beginning from Moses and from all the prophets, he explained to them in all the Scriptures the things concerning himself.

They drew near to the village, where they were going, and he acted like he would go further.

They urged him, saying, "Stay with us, for it is almost evening, and the day is almost over."

He went in to stay with them. It happened, that when he had sat down at the table with them, he took the bread and gave thanks. Breaking it, he gave to them. Their eyes were opened, and they recognized him, and he vanished out of their sight. They said one to another, "Weren't our hearts burning within us, while he spoke to us along the way, and while he opened the Scriptures to us?"

They rose up that very hour, returned to Jerusalem, and found the eleven gathered together, and those who were with them, saying, "The Lord is risen indeed, and has appeared to Simon!" They related the things that happened along the way, and how he was recognized by them in the breaking of the bread.

As they said these things, Jesus himself stood among them, and said to them, "Peace be to you."

But they were terrified and filled with fear, and supposed they had seen a spirit.

He said to them, "Why are you troubled? Why do doubts arise in your hearts? See my hands and my feet, that it is truly me. Touch me and see, for a spirit doesn't have flesh and bones, as you see that I have." When he had said this, he showed them his hands and his feet. While they still didn't believe for joy, and wondered, he said to them, "Do you have anything here to eat?"

They gave him a piece of a broiled fish and some honeycomb. He took them, and ate in front of them. He said to them, "This is what I told you, while I was still with you, that all things which are written in the law of Moses, the prophets, and the psalms, concerning me must be fulfilled."

Jesus therefore said to them again, "Peace be to you. As the Father has sent me, even so I send you." When he had said this, he breathed on them, and said to them, "Receive the Holy Spirit! If you forgive anyone's sins, they have been forgiven them. If you retain anyone's sins, they have been retained."

But Thomas, one of the twelve, called Didymus, wasn't with them when Jesus came. The other disciples therefore said to him, "We have seen the Lord!"

But he said to them, "Unless I see in his hands the print of the nails, and put my hand into his side, I will not believe."

After eight days again his disciples were inside, and Thomas was with them. Jesus came, the doors being locked, and stood in the midst, and said, "Peace be to you." Then he said to Thomas, "Reach here your finger, and see my hands. Reach here your hand, and put it into my side. Don't be unbelieving, but believing."

Thomas answered him, "My Lord and my God!"

Jesus said to him, "Because you have seen me, you have believed. Blessed are those who have not seen, and have believed."

Therefore Jesus did many other signs in the presence of his disciples, which are not written in this book; but these are written, that you may believe that Jesus is the Christ, the Son of God, and that believing you may have life in his name.

Jesus again made an appearance before some of the apostles at the sea of Tiberius. When He told the apostles to cast their nets on the right side of the boat, they had a great catch of fish, and then they were able to recognize who He was. Bringing the net to shore, they began to cook some of the fish.

This is now the third time that Jesus was revealed to his disciples, after he had risen from the dead.

So when they had eaten their breakfast, Jesus said to Simon Peter, "Simon, son of Jonah, do you love me more than these?"

He said to him, "Yes, Lord; you know that I have affection for you."

He said to him, "Feed my lambs." He said to him again a second time, "Simon, son of Jonah, do you love me?"

He said to him, "Yes, Lord; you know that I have affection for you."

He said to him, "Tend my sheep." He said to him the third time, "Simon, son of Jonah, do you have affection for me?"

Peter was grieved because he asked him the third time, "Do you have affection for me?" He said to him, "Lord, you know everything. You know that I have affection for you."

Jesus said to him, "Feed my sheep.

But the eleven disciples went into Galilee, to the mountain where Jesus had sent them. When they saw him, they bowed down to him, but some doubted. Jesus came to them and spoke to them, saying, "All authority has been given to me in heaven and on earth. Go, and make disciples of all nations, baptizing them in the name of the Father and of the Son and of the Holy Spirit, teaching them to observe all things that I commanded you. Behold, I am with you always, even to the end of the age."

He who believes and is baptized will be saved; but he who disbelieves will be condemned. These signs will accompany those who believe: in my name they will cast out demons; they will speak with new languages; they will take up serpents; and if they drink any deadly thing, it will in no way hurt them; they will lay hands on the sick, and they will recover."

On another occasion, Jesus appeared to more than 500 disciples at one time. He also appeared to James, and on another occasion to all of the apostles. Although sometimes short and fleeting, his appearances were important in firmly establishing the truth of his resurrection. Finally, the time came for Jesus to ascend to heaven permanently.

Then he opened their minds, that they might understand the Scriptures. He said to them, "Thus it is written, and thus it was necessary for the Christ to suffer and to rise from the dead the third day, and that repentance and remission of sins should be preached in his name to all the nations, beginning at Jerusalem. You are witnesses of these things. Behold, I send forth the promise of my Father on you. But wait in the city of Jerusalem until you are clothed with power from on high."

He led them out as far as Bethany, and he lifted up his hands, and blessed them. It happened, while he blessed them, that he withdrew from them, and was carried up into heaven.

They worshiped him, and returned to Jerusalem with great joy, and were continually in the temple, praising and blessing God.

There are also many other things which Jesus did, which if they would all be written, I suppose that even the world itself wouldn't have room for the books that would be written.

32 THE NEW BEGINNING

Establishment of the Church

The history of the early church was recorded in the Bible by the disciple Luke, a physician from the Greek city of Antioch. He wrote the gospel of Luke and the book of Acts., which were addressed to a man known as Theophilus. In the Book of the Acts of the Apostles, Luke recorded the amazing beginning and growth of Christianity after the resurrection of Jesus Christ. The book begins with the ascension of Jesus to Heaven, and follows up with the church encountering an amazing demonstration of power by the Holy Spirit.

The first book I wrote, Theophilus, concerned all that Jesus began both to do and to teach, until the day in which he was received up, after he had given commandment through the Holy Spirit to the apostles whom he had chosen. To these he also showed himself alive after he suffered, by many proofs, appearing to them over a period of forty days, and speaking about God's Kingdom. Being assembled together with them, he commanded them, "Don't depart from Jerusalem, but wait for the promise of the Father, which you heard from me. For John indeed baptized in water, but you will be baptized in the Holy Spirit not many days from now."

Therefore when they had come together, they asked him, "Lord, are you now restoring the kingdom to Israel?"

He said to them, "It isn't for you to know times or seasons which the Father has set within his own authority. But you will receive power when the Holy Spirit has come upon you. You will be witnesses to me in Jerusalem, in all Judea and Samaria, and to the uttermost parts of the earth."

When he had said these things, as they were looking, he was taken up, and a cloud received him out of their sight. While they were looking steadfastly into the sky as he went, behold, two men stood by them in white clothing, who also said, "You men of Galilee, why do you stand looking into the sky? This Jesus, who was received up from you into the sky will come back in the same way as you saw him going into the sky."

Now when the day of Pentecost had come, they were all with one accord in one place. Suddenly there came from the sky a sound like the rushing of a mighty wind, and it filled all the house where they were sitting. Tongues like fire appeared and were distributed to them, and one sat on each of them. They were all filled with the Holy Spirit, and began to speak with other languages, as the Spirit gave them the ability to speak. Now there were dwelling in Jerusalem Jews, devout men, from every nation under the sky. When this sound was heard, the multitude came together, and were bewildered, because everyone heard them speaking in his own language. They were all amazed and marveled, saying to one another, "Behold, aren't all these who speak Galileans? How do we hear, everyone in our own native language?

They were all amazed, and were perplexed, saying one to another, "What does this mean?" Others, mocking, said, "They are filled with new wine."

But Peter, standing up with the eleven, lifted up his voice, and spoke out to them, "You men of Judea, and all you who dwell at Jerusalem, let this be known to you, and listen to my words. For these aren't drunken, as you suppose, seeing it is only the third hour of the day. But this is what has been spoken through the prophet Joel:

'It will be in the last days, says God,
that I will pour out my Spirit on all flesh.
Your sons and your daughters will prophesy.
Your young men will see visions.
Your old men will dream dreams.
Yes, and on my servants and on my handmaidens in those days,
I will pour out my Spirit, and they will prophesy.
I will show wonders in the sky above,
and signs on the earth beneath;
blood, and fire, and billows of smoke.
The sun will be turned into darkness,
and the moon into blood,
before the great and glorious day of the Lord comes.
It will be, that whoever will call on the name of the Lord will be saved.'

"Men of Israel, hear these words! Jesus of Nazareth, a man approved by God to you by mighty works and wonders and signs which God did by him in the midst of you, even as you yourselves know, him, being delivered up by the determined counsel and foreknowledge of God, you have taken by the hand of lawless men, crucified and killed; whom God raised up, having freed him from the agony of death, because it was not possible that he should be held by it.

"Brothers, I may tell you freely of the patriarch David, that he both died and was buried, and his tomb is with us to this day. Therefore, being a prophet, and knowing that God had sworn with an oath to him that of the fruit of his body, according to the flesh, he would raise up the Christ to sit on his throne, he foreseeing this spoke about the resurrection of the Christ, that neither was his soul left in Hades, nor did his flesh see decay. This Jesus God raised up, to which we all are witnesses. Being therefore exalted by the right hand of God, and having received from the Father the promise of the Holy Spirit, he has poured out this, which you now see and hear

"Let all the house of Israel therefore know certainly that God has made him both Lord and Christ, this Jesus whom you crucified."

Now when they heard this, they were cut to the heart, and said to Peter and the rest of the apostles, "Brothers, what shall we do?"

Peter said to them, "Repent, and be baptized, every one of you, in the name of Jesus Christ for the forgiveness of sins, and you will receive the gift of the Holy Spirit. For the promise is to you, and to your children, and to all who are far off, even as many as the Lord our God will call to himself." With many other words he testified, and exhorted them, saying, "Save yourselves from this crooked generation!"

Then those who gladly received his word were baptized. There were added that day about three thousand souls. They continued steadfastly in the apostles' teaching and fellowship, in the breaking of bread, and prayer. Fear came on every soul, and many wonders and signs were done through the apostles. All who believed were together, and had all things in common. They sold their possessions and goods, and distributed them to all, according as anyone had need. Day by day, continuing steadfastly with one accord in the temple, and breaking bread at home, they took their food with gladness and singleness of heart, praising God, and having favor with all the people. The Lord added to the assembly day by day those who were being saved.

Peter and John were going up into the temple at the hour of prayer, the ninth hour. A certain man who was lame from his mother's womb was being carried, whom they laid daily at the door of the temple which is called Beautiful, to ask gifts for the needy of those who entered into the temple. Seeing Peter and John about to go into the temple, he asked to receive gifts for the needy. Peter, fastening his eyes on him, with John, said, "Look at us." He listened to them, expecting to receive something from them. But Peter said, "Silver and gold have I none, but what I have, that I give you. In the name of Jesus Christ of Nazareth, get up and walk!" He took him by the right hand, and raised him up. Immediately his feet and his ankle bones received strength. Leaping up, he stood, and began to walk. He entered with them into the temple, walking, leaping, and praising God. All the people saw him walking and praising God. They recognized him, that it was he who used to sit begging for gifts for the needy at the Beautiful Gate of the temple. They were filled with wonder and amazement at what had happened to him. As the lame man who was healed held on to Peter and John, all the people ran together to them in the porch that is called Solomon's, greatly wondering.

When Peter saw it, he responded to the people, "You men of Israel, why do you marvel at this man? Why do you fasten your eyes on us, as though by our own power or godliness we had made him walk? The God of Abraham, Isaac, and Jacob, the God of our fathers, has glorified his Servant Jesus, whom you delivered up, and denied in the presence of Pilate, when he had determined to release him. But you denied the Holy and Righteous One, and asked for a murderer to be granted to you, and killed the Prince of life, whom God raised from the dead, to which we are witnesses. By faith in his name, his name has made this man strong, whom you see and know. Yes, the faith which is through him has given him this perfect soundness in the presence of you all.

"Now, brothers, I know that you did this in ignorance, as did also your rulers. But the things which God announced by the mouth of all his prophets, that Christ should suffer, he thus fulfilled.

"Repent therefore, and turn again, that your sins may be blotted out, so that there may come times of refreshing from the presence of the Lord, and that he may send Christ Jesus, who was ordained for you before.

As they spoke to the people, the priests and the captain of the temple and the Sadducees came to them, being upset because they taught the people and proclaimed in Jesus the resurrection from the dead. They laid hands on them, and put them in custody until the next day, for it was now evening. But many of those who heard the word believed, and the number of the men came to be about five thousand.

It happened in the morning, that their rulers, elders, and scribes were gathered together in Jerusalem. Annas the high priest was there, with Caiaphas, John, Alexander, and as many as were relatives of the high priest. When they had stood them in the middle of them, they inquired, "By what power, or in what name, have you done this?"

Then Peter, filled with the Holy Spirit, said to them, "You rulers of the people, and elders of Israel, if we are examined today concerning a good deed done to a crippled man, by what means this man has been healed, be it known to you all, and to all the people of Israel, that in the name of Jesus Christ of Nazareth, whom you crucified, whom God raised from the dead, in him does this man stand here before you whole. He is 'the stone which was regarded as worthless by you, the builders, which has become the head of the corner.' There is salvation in none other, for neither is there any other name under heaven, that is given among men, by which we must be saved!"

Now when they saw the boldness of Peter and John, and had perceived that they were unlearned and ignorant men, they marveled. They recognized that they had been with Jesus. Seeing the man who was healed standing with them, they could say nothing against it. But when they had commanded them to go aside out of the council, they conferred among themselves, saying, "What shall we do to these men? Because indeed a notable miracle has been done through them, as can be plainly seen by all who dwell in Jerusalem, and we can't deny it. But so that this spreads no further among the people, let's threaten them, that from now on they don't speak to anyone in this name." They called them, and commanded them not to speak at all nor teach in the name of Jesus.

But Peter and John answered them, "Whether it is right in the sight of God to listen to you rather than to God, judge for yourselves, for we can't help telling the things which we saw and heard."

When they had further threatened them, they let them go, finding no way to punish them, because of the people; for everyone glorified God for that which was done.

For the man on whom this miracle of healing was performed was more than forty years old.

Being let go, they came to their own company, and reported all that the chief priests and the elders had said to them.

When they had prayed, the place was shaken where they were gathered together. They were all filled with the Holy Spirit, and they spoke the word of God with boldness.

The multitude of those who believed were of one heart and soul. Not one of them claimed that anything of the things which he possessed was his own, but they had all things in common. With great power, the apostles gave their testimony of the resurrection of the Lord Jesus. Great grace was on them all. For neither was there among them any who lacked, for as many as were owners of lands or houses sold them, and brought the proceeds of the things that were sold, and laid them at the apostles' feet, and distribution was made to each, according as anyone had need.

By the hands of the apostles many signs and wonders were done among the people. They were all with one accord in Solomon's porch. None of the rest dared to join them, however the people honored them. More believers were added to the Lord, multitudes of both men and women. They even carried out the sick into the streets, and laid them on cots and mattresses, so that as Peter came by, at the least his shadow might overshadow some of them. Multitudes also came together from the cities around Jerusalem, bringing sick people, and those who were tormented by unclean spirits: and they were all healed.

But the high priest rose up, and all those who were with him (which is the sect of the Sadducees), and they were filled with jealousy, and laid hands on the apostles, and put them in public custody. But an angel of the Lord opened the prison doors by night, and brought them out, and said, "Go stand and speak in the temple to the people all the words of this life."

When they heard this, they entered into the temple about daybreak, and taught. But the high priest came, and those who were with him, and called the council together, and all the senate of the children of Israel, and sent to the prison to have them brought. But the officers who came didn't find them in the prison. They returned and reported, "We found the prison shut and locked, and the guards standing before the doors, but when we opened them, we found no one inside!"

Now when the high priest, the captain of the temple, and the chief priests heard these words, they were very perplexed about them and what might become of this. One came and told them, "Behold, the men whom you put in prison are in the temple, standing and teaching the people." Then the captain went with the officers, and brought them without violence, for they were afraid that the people might stone them.

When they had brought them, they set them before the council. The high priest questioned them, saying, "Didn't we strictly command you not to teach in this name? Behold, you have filled Jerusalem with your teaching, and intend to bring this man's blood on us."

But Peter and the apostles answered, "We must obey God rather than men. The God of our fathers raised up Jesus, whom you killed, hanging him on a tree. God exalted him with his right hand to be a Prince and a Savior, to give repentance to Israel, and remission of sins. We are His witnesses of these things; and so also is the Holy Spirit, whom God has given to those who obey him."

But they, when they heard this, were cut to the heart, and determined to kill them. But one stood up in the council, a Pharisee named Gamaliel, a teacher of the law, honored by all the people, and commanded to put the apostles out for a little while. He said to them, "You men of Israel, be careful concerning these men, what you are about to do. For before these days Theudas rose up, making himself out to be somebody; to whom a number of men, about four hundred, joined themselves: who was slain; and all, as many as obeyed him, were dispersed, and came to nothing. After this man, Judas of Galilee rose up in the days of the enrollment, and drew away some people after him. He also perished, and all, as many as obeyed him, were scattered abroad. Now I tell you, withdraw from these men, and leave them alone. For if this counsel or this work is of men, it will be overthrown. But if it is of God, you will not be able to overthrow it, and you would be found even to be fighting against God!"

They agreed with him. Summoning the apostles, they beat them and commanded them not to speak in the name of Jesus, and let them go. They therefore departed from the presence of the council, rejoicing that they were counted worthy to suffer dishonor for Jesus' name.

Every day, in the temple and at home, they never stopped teaching and preaching Jesus, the Christ.

As the early church grew, seven men were tasked to help with organizational needs, so that the apostles could devote themselves to the word of God. Among these men were Philip and the disciple Stephen, who was described as a man "full of faith and the Holy Spirit."

Stephen, full of faith and power, performed great wonders and signs among the people. But some of those who were of the synagogue called "The Libertines," and of the Cyrenians, of the Alexandrians, and of those of Cilicia and Asia arose, disputing with Stephen. They weren't able to withstand the wisdom and the Spirit by which he spoke. Then they secretly induced men to say, "We have heard him speak blasphemous words against Moses and God." They stirred up the people, the elders, and the scribes, and came against him and seized him, and brought him in to the council, and set up false witnesses who said, "This man never stops speaking blasphemous words against this holy place and the law. For we have heard him say that this Jesus of Nazareth will destroy this place, and will change the customs which Moses delivered to us." All who sat in the council, fastening their eyes on him, saw his face like it was the face of an angel.

The high priest said, "Are these things so?"

Stephen delivered a powerful address to the Jewish council, in which he traveled through the scriptures, showing how they pointed to Jesus Christ as the Messiah. From the time of Abraham, to Moses and the early kings of Israel, Stephen showed that God's people had a long history of rejecting God's messengers. Having set the stage, Stephen then holds back nothing in his scathing rebuke of the unbelieving religious leaders of the day. For this he paid the ultimate price.

"You stiff-necked and uncircumcised in heart and ears, you always resist the Holy Spirit! As your fathers did, so you do. Which of the prophets didn't your fathers persecute? They killed those who foretold the coming of the Righteous One, of whom you have now become betrayers and murderers. You received the law as it was ordained by angels, and didn't keep it!"

Now when they heard these things, they were cut to the heart, and they gnashed at him with their teeth. But he, being full of the Holy Spirit, looked up steadfastly into heaven, and saw the glory of God, and Jesus standing on the right hand of God, and said, "Behold, I see the heavens opened, and the Son of Man standing at the right hand of God!"

But they cried out with a loud voice, and stopped their ears, and rushed at him with one accord. They threw him out of the city, and stoned him. The witnesses placed their garments at the feet of a young man named Saul. They stoned Stephen as he called out, saying, "Lord Jesus, receive my spirit!" He kneeled down, and cried with a loud voice, "Lord, don't hold this sin against them!" When he had said this, he fell asleep.

Saul was consenting to his death. A great persecution arose against the assembly which was in Jerusalem in that day. They were all scattered abroad throughout the regions of Judea and Samaria, except for the apostles. Devout men buried Stephen, and lamented greatly over him. But Saul ravaged the assembly, entering into every house, and dragged both men and women off to prison. Therefore those who were scattered abroad went around preaching the word. Philip went down to the city of Samaria, and proclaimed to them the Christ. The multitudes listened with one accord to the things that were spoken by Philip, when they heard and saw the signs which he did. For unclean spirits came out of many of those who had them. They came out, crying with a loud voice. Many who had been paralyzed and lame were healed. There was great joy in that city.

But an angel of the Lord spoke to Philip, saying, "Arise, and go toward the south to the way that goes down from Jerusalem to Gaza. This is a desert."

He arose and went; and behold, there was a man of Ethiopia, a eunuch of great authority under Candace, queen of the Ethiopians, who was over all her treasure, who had come to Jerusalem to worship. He was returning and sitting in his chariot, and was reading the prophet Isaiah.

The Spirit said to Philip, "Go near, and join yourself to this chariot."

Philip ran to him, and heard him reading Isaiah the prophet, and said, "Do you understand what you are reading?"

He said, "How can I, unless someone explains it to me?" He begged Philip to come up and sit with him. Now the passage of the Scripture which he was reading was this,

"He was led as a sheep to the slaughter.

As a lamb before his shearer is silent,

so he doesn't open his mouth.

In his humiliation, his judgment was taken away.

Who will declare His generation?

For his life is taken from the earth."

The eunuch answered Philip, "Who is the prophet talking about? About himself, or about someone else?"

Philip opened his mouth, and beginning from this Scripture, preached to him Jesus. As they went on the way, they came to some water, and the eunuch said, "Behold, here is water. What is keeping me from being baptized?"

He commanded the chariot to stand still, and they both went down into the water, both Philip and the eunuch, and he baptized him.

When they came up out of the water, the Spirit of the Lord caught Philip away, and the eunuch didn't see him any more, for he went on his way rejoicing.

But Saul, still breathing threats and slaughter against the disciples of the Lord, went to the high priest, and asked for letters from him to the synagogues of Damascus, that if he found any who were of the Way, whether men or women, he might bring them bound to Jerusalem. As he traveled, it happened that he got close to Damascus, and suddenly a light from the sky shone around him. He fell on the earth, and heard a voice saying to him, "Saul, Saul, why do you persecute me?"

He said, "Who are you, Lord?"

The Lord said, "I am Jesus, whom you are persecuting. But rise up, and enter into the city, and you will be told what you must do."

The men who traveled with him stood speechless, hearing the sound, but seeing no one. Saul arose from the ground, and when his eyes were opened, he saw no one. They led him by the hand, and brought him into Damascus. He was without sight for three days, and neither ate nor drank.

Now there was a certain disciple at Damascus named Ananias. The Lord said to him in a vision, "Ananias!"

He said, "Behold, it's me, Lord."

The Lord said to him, "Arise, and go to the street which is called Straight, and inquire in the house of Judah for one named Saul, a man of Tarsus. For behold, he is praying, and in a vision he has seen a man named Ananias coming in, and laying his hands on him, that he might receive his sight."

But Ananias answered, "Lord, I have heard from many about this man, how much evil he did to your saints at Jerusalem. Here he has authority from the chief priests to bind all who call on your name."

But the Lord said to him, "Go your way, for he is my chosen vessel to bear my name before the nations and kings, and the children of Israel. For I will show him how many things he must suffer for my name's sake."

Ananias departed, and entered into the house. Laying his hands on him, he said, "Brother Saul, the Lord, who appeared to you on the road by which you came, has sent me, that you may receive your sight, and be filled with the Holy Spirit." Immediately something like scales fell from his eyes, and he received his sight. He arose and was baptized. He took food and was strengthened. Saul stayed several days with the disciples who were at Damascus. Immediately in the synagogues he proclaimed the Christ, that he is the Son of God. All who heard him were amazed, and said, "Isn't this he who in Jerusalem made havoc of those who called on this name? And he had come here intending to bring them bound before the chief priests!"

But Saul increased more in strength, and confounded the Jews who lived at Damascus, proving that this is the Christ. When many days were fulfilled, the Jews conspired together to kill him, but their plot became known to Saul. They watched the gates both day and night that they might kill him, but his disciples took him by night, and let him down through the wall, lowering him in a basket. When Saul had come to Jerusalem, he tried to join himself to the disciples; but they were all afraid of him, not believing that he was a disciple. But Barnabas took him, and brought him to the apostles, and declared to them how he had seen the Lord in the way, and that he had spoken to him, and how at Damascus he had preached boldly in the name of Jesus. He was with them entering into Jerusalem, preaching boldly in the name of the Lord Jesus. He spoke and disputed against the Hellenists, but they were seeking to kill him. When the brothers knew it, they brought him down to Caesarea, and sent him off to Tarsus. So the assemblies throughout all Judea and Galilee and Samaria had peace, and were built up. They were multiplied, walking in the fear of the Lord and in the comfort of the Holy Spirit.

The conversion of Saul (later known as Paul) was a key moment in the history of the early church. The man who had been persecuting Christians became an apostle and a leading force in adding more converts to the church. Also, Peter was performing amazing miracles, which confirmed the word of God to the early disciples. But it was Cornelius, a devout centurion soldier, who became the first Gentile (non Jewish) convert to Christianity.

Now there was a certain man in Caesarea, Cornelius by name, a centurion of what was called the Italian Regiment, a devout man, and one who feared God with all his house, who gave gifts for the needy generously to the people, and always prayed to God. At about the ninth hour of the day, he clearly saw in a vision an angel of God coming to him, and saying to him, "Cornelius!"

He, fastening his eyes on him, and being frightened, said, "What is it, Lord?"

He said to him, "Your prayers and your gifts to the needy have gone up for a memorial before God. Now send men to Joppa, and get Simon, who is surnamed Peter. He lodges with one Simon, a tanner, whose house is by the seaside."

When the angel who spoke to him had departed, Cornelius called two of his household servants and a devout soldier of those who waited on him continually. Having explained everything to them, he sent them to Joppa. Now on the next day as they were on their journey, and got close to the city, Peter went up on the housetop to pray at about noon. He became hungry and desired to eat, but while they were preparing, he fell into a trance. He saw heaven opened and a certain container descending to him, like a great sheet let down by four corners on the earth, in which were all kinds of four-footed animals of the earth, wild animals, reptiles, and birds of the sky. A voice came to him, "Rise, Peter, kill and eat!"

But Peter said, "Not so, Lord; for I have never eaten anything that is common or unclean."

A voice came to him again the second time, "What God has cleansed, you must not call unclean." This was done three times, and immediately the vessel was received up into heaven. Now while Peter was very perplexed in himself what the vision which he had seen might mean, behold, the men who were sent by Cornelius, having made inquiry for Simon's house, stood before the gate, and called and asked whether Simon, who was surnamed Peter, was lodging there. While Peter was pondering the vision, the Spirit said to him, "Behold, three men seek you. But arise, get down, and go with them, doubting nothing; for I have sent them."

Peter went down to the men, and said, "Behold, I am he whom you seek. Why have you come?"

They said, "Cornelius, a centurion, a righteous man and one who fears God, and well spoken of by all the nation of the Jews, was directed by a holy angel to invite you to his house, and to listen to what you say." So he called them in and lodged them. On the next day Peter arose and went out with them, and some of the brothers from Joppa accompanied him. On the next day they entered into

Caesarea. Cornelius was waiting for them, having called together his relatives and his near friends. When it happened that Peter entered, Cornelius met him, fell down at his feet, and worshiped him. But Peter raised him up, saying, "Stand up! I myself am also a man." As he talked with him, he went in and found many gathered together.

Peter opened his mouth and said, "Truly I perceive that God doesn't show favoritism; but in every nation he who fears him and works righteousness is acceptable to him.

The word which he sent to the children of Israel, preaching good news of peace by Jesus Christ - he is Lord of all - you yourselves know what happened, which was proclaimed throughout all Judea, beginning from Galilee, after the baptism which John preached; even Jesus of Nazareth, how God anointed him with the Holy Spirit and with power, who went about doing good and healing all who were oppressed by the devil, for God was with him.

We are witnesses of everything he did both in the country of the Jews, and in Jerusalem; whom they also killed, hanging him on a tree. God raised him up the third day, and gave him to be revealed, not to all the people, but to witnesses who were chosen before by God, to us, who ate and drank with him after he rose from the dead. He commanded us to preach to the people and to testify that this is he who is appointed by God as the Judge of the living and the dead. All the prophets testify about him, that through his name everyone who believes in him will receive remission of sins."

While Peter was still speaking these words, the Holy Spirit fell on all those who heard the word. They of the circumcision who believed were amazed, as many as came with Peter, because the gift of the Holy Spirit was also poured out on the Gentiles. For they heard them speaking in other languages and magnifying God.

Then Peter answered, "Can any man forbid the water, that these who have received the Holy Spirit as well as we should not be baptized?" He commanded them to be baptized in the name of Jesus Christ. Then they asked him to stay some days.

Peter soon told the other apostles and disciples about his dream and the subsequent conversion of Cornelius and his household. When they heard that the Holy Spirit had come upon them as it had upon the disciples on the Day of Pentecost, they realized that God had opened up the church to the Gentiles.

Those disciples who moved away from Jerusalem due to persecution were preaching and developing converts over a broad region. The very persecution designed to destroy the church was causing it to expand in many regions.

Now about that time, King Herod stretched out his hands to oppress some of the assembly. He killed James, the brother of John, with the sword. When he saw that it pleased the Jews, he proceeded to seize Peter also. This was during the days of unleavened bread. When he had arrested him, he put him in prison, and delivered him to four squads of four soldiers each to guard him, intending to bring him out to the people after the Passover. Peter therefore was kept in the prison, but constant prayer was made by the assembly to God for him. The same night when Herod was about to bring him out, Peter was sleeping between two soldiers, bound with two chains. Guards in front of the door kept the prison.

And behold, an angel of the Lord stood by him, and a light shone in the cell. He struck Peter on the side, and woke him up, saying, "Stand up quickly!" His chains fell off from his hands. The angel said to him, "Get dressed and put on your sandals." He did so. He said to him, "Put on your cloak, and follow me." And he went out and followed him. He didn't know that what was being done by the angel was real, but thought he saw a vision. When they were past the first and the second guard, they came to the iron gate that leads into the city, which opened to them by itself. They went out, and went down one street, and immediately the angel departed from him.

When Peter had come to himself, he said, "Now I truly know that the Lord has sent out his angel and delivered me out of the hand of Herod, and from everything the Jewish people were expecting." Thinking about that, he came to the house of Mary, the mother of John whose surname was Mark, where many were gathered together and were praying. When Peter knocked at the door of the gate, a maid named Rhoda came to answer. When she recognized Peter's voice, she didn't open the gate for joy, but ran in, and reported that Peter was standing in front of the gate.

They said to her, "You are crazy!" But she insisted that it was so. They said, "It is his angel." But Peter continued knocking. When they had opened, they saw him, and were amazed. But he, beckoning to them with his hand to be silent, declared to them how the Lord had brought him out of the prison. He said, "Tell these things to James, and to the brothers." Then he departed, and went to another place.

Now as soon as it was day, there was no small stir among the soldiers about what had become of Peter. When Herod had sought for him, and didn't find him, he examined the guards, and commanded that they should be put to death.

But the word of God grew and multiplied.

Barnabas and Saul returned to Jerusalem, when they had fulfilled their service, also taking with them John whose surname was Mark.

33 HITTING THE ROAD

The First and Second Missionary Journeys of Paul

After Saul had time to establish himself as a true believer among the Christians, he embarked on a series of missionary journeys to spread the gospel. Accompanied by trusted disciples on his journeys, Saul, soon to be known as Paul, was instrumental in establishing congregations throughout the Mediterranean region.

Now in the assembly that was at Antioch there were some prophets and teachers: Barnabas, Simeon who was called Niger, Lucius of Cyrene, Manaen the foster brother of Herod the tetrarch, and Saul. As they served the Lord and fasted, the Holy Spirit said, "Separate Barnabas and Saul for me, for the work to which I have called them."

Then, when they had fasted and prayed and laid their hands on them, they sent them away. So, being sent out by the Holy Spirit, they went down to Seleucia. From there they sailed to Cyprus. When they were at Salamis, they proclaimed the word of God in the Jewish synagogues. They had also John as their attendant. When they had gone through the island to Paphos, they found a certain sorcerer, a false prophet, a Jew, whose name was Bar Jesus, who was with the proconsul, Sergius Paulus, a man of understanding. This man summoned Barnabas and Saul, and sought to hear the word of God. But Elymas the sorcerer (for so is his name by interpretation) withstood them, seeking to turn aside the proconsul from the faith. But Saul, who is also called Paul, filled with the Holy Spirit, fastened his eyes on him, and said, "Full of all deceit and all cunning, you son of the devil, you enemy of all righteousness, will you not cease to pervert the right ways of the Lord? Now, behold, the hand of the Lord is on you, and you will be blind, not seeing the sun for a season!"

Immediately a mist and darkness fell on him. He went around seeking someone to lead him by the hand. Then the proconsul, when he saw what was done, believed, being astonished at the teaching of the Lord.

Now Paul and his company set sail from Paphos, and came to Perga in Pamphylia. John departed from them and returned to Jerusalem. But they, passing on from Perga, came to Antioch of Pisidia. They went into the synagogue on the Sabbath day, and sat down. After the reading of the law and the prophets, the rulers of the synagogue sent to them, saying, "Brothers, if you have any word of exhortation for the people, speak."

Paul stood up, and beckoning with his hand said, "Men of Israel, and you who fear God, listen. God has brought salvation to Israel according to his promise, before his coming, when John had first preached the baptism of repentance to Israel. As John was fulfilling his course, he said, 'What do you suppose that I am? I am not he. But behold, one comes after me the sandals of whose feet I am not worthy to untie.' Brothers, children of the stock of Abraham, and those among you who fear God, the word of this salvation is sent out to you.

For those who dwell in Jerusalem, and their rulers, because they didn't know him, nor the voices of the prophets which are read every Sabbath, fulfilled them by condemning him. Though they found no cause for death, they still asked Pilate to have him killed. When they had fulfilled all things that were written about him, they took him down from the tree, and laid him in a tomb. But God raised him from the dead, and he was seen for many days by those who came up with him from Galilee to Jerusalem, who are his witnesses to the people. We bring you good news of the promise made to the fathers, that God has fulfilled the same to us, their children, in that he raised up Jesus.

Be it known to you therefore, brothers, that through this man is proclaimed to you remission of sins, and by him everyone who believes is justified from all things, from which you could not be justified by the law of Moses.

So when the Jews went out of the synagogue, the Gentiles begged that these words might be preached to them the next Sabbath. Now when the synagogue broke up, many of the Jews and of the devout proselytes followed Paul and Barnabas; who, speaking to them, urged them to continue in the grace of God. The next Sabbath almost the whole city was gathered together to hear the word of God. But when the Jews saw the multitudes, they were filled with jealousy, and contradicted the things which were spoken by Paul, and blasphemed.

Paul and Barnabas spoke out boldly, and said, "It was necessary that God's word should be spoken to you first. Since indeed you thrust it from you, and judge yourselves unworthy of eternal life, behold, we turn to the Gentiles. For so has the Lord commanded us, saying,

'I have set you as a light for the Gentiles, that you should bring salvation to the uttermost parts of the earth.'"

As the Gentiles heard this, they were glad, and glorified the word of God. As many as were appointed to eternal life believed. The Lord's word was spread abroad throughout all the region. But the Jews stirred up the devout and prominent women and the chief men of the city, and stirred up a persecution against Paul and Barnabas, and threw them out of their borders. But they shook off the dust of their feet against them, and came to Iconium. The disciples were filled with joy with the Holy Spirit.

It happened in Iconium that they entered together into the synagogue of the Jews, and so spoke that a great multitude both of Jews and of Greeks believed. But the disbelieving Jews stirred up and embittered the souls of the Gentiles against the brothers. Therefore they stayed there a long time, speaking boldly in the Lord, who testified to the word of his grace, granting signs and wonders to be done by their hands. But the multitude of the city was divided. Part sided with the Jews, and part with the apostles. When some of both the Gentiles and the Jews, with their rulers, made a violent attempt to mistreat and stone them, they became aware of it, and fled to the cities of Lycaonia, Lystra, Derbe, and the surrounding region. There they preached the Good News.

At Lystra a certain man sat, impotent in his feet, a cripple from his mother's womb, who never had walked. He was listening to Paul speaking, who, fastening eyes on him, and seeing that he had faith to be made whole, said with a loud voice, "Stand upright on your feet!" He leaped up and walked. When the multitude saw what Paul had done, they lifted up their voice, saying in the language of Lycaonia, "The gods have come down to us in the likeness of men!" They called Barnabas "Jupiter," and Paul "Mercury," because he was the chief speaker. The priest of Jupiter, whose temple was in front of their city, brought oxen and garlands to the gates, and would have made a sacrifice along with the multitudes. But when the apostles, Barnabas and Paul, heard of it, they tore their clothes, and sprang into the multitude, crying out, "Men, why are you doing these things? We also are men of like passions with you, and bring you good news, that you should turn from these vain things to the living God, who made the sky and the earth and the sea, and all that is in them; who in the generations gone by allowed all the nations to walk in their own ways. Yet he didn't leave himself without witness, in that he did good and gave you rains from the sky and fruitful seasons, filling our hearts with food and gladness."

Even saying these things, they hardly stopped the multitudes from making a sacrifice to them. But some Jews from Antioch and Iconium came there, and having persuaded the multitudes, they stoned Paul, and dragged him out of the city, supposing that he was dead.

But as the disciples stood around him, he rose up, and entered into the city.

After nearly being killed for preaching Christ, Paul left Lystra and eventually returned to his "home base" of Antioch. There, they appointed elders to lead the church and stayed a long time, reporting on the events of their journey.

During this time, Paul and Barnabas were forced to make a trip to Jerusalem to deal with the teachings of some of the men there, who were attempting to force the converted Christians to be circumcised according to the practices of Judaism. In Jerusalem, a conference convened and the topic was discussed in detail. The church leaders agreed that circumcision and other Jewish practices were no longer a requirement for the Gentile converts.

As Paul prepared for his second missionary journey, he had a disagreement with Barnabas, who wanted to take John Mark. Paul did not want to take John Mark, because he had left them midway through their first missionary journey. So Barnabas took John Mark and set sail for Cyprus, and Paul selected Silas to accompany him on his journey. (Paul and Mark later reconciled, and Mark accompanied Paul when he traveled to Rome.) In a vision, the Holy Spirit called Paul to go to Macedonia, and he traveled to the city of Philippi.

On the Sabbath day we went forth outside of the city by a riverside, where we supposed there was a place of prayer, and we sat down, and spoke to the women who had come together. A certain woman named Lydia, a seller of purple, of the city of Thyatira, one who worshiped God, heard us; whose heart the Lord opened to listen to the things which were spoken by Paul. When she and her household were baptized, she begged us, saying, "If you have judged me to be faithful to the Lord, come into my house, and stay." So she persuaded us.

It happened, as we were going to prayer, that a certain girl having a spirit of divination met us, who brought her masters much gain by fortune telling. Following Paul and us, she cried out, "These men are servants of the Most High God, who proclaim to us a way of salvation!" She was doing this for many days.

But Paul, becoming greatly annoyed, turned and said to the spirit, "I command you in the name of Jesus Christ to come out of her!" It came out that very hour. But when her masters saw that the hope of their gain was gone, they seized Paul and Silas, and dragged them into the marketplace before the rulers. When they had brought them to the magistrates, they said, "These men, being Jews, are agitating our city, and set forth customs which it is not lawful for us to accept or to observe, being Romans."

The multitude rose up together against them, and the magistrates tore their clothes off of them, and commanded them to be beaten with rods. When they had laid many stripes on them, they threw them into prison, charging the jailer to keep them safely, who, having received such a command, threw them into the inner prison, and secured their feet in the stocks.

But about midnight Paul and Silas were praying and singing hymns to God, and the prisoners were listening to them. Suddenly there was a great earthquake, so that the foundations of the prison were shaken; and immediately all the doors were opened, and everyone's bonds were loosened. The jailer, being roused out of sleep and seeing the prison doors open, drew his sword and was about to kill himself, supposing that the prisoners had escaped. But Paul cried with a loud voice, saying, "Don't harm yourself, for we are all here!"

He called for lights and sprang in, and, fell down trembling before Paul and Silas, and brought them out and said, "Sirs, what must I do to be saved?"

They said, "Believe in the Lord Jesus Christ, and you will be saved, you and your household." They spoke the word of the Lord to him, and to all who were in his house.

He took them the same hour of the night, and washed their stripes, and was immediately baptized, he and all his household. He brought them up into his house, and set food before them, and rejoiced greatly, with all his household, having believed in God.

But when it was day, the magistrates sent the sergeants, saying, "Let those men go." The jailer reported these words to Paul, saying, "The magistrates have sent to let you go; now therefore come out, and go in peace."

But Paul said to them, "They have beaten us publicly, without a trial, men who are Romans, and have cast us into prison! Do they now release us secretly? No, most certainly, but let them come themselves and bring us out!"

The sergeants reported these words to the magistrates, and they were afraid when they heard that they were Romans, and they came and begged them. When they had brought them out, they asked them to depart from the city. They went out of the prison, and entered into Lydia's house. When they had seen the brothers, they encouraged them, and departed.

Now when they had passed through Amphipolis and Apollonia, they came to Thessalonica, where there was a Jewish synagogue. Paul, as was his custom, went in to them, and for three Sabbath days reasoned with them from the Scriptures, explaining and demonstrating that the Christ had to suffer and rise again from the dead, and saying, "This Jesus, whom I proclaim to you, is the Christ."

Some of them were persuaded, and joined Paul and Silas, of the devout Greeks a great multitude, and not a few of the chief women. But the unpersuaded Jews took along some wicked men from the marketplace, and gathering a crowd, set the city in an uproar. Assaulting the house of Jason, they sought to bring them out to the people. When they didn't find them, they dragged Jason and certain brothers before the rulers of the city, crying, "These who have turned the world upside down have come here also, whom Jason has received. These all act contrary to the decrees of Caesar, saying that there is another king, Jesus!" The multitude and the rulers of the city were troubled when they heard these things. When they had taken security from Jason and the rest, they let them go. The brothers immediately sent Paul and Silas away by night to Berea. When they arrived, they went into the Jewish synagogue.

Now these were more noble than those in Thessalonica, in that they received the word with all readiness of the mind, examining the Scriptures daily to see whether these things were so. Many of them therefore believed; also of the prominent Greek women, and not a few men.

Unfortunately, although Paul received a good reception in Berea, several Jews from Thessalonica traveled to Berea and created a stir against Paul, causing him to leave the city. Paul was given a chance to preach to the philosophers in the great Greek city of Athens. He appealed to their love of idols, starting his discourse by mentioning an idol he had seen that was addressed to "an unknown God." He then proclaimed that there was but one true God, and that He commands men everywhere to repent. When the Athenian scholars heard Paul mention the resurrection, many mocked him, but some believed.

From Athens, Paul traveled to Corinth, where he made disciples, including Aquila and Priscilla, who practiced the same trade of tent making with Paul. When he was opposed by many of the Jews, Paul decided to focus on preaching to the Gentiles in the city.

Many of the Corinthians, when they heard, believed and were baptized. The Lord said to Paul in the night by a vision, "Don't be afraid, but speak and don't be silent; for I am with you, and no one will attack you to harm you, for I have many people in this city."

He lived there a year and six months, teaching the word of God among them.

But when Gallio was proconsul of Achaia, the Jews with one accord rose up against Paul and brought him before the judgment seat, saying, "This man persuades men to worship God contrary to the law."

But when Paul was about to open his mouth, Gallio said to the Jews, "If indeed it were a matter of wrong or of wicked crime, you Jews, it would be reasonable that I should bear with you; but if they are questions about words and names and your own law, look to it yourselves. For I don't want to be a judge of these matters." He drove them from the judgment seat.

Then all the Greeks laid hold on Sosthenes, the ruler of the synagogue, and beat him before the judgment seat. Gallio didn't care about any of these things.

Paul, having stayed after this many more days, took his leave of the brothers, and sailed from there for Syria, together with Priscilla and Aquila. He shaved his head in Cenchreae, for he had a vow. He came to Ephesus, and he left them there; but he himself entered into the synagogue, and reasoned with the Jews. When they asked him to stay with them a longer time, he declined; but taking his leave of them, and saying, "I must by all means keep this coming feast in Jerusalem, but I will return again to you if God wills," he set sail from Ephesus.

When Paul first visited Thessalonica, he taught only three weeks in the synagogue before he was run out of town by trouble-making Jews, who were accusing him of causing "trouble all over the world." These men even followed them to Berea, stirring up trouble there. Still, Paul was successful in starting a congregation in the city.

In one of the earliest of the Biblical epistles, Paul wrote to this young church, only some 20 years after the death of Jesus. He started by answering some who had questioned his motives, and had accused him of preaching for flattery and financial gain. Paul reminded them that he had worked diligently there, making his own living, to avoid becoming a financial burden. Paul went out of his way to thank the church in Thessalonica for their continued faithfulness and progress. The excerpts presented here show that although Paul could not be with them in person, he was with them in heart.

Paul, Silvanus, and Timothy, to the assembly of the Thessalonians in God the Father and the Lord Jesus Christ: Grace to you and peace from God our Father and the Lord Jesus Christ.

We always give thanks to God for all of you, mentioning you in our prayers, remembering without ceasing your work of faith and labor of love and patience of hope in our Lord Jesus Christ, before our God and Father. We know, brothers loved by God, that you are chosen, and that our Good News came to you not in word only, but also in power, and in the Holy Spirit, and with much assurance. You know what kind of men we showed ourselves to be among you for your sake. You became imitators of us, and of the Lord, having received the word in much affliction, with joy of the Holy Spirit, so that you became an example to all who believe in Macedonia and in Achaia.

But even as we have been approved by God to be entrusted with the Good News, so we speak; not as pleasing men, but God, who tests our hearts. For neither were we at any time found using words of flattery, as you know, nor a cloak of covetousness (God is witness), nor seeking glory from men (neither from you nor from others), when we might have claimed authority as apostles of Christ. But we were gentle among you, like a nursing mother cherishes her own children.

Even so, affectionately longing for you, we were well pleased to impart to you, not the Good News of God only, but also our own souls, because you had become very dear to us. For you remember, brothers, our labor and travail; for working night and day, that we might not burden any of you, we preached to you the Good News of God. You are witnesses with God, how holy, righteously, and blamelessly we behaved ourselves toward you who believe.

But we, brothers, being bereaved of you for a short season, in presence, not in heart, tried even harder to see your face with great desire, because we wanted to come to you—indeed, I, Paul, once and again—but Satan hindered us. For what is our hope, or joy, or crown of rejoicing? Isn't it even you, before our Lord Jesus at his coming? For you are our glory and our joy.

Therefore when we couldn't stand it any longer, we thought it good to be left behind at Athens alone, and sent Timothy, our brother and God's servant in the Good News of Christ, to establish you, and to comfort you concerning your faith; that no one be moved by these afflictions. For you know that we are appointed to this task. For most certainly, when we were with you, we told you beforehand that we are to suffer affliction, even as it happened, and you know. For this cause I also, when I couldn't stand it any longer, sent that I might know your faith, for fear that by any means the tempter had tempted you, and our labor would have been in vain. But when Timothy came just now to us from you, and brought us glad news of your faith and love, and that you have good memories of us always, longing to see us, even as we also long to see you; for this cause, brothers, we were comforted over you in all our distress and affliction through your faith.

But we don't want you to be ignorant, brothers, concerning those who have fallen asleep, so that you don't grieve like the rest, who have no hope. For if we believe that Jesus died and rose again, even so God will bring with him those who have fallen asleep in Jesus. For this we tell you by the word of the Lord, that we who are alive, who are left to the coming of the Lord, will in no way precede those who have fallen asleep. For the Lord himself will descend from heaven with a shout, with the voice of the archangel, and with God's trumpet. The dead in Christ will rise first, then we who are alive, who are left, will be caught up together with them in the clouds, to meet the Lord in the air. So we will be with the Lord forever. Therefore comfort one another with these words.

But concerning the times and the seasons, brothers, you have no need that anything be written to you. For you yourselves know well that the day of the Lord comes like a thief in the night.

Rejoice always. Pray without ceasing. In everything give thanks, for this is the will of God in Christ Jesus toward you. Don't quench the Spirit. Don't despise prophesies. Test all things, and hold firmly that which is good. Abstain from every form of evil.

May the God of peace himself sanctify you completely. May your whole spirit, soul, and body be preserved blameless at the coming of our Lord Jesus Christ.

He who calls you is faithful, who will also do it. Brothers, pray for us. Greet all the brothers with a holy kiss. I solemnly command you by the Lord that this letter be read to all the holy brothers.

The grace of our Lord Jesus Christ be with you. Amen.

Shortly after Paul wrote his first letter to the Thessalonian brethren, he found it necessary to send a second letter. This time, Paul took on a slightly sterner tone. It seems likely that the brethren in Thessalonica had misunderstood that Paul had taught that the second coming of Christ was at hand, or even had already occurred. Paul corrected this and clarified that things that were to happen were still before the "end days."

Paul, Silvanus, and Timothy, to the assembly of the Thessalonians in God our Father, and the Lord Jesus Christ: Grace to you and peace from God our Father and the Lord Jesus Christ.

Now, brothers, concerning the coming of our Lord Jesus Christ, and our gathering together to him, we ask you not to be quickly shaken in your mind, nor yet be troubled, either by spirit, or by word, or by letter as from us, saying that the day of Christ had come. Let no one deceive you in any way. For it will not be, unless the departure comes first, and the man of sin is revealed, the son of destruction, he who opposes and exalts himself against all that is called God or that is worshiped; so that he sits as God in the temple of God, setting himself up as God. Don't you remember that, when I was still with you, I told you these things? Now you know what is restraining him, to the end that he may be revealed in his own season. For the mystery of lawlessness already works. Only there is one who restrains now, until he is taken out of the way. Then the lawless one will be revealed, whom the Lord will kill with the breath of his mouth, and destroy by the manifestation of his coming.

So then, brothers, stand firm, and hold the traditions which you were taught by us, whether by word, or by letter.

Now our Lord Jesus Christ himself, and God our Father, who loved us and gave us eternal comfort and good hope through grace, comfort your hearts and establish you in every good work and word.

Now we command you, brothers, in the name of our Lord Jesus Christ, that you withdraw yourselves from every brother who walks in rebellion, and not after the tradition which they received from us. For you know how you ought to imitate us. For we didn't behave ourselves rebelliously among you, neither did we eat bread from anyone's hand without paying for it, but in labor and travail worked night and day, that we might not burden any of you.

The greeting of me, Paul, with my own hand, which is the sign in every letter: this is how I write. The grace of our Lord Jesus Christ be with you all. Amen.

34 SUPPORTING YOUNG CHURCHES

The Third Missionary Journey and More Letters of Paul

When he had landed at Caesarea, he went up and greeted the assembly, and went down to Antioch. Having spent some time there, he departed, and went through the region of Galatia, and Phrygia, in order, establishing all the disciples. Now a certain Jew named Apollos, an Alexandrian by race, an eloquent man, came to Ephesus. He was mighty in the Scriptures. This man had been instructed in the way of the Lord; and being fervent in spirit, he spoke and taught accurately the things concerning Jesus, although he knew only the baptism of John. He began to speak boldly in the synagogue. But when Priscilla and Aquila heard him, they took him aside, and explained to him the way of God more accurately.

When he had determined to pass over into Achaia, the brothers encouraged him, and wrote to the disciples to receive him. When he had come, he greatly helped those who had believed through grace; for he powerfully refuted the Jews, publicly showing by the Scriptures that Jesus was the Christ.

It happened that, while Apollos was at Corinth, Paul, having passed through the upper country, came to Ephesus, and found certain disciples. He said to them, "Did you receive the Holy Spirit when you believed?"

They said to him, "No, we haven't even heard that there is a Holy Spirit."

He said, "Into what then were you baptized?"

They said, "Into John's baptism."

Paul said, "John indeed baptized with the baptism of repentance, saying to the people that they should believe in the one who would come after him, that is, in Jesus."

When they heard this, they were baptized in the name of the Lord Jesus. When Paul had laid his hands on them, the Holy Spirit came on them, and they spoke with other languages and prophesied. They were about twelve men in all.

He entered into the synagogue, and spoke boldly for a period of three months, reasoning and persuading about the things concerning the Kingdom of God.

But when some were hardened and disobedient, speaking evil of the Way before the multitude, he departed from them, and separated the disciples, reasoning daily in the school of Tyrannus. This continued for two years, so that all those who lived in Asia heard the word of the Lord Jesus, both Jews and Greeks.

God worked special miracles by the hands of Paul, so that even handkerchiefs or aprons were carried away from his body to the sick, and the evil spirits went out. But some of the itinerant Jews, exorcists, took on themselves to invoke over those who had the evil spirits the name of the Lord Jesus, saying, "We adjure you by Jesus whom Paul preaches." There were seven sons of one Sceva, a Jewish chief priest, who did this.

The evil spirit answered, "Jesus I know, and Paul I know, but who are you?" The man in whom the evil spirit was leaped on them, and overpowered them, and prevailed against them, so that they fled out of that house naked and wounded. This became known to all, both Jews and Greeks, who lived at Ephesus. Fear fell on them all, and the name of the Lord Jesus was magnified. Many also of those who had believed came, confessing, and declaring their deeds. Many of those who practiced magical arts brought their books together and burned them in the sight of all. They counted their price, and found it to be fifty thousand pieces of silver. So the word of the Lord was growing and becoming mighty.

Now after these things had ended, Paul determined in the spirit, when he had passed through Macedonia and Achaia, to go to Jerusalem, saying, "After I have been there, I must also see Rome."

Having sent into Macedonia two of those who served him, Timothy and Erastus, he himself stayed in Asia for a while.

About that time there arose no small stir concerning the Way. For a certain man named Demetrius, a silversmith, who made silver shrines of Artemis, brought no little business to the craftsmen, whom he gathered together, with the workmen of like occupation, and said, "Sirs, you know that by this business we have our wealth. You see and hear, that not at Ephesus alone, but almost throughout all Asia, this Paul has persuaded and turned away many people, saying that they are no gods, that are made with hands. Not only is there danger that this our trade come into disrepute, but also that the temple of the great goddess Artemis will be counted as nothing, and her majesty destroyed, whom all Asia and the world worships."

When they heard this they were filled with anger, and cried out, saying,

"Great is Artemis of the Ephesians!" The whole city was filled with confusion, and they rushed with one accord into the theater, having seized Gaius and Aristarchus, men of Macedonia, Paul's companions in travel. When Paul wanted to enter in to the people, the disciples didn't allow him. Certain also of the Asiarchs, being his friends, sent to him and begged him not to venture into the theater. Some therefore cried one thing, and some another, for the assembly was in confusion. Most of them didn't know why they had come together. They brought Alexander out of the multitude, the Jews putting him forward. Alexander beckoned with his hand, and would have made a defense to the people. But when they perceived that he was a Jew, all with one voice for a time of about two hours cried out, "Great is Artemis of the Ephesians!"

When the town clerk had quieted the multitude, he said, "You men of Ephesus, what man is there who doesn't know that the city of the Ephesians is temple keeper of the great goddess Artemis, and of the image which fell down from Zeus? Seeing then that these things can't be denied, you ought to be quiet, and to do nothing rash. For you have brought these men here, who are neither robbers of temples nor blasphemers of your goddess. If therefore Demetrius and the craftsmen who are with him have a matter against anyone, the courts are open, and there are proconsuls. Let them press charges against one another. But if you seek anything about other matters, it will be settled in the regular assembly. For indeed we are in danger of being accused concerning this day's riot, there being no cause. Concerning it, we wouldn't be able to give an account of this commotion." When he had thus spoken, he dismissed the assembly.

After the uproar had ceased, Paul sent for the disciples, took leave of them, and departed to go into Macedonia. When he had gone through those parts, and had encouraged them with many words, he came into Greece.

After three months in Greece, it was determined that a plot was made by some Jews to attack Paul as he traveled to Syria; so instead, Paul returned through Macedonia. Paul went from Philippi to Troas, and from there sailed to Miletus, making several stops along the way.

For Paul had determined to sail past Ephesus, that he might not have to spend time in Asia; for he was hastening, if it were possible for him, to be in Jerusalem on the day of Pentecost.

From Miletus he sent to Ephesus, and called to himself the elders of the assembly. When they had come to him, he said to them, "You yourselves know, from the first day that I set foot in Asia, how I was with you all the time, serving the Lord with all humility, with many tears, and with trials which happened to me by the plots of the Jews; how I didn't shrink from declaring to you anything that was profitable, teaching you publicly and from house to house, testifying both to Jews and to Greeks repentance toward God, and faith toward our Lord Jesus. Now, behold, I go bound by the Spirit to Jerusalem, not knowing what will happen to me there; except that the Holy Spirit testifies in every city, saying that bonds and afflictions wait for me. But these things don't count; nor do I hold my life dear to myself, so that I may finish my race with joy, and the ministry which I received from the Lord Jesus, to fully testify to the Good News of the grace of God.

"Now, behold, I know that you all, among whom I went about preaching the Kingdom of God, will see my face no more. Therefore I testify to you this day that I am clean from the blood of all men, for I didn't shrink from declaring to you the whole counsel of God. Take heed, therefore, to yourselves, and to all the flock, in which the Holy Spirit has made you overseers, to shepherd the assembly of the Lord and God which he purchased with his own blood.

For I know that after my departure, vicious wolves will enter in among you, not sparing the flock. Men will arise from among your own selves, speaking perverse things, to draw away the disciples after them. Therefore watch, remembering that for a period of three years I didn't cease to admonish everyone night and day with tears.

When he had spoken these things, he knelt down and prayed with them all. They all wept a lot, and fell on Paul's neck and kissed him, sorrowing most of all because of the word which he had spoken, that they should see his face no more. And they accompanied him to the ship.

On the next day, we, who were Paul's companions, departed, and came to Caesarea.

We entered into the house of Philip the evangelist, who was one of the seven, and stayed with him. Now this man had four virgin daughters who prophesied. As we stayed there some days, a certain prophet named Agabus came down from Judea. Coming to us, and taking Paul's belt, he bound his own feet and hands, and said, "Thus says the Holy Spirit: 'So will the Jews at Jerusalem bind the man who owns this belt, and will deliver him into the hands of the Gentiles.'"

When we heard these things, both we and they of that place begged him not to go up to Jerusalem. Then Paul answered, "What are you doing, weeping and breaking my heart? For I am ready not only to be bound, but also to die at Jerusalem for the name of the Lord Jesus."

When he would not be persuaded, we ceased, saying, "The Lord's will be done."

After these days we took up our baggage and went up to Jerusalem. Some of the disciples from Caesarea also went with us, bringing one Mnason of Cyprus, an early disciple, with whom we would stay.

When we had come to Jerusalem, the brothers received us gladly.

Paul had labored for 18 months in Corinth, in what must have been one of the most difficult mission efforts of his long career. Corinth was a major city of around 700,000 people at that time, situated on a major road hub, being the entry point to the Peloponnesian peninsula, at the southern tip of what is now modern-day Greece. It had a diverse culture, and was greatly influenced by idolatry, money, and power.

Corinth was known for sin and depravity. In fact, the Greek verb "to Corinthianize" meant to live immorally. A city temple honoring Venus, the goddess of love, employed more than 1,000 "religious prostitutes."

Despite these difficulties, the church in Corinth grew and prospered. Yet, after Paul left, they soon ran into deep troubles, such as division, sexual immorality among their members, misuse of spiritual gifts, and an overall lack of unity. In the excerpts presented here, we see that Paul addressed these issues in his first letter to this struggling church.

Paul, called to be an apostle of Jesus Christ through the will of God, and our brother Sosthenes, to the assembly of God which is at Corinth; those who are sanctified in Christ Jesus, called to be saints, with all who call on the name of our Lord Jesus Christ in every place, both theirs and ours: Grace to you and peace from God our Father and the Lord Jesus Christ.

Now I beg you, brothers, through the name of our Lord, Jesus Christ, that you all speak the same thing and that there be no divisions among you, but that you be perfected together in the same mind and in the same judgment. For it has been reported to me concerning you, my brothers, by those who are from Chloe's household, that there are contentions among you. Now I mean this, that each one of you says, "I follow Paul," "I follow Apollos," "I follow Cephas," and, "I follow Christ." Is Christ divided? Was Paul crucified for you? Or were you baptized into the name of Paul?

For the word of the cross is foolishness to those who are dying, but to us who are saved it is the power of God.

For seeing that in the wisdom of God, the world through its wisdom didn't know God, it was God's good pleasure through the foolishness of the preaching to save those who believe. For Jews ask for signs, Greeks seek after wisdom, but we preach Christ crucified; a stumbling block to Jews, and foolishness to Greeks, but to those who are called, both Jews and Greeks, Christ is the power of God and the wisdom of God.

When I came to you, brothers, I didn't come with excellence of speech or of wisdom, proclaiming to you the testimony of God. For I determined not to know anything among you, except Jesus Christ, and him crucified. I was with you in weakness, in fear, and in much trembling. My speech and my preaching were not in persuasive words of human wisdom, but in demonstration of the Spirit and of power, that your faith wouldn't stand in the wisdom of men, but in the power of God.

Brothers, I couldn't speak to you as to spiritual, but as to fleshly, as to babies in Christ. I fed you with milk, not with meat; for you weren't yet ready. Indeed, not even now are you ready, for you are still fleshly. For insofar as there is jealousy, strife, and factions among you, aren't you fleshly, and don't you walk in the ways of men? For when one says, "I follow Paul," and another, "I follow Apollos," aren't you fleshly? Who then is Apollos, and who is Paul, but servants through whom you believed; and each as the Lord gave to him? I planted. Apollos watered. But God gave the increase.

According to the grace of God which was given to me, as a wise master builder I laid a foundation, and another builds on it. But let each man be careful how he builds on it. For no one can lay any other foundation than that which has been laid, which is Jesus Christ.

Don't you know that you are a temple of God, and that God's Spirit lives in you? If anyone destroys the temple of God, God will destroy him; for God's temple is holy, which you are.

It is actually reported that there is sexual immorality among you, and such sexual immorality as is not even named among the Gentiles, that one has his father's wife. You are puffed up, and didn't rather mourn, that he who had done this deed might be removed from among you. For I most certainly, as being absent in body but present in spirit, have already, as though I were present, judged him who has done this thing. In the name of our Lord Jesus Christ, you being gathered together, and my spirit, with the power of our Lord Jesus Christ, are to deliver such a one to Satan for the destruction of the flesh, that the spirit may be saved in the day of the Lord Jesus.

But as it is, I wrote to you not to associate with anyone who is called a brother who is a sexual sinner, or covetous, or an idolater, or a slanderer, or a drunkard, or an extortioner. Don't even eat with such a person. For what have I to do with also judging those who are outside? Don't you judge those who are within? But those who are outside, God judges. "Put away the wicked man from among yourselves."

Or don't you know that the unrighteous will not inherit the Kingdom of God? Don't be deceived. Neither the sexually immoral, nor idolaters, nor adulterers, nor male prostitutes, nor homosexuals, nor thieves, nor covetous, nor drunkards, nor slanderers, nor extortioners, will inherit the Kingdom of God. Such were some of you, but you were washed. But you were sanctified. But you were justified in the name of the Lord Jesus, and in the Spirit of our God.

Flee sexual immorality! "Every sin that a man does is outside the body," but he who commits sexual immorality sins against his own body. Or don't you know that your body is a temple of the Holy Spirit which is in you, which you have from God? You are not your own, for you were bought with a price. Therefore glorify God in your body and in your spirit, which are God's.

Now concerning the things about which you wrote to me: it is good for a man not to touch a woman. But, because of sexual immoralities, let each man have his own wife, and let each woman have her own husband. Let the husband render to his wife the affection owed her, and likewise also the wife to her husband. The wife doesn't have authority over her own body, but the husband. Likewise also the husband doesn't have authority over his own body, but the wife. Don't deprive one another, unless it is by consent for a season, that you may give yourselves to fasting and prayer, and may be together again, that Satan doesn't tempt you because of your lack of self-control.

Don't you know that those who run in a race all run, but one receives the prize? Run like that, that you may win. Every man who strives in the games exercises self-control in all things. Now they do it to receive a corruptible crown, but we an incorruptible. I therefore run like that, as not uncertainly. I fight like that, as not beating the air, but I beat my body and bring it into submission, lest by any means, after I have preached to others, I myself should be rejected.

No temptation has taken you except what is common to man. God is faithful, who will not allow you to be tempted above what you are able, but will with the temptation also make the way of escape, that you may be able to endure it.

Whether therefore you eat, or drink, or whatever you do, do all to the glory of God. Give no occasions for stumbling, either to Jews, or to Greeks, or to the assembly of God;

For I received from the Lord that which also I delivered to you, that the Lord Jesus on the night in which he was betrayed took bread. When he had given thanks, he broke it, and said, "Take, eat. This is my body, which is broken for you. Do this in memory of me." In the same way he also took the cup, after supper, saying, "This cup is the new covenant in my blood. Do this, as often as you drink, in memory of me." For as often as you eat this bread and drink this cup, you proclaim the Lord's death until he comes.

Now concerning spiritual things, brothers, I don't want you to be ignorant.

Now there are various kinds of gifts, but the same Spirit. There are various kinds of service, and the same Lord. There are various kinds of workings, but the same God, who works all things in all.

For as the body is one, and has many members, and all the members of the body, being many, are one body; so also is Christ. For in one Spirit we were all baptized into one body, whether Jews or Greeks, whether bond or free; and were all given to drink into one Spirit. For the body is not one member, but many.

If the foot would say, "Because I'm not the hand, I'm not part of the body," it is not therefore not part of the body. If the ear would say, "Because I'm not the eye, I'm not part of the body," it's not therefore not part of the body. If the whole body were an eye, where would the hearing be? If the whole were hearing, where would the smelling be? But now God has set the members, each one of them, in the body, just as he desired.

Now you are the body of Christ, and members individually.

If I speak with the languages of men and of angels, but don't have love, I have become sounding brass, or a clanging cymbal. If I have the gift of prophecy, and know all mysteries and all knowledge; and if I have all faith, so as to remove mountains, but don't have love, I am nothing. If I dole out all my goods to feed the poor, and if I give my body to be burned, but don't have love, it profits me nothing.

Love is patient and is kind; love doesn't envy. Love doesn't brag, is not proud, doesn't behave itself inappropriately, doesn't seek its own way, is not provoked, takes no account of evil; doesn't rejoice in unrighteousness, but rejoices with the truth; bears all things, believes all things, hopes all things, endures all things. Love never fails. But where there are prophecies, they will be done away with. Where there are various languages, they will cease. Where there is knowledge, it will be done away with.

Now I declare to you, brothers, the Good News which I preached to you, which also you received, in which you also stand, by which also you are saved, if you hold firmly the word which I preached to you—unless you believed in vain. For I delivered to you first of all that which I also received: that Christ died for our sins according to the Scriptures, that he was buried, that he was raised on the third day according to the Scriptures, and that he appeared to Cephas, then to the twelve. Then he appeared to over five hundred brothers at once, most of whom remain until now, but some have also fallen asleep. Then he appeared to James, then to all the apostles, and last of all, as to the child born at the wrong time, he appeared to me also. For I am the least of the apostles, who is not worthy to be called an apostle, because I persecuted the assembly of God. But by the grace of God I am what I am. His grace which was bestowed on me was not futile, but I worked more than all of them; yet not I, but the grace of God which was with me. Whether then it is I or they, so we preach, and so you believed.

Now if Christ is preached, that he has been raised from the dead, how do some among you say that there is no resurrection of the dead? But if there is no resurrection of the dead, neither has Christ been raised. If Christ has not been raised, then our preaching is in vain, and your faith also is in vain. Yes, we are found false witnesses of God, because we testified about God that he raised up Christ, whom he didn't raise up, if it is so that the dead are not raised. For if the dead aren't raised, neither has Christ been raised. If Christ has not been raised, your faith is vain; you are still in your sins. Then they also who are fallen asleep in Christ have perished. If we have only hoped in Christ in this life, we are of all men most pitiable.

But now Christ has been raised from the dead. He became the first fruits of those who are asleep. For since death came by man, the resurrection of the dead also came by man. For as in Adam all die, so also in Christ all will be made alive. But each in his own order: Christ the first fruits, then those who are Christ's, at his coming. Then the end comes, when he will deliver up the Kingdom to God, even the Father; when he will have abolished all rule and all authority and power. For he must reign until he has put all his enemies under his feet. The last enemy that will be abolished is death.

Behold, I tell you a mystery. We will not all sleep, but we will all be changed, in a moment, in the twinkling of an eye, at the last trumpet. For the trumpet will sound, and the dead will be raised incorruptible, and we will be changed. For this corruptible must put on incorruption, and this mortal must put on immortality.

But when this corruptible will have put on incorruption, and this mortal will have put on immortality, then what is written will happen:

"Death is swallowed up in victory."

"Death, where is your sting?

Hades, where is your victory?"

The sting of death is sin, and the power of sin is the law. But thanks be to God, who gives us the victory through our Lord Jesus Christ. Therefore, my beloved brothers, be steadfast, immovable, always abounding in the Lord's work, because you know that your labor is not in vain in the Lord.

Watch! Stand firm in the faith! Be courageous! Be strong! Let all that you do be done in love.

Paul's first letter to the church at Corinth had an amazing effect. The church took his words seriously, and began to correct the problems among their members.

In his second letter to this church, Paul was thankful for their change of heart, yet he was surprisingly candid about his own personal struggles and persecution. He challenged the church at Corinth to remain strong in the face of persecution.

Here, some excerpts from this letter give insight into the ability of Paul to plead for followers to keep their focus on Christ, in the midst of difficult circumstances.

Paul, an apostle of Christ Jesus through the will of God, and Timothy our brother, to the assembly of God which is at Corinth, with all the saints who are in the whole of Achaia: Grace to you and peace from God our Father and the Lord Jesus Christ.

But I determined this for myself, that I would not come to you again in sorrow.

For out of much affliction and anguish of heart I wrote to you with many tears, not that you should be made sorry, but that you might know the love that I have so abundantly for you.

You are our letter, written in our hearts, known and read by all men; being revealed that you are a letter of Christ, served by us, written not with ink, but with the Spirit of the living God; not in tablets of stone, but in tablets that are hearts of flesh.

But we have this treasure in clay vessels, that the exceeding greatness of the power may be of God, and not from ourselves. We are pressed on every side, yet not crushed; perplexed, yet not to despair; pursued, yet not forsaken; struck down, yet not destroyed; always carrying in the body the putting to death of the Lord Jesus, that the life of Jesus may also be revealed in our body. For we who live are always delivered to death for Jesus' sake, that the life also of Jesus may be revealed in our mortal flesh. So then death works in us, but life in you.

Therefore we don't faint, but though our outward man is decaying, yet our inward man is renewed day by day. For our light affliction, which is for the moment, works for us more and more exceedingly an eternal weight of glory; while we don't look at the things which are seen, but at the things which are not seen. For the things which are seen are temporal, but the things which are not seen are eternal.

For we know that if the earthly house of our tent is dissolved, we have a building from God, a house not made with hands, eternal, in the heavens.

Therefore we are always confident and know that while we are at home in the body, we are absent from the Lord; for we walk by faith, not by sight. We are courageous, I say, and are willing rather to be absent from the body, and to be at home with the Lord.

Therefore if anyone is in Christ, he is a new creation. The old things have passed away. Behold, all things have become new. But all things are of God, who reconciled us to himself through Jesus Christ, and gave to us the ministry of reconciliation; namely, that God was in Christ reconciling the world to himself, not reckoning to them their trespasses, and having committed to us the word of reconciliation. We are therefore ambassadors on behalf of Christ, as though God were entreating by us: we beg you on behalf of Christ, be reconciled to God.

For though I made you sorry with my letter, I do not regret it, though I did regret it. For I see that my letter made you sorry, though just for a while. I now rejoice, not that you were made sorry, but that you were made sorry to repentance. For you were made sorry in a godly way, that you might suffer loss by us in nothing. For godly sorrow works repentance to salvation, which brings no regret. But the sorrow of the world works death.

For you know the grace of our Lord Jesus Christ, that, though he was rich, yet for your sakes he became poor, that you through his poverty might become rich.

Remember this: he who sows sparingly will also reap sparingly. He who sows bountifully will also reap bountifully. Let each man give according as he has determined in his heart; not grudgingly, or under compulsion; for God loves a cheerful giver. And God is able to make all grace abound to you, that you, always having all sufficiency in everything, may abound to every good work.

Now thanks be to God for his unspeakable gift!

I say again, let no one think me foolish. But if so, yet receive me as foolish, that I also may boast a little. That which I speak, I don't speak according to the Lord, but as in foolishness, in this confidence of boasting.

Five times from the Jews I received forty stripes minus one. Three times I was beaten with rods. Once I was stoned. Three times I suffered shipwreck. I have been a night and a day in the deep. I have been in travels often, perils of rivers, perils of robbers, perils from my countrymen, perils from the Gentiles, perils in the city, perils in the wilderness, perils in the sea, perils among false brothers; in labor and travail, in watchings often, in hunger and thirst, in fastings often, and in cold and nakedness.

By reason of the exceeding greatness of the revelations, that I should not be exalted excessively, there was given to me a thorn in the flesh, a messenger of Satan to torment me, that I should not be exalted excessively. Concerning this thing, I begged the Lord three times that it might depart from me. He has said to me, "My grace is sufficient for you, for my power is made perfect in weakness." Most gladly therefore I will rather glory in my weaknesses, that the power of Christ may rest on me.

Therefore I take pleasure in weaknesses, in injuries, in necessities, in persecutions, in distresses, for Christ's sake. For when I am weak, then am I strong.

Finally, brothers, rejoice. Be perfected, be comforted, be of the same mind, live in peace, and the God of love and peace will be with you. Greet one another with a holy kiss. All the saints greet you. The grace of the Lord Jesus Christ, the love of God, and the fellowship of the Holy Spirit, be with you all. Amen.

Paul wrote a letter to the church at Galatia, warning them that they were sliding into a trap. Some men were stressing the Jewish law, and a consensus had developed that the Jewish Christians were more "worthy" than their Gentile neighbors.

In his letter to these Galatian brethren, Paul defended the freedom of Christianity against the bonds of Jewish law. At times he seemed angry, as he forcefully made his points. Although they were not suffering from the same levels of depravity as their Corinthian brethren, Paul saw the need to lovingly scold them for deserting what was carefully taught to them. He elegantly made the point that there is no "class warfare" or prejudice in Christianity - we are all the same, whether Jew or Greek, slave or free, man or woman - we are all one in Christ Jesus.

Paul, an apostle (not from men, neither through man, but through Jesus Christ, and God the Father, who raised him from the dead), and all the brothers who are with me, to the assemblies of Galatia: Grace to you and peace from God the Father, and our Lord Jesus Christ, who gave himself for our sins, that he might deliver us out of this present evil age, according to the will of our God and Father— to whom be the glory forever and ever. Amen.

I marvel that you are so quickly deserting him who called you in the grace of Christ to a different "good news"; and there isn't another "good news." Only there are some who trouble you, and want to pervert the Good News of Christ. But even though we, or an angel from heaven, should preach to you any "good news" other than that which we preached to you, let him be cursed. As we have said before, so I now say again: if any man preaches to you any "good news" other than that which you received, let him be cursed.

"We, being Jews by nature, and not Gentile sinners, yet knowing that a man is not justified by the works of the law but through faith in Jesus Christ, even we believed in Christ Jesus, that we might be justified by faith in Christ, and not by the works of the law, because no flesh will be justified by the works of the law. But if, while we sought to be justified in Christ, we ourselves also were found sinners, is Christ a servant of sin? Certainly not! For if I build up again those things which I destroyed, I prove myself a law-breaker. For I, through the law, died to the law, that I might live to God. I have been crucified with Christ, and it is no longer I that live, but Christ living in me. That life which I now live in the flesh, I live by faith in the Son of God, who loved me, and gave himself up for

me.

Foolish Galatians, who has bewitched you not to obey the truth, before whose eyes Jesus Christ was openly set forth among you as crucified? I just want to learn this from you. Did you receive the Spirit by the works of the law, or by hearing of faith? Are you so foolish? Having begun in the Spirit, are you now completed in the flesh? Did you suffer so many things in vain, if it is indeed in vain? He therefore who supplies the Spirit to you, and works miracles among you, does he do it by the works of the law, or by hearing of faith?

Christ redeemed us from the curse of the law, having become a curse for us. For it is written, "Cursed is everyone who hangs on a tree," that the blessing of Abraham might come on the Gentiles through Christ Jesus; that we might receive the promise of the Spirit through faith.

What then is the law? It was added because of transgressions, until the seed should come to whom the promise has been made. It was ordained through angels by the hand of a mediator. Now a mediator is not between one, but God is one. Is the law then against the promises of God? Certainly not! For if there had been a law given which could make alive, most certainly righteousness would have been of the law. But the Scriptures imprisoned all things under sin, that the promise by faith in Jesus Christ might be given to those who believe.

But before faith came, we were kept in custody under the law, confined for the faith which should afterwards be revealed. So that the law has become our tutor to bring us to Christ, that we might be justified by faith. But now that faith has come, we are no longer under a tutor. For you are all children of God, through faith in Christ Jesus. For as many of you as were baptized into Christ have put on Christ. There is neither Jew nor Greek, there is neither slave nor free man, there is neither male nor female; for you are all one in Christ Jesus.

Stand firm therefore in the liberty by which Christ has made us free, and don't be entangled again with a yoke of bondage.

But if you are led by the Spirit, you are not under the law. Now the works of the flesh are obvious, which are: adultery, sexual immorality, uncleanness, lustfulness, idolatry, sorcery, hatred, strife, jealousies, outbursts of anger, rivalries, divisions, heresies, envyings, murders, drunkenness, orgies, and things like these; of which I forewarn you, even as I also forewarned you, that those who practice such things will not inherit the Kingdom of God.

But the fruit of the Spirit is love, joy, peace, patience, kindness, goodness, faith, gentleness, and self-control. Against such things there is no law.

The grace of our Lord Jesus Christ be with your spirit, brothers. Amen.

Paul desired to visit the church in Rome, which is unique in that it seemed to have been established without any apostolic presence. It may be that early Christians, returning to Rome after the establishment of the church in Jerusalem on Pentecost, continued to meet together and make converts. Located in the seat of power for the mighty Roman empire, this congregation was uniquely positioned to have great influence on the early church.

Paul wrote a letter to the church in Rome, which contained a brilliant synopsis of the scope of Christian doctrine.

Paul, a servant of Jesus Christ, called to be an apostle, set apart for the Good News of God, which he promised before through his prophets in the holy Scriptures, concerning his Son, who was born of the seed of David according to the flesh, who was declared to be the Son of God with power, according to the Spirit of holiness, by the resurrection from the dead, Jesus Christ our Lord, through whom we received grace and apostleship, for obedience of faith among all the nations, for his name's sake; among whom you are also called to belong to Jesus Christ; to all who are in Rome, beloved of God, called to be saints: Grace to you and peace from God our Father and the Lord Jesus Christ.

For I am not ashamed of the Good News of Christ, for it is the power of God for salvation for everyone who believes; for the Jew first, and also for the Greek. For in it is revealed God's righteousness from faith to faith. As it is written, "But the righteous shall live by faith.

But glory, honor, and peace go to every man who works good, to the Jew first, and also to the Greek. For there is no partiality with God. For as many as have sinned without law will also perish without the law. As many as have sinned under the law will be judged by the law.

For he is not a Jew who is one outwardly, neither is that circumcision which is outward in the flesh; but he is a Jew who is one inwardly, and circumcision is that of the heart, in the spirit not in the letter; whose praise is not from men, but from God.

Now we know that whatever things the law says, it speaks to those who are under the law, that every mouth may be closed, and all the world may be brought under the judgment of God. Because by the works of the law, no flesh will be justified in his sight. For through the law comes the knowledge of sin. But now apart from the law, a righteousness of God has been revealed, being testified by the law and the prophets; even the righteousness of God through faith in Jesus Christ to all and on all those who believe. For there is no distinction, for all have sinned, and fall short of the glory of God; being justified freely by his grace through the redemption that is in Christ Jesus; whom God set forth to be an atoning sacrifice, through faith in his blood, for a demonstration of his righteousness through the passing over of prior sins, in God's forbearance; to demonstrate his righteousness at this present time; that he might himself be just, and the justifier of him who has faith in Jesus.

Where then is the boasting? It is excluded. By what kind of law? Of works? No, but by a law of faith. We maintain therefore that a man is justified by faith apart from the works of the law.

What then will we say that Abraham, our forefather, has found according to the flesh? For if Abraham was justified by works, he has something to boast about, but not toward God. For what does the Scripture say? "Abraham believed God, and it was accounted to him for righteousness." Now to him who works, the reward is not counted as grace, but as something owed. But to him who doesn't work, but believes in him who justifies the ungodly, his faith is accounted for righteousness. Even as David also pronounces blessing on the man to whom God counts righteousness apart from works,

"Blessed are they whose iniquities are forgiven,

whose sins are covered.

Blessed is the man whom the Lord will by no means charge with sin."

Being therefore justified by faith, we have peace with God through our Lord Jesus Christ; through whom we also have our access by faith into this grace in which we stand. We rejoice in hope of the glory of God. Not only this, but we also rejoice in our sufferings, knowing that suffering works perseverance; and perseverance, proven character; and proven character, hope: and hope doesn't disappoint us, because God's love has been poured out into our hearts through the Holy Spirit who was given to us. For while we were yet weak, at the right time Christ died for the ungodly. For one will hardly die for a righteous man. Yet perhaps for a righteous person someone would even dare to die. But God commends his own love toward us, in that while we were yet sinners, Christ died for us.

Much more then, being now justified by his blood, we will be saved from God's wrath through him. For if, while we were enemies, we were reconciled to God through the death of his Son, much more, being reconciled, we will be saved by his life.

Not only so, but we also rejoice in God through our Lord Jesus Christ, through whom we have now received the reconciliation.

But the free gift isn't like the trespass. For if by the trespass of the one the many died, much more did the grace of God, and the gift by the grace of the one man, Jesus Christ, abound to the many.

What shall we say then? Shall we continue in sin, that grace may abound? May it never be! We who died to sin, how could we live in it any longer? Or don't you know that all we who were baptized into Christ Jesus were baptized into his death? We were buried therefore with him through baptism to death, that just like Christ was raised from the dead through the glory of the Father, so we also might walk in newness of life. For if we have become united with him in the likeness of his death, we will also be part of his resurrection; knowing this, that our old man was crucified with him, that the body of sin might be done away with, so that we would no longer be in bondage to sin. For he who has died has been freed from sin. But if we died with Christ, we believe that we will also live with him; knowing that Christ, being raised from the dead, dies no more. Death no more has dominion over him! For the death that he died, he died to sin one time; but the life that he lives, he lives to God. Thus consider yourselves also to be dead to sin, but alive to God in Christ Jesus our Lord.

But thanks be to God, that, whereas you were bondservants of sin, you became obedient from the heart to that form of teaching whereunto you were delivered. Being made free from sin, you became bondservants of righteousness.

But now, being made free from sin, and having become servants of God, you have your fruit of sanctification, and the result of eternal life. For the wages of sin is death, but the free gift of God is eternal life in Christ Jesus our Lord.

There is therefore now no condemnation to those who are in Christ Jesus, who don't walk according to the flesh, but according to the Spirit. For the law of the Spirit of life in Christ Jesus made me free from the law of sin and of death. For what the law couldn't do, in that it was weak through the flesh, God did, sending his own Son in the likeness of sinful flesh and for sin, he condemned sin in the flesh; that the ordinance of the law might be fulfilled in us, who walk not after the flesh, but after the Spirit.

The Spirit himself testifies with our spirit that we are children of God; and if children, then heirs; heirs of God, and joint heirs with Christ; if indeed we suffer with him, that we may also be glorified with him. For I consider that the sufferings of this present time are not worthy to be compared with the glory which will be revealed toward us.

We know that all things work together for good for those who love God, to those who are called according to his purpose.

What then shall we say about these things? If God is for us, who can be against us? He who didn't spare his own Son, but delivered him up for us all, how would he not also with him freely give us all things? Who could bring a charge against God's chosen ones? It is God who justifies. Who is he who condemns? It is Christ who died, yes rather, who was raised from the dead, who is at the right hand of God, who also makes intercession for us.

Who shall separate us from the love of Christ? Could oppression, or anguish, or persecution, or famine, or nakedness, or peril, or sword? Even as it is written,

"For your sake we are killed all day long. We were accounted as sheep for the slaughter." No, in all these things, we are more than conquerors through him who loved us. For I am persuaded, that neither death, nor life, nor angels, nor principalities, nor things present, nor things to come, nor powers, nor height, nor depth, nor any other created thing, will be able to separate us from the love of God, which is in Christ Jesus our Lord.

Therefore I urge you, brothers, by the mercies of God, to present your bodies a living sacrifice, holy, acceptable to God, which is your spiritual service. Don't be conformed to this world, but be transformed by the renewing of your mind, so that you may prove what is the good, well-pleasing, and perfect will of God. For I say, through the grace that was given me, to every man who is among you, not to think of himself more highly than he ought to think; but to think reasonably, as God has apportioned to each person a measure of faith. For even as we have many members in one body, and all the members don't have the same function, so we, who are many, are one body in Christ, and individually members one of another.

Let love be without hypocrisy. Abhor that which is evil. Cling to that which is good. In love of the brothers be tenderly affectionate one to another; in honor preferring one another; not lagging in diligence; fervent in spirit; serving the Lord; rejoicing in hope; enduring in troubles; continuing steadfastly in prayer; contributing to the needs of the saints; given to hospitality. Bless those who persecute you; bless, and don't curse. Rejoice with those who rejoice. Weep with those who weep.

Don't be overcome by evil, but overcome evil with good.

Let every soul be in subjection to the higher authorities, for there is no authority except from God, and those who exist are ordained by God. Therefore he who resists the authority, withstands the ordinance of God; and those who withstand will receive to themselves judgment.

But you, why do you judge your brother? Or you again, why do you despise your brother? For we will all stand before the judgment seat of Christ. For it is written, "'As I live,' says the Lord, 'to me every knee will bow. Every tongue will confess to God.'" So then each one of us will give account of himself to God.

Therefore also I was hindered these many times from coming to you, but now, no longer having any place in these regions, and having these many years a longing to come to you, whenever I journey to Spain, I will come to you. For I hope to see you on my journey, and to be helped on my way there by you, if first I may enjoy your company for a while. But now, I am going to Jerusalem, serving the saints.

I know that, when I come to you, I will come in the fullness of the blessing of the Good News of Christ.

Now I beg you, brothers, by our Lord Jesus Christ, and by the love of the Spirit, that you strive together with me in your prayers to God for me, that I may be delivered from those who are disobedient in Judea, and that my service which I have for Jerusalem may be acceptable to the saints; that I may come to you in joy through the will of God, and together with you, find rest. Now the God of peace be with you all. Amen.

35 THE PATH TO DESTINY

Paul Heads for Rome

Having arrived in Jerusalem, Paul reported to the apostle James and the disciples news of his journeys, particularly how God was working through him to reach the Gentiles. When they heard and saw this, they glorified God. But Paul was informed of false rumors, that he was supposedly teaching the Jewish Christians to forsake the keeping of their Israelite customs. Paul was advised to take a vow of purification, in order to demonstrate his continued respect for the Jewish customs.

Then Paul took the men, and the next day, purified himself and went with them into the temple, declaring the fulfillment of the days of purification, until the offering was offered for every one of them. When the seven days were almost completed, the Jews from Asia, when they saw him in the temple, stirred up all the multitude and laid hands on him, crying out, "Men of Israel, help! This is the man who teaches all men everywhere against the people, and the law, and this place. Moreover, he also brought Greeks into the temple, and has defiled this holy place!" For they had seen Trophimus, the Ephesian, with him in the city, and they supposed that Paul had brought him into the temple.

All the city was moved, and the people ran together. They seized Paul and dragged him out of the temple. Immediately the doors were shut. As they were trying to kill him, news came up to the commanding officer of the regiment that all Jerusalem was in an uproar. Immediately he took soldiers and centurions, and ran down to them. They, when they saw the chief captain and the soldiers, stopped beating Paul. Then the commanding officer came near, arrested him, commanded him to be bound with two chains, and inquired who he was and what he had done. Some shouted one thing, and some another, among the crowd. When he couldn't find out the truth because of the noise, he commanded him to be brought into the barracks.

When he came to the stairs, it happened that he was carried by the soldiers because of the violence of the crowd; for the multitude of the people followed after, crying out, "Away with him!" As Paul was about to be brought into the barracks, he asked the commanding officer, "May I speak to you?"

He said, "Do you know Greek? Aren't you then the Egyptian, who before these days stirred up to sedition and led out into the wilderness the four thousand men of the Assassins?"

But Paul said, "I am a Jew, from Tarsus in Cilicia, a citizen of no insignificant city. I beg you, allow me to speak to the people."

When he had given him permission, Paul, standing on the stairs, beckoned with his hand to the people. When there was a great silence, he spoke to them in the Hebrew language, saying,

"Brothers and fathers, listen to the defense which I now make to you."

When they heard that he spoke to them in the Hebrew language, they were even more quiet. He said, "I am indeed a Jew, born in Tarsus of Cilicia, but brought up in this city at the feet of Gamaliel, instructed according to the strict tradition of the law of our fathers, being zealous for God, even as you all are this day. I persecuted this Way to the death, binding and delivering into prisons both men and women. As also the high priest and all the council of the elders testify, from whom also I received letters to the brothers, and traveled to Damascus to bring them also who were there to Jerusalem in bonds to be punished. It happened that, as I made my journey, and came close to Damascus, about noon, suddenly there shone from the sky a great light around me. I fell to the ground, and heard a voice saying to me, 'Saul, Saul, why are you persecuting me?' I answered, 'Who are you, Lord?' He said to me, 'I am Jesus of Nazareth, whom you persecute.'

"Those who were with me indeed saw the light and were afraid, but they didn't understand the voice of him who spoke to me. I said, 'What shall I do, Lord?' The Lord said to me, 'Arise, and go into Damascus. There you will be told about all things which are appointed for you to do.' When I couldn't see for the glory of that light, being led by the hand of those who were with me, I came into Damascus. One Ananias, a devout man according to the law, well reported of by all the Jews who lived in Damascus, came to me, and standing by me said to me, 'Brother Saul, receive your sight!' In that very hour I looked up at him. He said, 'The God of our fathers has appointed you to know his will, and to see the Righteous One, and to hear a voice from his mouth. For you will be a witness for him to all men of what you have seen and heard. Now why do you wait? Arise, be baptized, and wash away your sins, calling on the name of the Lord.'

"It happened that, when I had returned to Jerusalem, and while I prayed in the temple, I fell into a trance, and saw him saying to me, 'Hurry and get out of Jerusalem quickly, because they will not receive testimony concerning me from you.' I said, 'Lord, they themselves know that I imprisoned and beat in every synagogue those who believed in you. When the blood of Stephen, your witness, was shed, I also was standing by, and consenting to his death, and guarding the cloaks of those who killed him.'

"He said to me, 'Depart, for I will send you out far from here to the Gentiles.'"

They listened to him until he said that; then they lifted up their voice, and said, "Rid the earth of this fellow, for he isn't fit to live!"

As they cried out, and threw off their cloaks, and threw dust into the air, the commanding officer commanded him to be brought into the barracks, ordering him to be examined by scourging, that he might know for what crime they shouted against him like that. When they had tied him up with thongs, Paul asked the centurion who stood by, "Is it lawful for you to scourge a man who is a Roman, and not found guilty?"

When the centurion heard it, he went to the commanding officer and told him, "Watch what you are about to do, for this man is a Roman!"

The commanding officer came and asked him, "Tell me, are you a Roman?"

He said, "Yes."

The commanding officer answered, "I bought my citizenship for a great price."

Paul said, "But I was born a Roman."

Immediately those who were about to examine him departed from him, and the commanding officer also was afraid when he realized that he was a Roman, because he had bound him. But on the next day, desiring to know the truth about why he was accused by the Jews, he freed him from the bonds, and commanded the chief priests and all the council to come together, and brought Paul down and set him before them.

Paul, looking steadfastly at the council, said, "Brothers, I have lived before God in all good conscience until this day."

The high priest, Ananias, commanded those who stood by him to strike him on the mouth.

Then Paul said to him, "God will strike you, you whitewashed wall! Do you sit to judge me according to the law, and command me to be struck contrary to the law?"

Those who stood by said, "Do you malign God's high priest?"

Paul said, "I didn't know, brothers, that he was high priest. For it is written,

'You shall not speak evil of a ruler of your people.'" But when Paul perceived that the one part were Sadducees and the other Pharisees, he cried out in the council, "Men and brothers, I am a Pharisee, a son of Pharisees. Concerning the hope and resurrection of the dead I am being judged!"

When he had said this, an argument arose between the Pharisees and Sadducees, and the assembly was divided. For the Sadducees say that there is no resurrection, nor angel, nor spirit; but the Pharisees confess all of these. A great clamor arose, and some of the scribes of the Pharisees part stood up, and contended, saying, "We find no evil in this man. But if a spirit or angel has spoken to him, let's not fight against God!"

When a great argument arose, the commanding officer, fearing that Paul would be torn in pieces by them, commanded the soldiers to go down and take him by force from among them, and bring him into the barracks.

The following night, the Lord stood by him, and said, "Cheer up, Paul, for as you have testified about me at Jerusalem, so you must testify also at Rome."

When it was day, some of the Jews banded together, and bound themselves under a curse, saying that they would neither eat nor drink until they had killed Paul. There were more than forty people who had made this conspiracy. They came to the chief priests and the elders, and said, "We have bound ourselves under a great curse, to taste nothing until we have killed Paul. Now therefore, you with the council inform the commanding officer that he should bring him down to you tomorrow, as though you were going to judge his case more exactly. We are ready to kill him before he comes near."

But Paul's sister's son heard of their lying in wait, and he came and entered into the barracks and told Paul. Paul summoned one of the centurions, and said, "Bring this young man to the commanding officer, for he has something to tell him."

So he took him, and brought him to the commanding officer, and said, "Paul, the prisoner, summoned me and asked me to bring this young man to you, who has something to tell you."

The commanding officer took him by the hand, and going aside, asked him privately, "What is it that you have to tell me?"

He said, "The Jews have agreed to ask you to bring Paul down to the council tomorrow, as though intending to inquire somewhat more accurately concerning him. Therefore don't yield to them, for more than forty men lie in wait for him, who have bound themselves under a curse neither to eat nor to drink until they have killed him. Now they are ready, looking for the promise from you."

So the commanding officer let the young man go, charging him, "Tell no one that you have revealed these things to me." He called to himself two of the centurions, and said, "Prepare two hundred soldiers to go as far as Caesarea, with seventy horsemen, and two hundred men armed with spears, at the third hour of the night." He asked them to provide animals, that they might set Paul on one, and bring him safely to Felix the governor. He wrote a letter like this:

"Claudius Lysias to the most excellent governor Felix: Greetings.

"This man was seized by the Jews, and was about to be killed by them, when I came with the soldiers and rescued him, having learned that he was a Roman. Desiring to know the cause why they accused him, I brought him down to their council. I found him to be accused about questions of their law, but not to be charged with anything worthy of death or of imprisonment. When I was told that the Jews lay in wait for the man, I sent him to you immediately, charging his accusers also to bring their accusations against him before you. Farewell."

So the soldiers, carrying out their orders, took Paul and brought him by night to Antipatris. But on the next day they left the horsemen to go with him, and returned to the barracks. When they came to Caesarea and delivered the letter to the governor, they also presented Paul to him. When the governor had read it, he asked what province he was from. When he understood that he was from Cilicia, he said, "I will hear you fully when your accusers also arrive." He commanded that he be kept in Herod's palace.

The Jews made their case against Paul before the governor, Felix. They accused Paul of being a ringleader of insurrections, and of profaning the temple. Paul then made his defense, showing how he was raised as a Jew, and that he continued to follow Jewish customs. Paul also discussed that he was worshiping peacefully in the temple when he was arrested.

Felix delayed his judgment; but Paul had a second chance to lay out his case when Felix brought his Jewish wife, Drusilla, to meet Paul.

As he reasoned about righteousness, self-control, and the judgment to come, Felix was terrified, and answered, "Go your way for this time, and when it is convenient for me, I will summon you." Meanwhile, he also hoped that money would be given to him by Paul, that he might release him. Therefore also he sent for him more often, and talked with him. But when two years were fulfilled, Felix was succeeded by Porcius Festus, and desiring to gain favor with the Jews, Felix left Paul in bonds.

Shortly after Festus became governor, the Jews met with him, asking him to hear their case against Paul. They had hoped he would move Paul to Jerusalem, for they were planning to attack and kill Paul on this trip. But Festus was determined to keep Paul in Caesarea, and it was there that Felix called for Paul and his accusers. The Jews made many accusations against Paul, but none of them could be proven. Festus then gave Paul a chance to return to Jerusalem to be judged there, but Paul, being a Roman citizen, invoked his privilege of appealing to Caesar in Rome.

However Paul was not finished in Caesarea. The Jewish king Herod and his wife Bernice came to town, and they were invited by Festus to meet Paul and to hear his story. When summoned before the king, Paul told his life story, including the account of his conversion on the road to Damascus, and that Jesus was the Messiah who was prophesied in the Old Testament.

As he thus made his defense, Festus said with a loud voice, "Paul, you are crazy! Your great learning is driving you insane!"

But he said, "I am not crazy, most excellent Festus, but boldly declare words of truth and reasonableness. For the king knows of these things, to whom also I speak freely. For I am persuaded that none of these things is hidden from him, for this has not been done in a corner. King Agrippa, do you believe the prophets? I know that you believe."

Agrippa said to Paul, "With a little persuasion are you trying to make me a Christian?"

Paul said, "I pray to God, that whether with little or with much, not only you, but also all that hear me this day, might become such as I am, except for these bonds."

The king rose up with the governor, and Bernice, and those who sat with them. When they had withdrawn, they spoke one to another, saying, "This man does nothing worthy of death or of bonds." Agrippa said to Festus, "This man might have been set free if he had not appealed to Caesar."

When it was determined that we should sail for Italy, they delivered Paul and certain other prisoners to a centurion named Julius, of the Augustan band. Embarking in a ship of Adramyttium, which was about to sail to places on the coast of Asia, we put to sea; Aristarchus, a Macedonian of Thessalonica, being with us. The next day, we touched at Sidon. Julius treated Paul kindly, and gave him permission to go to his friends and refresh himself. Putting to sea from there, we sailed under the lee of Cyprus, because the winds were contrary. When we had sailed across the sea which is off Cilicia and Pamphylia, we came to Myra, a city of Lycia. There the centurion found a ship of Alexandria sailing for Italy, and he put us on board. When we had sailed slowly many days, and had come with difficulty opposite Cnidus, the wind not allowing us further, we sailed under the lee of Crete, opposite Salmone. With difficulty sailing along it we came to a certain place called Fair Havens, near the city of Lasea.

When much time had passed and the voyage was now dangerous, because the Fast had now already gone by, Paul admonished them, and said to them, "Sirs, I perceive that the voyage will be with injury and much loss, not only of the cargo and the ship, but also of our lives." But the centurion gave more heed to the master and to the owner of the ship than to those things which were spoken by Paul. Because the haven was not suitable to winter in, the majority advised going to sea from there, if by any means they could reach Phoenix, and winter there, which is a port of Crete, looking northeast and southeast.

When the south wind blew softly, supposing that they had obtained their purpose, they weighed anchor and sailed along Crete, close to shore. But before long, a stormy wind beat down from shore, which is called Euroclydon. When the ship was caught, and couldn't face the wind, we gave way to it, and were driven along. Running under the lee of a small island called Clauda, we were able, with difficulty, to secure the boat. After they had hoisted it up, they used cables to help reinforce the ship. Fearing that they would run aground on the Syrtis sand bars, they lowered the sea anchor, and so were driven along. As we labored exceedingly with the storm, the next day they began to throw things overboard. On the third day, they threw out the ship's tackle with their own hands. When neither sun nor stars shone on us for many days, and no small storm pressed on us, all hope that we would be saved was now taken away.

When they had been long without food, Paul stood up in the middle of them, and said, "Sirs, you should have listened to me, and not have set sail from Crete, and have gotten this injury and loss. Now I exhort you to cheer up, for there will be no loss of life among you, but only of the ship. For there stood by me this night an angel, belonging to the God whose I am and whom I serve, saying, 'Don't be afraid, Paul. You must stand before Caesar. Behold, God has granted you all those who sail with you.' Therefore, sirs, cheer up! For I believe God, that it will be just as it has been spoken to me. But we must run aground on a certain island."

But when the fourteenth night had come, as we were driven back and forth in the Adriatic Sea, about midnight the sailors surmised that they were drawing near to some land. They took soundings, and found twenty fathoms. After a little while, they took soundings again, and found fifteen fathoms. Fearing that we would run aground on rocky ground, they let go four anchors from the stern, and wished for daylight. As the sailors were trying to flee out of the ship, and had lowered the boat into the sea, pretending that they would lay out anchors from the bow, Paul said to the centurion and to the soldiers, "Unless these stay in the ship, you can't be saved." Then the soldiers cut away the ropes of the boat, and let it fall off.

While the day was coming on, Paul begged them all to take some food, saying, "This day is the fourteenth day that you wait and continue fasting, having taken nothing. Therefore I beg you to take some food, for this is for your safety; for not a hair will perish from any of your heads." When he had said this, and had taken bread, he gave thanks to God in the presence of all, and he broke it, and began to eat. Then they all cheered up, and they also took food. In all, we were two hundred seventy-six souls on the ship. When they had eaten enough, they lightened the ship, throwing out the wheat into the sea. When it was day, they didn't recognize the land, but they noticed a certain bay with a beach, and they decided to try to drive the ship onto it. Casting off the anchors, they left them in the sea, at the same time untying the rudder ropes. Hoisting up the foresail to the wind, they made for the beach. But coming to a place where two seas met, they ran the vessel aground. The bow struck and remained immovable, but the stern began to break up by the violence of the waves.

The soldiers' counsel was to kill the prisoners, so that none of them would swim out and escape. But the centurion, desiring to save Paul, stopped them from their purpose, and commanded that those who could swim should throw themselves overboard first to go toward the land; and the rest should follow, some on planks, and some on other things from the ship. So it happened that they all escaped safely to the land.

When we had escaped, then they learned that the island was called Malta. The natives showed us uncommon kindness; for they kindled a fire, and received us all, because of the present rain, and because of the cold. But when Paul had gathered a bundle of sticks and laid them on the fire, a viper came out because of the heat, and fastened on his hand. When the natives saw the creature hanging from his hand, they said one to another, "No doubt this man is a murderer, whom, though he has escaped from the sea, yet Justice has not allowed to live." However he shook off the creature into the fire, and wasn't harmed. But they expected that he would have swollen or fallen down dead suddenly, but when they watched for a long time and saw nothing bad happen to him, they changed their minds, and said that he was a god.

Now in the neighborhood of that place were lands belonging to the chief man of the island, named Publius, who received us, and courteously entertained us for three days. It happened that the father of Publius lay sick of fever and dysentery. Paul entered in to him, prayed, and laying his hands on him, healed him. Then when this was done, the rest also who had diseases in the island came, and were cured. They also honored us with many honors, and when we sailed, they put on board the things that we needed.

After three months, we set sail in a ship of Alexandria which had wintered in the island, whose sign was "The Twin Brothers." Touching at Syracuse, we stayed there three days. From there we circled around and arrived at Rhegium.

After one day, a south wind sprang up, and on the second day we came to Puteoli, where we found brothers, and were entreated to stay with them for seven days. So we came to Rome. From there the brothers, when they heard of us, came to meet us as far as The Market of Appius and The Three Taverns. When Paul saw them, he thanked God, and took courage. When we entered into Rome, the centurion delivered the prisoners to the captain of the guard, but Paul was allowed to stay by himself with the soldier who guarded him.

It happened that after three days Paul called together those who were the leaders of the Jews. When they had come together, he said to them, "I, brothers, though I had done nothing against the people, or the customs of our fathers, still was delivered prisoner from Jerusalem into the hands of the Romans, who, when they had examined me, desired to set me free, because there was no cause of death in me. But when the Jews spoke against it, I was constrained to appeal to Caesar, not that I had anything about which to accuse my nation. For this cause therefore I asked to see you and to speak with you. For because of the hope of Israel I am bound with this chain."

They said to him, "We neither received letters from Judea concerning you, nor did any of the brothers come here and report or speak any evil of you. But we desire to hear from you what you think. For, as concerning this sect, it is known to us that everywhere it is spoken against."

When they had appointed him a day, many people came to him at his lodging. He explained to them, testifying about the Kingdom of God, and persuading them concerning Jesus, both from the law of Moses and from the prophets, from morning until evening. Some believed the things which were spoken, and some disbelieved.

When he had said these words, the Jews departed, having a great dispute among themselves.

Paul stayed two whole years in his own rented house, and received all who were coming to him, preaching the Kingdom of God, and teaching the things concerning the Lord Jesus Christ with all boldness, without hindrance.

36 FREEDOM IN CHAINS

Paul's Prison Epistles

While imprisoned in Rome, Paul, calling himself "the prisoner of Christ Jesus on behalf of you Gentiles" wrote a letter to the church at Ephesus. Despite being in chains, Paul wrote an uplifting, encouraging letter that must have been received gladly by the Ephesians. Paul overcame his own situation, confirming powerfully that the Christian life is rich, fulfilling and worth the effort. In beautiful and soaring language, he laid out both doctrine and overall advice for Christian living, expressing hope that everyone would come to understand "Christ's love which surpasses knowledge."

Paul, an apostle of Christ Jesus through the will of God, to the saints who are at Ephesus, and the faithful in Christ Jesus: Grace to you and peace from God our Father and the Lord Jesus Christ.

Blessed be the God and Father of our Lord Jesus Christ, who has blessed us with every spiritual blessing in the heavenly places in Christ; even as he chose us in him before the foundation of the world, that we would be holy and without blemish before him in love;

For this cause I also, having heard of the faith in the Lord Jesus which is among you, and the love which you have toward all the saints, don't cease to give thanks for you, making mention of you in my prayers, that the God of our Lord Jesus Christ, the Father of glory, may give to you a spirit of wisdom and revelation in the knowledge of him; having the eyes of your hearts enlightened, that you may know what is the hope of his calling, and what are the riches of the glory of his inheritance in the saints, and what is the exceeding greatness of his power toward us who believe, according to that working of the strength of his might which he worked in Christ, when he raised him from the dead, and made him to sit at his right hand in the heavenly places, far above all rule, and authority, and power, and dominion, and every name that is named, not only in this age, but also in that which is to come. He put all things in subjection under his feet, and gave him to be head over all things for the assembly, which is his body, the fullness of him who fills all in all.

But God, being rich in mercy, for his great love with which he loved us, even when we were dead through our trespasses, made us alive together with Christ (by grace you have been saved), and raised us up with him, and made us to sit with him in the heavenly places in Christ Jesus, that in the ages to come he might show the exceeding riches of his grace in kindness toward us in Christ Jesus; for by grace you have been saved through faith, and that not of yourselves; it is the gift of God, not of works, that no one would boast. For we are his workmanship, created in Christ Jesus for good works, which God prepared before that we would walk in them.

He came and preached peace to you who were far off and to those who were near. For through him we both have our access in one Spirit to the Father. So then you are no longer strangers and foreigners, but you are fellow citizens with the saints, and of the household of God, being built on the foundation of the apostles and prophets, Christ Jesus himself being the chief cornerstone; in whom the whole building, fitted together, grows into a holy temple in the Lord; in whom you also are built together for a habitation of God in the Spirit.

For this cause, I bow my knees to the Father of our Lord Jesus Christ, from whom every family in heaven and on earth is named, that he would grant you, according to the riches of his glory, that you may be strengthened with power through his Spirit in the inward man; that Christ may dwell in your hearts through faith; to the end that you, being rooted and grounded in love, may be strengthened to comprehend with all the saints what is the breadth and length and height and depth, and to know Christ's love which surpasses knowledge, that you may be filled with all the fullness of God. Now to him who is able to do exceedingly abundantly above all that we ask or think, according to the power that works in us, to him be the glory in the assembly and in Christ Jesus to all generations forever and ever. Amen.

I therefore, the prisoner in the Lord, beg you to walk worthily of the calling with which you were called, with all lowliness and humility, with patience, bearing with one another in love; being eager to keep the unity of the Spirit in the bond of peace. There is one body, and one Spirit, even as you also were called in one hope of your calling; one Lord, one faith, one baptism, one God and Father of all, who is over all, and through all, and in us all.

Be therefore imitators of God, as beloved children. Walk in love, even as Christ also loved you, and gave himself up for us, an offering and a sacrifice to God for a sweet-smelling fragrance. But sexual immorality, and all uncleanness, or covetousness, let it not even be mentioned among you, as becomes saints; nor filthiness, nor foolish talking, nor jesting, which are not appropriate; but rather giving of thanks.

Wives, be subject to your own husbands, as to the Lord. For the husband is the head of the wife, and Christ also is the head of the assembly, being himself the savior of the body. But as the assembly is subject to Christ, so let the wives also be to their own husbands in everything.

Husbands, love your wives, even as Christ also loved the assembly, and gave himself up for it; that he might sanctify it, having cleansed it by the washing of water with the word, that he might present the assembly to himself gloriously, not having spot or wrinkle or any such thing; but that it should be holy and without blemish. Even so husbands also ought to love their own wives as their own bodies. He who loves his own wife loves himself.

For no man ever hated his own flesh; but nourishes and cherishes it, even as the Lord also does the assembly; because we are members of his body, of his flesh and bones. "For this cause a man will leave his father and mother, and will be joined to his wife. The two will become one flesh." This mystery is great, but I speak concerning Christ and of the assembly. Nevertheless each of you must also love his own wife even as himself; and let the wife see that she respects her husband.

Children, obey your parents in the Lord, for this is right. "Honor your father and mother," which is the first commandment with a promise: "that it may be well with you, and you may live long on the earth."

You fathers, don't provoke your children to wrath, but nurture them in the discipline and instruction of the Lord.

Finally, be strong in the Lord, and in the strength of his might. Put on the whole armor of God, that you may be able to stand against the wiles of the devil. For our wrestling is not against flesh and blood, but against the principalities, against the powers, against the world's rulers of the darkness of this age, and against the spiritual forces of wickedness in the heavenly places. Therefore put on the whole armor of God, that you may be able to withstand in the evil day, and, having done all, to stand. Stand therefore, having the utility belt of truth buckled around your waist, and having put on the breastplate of righteousness, and having fitted your feet with the preparation of the Good News of peace; above all, taking up the shield of faith, with which you will be able to quench all the fiery darts of the evil one. And take the helmet of salvation, and the sword of the Spirit, which is the word of God; with all prayer and requests, praying at all times in the Spirit, and being watchful to this end in all perseverance and requests for all the saints:

Peace be to the brothers, and love with faith, from God the Father and the Lord Jesus Christ. Grace be with all those who love our Lord Jesus Christ with incorruptible love. Amen.

Paul also wrote a short letter to the church at Philippi, which he had visited on his second missionary journey. Here, Lydia and the Philippian jailer and his family were converted to Christ. At this time, the church was well established, having "bishops (elders) and deacons." At a time when persecution of the church was rapidly increasing under the watch of the Roman emperor Nero, Paul sent out a letter proclaiming love and joy, and rejoicing in the blessings of Christianity.

Paul and Timothy, servants of Jesus Christ;

To all the saints in Christ Jesus who are at Philippi, with the overseers and servants: Grace to you, and peace from God, our Father, and the Lord Jesus Christ. I thank my God whenever I remember you, always in every request of mine on behalf of you all making my requests with joy, for your partnership in furtherance of the Good News from the first day until now; being confident of this very thing, that he who began a good work in you will complete it until the day of Jesus Christ.

This I pray, that your love may abound yet more and more in knowledge and all discernment; so that you may approve the things that are excellent; that you may be sincere and without offense to the day of Christ; being filled with the fruits of righteousness, which are through Jesus Christ, to the glory and praise of God.

For to me to live is Christ, and to die is gain.

If there is therefore any exhortation in Christ, if any consolation of love, if any fellowship of the Spirit, if any tender mercies and compassion, make my joy full, by being like-minded, having the same love, being of one accord, of one mind; doing nothing through rivalry or through conceit, but in humility, each counting others better than himself; each of you not just looking to his own things, but each of you also to the things of others.

Have this in your mind, which was also in Christ Jesus, who, existing in the form of God, didn't consider equality with God a thing to be grasped, but emptied himself, taking the form of a servant, being made in the likeness of men.

And being found in human form, he humbled himself, becoming obedient to death, yes, the death of the cross. Therefore God also highly exalted him, and gave to him the name which is above every name; that at the name of Jesus every knee should bow, of those in heaven, those on earth, and those under the earth, and that every tongue should confess that Jesus Christ is Lord, to the glory of

God the Father.

So then, my beloved, even as you have always obeyed, not only in my presence, but now much more in my absence, work out your own salvation with fear and trembling.

For it is God who works in you both to will and to work, for his good pleasure. Do all things without murmurings and disputes, that you may become blameless and harmless, children of God without blemish in the midst of a crooked and perverse generation, among whom you are seen as lights in the world, holding up the word of life; that I may have something to boast in the day of Christ, that I didn't run in vain nor labor in vain. Yes, and if I am poured out on the sacrifice and service of your faith, I rejoice, and rejoice with you all. In the same way, you also rejoice, and rejoice with me.

Brothers, I don't regard myself as yet having taken hold, but one thing I do. Forgetting the things which are behind, and stretching forward to the things which are before, I press on toward the goal for the prize of the high calling of God in Christ Jesus.

For our citizenship is in heaven, from where we also wait for a Savior, the Lord Jesus Christ; who will change the body of our humiliation to be conformed to the body of his glory, according to the working by which he is able even to subject all things to himself.

Finally, brothers, whatever things are true, whatever things are honorable, whatever things are just, whatever things are pure, whatever things are lovely, whatever things are of good report; if there is any virtue, and if there is any praise, think about these things. The things which you learned, received, heard, and saw in me: do these things, and the God of peace will be with you.

Greet every saint in Christ Jesus. The brothers who are with me greet you. All the saints greet you, especially those who are of Caesar's household. The grace of the Lord Jesus Christ be with you all. Amen.

Another "prison letter" was sent to the church at Colossae. It was written primarily to address doctrinal issues caused by men seeking to distort Christianity by bringing in influences from other "mysterious" religions with "philosophy and vain deceit." However, the letter also has wonderful prose glorifying Christ and encouraging the Colossians to remain faithful to Him only.

Paul, an apostle of Christ Jesus through the will of God, and Timothy our brother, to the saints and faithful brothers in Christ at Colossae: Grace to you and peace from God our Father, and the Lord Jesus Christ.

We give thanks to God the Father of our Lord Jesus Christ, praying always for you, having heard of your faith in Christ Jesus, and of the love which you have toward all the saints, because of the hope which is laid up for you in the heavens, of which you heard before in the word of the truth of the Good News,

For this cause, we also, since the day we heard this, don't cease praying and making requests for you, that you may be filled with the knowledge of his will in all spiritual wisdom and understanding, that you may walk worthily of the Lord, to please him in all respects, bearing fruit in every good work, and increasing in the knowledge of God; strengthened with all power, according to the might of his glory, for all endurance and perseverance with joy; giving thanks to the Father, who made us fit to be partakers of the inheritance of the saints in light; who delivered us out of the power of darkness, and translated us into the Kingdom of the Son of his love; in whom we have our redemption, the forgiveness of our sins; who is the image of the invisible God, the firstborn of all creation.

For by him all things were created, in the heavens and on the earth, things visible and things invisible, whether thrones or dominions or principalities or powers; all things have been created through him, and for him. He is before all things, and in him all things are held together. He is the head of the body, the assembly, who is the beginning, the firstborn from the dead; that in all things he might have the preeminence. For all the fullness was pleased to dwell in him; and through him to reconcile all things to himself, by him, whether things on the earth, or things in the heavens, having made peace through the blood of his cross.

For though I am absent in the flesh, yet am I with you in the spirit, rejoicing and seeing your order, and the steadfastness of your faith in Christ. As therefore you received Christ Jesus, the Lord, walk in him, rooted and built up in him, and established in the faith, even as you were taught, abounding in it in thanksgiving. Be careful that you don't let anyone rob you through his philosophy and vain deceit, after the tradition of men, after the elements of the world, and not after Christ.

For in him all the fullness of the Godhead dwells bodily, and in him you are made full, who is the head of all principality and power; in whom you were also circumcised with a circumcision not made with hands, in the putting off of the body of the sins of the flesh, in the circumcision of Christ; having been buried with him in baptism, in which you were also raised with him through faith in the working of God, who raised him from the dead. You were dead through your trespasses and the uncircumcision of your flesh. He made you alive together with him, having forgiven us all our trespasses, wiping out the handwriting in ordinances which was against us; and he has taken it out of the way, nailing it to the cross; having stripped the principalities and the powers, he made a show of them openly, triumphing over them in it.

If then you were raised together with Christ, seek the things that are above, where Christ is, seated on the right hand of God. Set your mind on the things that are above, not on the things that are on the earth. For you died, and your life is hidden with Christ in God. When Christ, our life, is revealed, then you will also be revealed with him in glory.

Put to death therefore your members which are on the earth: sexual immorality, uncleanness, depraved passion, evil desire, and covetousness, which is idolatry; for which things' sake the wrath of God comes on the children of disobedience. You also once walked in those, when you lived in them; but now you also put them all away: anger, wrath, malice, slander, and shameful speaking out of your mouth.

Put on therefore, as God's chosen ones, holy and beloved, a heart of compassion, kindness, lowliness, humility, and perseverance; bearing with one another, and forgiving each other, if any man has a complaint against any; even as Christ forgave you, so you also do.

Above all these things, walk in love, which is the bond of perfection. And let the peace of God rule in your hearts, to which also you were called in one body; and be thankful. Let the word of Christ dwell in you richly; in all wisdom teaching and admonishing one another with psalms, hymns, and spiritual songs, singing with grace in your heart to the Lord.

Whatever you do, in word or in deed, do all in the name of the Lord Jesus, giving thanks to God the Father, through him.

The salutation of me, Paul, with my own hand: remember my bonds. Grace be with you. Amen.

37 THAT WHICH WE HAVE TOUCHED

Letters from James, Peter and John

Sometimes called the "Proverbs of the New Testament," the book of James is full of advice for practical Christian living. The author of this epistle is thought to be the brother of Jesus Christ, who became a believer only after the resurrection, and later is mentioned as a leader in the church at Jerusalem. Stressing the walk of genuine believers, James compares worldly and Godly wisdom, asking the reader to choose God.

James, a servant of God and of the Lord Jesus Christ, to the twelve tribes which are in the Dispersion: Greetings. Count it all joy, my brothers, when you fall into various temptations, knowing that the testing of your faith produces endurance. Let endurance have its perfect work, that you may be perfect and complete, lacking in nothing. But if any of you lacks wisdom, let him ask of God, who gives to all liberally and without reproach; and it will be given to him. But let him ask in faith, without any doubting, for he who doubts is like a wave of the sea, driven by the wind and tossed. For let that man not think that he will receive anything from the Lord. He is a double-minded man, unstable in all his ways.

Blessed is the man who endures temptation, for when he has been approved, he will receive the crown of life, which the Lord promised to those who love him. Let no man say when he is tempted, "I am tempted by God," for God can't be tempted by evil, and he himself tempts no one. But each one is tempted, when he is drawn away by his own lust, and enticed. Then the lust, when it has conceived, bears sin; and the sin, when it is full grown, brings forth death.

So, then, my beloved brothers, let every man be swift to hear, slow to speak, and slow to anger; for the anger of man doesn't produce the righteousness of God. Therefore, putting away all filthiness and overflowing of wickedness, receive with humility the implanted word, which is able to save your souls. But be doers of the word, and not only hearers, deluding your own selves.

If anyone among you thinks himself to be religious while he doesn't bridle his tongue, but deceives his heart, this man's religion is worthless. Pure religion and undefiled before our God and Father is this: to visit the fatherless and widows in their affliction, and to keep oneself unstained by the world.

What good is it, my brothers, if a man says he has faith, but has no works? Can faith save him? And if a brother or sister is naked and in lack of daily food, and one of you tells them, "Go in peace, be warmed and filled"; and yet you didn't give them the things the body needs, what good is it? Even so faith, if it has no works, is dead in itself. Yes, a man will say, "You have faith, and I have works." Show me your faith without works, and I by my works will show you my faith.

You believe that God is one. You do well. The demons also believe, and shudder. But do you want to know, vain man, that faith apart from works is dead? Wasn't Abraham our father justified by works, in that he offered up Isaac his son on the altar? You see that faith worked with his works, and by works faith was perfected; and the Scripture was fulfilled which says, "Abraham believed God, and it was accounted to him as righteousness"; and he was called the friend of God. You see then that by works, a man is justified, and not only by faith.

Who is wise and understanding among you? Let him show by his good conduct that his deeds are done in gentleness of wisdom. But if you have bitter jealousy and selfish ambition in your heart, don't boast and don't lie against the truth. This wisdom is not that which comes down from above, but is earthly, sensual, and demonic. For where jealousy and selfish ambition are, there is confusion and every evil deed. But the wisdom that is from above is first pure, then peaceful, gentle, reasonable, full of mercy and good fruits, without partiality, and without hypocrisy. Now the fruit of righteousness is sown in peace by those who make peace.

Humble yourselves in the sight of the Lord, and he will exalt you.

Come now, you who say, "Today or tomorrow let's go into this city, and spend a year there, trade, and make a profit." Whereas you don't know what your life will be like tomorrow. For what is your life? For you are a vapor, that appears for a little time, and then vanishes away. For you ought to say, "If the Lord wills, we will both live, and do this or that."

Be patient therefore, brothers, until the coming of the Lord. Behold, the farmer waits for the precious fruit of the earth, being patient over it, until it receives the early and late rain. You also be patient. Establish your hearts, for the coming of the Lord is at hand.

Is any among you suffering? Let him pray. Is any cheerful? Let him sing praises. Is any among you sick? Let him call for the elders of the assembly, and let them pray over him, anointing him with oil in the name of the Lord, and the prayer of faith will heal him who is sick, and the Lord will raise him up. If he has committed sins, he will be forgiven. Confess your offenses to one another, and pray for one another, that you may be healed. The insistent prayer of a righteous person is powerfully effective.

Brothers, if any among you wanders from the truth, and someone turns him back, let him know that he who turns a sinner from the error of his way will save a soul from death, and will cover a multitude of sins.

The apostle Peter emerged from the life of a lowly fisherman in the town of Bethsaida to become one of the most prominent leaders and teachers in the early church. In his first epistle, Peter wrote to Christians who had been dispersed by the persecution of the church. Designed to help those enduring such sufferings, this book gives hope as it points out that the eternal reward will more than repay the troubles for those enduring temporary persecution on earth. As he wrote, "But because you are partakers of Christ's sufferings, rejoice; that at the revelation of his glory you also may rejoice with exceeding joy."

Peter, an apostle of Jesus Christ, to the chosen ones who are living as foreigners in the Dispersion in Pontus, Galatia, Cappadocia, Asia, and Bithynia, according to the foreknowledge of God the Father, in sanctification of the Spirit, that you may obey Jesus Christ and be sprinkled with his blood: Grace to you and peace be multiplied.

Blessed be the God and Father of our Lord Jesus Christ, who according to his great mercy became our father again to a living hope through the resurrection of Jesus Christ from the dead, to an incorruptible and undefiled inheritance that doesn't fade away, reserved in Heaven for you, who by the power of God are guarded through faith for a salvation ready to be revealed in the last time. Wherein you greatly rejoice, though now for a little while, if need be, you have been put to grief in various trials, that the proof of your faith, which is more precious than gold that perishes even though it is tested by fire, may be found to result in praise, glory, and honor at the revelation of Jesus Christ.

Therefore prepare your minds for action, be sober and set your hope fully on the grace that will be brought to you at the revelation of Jesus Christ— as children of obedience, not conforming yourselves according to your former lusts as in your ignorance, but just as he who called you is holy, you yourselves also be holy in all of your behavior; because it is written, "You shall be holy; for I am holy."

Putting away therefore all wickedness, all deceit, hypocrisies, envies, and all evil speaking, as newborn babies, long for the pure milk of the Word, that you may grow thereby, if indeed you have tasted that the Lord is gracious: coming to him, a living stone, rejected indeed by men, but chosen by God, precious. You also, as living stones, are built up as a spiritual house, to be a holy priesthood, to offer up spiritual sacrifices, acceptable to God through Jesus Christ.

But you are a chosen race, a royal priesthood, a holy nation, a people for God's own possession, that you may proclaim the excellence of him who called you out of darkness into his marvelous light: who in time past were no people, but now are God's people, who had not obtained mercy, but now have obtained mercy.

For what glory is it if, when you sin, you patiently endure beating? But if, when you do well, you patiently endure suffering, this is commendable with God. For to this you were called, because Christ also suffered for us, leaving you an example, that you should follow his steps, who did not sin, "neither was deceit found in his mouth." Who, when he was cursed, didn't curse back. When he suffered, didn't threaten, but committed himself to him who judges righteously; who his own self bore our sins in his body on the tree, that we, having died to sins, might live to righteousness; by whose stripes you were healed. For you were going astray like sheep; but now have returned to the Shepherd and Overseer of your souls.

Now who is he who will harm you, if you become imitators of that which is good? But even if you should suffer for righteousness' sake, you are blessed. "Don't fear what they fear, neither be troubled." But sanctify the Lord God in your hearts; and always be ready to give an answer to everyone who asks you a reason concerning the hope that is in you, with humility and fear: having a good conscience; that, while you are spoken against as evildoers, they may be disappointed who curse your good way of life in Christ.

For it is better, if it is God's will, that you suffer for doing well than for doing evil.

Because Christ also suffered for sins once, the righteous for the unrighteous, that he might bring you to God; being put to death in the flesh, but made alive in the spirit; in which he also went and preached to the spirits in prison, who before were disobedient, when God waited patiently in the days of Noah, while the ship was being built. In it, few, that is, eight souls, were saved through water. This is a symbol of baptism, which now saves you—not the putting away of the filth of the flesh, but the answer of a good conscience toward God, through the resurrection of Jesus Christ, who is at the right hand of God, having gone into heaven, angels and authorities and powers being made subject to him.

Beloved, don't be astonished at the fiery trial which has come upon you, to test you, as though a strange thing happened to you. But because you are partakers of Christ's sufferings, rejoice; that at the revelation of his glory you also may rejoice with exceeding joy. If you are insulted for the name of Christ, you are blessed; because the Spirit of glory and of God rests on you. On their part he is blasphemed, but on your part he is glorified.

Be sober and self-controlled. Be watchful. Your adversary, the devil, walks around like a roaring lion, seeking whom he may devour. Withstand him steadfast in your faith, knowing that your brothers who are in the world are undergoing the same sufferings. But may the God of all grace, who called you to his eternal glory by Christ Jesus, after you have suffered a little while, perfect, establish, strengthen, and settle you. To him be the glory and the power forever and ever. Amen.

Peter wrote a second letter, in which he warned the church of dangers from within - false teachers, mockers, and immorality. These were similar concerns as expressed by Paul and the other epistle authors. In this letter, Peter stressed the need to rely on knowledge to determine how to live. He also confirmed details about the future second coming of Jesus, to counteract "mockers" who were making fun of Christians for believing that Christ would come again. Peter told the readers to have faith in the return of Jesus, and to live "without blemish and blameless," as the second coming was incentive for holy living.

Simon Peter, a servant and apostle of Jesus Christ, to those who have obtained a like precious faith with us in the righteousness of our God and Savior, Jesus Christ:

Grace to you and peace be multiplied in the knowledge of God and of Jesus our Lord, seeing that his divine power has granted to us all things that pertain to life and godliness, through the knowledge of him who called us by his own glory and virtue.

For we did not follow cunningly devised fables, when we made known to you the power and coming of our Lord Jesus Christ, but we were eyewitnesses of his majesty. For he received from God the Father honor and glory, when the voice came to him from the Majestic Glory, "This is my beloved Son, in whom I am well pleased." We heard this voice come out of heaven when we were with him on the holy mountain.

We have the more sure word of prophecy; and you do well that you heed it, as to a lamp shining in a dark place, until the day dawns, and the morning star arises in your hearts: knowing this first, that no prophecy of Scripture is of private interpretation. For no prophecy ever came by the will of man: but holy men of God spoke, being moved by the Holy Spirit.

But false prophets also arose among the people, as false teachers will also be among you, who will secretly bring in destructive heresies, denying even the Master who bought them, bringing on themselves swift destruction. Many will follow their immoral ways, and as a result, the way of the truth will be maligned.

For if, after they have escaped the defilement of the world through the knowledge of the Lord and Savior Jesus Christ, they are again entangled in it and overcome, the last state has become worse for them than the first. For it would be better for them not to have known the way of righteousness, than, after knowing it, to turn back from the holy commandment delivered to them. But it has happened to them according to the true proverb, "The dog turns to his own vomit again," and "the sow that has washed to wallowing in the mire."

This is now, beloved, the second letter that I have written to you; and in both of them I stir up your sincere mind by reminding you; that you should remember the words which were spoken before by the holy prophets, and the commandments of us, the apostles of the Lord and Savior: knowing this first, that in the last days mockers will come, walking after their own lusts, and saying, "Where is the promise of his coming? For, from the day that the fathers fell asleep, all things continue as they were from the beginning of the creation."

But don't forget this one thing, beloved, that one day is with the Lord as a thousand years, and a thousand years as one day. The Lord is not slow concerning his promise, as some count slowness; but is patient with us, not wishing that any should perish, but that all should come to repentance. But the day of the Lord will come as a thief in the night; in which the heavens will pass away with a great noise, and the elements will be dissolved with fervent heat, and the earth and the works that are in it will be burned up. Therefore since all these things will be destroyed like this, what kind of people ought you to be in holy living and godliness, looking for and earnestly desiring the coming of the day of God, which will cause the burning heavens to be dissolved, and the elements will melt with fervent heat? But, according to his promise, we look for new heavens and a new earth, in which righteousness dwells.

Therefore, beloved, seeing that you look for these things, be diligent to be found in peace, without blemish and blameless in his sight.

But grow in the grace and knowledge of our Lord and Savior Jesus Christ. To him be the glory both now and forever. Amen.

The apostle John, in addition to penning the Gospel of John, also wrote three letters (epistles) to the church. Now late in his life, he was likely the only surviving apostle, and perhaps the only one to die a death of natural causes. As a "senior statesman" in the Church,

John usually spoke to the followers of Christ in simple, loving tones, seeking to lead them gently to the right path. But, at other times, he bristled with angry words - especially directed toward false teachers.

When he wrote his letters, the church was already under many attacks, both in the form of persecution and in false teaching. John particularly was disturbed by the Gnostics, who taught that everything physical or of this world was evil; a byproduct of this viewpoint was their denial that Christ came to earth in the flesh. John reminded the readers in his beginning statements that he saw and touched Jesus with his own hands.

That which was from the beginning, that which we have heard, that which we have seen with our eyes, that which we saw, and our hands touched, concerning the Word of life (and the life was revealed, and we have seen, and testify, and declare to you the life, the eternal life, which was with the Father, and was revealed to us); that which we have seen and heard we declare to you, that you also may have fellowship with us. Yes, and our fellowship is with the Father, and with his Son, Jesus Christ. And we write these things to you, that our joy may be fulfilled.

This is the message which we have heard from him and announce to you, that God is light, and in him is no darkness at all. If we say that we have fellowship with him and walk in the darkness, we lie, and don't tell the truth. But if we walk in the light, as he is in the light, we have fellowship with one another, and the blood of Jesus Christ, his Son, cleanses us from all sin. If we say that we have no sin, we deceive ourselves, and the truth is not in us. If we confess our sins, he is faithful and righteous to forgive us the sins, and to cleanse us from all unrighteousness. If we say that we haven't sinned, we make him a liar, and his word is not in us.

My little children, I write these things to you so that you may not sin. If anyone sins, we have a Counselor with the Father, Jesus Christ, the righteous. And he is the atoning sacrifice for our sins, and not for ours only, but also for the whole world. This is how we know that we know him: if we keep his commandments.

Don't love the world, neither the things that are in the world. If anyone loves the world, the Father's love isn't in him. For all that is in the world, the lust of the flesh, the lust of the eyes, and the pride of life, isn't the Father's, but is the world's. The world is passing away with its lusts, but he who does God's will remains forever.

Behold, how great a love the Father has bestowed on us, that we should be called children of God! For this cause the world doesn't know us, because it didn't know him. Beloved, now we are children of God, and it is not yet revealed

425

what we will be. But we know that, when he is revealed, we will be like him; for we will see him just as he is.

By this we know love, because he laid down his life for us. And we ought to lay down our lives for the brothers. This is his commandment, that we should believe in the name of his Son, Jesus Christ, and love one another, even as he commanded. He who keeps his commandments remains in him, and he in him. By this we know that he remains in us, by the Spirit which he gave us.

Beloved, don't believe every spirit, but test the spirits, whether they are of God, because many false prophets have gone out into the world. By this you know the Spirit of God: every spirit who confesses that Jesus Christ has come in the flesh is of God, and every spirit who doesn't confess that Jesus Christ has come in the flesh is not of God.

Beloved, let us love one another, for love is of God; and everyone who loves is born of God, and knows God. He who doesn't love doesn't know God, for God is love. By this God's love was revealed in us, that God has sent his one and only Son into the world that we might live through him. In this is love, not that we loved God, but that he loved us, and sent his Son as the atoning sacrifice for our sins. Beloved, if God loved us in this way, we also ought to love one another. No one has seen God at any time. If we love one another, God remains in us, and his love has been perfected in us.

We love him, because he first loved us. If a man says, "I love God," and hates his brother, he is a liar; for he who doesn't love his brother whom he has seen, how can he love God whom he has not seen? This commandment we have from him, that he who loves God should also love his brother.

Whoever believes that Jesus is the Christ is born of God. Whoever loves the Father also loves the child who is born of him. By this we know that we love the children of God, when we love God and keep his commandments. For this is the love of God, that we keep his commandments. His commandments are not grievous. For whatever is born of God overcomes the world. This is the victory that has overcome the world: your faith.

These things I have written to you who believe in the name of the Son of God, that you may know that you have eternal life, and that you may continue to believe in the name of the Son of God.

38 WORDS OF ENCOURAGEMENT

Letters to the Hebrew Christians and a Young Minister

The writer of the book of Hebrews spent much time going back to the Old Testament, showing how the prophets and heroes of the Bible who preceded Jesus were all looking ahead to his coming, and to the establishment of the spiritual kingdom. Here, the case was firmly made that the New Covenant, brought about by Jesus, was vastly superior to the covenant of Moses. The readers of this epistle can gain confidence in their faith and in their high priest - Christ Jesus.

God, having in the past spoken to the fathers through the prophets at many times and in various ways, has at the end of these days spoken to us by his Son, whom he appointed heir of all things, through whom also he made the worlds. His Son is the radiance of his glory, the very image of his substance, and upholding all things by the word of his power, when he had by himself made purification for our sins, sat down on the right hand of the Majesty on high; having become so much better than the angels, as he has inherited a more excellent name than they have.

Therefore we ought to pay greater attention to the things that were heard, lest perhaps we drift away. For if the word spoken through angels proved steadfast, and every transgression and disobedience received a just recompense; how will we escape if we neglect so great a salvation—which at the first having been spoken through the Lord, was confirmed to us by those who heard; God also testifying with them, both by signs and wonders, by various works of power, and by gifts of the Holy Spirit, according to his own will?

But we see him who has been made a little lower than the angels, Jesus, because of the suffering of death crowned with glory and honor, that by the grace of God he should taste of death for everyone. For it became him, for whom are all things, and through whom are all things, in bringing many children to glory, to make the author of their salvation perfect through sufferings.

Having then a great high priest, who has passed through the heavens, Jesus, the Son of God, let us hold tightly to our confession. For we don't have a high priest who can't be touched with the feeling of our infirmities, but one who has been in all points tempted like we are, yet without sin. Let us therefore draw near with boldness to the throne of grace, that we may receive mercy, and may find grace for help in time of need.

He, in the days of his flesh, having offered up prayers and petitions with strong crying and tears to him who was able to save him from death, and having been heard for his godly fear, though he was a Son, yet learned obedience by the things which he suffered. Having been made perfect, he became to all of those who obey him the author of eternal salvation, named by God a high priest after the order of Melchizedek.

Therefore leaving the teaching of the first principles of Christ, let us press on to perfection—not laying again a foundation of repentance from dead works, of faith toward God, of the teaching of baptisms, of laying on of hands, of resurrection of the dead, and of eternal judgment. This will we do, if God permits.

Now in the things which we are saying, the main point is this. We have such a high priest, who sat down on the right hand of the throne of the Majesty in the heavens, a servant of the sanctuary, and of the true tabernacle, which the Lord pitched, not man.

But Christ having come as a high priest of the coming good things, through the greater and more perfect tabernacle, not made with hands, that is to say, not of this creation, nor yet through the blood of goats and calves, but through his own blood, entered in once for all into the Holy Place, having obtained eternal redemption. For if the blood of goats and bulls, and the ashes of a heifer sprinkling those who have been defiled, sanctify to the cleanness of the flesh: how much more will the blood of Christ, who through the eternal Spirit offered himself without blemish to God, cleanse your conscience from dead works to serve the living God? For this reason he is the mediator of a new covenant, since a death has occurred for the redemption of the transgressions that were under the first covenant, that those who have been called may receive the promise of the eternal inheritance.

Inasmuch as it is appointed for men to die once, and after this, judgment, so Christ also, having been offered once to bear the sins of many, will appear a second time, without sin, to those who are eagerly waiting for him for salvation.

Now faith is assurance of things hoped for, proof of things not seen. For by this, the elders obtained testimony. By faith, we understand that the universe has been framed by the word of God, so that what is seen has not been made out of things which are visible.

By faith, Abel offered to God a more excellent sacrifice than Cain, through which he had testimony given to him that he was righteous, God testifying with respect to his gifts; and through it he, being dead, still speaks.

By faith, Enoch was taken away, so that he wouldn't see death, and he was not found, because God translated him. For he has had testimony given to him that before his translation he had been well pleasing to God.

Without faith it is impossible to be well pleasing to him, for he who comes to God must believe that he exists, and that he is a rewarder of those who seek him.

By faith, Noah, being warned about things not yet seen, moved with godly fear, prepared a ship for the saving of his house, through which he condemned the world, and became heir of the righteousness which is according to faith.

By faith, Abraham, when he was called, obeyed to go out to the place which he was to receive for an inheritance. He went out, not knowing where he went. By faith, he lived as an alien in the land of promise, as in a land not his own, dwelling in tents, with Isaac and Jacob, the heirs with him of the same promise. For he looked for the city which has the foundations, whose builder and maker is God. By faith, even Sarah herself received power to conceive, and she bore a child when she was past age, since she counted him faithful who had promised. Therefore as many as the stars of the sky in multitude, and as innumerable as the sand which is by the sea shore, were fathered by one man, and him as good as dead.

These all died in faith, not having received the promises, but having seen them and embraced them from afar, and having confessed that they were strangers and pilgrims on the earth. For those who say such things make it clear that they are seeking a country of their own. If indeed they had been thinking of that country from which they went out, they would have had enough time to return. But now they desire a better country, that is, a heavenly one. Therefore God is not ashamed of them, to be called their God, for he has prepared a city for them.

By faith, Moses, when he had grown up, refused to be called the son of Pharaoh's daughter, choosing rather to share ill treatment with God's people, than to enjoy the pleasures of sin for a time; accounting the reproach of Christ greater riches than the treasures of Egypt; for he looked to the reward.

What more shall I say? For the time would fail me if I told of Gideon, Barak, Samson, Jephthah, David, Samuel, and the prophets; who, through faith subdued kingdoms, worked out righteousness, obtained promises, stopped the mouths of lions, quenched the power of fire, escaped the edge of the sword, from weakness were made strong, grew mighty in war, and caused foreign armies to flee. Women received their dead by resurrection. Others were tortured, not accepting their deliverance, that they might obtain a better resurrection. Others were tried by mocking and scourging, yes, moreover by bonds and imprisonment. They were stoned. They were sawn apart. They were tempted. They were slain with the sword. They went around in sheep skins and in goat skins; being destitute, afflicted, ill-treated (of whom the world was not worthy), wandering in deserts, mountains, caves, and the holes of the earth. These all, having had testimony given to them through their faith, didn't receive the promise, God having provided some better thing concerning us, so that apart from us they should not be made perfect.

Therefore let us also, seeing we are surrounded by so great a cloud of witnesses, lay aside every weight and the sin which so easily entangles us, and let us run with patience the race that is set before us, looking to Jesus, the author and perfecter of faith, who for the joy that was set before him endured the cross, despising its shame, and has sat down at the right hand of the throne of God.

But you have come to Mount Zion, and to the city of the living God, the heavenly Jerusalem, and to innumerable multitudes of angels, to the general assembly and assembly of the firstborn who are enrolled in heaven, to God the Judge of all, to the spirits of just men made perfect, to Jesus, the mediator of a new covenant, and to the blood of sprinkling that speaks better than that of Abel.

Let brotherly love continue. Don't forget to show hospitality to strangers, for in doing so, some have entertained angels without knowing it. Remember those who are in bonds, as bound with them; and those who are ill-treated, since you are also in the body. Let marriage be held in honor among all, and let the bed be undefiled: but God will judge the sexually immoral and adulterers.

Remember your leaders, men who spoke to you the word of God, and considering the results of their conduct, imitate their faith. Jesus Christ is the same yesterday, today, and forever. Don't be carried away by various and strange teachings, for it is good that the heart be established by grace, not by food, through which those who were so occupied were not benefited.

Now may the God of peace, who brought again from the dead the great shepherd of the sheep with the blood of an eternal covenant, our Lord Jesus, make you complete in every good work to do his will, working in you that which is well pleasing in his sight, through Jesus Christ, to whom be the glory forever and ever. Amen.

In addition to establishing churches, Paul also worked to develop men to follow in his place. He did not want a leadership vacuum to evolve when he died. Two such men were Timothy and Titus. Paul wrote letters to both of these men that are preserved as epistles in the Bible.

As a young man, Timothy gained Paul's trust. His early development was under the watch of his mother and grandmother, both of whom were Christian believers. Then Paul took him under his wing. Timothy often traveled with Paul; in six of Paul's letters, he mentions that Timothy is by his side. In his letter to the Church at Philippi, Paul wrote of Timothy, "For I have no one else like-minded, who will truly care about you. For they all seek their own, not the things of Jesus Christ. But you know the proof of him, that, as a child serves a father, so he served with me in furtherance of the Good News."

In his letters to Timothy, Paul encouraged him to lead by living the example of an exemplary life. Paul knew that the challenges ahead for this young minister would be difficult, and he encouraged him to remain steadfast.

Paul, an apostle of Christ Jesus according to the commandment of God our Savior, and Christ Jesus our hope; to Timothy, my true child in faith: Grace, mercy, and peace, from God our Father and Christ Jesus our Lord.

As I urged you when I was going into Macedonia, stay at Ephesus that you might command certain men not to teach a different doctrine, neither to pay attention to myths and endless genealogies, which cause disputes, rather than God's stewardship, which is in faith— but the goal of this command is love, out of a pure heart and a good conscience and sincere faith; from which things some, having missed the mark, have turned aside to vain talking; desiring to be teachers of the law, though they understand neither what they say, nor about what they strongly affirm.

But we know that the law is good, if a man uses it lawfully, as knowing this, that law is not made for a righteous man, but for the lawless and insubordinate, for the ungodly and sinners, for the unholy and profane, for murderers of fathers and murderers of mothers, for manslayers, for the sexually immoral, for homosexuals, for slave-traders, for liars, for perjurers, and for any other thing contrary to the sound doctrine; according to the Good News of the glory of the blessed God, which was committed to my trust. And I thank him who enabled me, Christ Jesus our Lord, because he counted me faithful, appointing me to service;

I exhort therefore, first of all, that petitions, prayers, intercessions, and givings of thanks, be made for all men: for kings and all who are in high places; that we may lead a tranquil and quiet life in all godliness and reverence. For this is good and acceptable in the sight of God our Savior; who desires all people to be saved and come to full knowledge of the truth. For there is one God, and one mediator between God and men, the man Christ Jesus, who gave himself as a ransom for all; the testimony in its own times; to which I was appointed a preacher and an apostle (I am telling the truth in Christ, not lying), a teacher of the Gentiles in faith and truth.

I desire therefore that the men in every place pray, lifting up holy hands without anger and doubting. In the same way, that women also adorn themselves in decent clothing, with modesty and propriety; not just with braided hair, gold, pearls, or expensive clothing.

These things I write to you, hoping to come to you shortly; but if I wait long, that you may know how men ought to behave themselves in God's house, which is the assembly of the living God, the pillar and ground of the truth. Without controversy, the mystery of godliness is great:

God was revealed in the flesh, justified in the spirit,

seen by angels, preached among the nations,

believed on in the world, and received up in glory.

But the Spirit says expressly that in later times some will fall away from the faith, paying attention to seducing spirits and doctrines of demons, through the hypocrisy of men who speak lies, branded in their own conscience as with a hot iron; forbidding marriage and commanding to abstain from foods which God created to be received with thanksgiving by those who believe and know the truth. For every creature of God is good, and nothing is to be rejected, if it is received with thanksgiving. For it is sanctified through the word of God and prayer.

If you instruct the brothers of these things, you will be a good servant of Christ Jesus, nourished in the words of the faith, and of the good doctrine which you have followed.

Let no man despise your youth; but be an example to those who believe, in word, in your way of life, in love, in spirit, in faith, and in purity. Until I come, pay attention to reading, to exhortation, and to teaching.

But godliness with contentment is great gain. For we brought nothing into the world, and we certainly can't carry anything out. But having food and clothing, we will be content with that. But those who are determined to be rich fall into a temptation and a snare and many foolish and harmful lusts, such as drown men in ruin and destruction. For the love of money is a root of all kinds of evil. Some have been led astray from the faith in their greed, and have pierced themselves through with many sorrows.

But you, man of God, flee these things, and follow after righteousness, godliness, faith, love, patience, and gentleness. Fight the good fight of faith. Lay hold of the eternal life to which you were called, and you confessed the good confession in the sight of many witnesses.

Timothy, guard that which is committed to you, turning away from the empty chatter and oppositions of the knowledge which is falsely so called; which some professing have erred concerning the faith. Grace be with you. Amen.

In his second letter to the young evangelist Timothy, Paul continued to exhort him to remain steadfast in the teachings that he had received. Paul warned that the time would come when men would not want to hear the truth; but he expressed full confidence in the scriptures, and encouraged Timothy to follow his pattern by, in turn, teaching the gospel to other men.

Paul, an apostle of Jesus Christ through the will of God, according to the promise of the life which is in Christ Jesus, to Timothy, my beloved child: Grace, mercy, and peace, from God the Father and Christ Jesus our Lord.

Hold the pattern of sound words which you have heard from me, in faith and love which is in Christ Jesus. That good thing which was committed to you, guard through the Holy Spirit who dwells in us.

You therefore, my child, be strengthened in the grace that is in Christ Jesus. The things which you have heard from me among many witnesses, commit the same to faithful men, who will be able to teach others also. You therefore must endure hardship, as a good soldier of Christ Jesus.

Remember Jesus Christ, risen from the dead, of the seed of David, according to my Good News, in which I suffer hardship to the point of chains as a criminal. But God's word isn't chained.

Give diligence to present yourself approved by God, a workman who doesn't need to be ashamed, properly handling the Word of Truth.

Flee from youthful lusts; but pursue righteousness, faith, love, and peace with those who call on the Lord out of a pure heart. But refuse foolish and ignorant questionings, knowing that they generate strife. The Lord's servant must not quarrel, but be gentle towards all, able to teach, patient, in gentleness correcting those who oppose him: perhaps God may give them repentance leading to a full knowledge of the truth, and they may recover themselves out of the devil's snare, having been taken captive by him to his will.

From infancy, you have known the holy Scriptures which are able to make you wise for salvation through faith, which is in Christ Jesus. Every Scripture is God-breathed and profitable for teaching, for reproof, for correction, and for instruction in righteousness, that the man of God may be complete, thoroughly equipped for every good work.

I command you therefore before God and the Lord Jesus Christ, who will judge the living and the dead at his appearing and his Kingdom: preach the word; be urgent in season and out of season; reprove, rebuke, and exhort, with all patience and teaching.

For the time will come when they will not listen to the sound doctrine, but, having itching ears, will heap up for themselves teachers after their own lusts; and will turn away their ears from the truth, and turn aside to fables. But you be sober in all things, suffer hardship, do the work of an evangelist, and fulfill your ministry.

The Lord Jesus Christ be with your spirit. Grace be with you. Amen.

39 VICTORIOUS IN THE END!

The Revelation to John

The book of Revelation, also known as "the apocalypse," was penned by the apostle John, and was the last book written that is in the Bible. Primarily prophetic in nature, the book begins with direct instructions to seven churches in Asia Minor, then progresses into highly symbolic revelations about the future of the church. The book of Revelation is difficult to fully understand due to the symbolic language; many believe John wrote the book in that form to keep those who were persecuting the church from understanding the contents. Although scholars have taught many different interpretations of the prophesies of this book over time, the central core message is clear; there is a battle of spiritual warfare that envelops this world, but in the end, Jesus Christ will win the fight and emerge victorious. In this victory, the saints who worshiped and obeyed Christ will be given eternal life in heaven, in the presence of God.

This is the Revelation of Jesus Christ, which God gave him to show to his servants the things which must happen soon, which he sent and made known by his angel to his servant, John, who testified to God's word, and of the testimony of Jesus Christ, about everything that he saw.

Blessed is he who reads and those who hear the words of the prophecy, and keep the things that are written in it, for the time is at hand.

John, to the seven assemblies that are in Asia: Grace to you and peace, from God, who is and who was and who is to come; and from the seven Spirits who are before his throne; and from Jesus Christ, the faithful witness, the firstborn of the dead, and the ruler of the kings of the earth. To him who loves us, and washed us from our sins by his blood; and he made us to be a Kingdom, priests to his God and Father; to him be the glory and the dominion forever and ever. Amen.

Behold, he is coming with the clouds, and every eye will see him, including those who pierced him. All the tribes of the earth will mourn over him. Even so,

Amen.

"I am the Alpha and the Omega," says the Lord God, "who is and who was and who is to come, the Almighty."

I John, your brother and partner with you in oppression, Kingdom, and perseverance in Christ Jesus, was on the isle that is called Patmos because of God's Word and the testimony of Jesus Christ. I was in the Spirit on the Lord's day, and I heard behind me a loud voice, like a trumpet saying, "What you see, write in a book and send to the seven assemblies: to Ephesus, Smyrna, Pergamum, Thyatira, Sardis, Philadelphia, and to Laodicea."

I turned to see the voice that spoke with me. Having turned, I saw seven golden lampstands. And among the lampstands was one like a son of man, clothed with a robe reaching down to his feet, and with a golden sash around his chest. His head and his hair were white as white wool, like snow. His eyes were like a flame of fire. His feet were like burnished brass, as if it had been refined in a furnace. His voice was like the voice of many waters. He had seven stars in his right hand. Out of his mouth proceeded a sharp two-edged sword. His face was like the sun shining at its brightest. When I saw him, I fell at his feet like a dead man.

He laid his right hand on me, saying, "Don't be afraid. I am the first and the last, and the Living one. I was dead, and behold, I am alive forevermore. Amen. I have the keys of Death and of Hades. Write therefore the things which you have seen, and the things which are, and the things which will happen hereafter; the mystery of the seven stars which you saw in my right hand, and the seven golden lampstands. The seven stars are the angels of the seven assemblies. The seven lampstands are seven assemblies.

"To the angel of the assembly in Ephesus write:

"He who holds the seven stars in his right hand, he who walks among the seven golden lampstands says these things:

"I know your works, and your toil and perseverance, and that you can't tolerate evil men, and have tested those who call themselves apostles, and they are not, and found them false. You have perseverance and have endured for my name's sake, and have not grown weary. But I have this against you, that you left your first love. Remember therefore from where you have fallen, and repent and do the first works; or else I am coming to you swiftly, and will move your lampstand out of its place, unless you repent. But this you have, that you hate the works of the Nicolaitans, which I also hate. He who has an ear, let him hear what the Spirit says to the assemblies. To him who overcomes I will give to eat of the tree of life, which is in the Paradise of my God.

"To the angel of the assembly in Smyrna write:

"The first and the last, who was dead, and has come to life says these things:

"I know your works, oppression, and your poverty (but you are rich), and the blasphemy of those who say they are Jews, and they are not, but are a synagogue of Satan. Don't be afraid of the things which you are about to suffer. Behold, the devil is about to throw some of you into prison, that you may be tested; and you will have oppression for ten days. Be faithful to death, and I will give you the crown of life. He who has an ear, let him hear what the Spirit says to the assemblies. He who overcomes won't be harmed by the second death.

"To the angel of the assembly in Pergamum write:

"He who has the sharp two-edged sword says these things:

"I know your works and where you dwell, where Satan's throne is. You hold firmly to my name, and didn't deny my faith in the days of Antipas my witness, my faithful one, who was killed among you, where Satan dwells. But I have a few things against you, because you have there some who hold the teaching of Balaam, who taught Balak to throw a stumbling block before the children of Israel, to eat things sacrificed to idols, and to commit sexual immorality. So you also have some who hold to the teaching of the Nicolaitans likewise. Repent therefore, or else I am coming to you quickly, and I will make war against them with the sword of my mouth. He who has an ear, let him hear what the Spirit says to the assemblies. To him who overcomes, to him I will give of the hidden manna, and I will give him a white stone, and on the stone a new name written, which no one knows but he who receives it.

"To the angel of the assembly in Thyatira write:

"The Son of God, who has his eyes like a flame of fire, and his feet are like burnished brass, says these things:

"I know your works, your love, faith, service, patient endurance, and that your last works are more than the first. But I have this against you, that you tolerate your woman, Jezebel, who calls herself a prophetess. She teaches and seduces my servants to commit sexual immorality, and to eat things sacrificed to idols. I gave her time to repent, but she refuses to repent of her sexual immorality. Behold, I will throw her into a bed, and those who commit adultery with her into great oppression, unless they repent of her works. I will kill her children with Death, and all the assemblies will know that I am he who searches the minds and hearts. I will give to each one of you according to your deeds. But to you I say, to the rest who are in Thyatira, as many as don't have this teaching, who don't know what some call 'the deep things of Satan,' to you I say, I am not putting any other burden on you. Nevertheless, hold that which you have firmly until I come. He who overcomes, and he who keeps my works to the end, to him I will give authority over the nations. He will rule them with a rod of iron, shattering them like clay pots; as I also have received of my Father: and I will give him the morning star. He who has an ear, let him hear what the Spirit says to the assemblies.

"And to the angel of the assembly in Sardis write:

"He who has the seven Spirits of God, and the seven stars says these things:

"I know your works, that you have a reputation of being alive, but you are dead. Wake up, and keep the things that remain, which you were about to throw away, for I have found no works of yours perfected before my God. Remember therefore how you have received and heard. Keep it, and repent. If therefore you won't watch, I will come as a thief, and you won't know what hour I will come upon you. Nevertheless you have a few names in Sardis that did not defile their garments. They will walk with me in white, for they are worthy. He who overcomes will be arrayed in white garments, and I will in no way blot his name out of the book of life, and I will confess his name before my Father, and before his angels. He who has an ear, let him hear what the Spirit says to the assemblies.

"To the angel of the assembly in Philadelphia write:

"He who is holy, he who is true, he who has the key of David, he who opens and no one can shut, and who shuts and no one opens, says these things:

"I know your works (behold, I have set before you an open door, which no one can shut), that you have a little power, and kept my word, and didn't deny my name. Behold, I give of the synagogue of Satan, of those who say they are Jews, and they are not, but lie. Behold, I will make them to come and worship before your feet, and to know that I have loved you. Because you kept my command to endure, I also will keep you from the hour of testing, which is to come on the whole world, to test those who dwell on the earth. I am coming quickly! Hold firmly that which you have, so that no one takes your crown. He who overcomes, I will make him a pillar in the temple of my God, and he will go out from there no more. I will write on him the name of my God, and the name of the city of my God, the new Jerusalem, which comes down out of heaven from my God, and my own new name. He who has an ear, let him hear what the Spirit says to the assemblies.

"To the angel of the assembly in Laodicea write:

"The Amen, the Faithful and True Witness, the Head of God's creation, says these things:

"I know your works, that you are neither cold nor hot. I wish you were cold or hot. So, because you are lukewarm, and neither hot nor cold, I will vomit you out of my mouth. Because you say, 'I am rich, and have gotten riches, and have need of nothing;' and don't know that you are the wretched one, miserable, poor, blind, and naked; I counsel you to buy from me gold refined by fire, that you may become rich; and white garments, that you may clothe yourself, and that the shame of your nakedness may not be revealed; and eye salve to anoint your eyes, that you may see. As many as I love, I reprove and chasten. Be zealous therefore, and repent. Behold, I stand at the door and knock. If anyone hears my voice and opens the door, then I will come in to him, and will dine with him, and he with me. He who overcomes, I will give to him to sit down with me on my throne, as I also overcame, and sat down with my Father on his throne. He who has an ear, let him hear what the Spirit says to the assemblies."

After these things I looked and saw a door opened in heaven, and the first voice that I heard, like a trumpet speaking with me, was one saying, "Come up here, and I will show you the things which must happen after this."

Immediately I was in the Spirit. Behold, there was a throne set in heaven, and one sitting on the throne that looked like a jasper stone and a sardius. There was a rainbow around the throne, like an emerald to look at. Around the throne were twenty-four thrones. On the thrones were twenty-four elders sitting, dressed in white garments, with crowns of gold on their heads. Out of the throne proceed lightnings, sounds, and thunders. There were seven lamps of fire burning before his throne, which are the seven Spirits of God. Before the throne was something like a sea of glass, similar to crystal. In the midst of the throne, and around the throne were four living creatures full of eyes before and behind. The first creature was like a lion, and the second creature like a calf, and the third creature had a face like a man, and the fourth was like a flying eagle. The four living creatures, each one of them having six wings, are full of eyes around and within. They have no rest day and night, saying, "Holy, holy, holy is the Lord God, the Almighty, who was and who is and who is to come!"

When the living creatures give glory, honor, and thanks to him who sits on the throne, to him who lives forever and ever, the twenty-four elders fall down before him who sits on the throne, and worship him who lives forever and ever, and throw their crowns before the throne, saying, "Worthy are you, our Lord and God, the Holy One, to receive the glory, the honor, and the power, for you created all things, and because of your desire they existed, and were created!"

I saw, in the right hand of him who sat on the throne, a book written inside and outside, sealed shut with seven seals. I saw a mighty angel proclaiming with a loud voice, "Who is worthy to open the book, and to break its seals?" No one in heaven above, or on the earth, or under the earth, was able to open the book, or to look in it. And I wept much, because no one was found worthy to open the book, or to look in it. One of the elders said to me, "Don't weep. Behold, the Lion who is of the tribe of Judah, the Root of David, has overcome; he who opens the book and its seven seals." I saw in the midst of the throne and of the four living creatures, and in the midst of the elders, a Lamb standing, as though it had been slain, having seven horns, and seven eyes, which are the seven Spirits of God, sent out into all the earth. Then he came, and he took it out of the right hand of him who sat on the throne. Now when he had taken the book, the four living creatures and the twenty-four elders fell down before the Lamb, each one having a harp, and golden bowls full of incense, which are the prayers of the saints. They sang a new song, saying,

"You are worthy to take the book,
and to open its seals:
for you were killed,
and bought us for God with your blood,
out of every tribe, language, people, and nation,
and made us kings and priests to our God,
and we will reign on earth."

I saw, and I heard something like a voice of many angels around the throne, the living creatures, and the elders; and the number of them was ten thousands of ten thousands, and thousands of thousands; saying with a loud voice, "Worthy is the Lamb who has been killed to receive the power, wealth, wisdom, strength, honor, glory, and blessing!"

I heard every created thing which is in heaven, on the earth, under the earth, on the sea, and everything in them, saying, "To him who sits on the throne, and to the Lamb be the blessing, the honor, the glory, and the dominion, forever and ever! Amen!"

The four living creatures said, "Amen!" The elders fell down and worshiped.

John then described an amazing series of events, where the Lamb opened the seals, and riders emerged on white, red, black and pale horses. He described the souls of persecuted Christians under the altar, crying out for vengeance. A great earthquake occurred, and four angels appeared at the corners of the earth, holding back the wind. This symbolic word picture continued, with images of multi-headed beasts, dragons, angels, plagues, and other scenes unfolding in dramatic form. Clearly a great battle between good and evil was being described.

I heard something like the voice of a great multitude, and like the voice of many waters, and like the voice of mighty thunders, saying, "Hallelujah! For the Lord our God, the Almighty, reigns! Let us rejoice and be exceedingly glad, and let us give the glory to him. For the marriage of the Lamb has come, and his wife has made herself ready." It was given to her that she would array herself in bright, pure, fine linen: for the fine linen is the righteous acts of the saints.

He said to me, "Write, 'Blessed are those who are invited to the marriage supper of the Lamb.'" He said to me, "These are true words of God."

I fell down before his feet to worship him. He said to me, "Look! Don't do it! I am a fellow bondservant with you and with your brothers who hold the testimony of Jesus. Worship God, for the testimony of Jesus is the Spirit of Prophecy."

I saw the heaven opened, and behold, a white horse, and he who sat on it is called Faithful and True. In righteousness he judges and makes war. His eyes are a flame of fire, and on his head are many crowns. He has names written and a name written which no one knows but he himself. He is clothed in a garment sprinkled with blood. His name is called "The Word of God." The armies which are in heaven followed him on white horses, clothed in white, pure, fine linen. Out of his mouth proceeds a sharp, double-edged sword, that with it he should strike the nations. He will rule them with an iron rod. He treads the wine press of the fierceness of the wrath of God, the Almighty. He has on his garment and on his thigh a name written, "KING OF KINGS, AND LORD OF LORDS."

I saw a great white throne, and him who sat on it, from whose face the earth and the heaven fled away. There was found no place for them. I saw the dead, the great and the small, standing before the throne, and they opened books. Another book was opened, which is the book of life. The dead were judged out of the things which were written in the books, according to their works. The sea gave up the dead who were in it. Death and Hades gave up the dead who were in them. They were judged, each one according to his works. Death and Hades were thrown into the lake of fire. This is the second death, the lake of fire. If anyone was not found written in the book of life, he was cast into the lake of fire.

I saw a new heaven and a new earth: for the first heaven and the first earth have passed away, and the sea is no more. I saw the holy city, New Jerusalem, coming down out of heaven from God, prepared like a bride adorned for her husband. I heard a loud voice out of heaven saying, "Behold, God's dwelling is with people, and he will dwell with them, and they will be his people, and God himself will be with them as their God. He will wipe away from them every tear from their eyes. Death will be no more; neither will there be mourning, nor crying, nor pain, any more. The first things have passed away."

He who sits on the throne said, "Behold, I am making all things new." He said, "Write, for these words of God are faithful and true."

He said to me, "It is done! I am the Alpha and the Omega, the Beginning and the End. I will give freely to him who is thirsty from the spring of the water of life.

He who overcomes, I will give him these things. I will be his God, and he will

441

be my son. But for the cowardly, unbelieving, sinners, abominable, murderers, sexually immoral, sorcerers, idolaters, and all liars, their part is in the lake that burns with fire and sulfur, which is the second death."

One of the seven angels who had the seven bowls, who were loaded with the seven last plagues came, and he spoke with me, saying, "Come here. I will show you the wife, the Lamb's bride." He carried me away in the Spirit to a great and high mountain, and showed me the holy city, Jerusalem, coming down out of heaven from God, having the glory of God. Her light was like a most precious stone, as if it were a jasper stone, clear as crystal; having a great and high wall; having twelve gates, and at the gates twelve angels; and names written on them, which are the names of the twelve tribes of the children of Israel. On the east were three gates; and on the north three gates; and on the south three gates; and on the west three gates. The wall of the city had twelve foundations, and on them twelve names of the twelve Apostles of the Lamb.

He who spoke with me had for a measure, a golden reed, to measure the city, its gates, and its walls. The city lies foursquare, and its length is as great as its breadth. He measured the city with the reed, Twelve thousand twelve stadia. Its length, breadth, and height are equal. Its wall is one hundred forty-four cubits, by the measure of a man, that is, of an angel. The construction of its wall was jasper. The city was pure gold, like pure glass. The foundations of the city's wall were adorned with all kinds of precious stones. The first foundation was jasper; the second, sapphire; the third, chalcedony; the fourth, emerald; the fifth, sardonyx; the sixth, sardius; the seventh, chrysolite; the eighth, beryl; the ninth, topaz; the tenth, chrysoprasus; the eleventh, jacinth; and the twelfth, amethyst. The twelve gates were twelve pearls. Each one of the gates was made of one pearl. The street of the city was pure gold, like transparent glass.

I saw no temple in it, for the Lord God, the Almighty, and the Lamb, are its temple. The city has no need for the sun, neither of the moon, to shine, for the very glory of God illuminated it, and its lamp is the Lamb. The nations will walk in its light. The kings of the earth bring the glory and honor of the nations into it. Its gates will in no way be shut by day (for there will be no night there), and they shall bring the glory and the honor of the nations into it so that they may enter. There will in no way enter into it anything profane, or one who causes an abomination or a lie, but only those who are written in the Lamb's book of life.

He showed me a river of water of life, clear as crystal, proceeding out of the throne of God and of the Lamb, in the middle of its street. On this side of the river and on that was the tree of life, bearing twelve kinds of fruits, yielding its fruit every month. The leaves of the tree were for the healing of the nations. There will be no curse any more. The throne of God and of the Lamb will be in it, and his servants serve him. They will see his face, and his name will be on their foreheads. There will be no night, and they need no lamp light; for the Lord God will illuminate them. They will reign forever and ever.

He said to me, "These words are faithful and true. The Lord God of the spirits of the prophets sent his angel to show to his bondservants the things which must happen soon."

"Behold, I come quickly. Blessed is he who keeps the words of the prophecy of this book."

Now I, John, am the one who heard and saw these things. When I heard and saw, I fell down to worship before the feet of the angel who had shown me these things. He said to me, "See you don't do it! I am a fellow bondservant with you and with your brothers, the prophets, and with those who keep the words of this book. Worship God." He said to me, "Don't seal up the words of the prophecy of this book, for the time is at hand. He who acts unjustly, let him act unjustly still. He who is filthy, let him be filthy still. He who is righteous, let him do righteousness still. He who is holy, let him be holy still."

"Behold, I come quickly. My reward is with me, to repay to each man according to his work. I am the Alpha and the Omega, the First and the Last, the Beginning and the End. Blessed are those who do his commandments, that they may have the right to the tree of life, and may enter in by the gates into the city. Outside are the dogs, the sorcerers, the sexually immoral, the murderers, the idolaters, and everyone who loves and practices falsehood. I, Jesus, have sent my angel to testify these things to you for the assemblies. I am the root and the offspring of David; the Bright and Morning Star."

The Spirit and the bride say, "Come!" He who hears, let him say, "Come!" He who is thirsty, let him come. He who desires, let him take the water of life freely. I testify to everyone who hears the words of the prophecy of this book, if anyone adds to them, may God add to him the plagues which are written in this book. If anyone takes away from the words of the book of this prophecy, may God take away his part from the tree of life, and out of the holy city, which are written in this book. He who testifies these things says, "Yes, I come quickly."

Amen! Yes, come, Lord Jesus.

The grace of the Lord Jesus Christ be with all the saints. Amen.

Thus ends the Bible, with an admonition for Jesus to return to initiate the great final judgment. With this finish, we finally see the entire grand picture of the Bible. God created the universe, the world, and mankind; we are the crowning glory of his work, as we were made in His own image. In order to have freedom to obey God, we were created with freewill, the ability to choose between good and evil. When Adam and Eve sinned, that sin separated them from

God, just as our sins separate us from God today.

In order to be reconciled to God, a sacrifice was required. The Old Testament animal sacrifices could not fully take away the sins of the people; a perfect sacrifice was required to once and for all time atone for our sins. Every man and woman needs this sacrifice, for "we have all sinned and fallen short of the glory of God." That sacrifice was Jesus Christ, the only begotten Son of God, who came to this earth in the form of a man and lived a perfect life. His death was that perfect sacrifice, and his resurrection shows us that God can also raise us from the dead at the end of time. In becoming free from the grave, Jesus overcame death itself.

God used the nation of Israel to prepare the way for the coming of Christ. He established his chosen people, setting them aside to keep a thread of purity in a world of unrighteousness. In this way, a pure lineage was protected, from Abraham through Jesus, the Messiah.

After the resurrection of Jesus, God established the church, the "bride of Christ," the body of believers who obey the gospel and follow Christ. Shortly after this happened, the door was opened for all men, both Jew and Gentile, to become co-heirs in this spiritual kingdom. Now, we wait diligently for the coming of Christ, to usher in the Day of Judgment and to initiate the heavenly reward of those faithful to God.

Thus, we see the plan of God, which spans from the beginning of creation to the future coming of Christ. Even from the time God created this world, He knew that the sacrifice of his Son would be required to redeem us from our sins. Despite our faults, God loved us enough to set this painful plan in motion. We were created to glorify God, who enjoys our loving worship of exercising our free will and showing our love for Him in response to His love for us. By obeying and loving Him, we fulfill our purpose. In return, God has prepared for us a wonderful place of eternal bliss.

This is the greatest story ever told.

This is God's love story.

BIBLE REFERENCE MAP

Chapter 1 - The Beginning
Transition
Gen 1:1 - 4:15
Transition
Gen 6:9-7:12, 7:20-8:5, 8:13-9:7, 9:11-9:18, 9:28
Transition
Gen 11:1-11:9
Transition

Chapter 2 – The Seed of a Nation
Gen 12:1-12:8
Transition
Gen 13:2-13:18
Transition
Gen 15:1-21:20, 22:1-22:18, 24:1-24:4, 24:9-24:27
Transition
Gen 25:20-25:34, 27:1-27:26, 27:30-27:45
Transition
Gen 30:22-30:34
Transition
Gen 31:22-31:49
Transition
Gen 32:3-33:11, 35:1-35:12, 35:16-35:19, 35:28-35:29

Chapter 3 – Dreams and Deliverance
Gen 37:3-37:13, 37:17-37:36, 39:1-39:23
Transition
Gen 41:14-42:15
Transition
Gen 43:1-43:5, 43:11-43:15, 43:26-44:18, 45:25-46:5, 46:28-46:30, 47:11-47:12
Transition
Gen 47:27-47:31
Transition
Gen 50:15-50:26

Chapter 4 – Israel in Bondage
Transition
Ex 1:8-3:15, 3:18-4:18, 4:27-5:9
Transition
Ex 7:1-7:13
Transition
Ex 7:14-7:25
Transition
Ex 10:27-11:8
Transition
Ex 12:3-12:14, 12:25-12:41

Chapter 5 – Out of Egypt
Ex 13:17-13:22
Transition
Ex 14:5-14:31
Transition
Ex 15:22-16:3, 16:6-16:15, 16:34-16:35, 17:1-17:13, 19:1-19:25
Transition
Ex 20:1-20:19, 24:3-24:8, 24:15-25:2, 25:8-25:9
Transition
Ex 28:1-28:4
Transition
Ex 32:1-33:3, 33:7-34:10, 34:27-34:35, 35:20-35:21
Transition
Ex 39:32-39:39, 39:42-39:43, 40:17, 40:34-40:38

Chapter 6 – The Covenant
Transition
Lev 6:1-6:7, 6:24-7:6
Transition
Lev 9:23-9:24
Transition
Lev 10:1-10:7
Transition
Lev 11:1-11:11, 11:26-11:28
Transition
Lev 16:1-16:10, 16:20-16:22, 18:1-18:5, 18:29-18:30
Transition
Lev 19:11-19:18, Lev 19:33-19:35, 23:22
Lev 24:17-24:22, 25:1-25:17, 25:39-25:43
Transition
Lev 26:6-26:17, 26:27-26:28, 26:36-26:46

Chapter 7 – Desert Wanderings
Transition
Num 1:1-1:3, 1:18-1:19
Transition
Num 1:45-1:54, 3:14-3:17, 3:39
Transition
Num 6:1-6:5, 7:1-7:5
Transition
Num 7:84-7:88,10:33-11:9, 11:21-11:23, 11:30-11:34, 9:15-9:17
Num 13:1-13:3, 13:25-14:20, 14:26-14:34
Transition
Num 20:1-20:12
Transition
Num 21:4-21:9
Transition
Num 22:18-22:35, 23:5-23:10
Transition
Num 25:1-25:13, 27:15-27:23
Transition
Num 33:50-33:55

Chapter 8 – Preparing for Conquest
Transition
Deut 1:1, 2:7, 4:1-4:4, 4:20-4:24, 4:32-4:40, 6:3-6:12, 6:20-6:23
Deut 7:16-7:21, 8:1-8:5, 9:1-9:6, 12:1-12:3, 27:1-27:10, 28:1-28:6
Deut 29:2-29:6, 30:11-30:20
Transition
Deut 31:1-31:8, 31:24-31:26, 32:48-32:52, 34:1-34:12

Chapter 9 – Finally Home
Transition
Joshua 1:1-1:3, 1:7-1:8, 1:10-1:11, 2:1-2:18
Transition
Joshua 2:22-2:24, 3:5-4:3, 4:14-4:19
Transition
Joshua 4:20-5:1, 5:10-5:12
Transition
Joshua 6:1-6:17, 6:20-6:24, 6:26-6:27
Transition
Joshua 8:1-8:2, 8:10-8:22, 8:25, 8:30-8:31, 8:34-8:35
Transition
Joshua 10:1-10:28, 10:40-11:15, 11:23
Transition
Joshua 21:43-21:45
Transition
Joshua 23:1-24:15, 24:24-24:31

Chapter 10 – Before The Kings

Transition
Judges 2:6-2:23, 3:7-3:12
Transition
Judges 4:1-4:24
Transition
Judges 6:1-6:24, 6:33-7:25, 8:28, 8:33-8:35
Transition
Judges 13:1-13:5, 13:24-16:31, 21:25

Chapter 11 – Your God, My God

Transition
Ruth 1:1-1:14
Transition
Ruth 1:16-1:22
Transition
Ruth 2:1-2:23
Transition
Ruth 3:1-4:17
Transition

Chapter 12 – Great Prophet, Disobedient King

Transition
I Samuel 1:1-1:28, 2:11, 2:18-2:21
Transition
I Samuel 3:1-4:18
Transition
I Samuel 6:13-6:15, 6:19-6:20
Transition
I Samuel 8:1-8:22
Transition
I Samuel 9:1-9:6, 9:14-9:21, 10:1, 10:17-10:25
Transition
I Samuel 11:1-11:11, 12:1-12:5, 13:1-13:14
Transition
I Samuel 15:1-15:4, 15:7-15:11
Transition
I Samuel 15:34-15:35

Chapter 13 – A New King

I Samuel 16:1-16:13
Transition
I Samuel 17:1-17:11, 17:16-18:7, 19:1-19:6
Transition
I Samuel 20:5, 20:11-20:12, 20:17-20:23
Transition
I Samuel 20:35-20:42

Chapter 16 – Wisdom and Prosperity

Transition
I Kings 1:1. 1:5-1:7, 1:11-1:17, 1:29-1:31, 1:38-1:40
I Kings 2:1-2:4, 2:10-2:12
Transition
I Kings 3:1-3:28, 4:20-5:12
Transition
I Kings 6:1, 6:11-6:13, 7:51
Transition
I Kings 8:1-8:6, 8:10-8:13, 8:22-8:24, 8:26-8:30, 8:54-8:61, 9:1-9:7
Transition
I Kings 10:1-10:10, 10:13-10:29
Transition
Proverbs 1:1-1:7, 2:1-2:8, 3:1-3:12
Proverbs 6:16-6:19, 6:27-6:29
Proverbs 11:30-11:31, 14:29, 14:34, 15:1
Proverbs 16:18, 16:25, 18:2, 18:22-19:2
Proverbs 20:7, 20:13, 20:19-20:22
Proverbs 21:1-21:7, 21:13-21:15, 21:19-21:21, 21:27-22:1
Proverbs 22:6, 22:22-22:25, 23:22-23:23, 23:29-23:32
Proverbs 27:1, 27:17, 28:6, 29:11
Transition
Ecclesiastes 1:1-1:10, 1:13a, 1:14, 1:16-2:2
Ecclesiastes 2:10-2:11, 2:16, 2:24, 3:1-3:8, 12:13-12:14

Chapter 17 – A Nation Divided

Transition
I Kings 11:1-11:13
Transition
I Kings 11:28-11:31, 11:34-11:35, 11:42-11:43
Transition
I Kings 12:1-12:14, 12:16-12:30
Transition
I Kings 13:1-13:6, 13:33-14:18, 14:20-14:21a
Transition
I Kings 14:22-14:28, 14:30-15:4, 15:8-15:21
II Chronicles 16:12, I Kings 15:24
Transition
I Kings 16:29-16:33, 17:1-18:2, 18:17-19:1
Transition
I Kings 19:3-19:21, 21:17-21:19, 21:23-21:28, 22:29-22:38

Chapter 18 – The Final Downfall

Transition
II Kings 2:1-2, 2:7-2:15
Transition
II Kings 4:1-4:20, 4:25, 4:27-4:37, 5:1-5:3, 5:9-5:15
Transition

Chapter 19 – The Trials of Job

Chapter 20 – I Desire Mercy

Transition
Ezekiel 36:22-36:28, 36:33-36:36
Transition
Ezekiel 37:1-37:14
Transition
Nahum 1:1-1:8, 1:14, 3:7
Transition
Haggai 1:3-1:7, 1:12-1:14, 2:10, 2:18-2:19
Transition
Zechariah 1:1-1:4, 1:16-1:17, 7:8-7:10, 8:7-8:8
Transition
Joel 1:1-1:4, 2:2, 2:11-2:13, 2:23-2:25
Transition
Obadiah 1:1-1:4, 1:6, 1:17-1:18
Transition
Malachi 1:1, 1:6-1:11, 1:14, 3:1-3:2a, 3:5-3:10

Chapter 23 – Return From Captivity

Transition
Ezra 1:1-2:1, 2:64-2:67, 3:1-3:4, 3:10-3:12
Transition
Ezra 4:1-4:6, 4:24
Transition
Ezra 5:1-5:5a, 5:7-6:9, 6:12b-6:18
Transition
Ezra 7:7-7:28
Transition
Ezra 8:35-9:6, 9:10, 10:1-10:5, 10:10-10:12
Transition
Nehemiah 1:1-1:6, 1:10-2:9
Transition
Nehemiah 2:10-2:18
Transition
Nehemiah 4:6-5:5
Transition
Nehemiah 5:6-5:12
Transition
Nehemiah 6:1-6:15, 7:1-7:3
Transition
Nehemiah 7:4-7:6, 7:66-7:67
Transition
Nehemiah 8:1-8:4a, 8:5-9:3, 10:28-10:29, 11:1-11:2
Transition

Chapter 24 – A Queen's Deliverance

Transition
Esther 1:1-1:5, 1:10-1:21, 2:1-2:11, 2:15-2:17, 2:21-3:6
Transition

Esther 3:8-3:13, 4:1-4:11
Transition
Esther 4:12-5:8
Transition
Esther 5:9-8:2
Transition
Esther 8:3-9:17
Transition

Chapter 25 – Birth of a Savior

Transition
John 1:1-1:5, 1:10-10:14
Luke 1:5-17, 1:26-35, 1:38a, 1:39-49, 1:56
Matt 1:19-25a
Luke 2:1-7, Luke 2:8-21
Transition
Matt 2:1-18
Transition
Luke 2:40-52

Chapter 26 – Everlasting Truths, Changed Lives

Matt 3:4
Luke 3:3, 3:15-18
Matt 3:13-17
Luke 3:23, 4:1-13
John 1:19-28
Transition
John 1:40-45, 2:1b-22
Transition
John 3:1-3:18
Luke 4:14
Transition
John 4:5-29, 4:39-42
Matt 4:17
John 4:46-54
Matt 4:13
Luke 5:1-11
Mark 1:21-34, 1:39, 1:40-45, 2:1-12, 2:13-14
Luke 5:29-32
Transition
Luke 6:12-16, 17-19

Chapter 27 – The Master Teacher

Transition
Matt 5:1-32, 5:38-48, 6:1-15, 6:19-21, 6:24-34
Luke 6:37-42
Matt 7:7-8, 7:13-15, 7:21-8:1
Luke 7:11-17, 7:18-19, 7:21-23

Mark 11:15-18
Luke 21:37-38
Mark 11:19-26, 12:1-12:9
Matt 21:28-32, 21:45-21:46, 22:15-22, 35-40, 23:1-12
Mark 12:41-44

Chapter 30 – In The Shadows

Matt 24:1-2, 25:1-12, 25:31-46, 26:1-5
Transition
Matt 26:14-16
Luke 22:7-13, 22:14-16
John 13:1-15, 13:21-38
Luke 22:17-20
John 14:1-7, 15:17-19, 15:26-27, 16:12-16, 17:1-4
Matt 26:30
Transition
Mark 14:32-36
Luke 22:43-44
Mark 14:37-42, 14:43-45
John 18:4-6
Matt 26:50b-56
Mark 14:53
John 18:19-23
Mark 14:55-64
Luke 22:63-65
John 18:15-18
Mark 14:66-70
Luke 22:59-62, 22:66-71
Transition
Matt 27:2
John 18:28-38
Luke 23:5-12
Mark 15:6-10
Matt 27:19
John 18:40-19:5
Luke 23:13-16
John 19:7-15
Matt 27:22-25

Chapter 31 – The Empty Tomb

Transition
Mark 15:15-21
Mark 15:22-23
Luke 23:32-34
John 19:19-27
Luke 23:39-43
Matt 27:39-44, 27:45-56
John 19:31-37

Mark 15:42-45
John 19:38b-42
Luke 23:55-56
Matt 27:62-66
Mark 16:1
Matt 28:2-4
Mark 16:2-8
John 20:2-18
Matt 28:9-15
Transition
Luke 24:13-44
John 20:21-31
Transition
John 21:14-17
Matt 28:16-20
Mark 16:16-18
Transition
Luke 24:45-52
John 21:25

Chapter 32 – The New Beginning
Transition
Acts 1:1-1:11, 2:1-2:8, 2:12-2:24, 2:29-2:33, 2:36-2:47
Acts 3:1-3:20, 4:1-4:23, 4:31-4:4:35, 5:1-5:42
Transition
Acts 6:8-7:1
Transition
Acts 7:51-8:8, 8:26-8:36, 8:38, 9:1-9:31
Transition
Acts 10:1-10:27, 10:34-10:48
Transition
Acts 12:1-12:19, 12:24-12:25

Chapter 33 – Hitting the Road
Transition
Acts 13:1-13:16, 13:23b-13:33a, 13:38-13:39, 13:42-14:20a
Transition
Acts 15:36
Transition
Acts 16:13-17:12
Transition
Acts 18:8b-18:11, 18:12-18:21
Transition
I Thess 1:1-1:7, 2:4-2:10, 2:17-3:7
I Thess 4:13-5:2, 5:16-5:28
Transition
II Thess 1:1-1:2, 2:1-2:8, 2:15-2:17
II Thess 3:6-3:8, 3:17-3:18

Chapter 34 – Supporting Young Churches
Acts 18:22-20:1
Transition
Acts 20:16-20:31, 20:36-20:38
Acts 21:8-21:17
Transition
I Cor 1:1-1:3, 1:10-1:13, 1:18, 1:21-1:24
I Cor 2:1-2:5, 3:1-3:6, 3:10-3:11, 3:16-3:17
I Cor 5:1-5:5, 5:11-5:13, 6:9-6:11, 6:18-7:5
I Cor 9:24-9:27, 10:13, 10:31
I Cor 11:23-11:26, 12:1, 12:4-12:6, 12:12-12:18, 12:27
I Cor 13:1-13:8, 15:1-15:26, 15:51-15:58, 16:13-16:14
Transition
II Cor 1:1-1:2, 2:1, 2:4, 3:2-3:2
II Cor 4:7-4:12, 4:16-5:1, 5:6-5:8, 5:17-5:20
II Cor 7:8-7:10, 8:9, 9:6-9:8, 9:15
II Cor 11:16-11:17, 11:24-11:27, 12:7-12:10, 13:11-13:14
Transition
Gal 1:1-1:9, 2:15-2:20, 3:1-3:5, 3:13-3:14, 3:19-3:28
Gal 5:1, 5:18-5:23, 6:18
Transition
Romans 1:1-1:7, 1:16-1:17, 2:10-2:12, 2:28-2:29
Romans 3:19-3:28, 4:1-4:8, 5:1-5:11, 5:15
Romans 6:1-6:11, 6:17-6:18, 6:22-6:23
Romans 8:1-8:4, 8:16-8:18, 8:28, 8:31-8:39
Romans 12:1-12:5, 12:9-12:15, 12:21-13:2
Romans 14:10-14:12, 15:22-15:25, 15:29-15:33

Chapter 35 – The Path to Destiny
Transition
Acts 21:26-23:35
Transition
Acts 24:25-24:27
Transition
Acts 26:24-28:24, 28:29-28:31

Chapter 36 – Freedom in Chains
Transition
Eph 1:1-1:4, 1:15-1:23, 2:4-2:10, 2:17-2:22
Eph 3:14-4:6, 5:1-5:4, 5:22-6:4, 6:10-6:18, 6:23-6:24
Transition
Phil 1:1-1:6, 1:9-1:11, 1:21
Phil 2:1-2:18, 3:13-3:14, 3:20-3:21, 4:8-4:9, 4:21-4:23
Transition
Col 1:1-1:5, 1:9-1:20, 2:5-2:15
Col 3:1-3:8, 3:12-3:17,4:18

Chapter 37 – That Which We Have Touched

Transition
James 1:1-1:8, 1:12-1:15, 1:19-1:22, 1:26-1:27
James 2:14-2:24, 3:13-3:18, 4:10, 4:13-4:15, 5:7-5:8
I Peter 1:1-1:7, 1:13-1:16, 2:1-2:5
I Peter 2:9-2:10, 2:20-2:25, 3:13-3:22
I Peter 4:12-4:14, 5:8-5:11
Transition
II Peter 1:1-1:3, 1:16-2:2, 2:20-3:4
II Peter 3:8-3:14, 3:18
I John 1:1-2:3, 2:15-2:17, 3:1-3:2, 3:16
I John 3:23-4:31, 4:7-4:12, 4:19-5:4, 5:13

Chapter 38 – Words of Encouragement

Transition
Heb 1:1-1:4, 2:1-2:4. 2:9-2:10, 4:14-4:16
Heb 5:7-5:10, 6:1-6:3, 8:1-8:2,
Heb 9:11-9:15, 9:27-9:28
Heb 11:1-116, 11:24-11:26, 11:32-12:2
Heb 12:22-12:24, 13:1-13:4, 13:7-13:9, 13:20-13:21
Transition
I Tim 1:1-1:12, 2:1-2:9, 3:14-4:6
I Tim 4:12-4:13, 6:6-6:12, 6:20-6:21
Transition
II Tim 1:1-1:2, 1:13-1:14, 2:1-2:3, 2:8-2:9
II Tim 2:15, 2:22-2:26, 3:15-4:5, 4:22
Transition

Chapter 39 – Victorious In the End!

Transition
Rev 1:1-5:14
Transition
Rev 19:6-19:16, Rev 20:11-22:21
Transition